NUMERICAL METHODS
WITH
FORTRAN 77

INTERNATIONAL COMPUTER SCIENCE SERIES

Consulting editors   **A D McGettrick**   University of Strathclyde

J van Leeuwen   University of Utrecht

SELECTED TITLES IN THE SERIES

NUMERICAL METHODS
WITH
FORTRAN 77
A Practical Introduction

L. V. Atkinson   P. J. Harley
J. D. Hudson

University of Sheffield

ADDISON-WESLEY
PUBLISHING
COMPANY

Wokingham, England · Reading, Massachusetts · Menlo Park, California
New York · Don Mills, Ontario · Amsterdam · Bonn
Sydney · Singapore · Tokyo · Madrid · San Juan

Cover designed by Crayon Design of Henley-on-Thames and printed by The Riverside Printing Co. (Reading) Ltd.
Typeset by Times Graphics, Singapore.
Printed in Great Britain by T. J. Press (Padstow), Cornwall.

First printed 1989.

British Library Cataloguing in Publication Data
Atkinson, Laurence V.
  Numerical methods with Fortran 77.
  1. Numerical methods. Applications of
  computer systems. Programming languages
  I. Title II. Harley, P. J. *1948–* III.
  Hudson, J. D. (Joseph Desmond) IV. Series
  519.4′028′5513

  ISBN 0-201-17430-8

Library of Congress Cataloging in Publication Data
Atkinson, Laurence.
  Numerical methods with Fortran 77: a practical introduction/
  L. V. Atkinson, P. J. Harley, J. D. Hudson.
      p.   cm. – (International computer science series)
    Bibliography: p.
    Includes index.
    ISBN 0-201-17430-8
    1. FORTRAN (Computer program language) 2. Numerical calculations –
  Data processing. I. Harley, P. J., 1948– . II. Hudson, J. D.,
  Ph.D. III. Title. IV. Series.
  QA76.73.F25A84   1989
  519.4′028′55133–do19   88–39259
                                                              CIP

Preface

The vast majority of mathematical models describing physical processes cannot be solved analytically. The only way to obtain any idea of the behaviour of a solution is to approximate the problem in such a way that numbers representing the solution can be produced. The process of obtaining the solution is then reduced to a series of arithmetic operations and such a process is called a *numerical method*.

The purpose of this book is twofold: to derive numerical methods and to describe their implementation in FORTRAN 77. An attempt has been made to keep analysis of the methods as simple and straightforward as possible; where results are more difficult to obtain, they are quoted and references for further reading are given. The programming of the methods is covered in much greater detail than is usual in texts on this subject. Starting from a mathematical algorithm for a numerical method, a program plan is constructed and then a FORTRAN subprogram is modelled upon this plan. Emphasis has been placed on program style and readability; in particular, use has been made of control constructs which minimize the number of GO TO statements and avoid backward jumps completely. Indentation has been used to highlight these constructs and meaningful variable names have been used throughout.

For readers not fully familiar with FORTRAN 77, Chapter 1 presents a summary of most features of the language and gives examples of some aspects particularly relevant to the implementation of numerical methods. In Chapter 2, the steps taken in a structured approach to programming numerical methods are illustrated. This chapter is important because it lays the foundations for the style of programming used throughout the book.

One fundamental feature of a numerical method is that it may not produce the 'right' answer. Two types of error are incurred: in general, a numerical method produces only an approximation to the right answer and, in addition, this approximation may be affected by the rounding inherent in computer arithmetic. The nature and control of these errors are discussed in Chapter 3.

Chapter 4 concerns non-linear equations and discusses several methods for solving a single equation in a single unknown. Chapter 5 considers systems of linear equations: the solution of n equations in n unknowns.

The behaviour of some of the methods of Chapter 5 depends upon the eigenvalues of the coefficient matrix; Chapter 6 presents techniques for determining both eigenvalues and eigenvectors.

Chapter 7 discusses problems of interpolation, function approximation and data fitting. Chapter 8 introduces numerical differentiation and integration; most of the methods of Chapter 8 are based on results given in Chapter 7. Chapter 9 considers the numerical solution of ordinary differential equations and, as might be expected, has links with Chapter 8; both initial-value and boundary-value problems are discussed.

Presented in appendices are solutions to selected exercises, some useful mathematical results, a list of FORTRAN 77 intrinsic functions and a list of subprograms appearing as figures within the book. References made throughout the text are collected in a bibliography.

This book assumes a working knowledge of FORTRAN 77 and a familiarity with elementary undergraduate calculus and algebra. The aim is to introduce several numerical techniques and encourage their implementation on a computer to reinforce the reader's understanding. Upon reaching the end of the book, the reader new to numerical analysis should have acquired a basic understanding of modern numerical techniques and be able to program them in FORTRAN 77. The continued exposure to FORTRAN 77 and its practical application should be of benefit to all FORTRAN programmers.

L. V. Atkinson
P. J. Harley
J. D. Hudson

University of Sheffield
March 1988

Software library

The subprograms presented in this book are available in machine readable form from the authors. Enquiries should be addressed to

Dr J. D. Hudson
Department of Applied and Computational Mathematics
The University of Sheffield
Sheffield S10 2TN
UK

Contents

Chapter 1
A summary of FORTRAN 77

This book assumes a familiarity with FORTRAN 77 but, for completeness, includes a summary of its main features and an indication of the way in which they are applied to numerical methods. Special emphasis is placed on programming style, and particular attention is paid to program transparency. A program is said to be transparent if it is easy to understand and its intended effect is clear. All the programs in this book conform to the ANSI X3.9 FORTRAN 77 standard.

1.1 Program body

In general, all letters used in a FORTRAN program must be upper case; the use of lower-case letters is restricted to comments and, if the output device allows it, to the output of text. Most statements must be preceded by at least six spaces because the first six character positions are reserved for special purposes which will be described later. Furthermore, because any characters beyond position 72 are ignored, no line should contain more than 72 characters (including spaces). A facility, described in Section 1.1.2, is available for dealing with very long statements.

A simple FORTRAN 77 program takes the form

```
PROGRAM name
statement 1
statement 2
    ⋮
END
```

The first line is optional, but its inclusion is recommended because it allows the programmer to name a program and thereby distinguish it from other programs. The program name, as for all other names used within a FORTRAN program, must begin with a letter and can be followed by up to five additional alphanumeric characters (i.e. letters or digits). The END marks the textual end of the program and, if control reaches this line at run-time, program execution is terminated.

1.1.1 Subprograms

In most cases, it is convenient to divide a program into a number of segments or subprograms. Thus, in general, a program will contain the main subprogram as outlined above and this will be followed by one or more subprograms (see Functions and subroutines, Section 1.12). In general, it is recommended that the main subprogram simply inputs the initial data for the program and outputs the final results, while all the computations are carried out by separate subprograms. Indeed, if there are many values to be input or many to be output, subprograms should be used for these tasks also. This book therefore concentrates on the development of subprograms although, in the early chapters, complete programs will also be constructed.

1.1.2 Continuation lines

To overcome the problem of very long statements, it is permissible to continue a statement on subsequent lines and it is not necessary (or even advisable in most cases) to reach column 72 before breaking a statement. Each 'continuation line' is marked by inserting any character except a space or a zero in position 6 of that line, the first five characters being spaces. Up to 19 continuation lines are permitted.

1.1.3 Statement labels

Where necessary, a statement may be labelled with an integer in the range 1 to 99999. A label may appear anywhere in columns 1 to 5 but, for neatness of layout, all labels in this book will be left justified. The labels used within a subprogram must be unique but need not appear in any particular order. However, some system for choosing labels should be adopted, particularly in long programs, to avoid the possibility of using the same label for two or more statements. Throughout this book, the integers 10, 20, 30 . . . are normally used to label appropriate statements; exceptions to this general rule are indicated where necessary.

1.1.4 Comments

At some points in a program, it is often helpful to insert comments which indicate the purpose of the next few statements for the benefit of another reader (or even the programmer at a later date). This can be accomplished by inserting either C or * in column 1 of the line containing the comment, thus causing the compiler to ignore this line. Some programmers precede every FORTRAN statement by several lines of comments in the hope that this will make the program easier to follow. However, this practice can often have the opposite effect because the program becomes unnecessarily long and the actual FORTRAN statements are obscured by the numerous comments. In any case, a well written program should be largely self-explanatory. This book therefore uses comment statements only sparingly and they are written in lower-case letters enclosed in braces, { }, so that the FORTRAN statements are still visually prominent.

Program layout can be improved by judicious use of blank lines to break the program into small easy-to-read fragments. Some compilers may remove such blank lines from any list file they produce but this can be overcome by inserting C or * in column 1 of an otherwise blank line.

1.2 Constants

Several types of constant are available in FORTRAN 77. All are described below but, in general, programs for numerical methods require the use of only the first two.

Integer constants are numeric constants that contain neither a decimal point nor an exponent (e.g. 17, -3). Their permitted range depends on the particular compiler in use and, within this range, integer values are represented exactly.

Real constants are numeric constants that contain a decimal point or an exponent or both (e.g. 1.1, -0.0123, 1E-10, 4.5678E4, 0.1357E-5). The exponential form is particularly useful for handling very large or very small numbers. In general it takes the form aEn which represents $a \times 10^n$, where n must be an integer constant. note that real values are stored correct to a finite number of significant figures and this number depends on the compiler in use, as also does the values' permitted range.

Logical constants, written either .TRUE. or .FALSE., are used to denote 'truth' values.

Complex constants allow us to represent a complex number $z = x + iy$ where $i^2 = -1$. They are written in the form (x,y) where x and y are real constants, e.g. (4.6,-3.2), (2E6,4E-3).

String constants are used to represent text and are always written inside single quotes, e.g. 'MONDAY', 'JULY', ','.

Double precision constants represent a number with a higher degree of accuracy than is possible with real constants – although the accuracy is not necessarily doubled! They are written in floating point form using a D instead of an E, e.g. 1.2233D6, 2.1D-8.

Finally, FORTRAN 77 allows the use of named constants, e.g. PI. These are described in Section 1.6.

1.3 Variables

These correspond to the individual memory locations in the computer. A variable name consists of any letter followed by up to five alphanumeric characters: it is recommended that names are chosen in a meaningful way to convey the information they hold (e.g. AMPS, VOLTS, STRESS, STRAIN). As with constants, variables can be of different types and it is important that the correct type is used at all times; failure to do so can cause a program to fail on compilation or, even worse, to produce incorrect results. Type specifications are used to declare the type of each variable used in the program.

1.3.1 Type specifications

These consist of a 'type' followed by a list of variables which are to be of that type. They must appear before any executable statement in the subprogram. For example,

```
INTEGER   COUNT,YEAR
REAL      OHMS,ROOT,X
LOGICAL   MALE,SOLVED
```

```
COMPLEX   Z
CHARACTER COMMA*1,MONTH*4
DOUBLE PRECISION PROD
```

In the character specification, the integer after the * denotes the number of characters to be stored in the associated character variable. Simpler forms of this statement are available for the case where two or more variables have the same length.

Note that it is not necessary to specify INTEGER and REAL variables explicitly. If these specifications are omitted, the compiler will assume that any variable whose name begins with one of the letters I, J, K, L, M or N is of type INTEGER. Similarly, a variable whose name begins with any other letter is assumed to be REAL unless declared otherwise. Many programmers make full use of this feature, but this implicit declaration of REAL and INTEGER variables is a common source of errors and it is strongly recommended that all variables are declared explicitly – a convention adopted throughout this book. It is also recommended that, where possible, the programmer should use a compiler that rejects programs containing variables not declared explicitly. Not only does this guard against the inadvertent use of variables of the wrong type, it also provides a check on typing and spelling errors. Throughout this book variables are listed in alphabetical order because this makes it easier to check that all variables have been specified.

1.4 Arrays

Arrays provide an alternative technique for naming the memory locations in the computer. FORTRAN 77 allows us to set up one-dimensional arrays which correspond to the mathematical concept of a vector. Array names are formed in exactly the same way as variable names. Arrays may be of any type described in Section 1.3.1 but the type specifications must also indicate the maximum number of elements required for each array. Thus, for example, the declarations

```
INTEGER K(20)
REAL    A(10)
```

indicate that K is a vector with 20 integer elements K(1),K(2),..., K(20) and A is a vector with 10 real elements A(1),A(2),..., A(10). To use an integer other than unity to address the first element of an array, simply modify the type specifications as in

```
REAL C(-10:10)
```

which would set up a real array with elements C(-10),C(-9), ...,C(10).

FORTRAN 77 also allows us to set up two-dimensional arrays corresponding to the mathematical concept of matrices. For example, the specification

```
REAL D(3,5),E(0:1,0:2)
```

declares 15 real variables:

```
D(1,1) D(1,2) D(1,3) D(1,4) D(1,5)
D(2,1) D(2,2) D(2,3) D(2,4) D(2,5)
D(3,1) D(3,2) D(3,3) D(3,4) D(3,5)
```

and six real variables:

```
E(0,0) E(0,1) E(0,2)
E(1,0) E(1,1) E(1,2)
```

This feature may be extended because FORTRAN 77 allows the use of up to seven subscripts after an array name. However, it should be noted that the elements of a multidimensional array are stored in column order as a one-dimensional array; consequently the subscripts vary most rapidly from left to right. Thus, for example, the elements of the array defined by

```
LOGICAL DONE(3,2)
```

would be stored in the order

```
DONE(1,1) DONE(2,1) DONE(3,1) DONE(1,2) DONE(2,2) DONE(3,2)
```

This fact need not concern the programmer except possibly when inputting or outputting multidimensional arrays or passing arrays as arguments to subroutines and function subprograms; further discussion is deferred until Sections 1.10–1.12. Finally, it should be noted that the time taken to access an array element increases with the number of dimensions.

1.5 Assignment statements

There are three types of assignment statement in FORTRAN 77 – arithmetic, logical and character. All have the general form

variable = *expression*

Only arithmetic assignments are commonly used in programming numerical methods and the following discussion is restricted to this one case. The expression on the right-hand side of the statement may be:

(1)   a single constant;
(2)   a single variable, or array element, which has previously been assigned a value;
(3)   an arithmetic expression using one or more of the operators $+$, $-$, $*$, $/$ and $**$.

The operator $**$ denotes exponentiation (raising to a power). Note that a negative number cannot be raised to a real power.

In general, the type of variable on the left-hand side of the assignment statement should agree with that of the expression on the right-hand side. If a constant or variable of one type is combined with another of the same type using one of the arithmetic operators, the result will also be of that type. Thus, assuming that the variables I1 and I2 have been specified as INTEGER and R1 and R2 as REAL, we may write assignment statements such as

```
I1 = 1
I2 = I1 + 7
R1 = 3.7
R2 = R1**0.25
```

Only in exceptional circumstances should an integer be divided by another integer because the fractional part of the result will be lost. Thus, for example, the statement

```
I1 = 8/3
```

will assign the value 2 to the variable I1.

1.5.1 Mixed-mode expressions

It is permissible to assign an integer quantity to a real variable as in the statement

```
R1 = 1
```

because the computer will automatically convert 1 to 1.0 and then assign the latter value to R1. However, the statement

```
R1 = 8/3
```

would assign the incorrect value 2.0 to R1 because of the integer division. If a real quantity is assigned to an integer variable, the fractional part of the real

Table 1.1 Resultant types for mixed-mode arithmetic.

	Integer	*Real*	*Complex*	*Double precision*
Integer	integer	real	complex	double precision
Real	real	real	complex	double precision
Complex	complex	complex	complex	×
Double precision	double precision	double precision	×	double precision

quantity will be lost. Thus the statement

    I1 = 3.7

will assign the value 3 to the integer variable I1. Although this feature is useful occasionally, it can lead to incorrect results if used inadvertently and is a common source of error in many FORTRAN programs. Even statements like

    I2 = 7.5/2.5

should be avoided because the computer may calculate the right-hand side to be 2.9999... and consequently assign the value 2 to I2.

When a constant or a variable of one type is combined with another of a different type, the result will be of the type indicated in Table 1.1, where × denotes an illegal operation. Thus, for example, the arithmetic expressions

    2*9.3   10-7.3   R1*I1

are real and should not be assigned to an integer variable.

1.5.2 Order of priority

When more than one operator is used in an arithmetic expression, any exponentiations are performed first, then multiplications and divisions – with equal priority. Finally additions and subtractions are carried out – again with equal priority. Within a group of operators with equal priority, calculations are carried out in left-to-right order unless the operators are exponentiations, when right-to-left priority is assumed. Thus in the statement

    X = A+B**C/D*E-F

the operators would be applied in the order

    B**C   B**C/D   (B**C/D)*E   A+(B**C/D)*E   A+(B**C/D)*E-F

but in the statement

    Y = A**B**C*D*E

they would be carried out in the order

    B**C   A**(B**C)   A**(B**C)*D   A**(B**C)*D*E

Round brackets can be used to change the order of priority and have the usual algebraic interpretation. Thus the statement

    X = (A+B)**C/(D-E)

would raise (A+B) to the power C and then divide the result by the difference D-E.

When writing complicated arithmetic expressions, the danger of producing incorrect results from accidental integer division becomes even more acute. For example, to calculate the cube root of a number, it is easy to write

    XTHIRD = X**(1/3)

instead of

    XTHIRD = X**(1.0/3.0)

or

    XTHIRD = X**(1.0/3)

but, assuming XTHIRD to be real, the first version will assign the value 1.0 to XTHIRD regardless of the type (or even the value!) of the variable X.

1.5.3 Intrinsic functions

FORTRAN 77 has many standard functions available for immediate use. A list of those likely to be required for programming numerical methods is given in Appendix B. To use any of these functions within an expression, it is necessary only to write its name, followed by the argument(s) in parentheses. Thus, for example, the statement

    SINX = SIN(X)

will compute the sine of the value stored in the variable X (assumed to be in radians) and assign the result to the variable SINX. More complicated expressions such as

```
FX = SQRT(ABS(SIN(X)-X)) + EXP(-0.5*X)
```

may also be constructed, assuming that the variable X has previously been assigned a numerical value.

If an intrinsic function is to be passed as an argument to a subprogram, its name must appear in an INTRINSIC specification. Following the convention of full explicit declaration mentioned in Section 1.3.1, *all* intrinsic functions used will be specified. Thus, a subprogram containing the above assignment to FX would include the line

```
INTRINSIC ABS, EXP, SIN, SQRT
```

Information on the appropriate type(s) of argument(s) and on the type of result produced by each function is given in Appendix B.

1.6 The PARAMETER statement

Any value given to a variable by an assignment statement may, of course, be changed by subsequent assignment statements as and when necessary. However, if a variable is required to hold the same value throughout the running of the program, it can be protected from inadvertent change by defining it in a PARAMETER statement which has the general form

```
PARAMETER (name1=value1, name2=value2, . . .)
```

where *name1*, *name2*, . . . are variable names of appropriate type and *value1*, *value2*, . . . are constants, constant expressions or character expressions. The items *name1*, *name2*, . . . then become named constants. For example, a constant PI could be named by the statement

```
PARAMETER (PI=3.1415926536)
```

Once a named constant has been defined, it can be used to define others as in

```
PARAMETER (PI=3.1415926536, PIBY2=PI/2, PISQRD=PI*PI)
```

Note that, inside a PARAMETER statement, the exponentiation operator ** can be used only with an integer exponent.

PARAMETER statements play an important role in the programs given in later chapters and they are mentioned again in Section 1.9.2.

1.7   The GO TO **statement**

This has the general form

    GO TO *n*

where *n* is the label of an executable statement, and simply transfers control to
that statement. It is strongly recommended, in the interests of program clarity,
that these statements are used as sparingly as possible.

1.8   IF **statements**

1.8.1   The logical IF

This is the simplest form of IF statement available in FORTRAN 77 and takes
the form

    IF (*logical constant or logical expression*) *statement*

where a logical expression is one whose value is either .TRUE. or .FALSE..
     The action of the statement is straightforward: if the logical constant or
expression is true, the associated statement is executed; otherwise it is ignored. A
simple logical expression is formed by comparing two arithmetic expressions
using one of the following relational operators:

    .GE. (greater than or equal to)
    .GT. (greater than)
    .LE. (less than or equal to)
    .LT. (less than)
    .EQ. (equal to)
    .NE. (not equal to)

Thus, assuming that numerical values have previously been assigned to the
variables A, B and C, examples of logical IF statements are:

    IF (A.GT.4) D=6
    IF ((A+B).LE.9.3) E=A-B
    IF ((B*B).GT.(4*A*C)) DISPOS=.TRUE.

In the last two examples, the inner parentheses are optional because arithmetic
operators have priority over relational operators. However, if included, they can
help to make a program easier to read. Note that two real quantities should never
be tested for equality because rounding errors (discussed in Chapter 3) can lead
to erroneous results. Instead, the modulus of their difference should be compared

with some very small number. Thus, for example, given

```
K = 0
X = 2.1
Y = X/3
```

the statement

```
IF (X.EQ.3*Y) K=10
```

may not affect the value of K, whereas the statement

```
IF (ABS(X-3*Y).LT.0.00001) K=10
```

would produce the expected result and set K to 10.

More complicated logical expressions may be formed by making use of **logical operators**. The most useful of these are

```
.AND.    and    .OR.
```

which occur in expressions such as

```
X.GE.0 .AND. X.LT.1
X.LE.0 .OR. Y.LE.0
```

Note that relational operators always have priority over logical operators. A logical expression may contain more than one logical operator. For example, we may write

```
X.GT.5 .AND. Y.GT.10 .OR. Z.GT.15
```

Here the .AND. is given higher priority than the .OR.. Parentheses may be used to emphasize this order of priority, as in

```
(X.GT.5 .AND. Y.GT.10) .OR. Z.GT.15
```

or even to change it, as in

```
X.GT.5 .AND. (Y.GT.10 .OR. Z.GT.15)
```

Another logical operator (with the highest priority of all logical operators) is .NOT. and this can be used to invert the value of a logical constant or logical expression. Thus, for example, if DONE is a logical variable, the statement

```
IF (.NOT.DONE) GO TO 100
```

will send control to the statement labelled 100 if DONE is false.

Two other logical operators available in FORTRAN 77 are

.EQV.   and   .NEQV.

These have the lowest priority of all the operators and are used to compare two logical expressions. If these are both true or both false, the .EQV. operator will produce the value .TRUE. and the .NEQV. operator will produce the value .FALSE.. For example, the expression

X.GT.4 .EQV. Y.GT.6

will evaluate to .TRUE. if

$X > 4$ and $Y > 6$

or if

$X \leqslant 4$ and $Y \leqslant 6$

and to .FALSE. otherwise.

1.8.2 The block IF structure

A disadvantage of the logical IF statement is that only one statement can be executed if the logical expression (or logical constant) turns out to be true. This can be overcome by using a block IF which, in its simplest form, is

```
IF (logical expression) THEN
   statements
END IF
```

In this case, if the logical expression is true, all the statements up to the END IF are executed. Otherwise these statements are ignored. Thus, for example, to calculate the real roots of a quadratic equation $ax^2 + bx + c = 0$, we could write the program fragment

```
DISC = B*B-4*A*C
IF (DISC.GE.0) THEN
   ROOT1 = (-B+SQRT(DISC))/(2*A)
   ROOT2 = (-B-SQRT(DISC))/(2*A)
END IF
```

Note the use of indentation to make the program easier to read.

Multiple decisions are best dealt with by the more general form of the block IF which is

```
IF (logical expression) THEN
   statements
ELSE IF (logical expression) THEN
   statements

   ⋮

ELSE IF (logical expression) THEN
   statements
ELSE
   statements
END IF
```

There may be any number of ELSE IF statements and the final ELSE may be omitted. Thus a more comprehensive program fragment for the solution of a quadratic equation takes the form:

```
      DISC = B*B-4*A*C
      IF (ABS(DISC).LE.1E-10) THEN
C        { double root}
         ROOT = -B/(2*A)
      ELSE IF (DISC.GT.0) THEN
C        { distinct real roots}
         ROOT1 = (-B+SQRT(DISC))/(2*A)
         ROOT2 = (-B-SQRT(DISC))/(2*A)
      ELSE
C        { complex roots}
         RPART = -B/(2*A)
         CPART = SQRT(-DISC)/(2*A)
      END IF
```

In some circumstances, program readability may be improved if separate IF statements are used and the number of ELSEs reduced. It could be argued that the effect of the following fragment is more readily apparent than in the example above.

```
      DISC = B*B-4*A*C
      IF (ABS(DISC).LE.1E-10) ROOT = -B/(2*A)
      IF (DISC.GT.1E-10) THEN
C        {distinct real roots}
         ROOT1 = (-B+SQRT(DISC))/(2*A)
         ROOT2 = (-B-SQRT(DISC))/(2*A)
      END IF
      IF (DISC.LT.-1E-10) THEN
C        {complex roots}
         RPART = -B/(2*A)
         CPART = SQRT(-DISC)/(2*A)
      END IF
```

1.9   Loops

FORTRAN 77 offers only one explicit loop facility and this is the DO statement.

1.9.1   DO loop

We shall use this in the general form:

```
      DO n, v = e₁,e₂,e₃
         statements
n        CONTINUE
```

where n is the label of a CONTINUE statement, v is a local integer variable (the control variable), and e_1, e_2, e_3 are integer constants or expressions. For clarity, the statements within the loop body are indented.

The loop body is obeyed for v taking successive values:

$$e_1, \ e_1+e_3, \ e_1+2e_3, \ . \ . \ .$$

If e_3 is positive, the process continues so long as v does not exceed e_2; if e_3 is negative, the process continues so long as v is not less than e_2.

The body of the loop

```
      DO 10, I=1,N,1
         ...
10       CONTINUE
```

will be obeyed for I taking values 1, 2, 3, . . . up to N. The body of the loop

```
      DO 20, NEXT=TOP,BOTTOM,-3
         ...
20       CONTINUE
```

will be performed for NEXT taking values TOP, TOP-3, TOP-6, . . . , finishing with the last value in this sequence which is not less than the value of BOTTOM.

If the increment is unity, it may be omitted. The first loop above can be written

```
      DO 10, I=1,N
         ...
10       CONTINUE
```

If control leaves the loop body via a GO TO statement, the control variable retains its current value; if the loop terminates naturally, the value of the control variable becomes undefined.

Note that FORTRAN 77 allows the control variable to be of type REAL but, because of the possible rounding problems mentioned in Section 1.8.1, this is not to be recommended and only control variables of type INTEGER will be used in this book.

1.9.2   Repeat—until loop

The DO loop is a natural vehicle for any loop where we know in advance, or can easily determine, how many times we want the loop body to be obeyed. Often, however, we do not know how many times we wish a loop body to be obeyed. An iterative process is a typical example; we must continue computing new values until convergence is achieved.

When planning such a program, a notation of the form

    repeat
      . . . { *perform one iteration* }
    until . . . { *converged* }

will be used or, if some maximum number of iterations has been specified, the form

    repeat (*not exceeding max iterations*)
      . . . { *perform one iteration* }
    until . . . { *converged* }

For the actual FORTRAN 77 program, the repeat—until construct will be transformed into a DO loop of the following form:

```
      DO 10, I=1,MAXITS
         ...
         IF (...) GO TO 11
10    CONTINUE
11       ...
```

Note that, for the statement which is the destination of the GO TO statement, we have chosen a label 1 greater than that of the CONTINUE statement used to mark the end of the loop body. This is a convention which we shall adopt consistently: there will never be more than one statement to which control can be transferred explicitly and its label will be 1 greater than that marking the end of the loop.

Usually, we wish to know whether convergence was achieved (in which case control left the loop via the GO TO) or the limit placed upon the number of iterations was reached without convergence being achieved (in which case the loop terminated naturally). We record this information in an integer variable called STATUS and, corresponding to each state of interest, introduce a named constant within a PARAMETER statement. The values of these constants are arbitrary (provided they are distinct) but we shall normally use 0 for the state corresponding to a successful outcome and consecutive integers from 1 upwards for the others. In the above example, there are two states of interest – 'converged' and 'limit reached'.

```
      PARAMETER (CONVGD=0,LIMIT=1)
      ...
      DO 10, I=1,MAXITS
        ...
        IF (...) THEN
          STATUS=CONVGD
          GO TO 11
        END IF
10    CONTINUE
      STATUS=LIMIT
11    ...
```

In some situations, a loop may not involve a natural upper bound to its number of executions. Such a loop could be implemented with an IF statement and a backward jump but we prefer to use an explicit loop statement – the DO loop. To allow a sufficient number of repetitions, we shall make use of some suitably large value for the upper bound.

1.10 Input

FORTRAN 77 provides both formatted input, where the precise layout of the input data is specified within the program, and unformatted input, where no layout is specified. Throughout this book we concern ourselves with unformatted input only. For details of the more advanced features of input, the reader is referred to Ellis (1982).

For simple variables we shall use a statement of the form

```
      READ *, V₁, V₂, ..., Vₙ
```

where each v_i is a variable name. With this form of READ statement, input is taken from the 'standard input unit' and, for a terminal or microprocessor, this will be the keyboard.

The data values are supplied at run-time, starting on a new line. The values must be separated by spaces, commas or ends of lines and are assigned to the variables in the order in which they appear in the READ statement. For example, in the context of

```
      INTEGER MAX,MIN
      REAL    VOLUME
```

and given the data

```
      10  40  67.892
```

the statement

```
READ *, MIN, MAX, VOLUME
```

will assign the value 10 to MIN, 40 to MAX and 67.892 to VOLUME.

1.10.1 Inputting arrays

One way to read values into an array is to read one value each time round a loop. Values could be read into the array

```
REAL A(25)
```

by the loop

```
      DO 10, I=1,25
         READ *, A(I)
10    CONTINUE
```

This requires that the data values be supplied one per line. If we wished to supply more than one value per line, we would use a READ statement which refers to the whole array. There are two ways to achieve this. One is to quote the name of the array rather than specify an element:

```
READ *, A
```

This has the effect of reading a value for every element of the array; the values are assigned to the array elements in the order

```
A(1) A(2) A(3) ... A(25)
```

The second technique employs a DO-**implied list**:

```
READ *, (A(I),I=1,25)
```

As written, this statement has the same effect as the previous one but an advantage of this form is that it is not necessary to read values for the whole array. If N and M have values in the range 1 to 25 and M > N, the statement

```
READ *, (A(I),I=N,M)
```

will read values for elements

```
A(N) A(N+1) ... A(M)
```

Furthermore, elements can be considered in reverse order; the statement

```
READ *, (A(I),I=16,6,-2)
```

will read values for six elements in the order

```
A(16)   A(14)   A(12)   A(10)   A(8)   A(6)
```

A similar situation applies for arrays of more than one dimension. Given the declaration

```
REAL A(5,10)
```

the statement

```
READ *, A
```

will read 50 real values and assign them, in turn, to the elements

```
A(1,1) A(2,1) A(3,1) A(4,1) A(5,1) A(1,2) A(2,2) . . . A(4,10) A(5,10)
```

As stated in Section 1.4, the array elements are considered in column-wise order.

If values are to be read into only part of an array, or are to be assigned to the array elements in a different order, a nested DO-implied list can be used. The statement

```
READ *, ((A(I,J),I=1,5),J=3,7,2)
```

will read values into columns 3, 5 and 7 of the array. Note that I varies more rapidly than J; this corresponds to the depth of nesting.

The statement

```
READ *, ((A(I,J),J=1,10),I=1,5)
```

will read values into every element of the array, in row-wise order

```
A(1,1)   A(1,2)   ...   A(1,10)   A(2,1)   A(2,2)   ...   A(5,9)   A(5,10)
```

Of course, we could use two nested DO loops:

```
     DO 10, I=1,5
       DO 20, J=1,10
         READ *, A(I,J)
20       CONTINUE
10     CONTINUE
```

but then we would have to supply every value on a new line. Another possibility is to use a DO-implied list inside a DO loop:

```
      DO 10, I=1,5
        READ *, (A(I,J),J=1,10)
10    CONTINUE
```

With this form, the first value of each row must be on a new line.

1.10.2 Inputting from a file

Before data can be read from a file, the file must be opened and must have a unit number assigned. For example, a file called INF would be opened as unit 8 by the statement

```
      OPEN (8,FILE='INF')
```

Data could then be read from this file by a READ statement quoting unit 8 as its input device; in place of

```
      READ *,
```

we would use

```
      READ (8,*)
```

The range of permissible unit numbers for files is implementation dependent and some implementations may even require additional information.

When program execution terminates, all open files should be closed automatically. However, some implementations fail to do this and so it is good practice to close files explicitly; the file above would be closed by the statement

```
      CLOSE (8)
```

1.11 Output

Output can be produced by PRINT or WRITE statements. The PRINT statement gives the programmer no control over the format of results, and throughout this text it is used only to prompt the user to type data, as in the following example:

```
      PRINT *,'What is the order of the system?'
```

To output results of computations, we use the 'standard output device' and the WRITE statement, in the general form

```
      WRITE (*,f) v1, v2, ..., vn
```

where each v_i is a variable name and f is the label of a FORMAT statement of the form

```
f       FORMAT (1X, ed1, ed2, ..., edn)
```

where each ed_i is an **edit descriptor**. In this book, simple edit descriptors of the following forms will be used:

nX   to output n spaces,

In   to output an integer occupying n character positions,

Fn.d   to output a real value occupying n character positions and with d decimal places,

'...'   to output a string.

The first character of an output record acts as a *carriage control* character and, in particular, a space character is interpreted as meaning 'move to the next line'. The use of 1X as above makes the control character a space, thereby ensuring that each output record starts a new line.

For a real variable AVE and two integer variables N1 and N2, the statements

```
      N1=45
      N2=8
      AVE=(N1+N2)/2.0
      WRITE (*,2010) N1,N2,AVE
2010  FORMAT (1X,'The average of ',I3,' and ',I3,' is ',F6.2)
```

would produce the following output:

```
The average of  45 and   8 is  26.50
```

Each of the two integers occupies three character positions (because of I3); the real value occupies six character positions and has two decimal places (because of F6.2).

It is good practice to use different numerical ranges for labels with different purposes. For output FORMAT statements, we shall use labels in the range 2000 – 2990 in the following chapters.

If more values are to be output than are allowed for in the FORMAT statement, the FORMAT statement is re-entered. In conjunction with the format specification

```
2020  FORMAT (1X,I7,I7,I7)
```

the statement

```
WRITE (*,2020) N1,N2,N3,N4,N5,N6,N7,N8
```

will produce output on three lines with N1, N2 and N3 on the first line, N4, N5 and N6 on the second and N7 and N8 on the third.

Rather than repeat an edit descriptor or sequence of edit descriptors, a **repeat count** can be used. The statement

```
2020    FORMAT (1X,3I7)
```

is equivalent to that above.

Within an output FORMAT statement, the symbol / may replace a comma and has the effect of terminating the current output record and starting a new one. The first character of the new output record will be interpreted as a carriage control character. For example, the following WRITE and FORMAT pair produces output on two lines, the heading on one and the values on the next:

```
        WRITE (*,2030) A,B,C
2030    FORMAT (1X,'   A        B        C'/1X,3F9.3)
```


1.11.1 Outputting arrays

As for input, array elements are considered in column order if only the array name is quoted. Thus, in conjunction with the type specification

```
    REAL A(5,10)
```

and the format specification

```
2030    FORMAT (1X,5F10.3)
```

the statement

```
    WRITE (*,2030) A
```

will produce ten rows and five columns. If the array A is used to represent a matrix, the output will be in the form of the transpose

```
    A(1,1)    A(2,1)    A(3,1)    A(4,1)    A(5,1)
    A(1,2)    A(2,2)    A(3,2)    A(4,2)    A(5,2)
      :         :         :         :         :
    A(1,10)   A(2,10)   A(3,10)   A(4,10)   A(5,10)
```

To output values in a different order or to output only part of an array, a DO-implied list can be used. In conjunction with the format specification

```
2040   FORMAT (1X,10F7.2)
```

the statements

```
       DO 10, I=1,5
         WRITE (*,2040) (A(I,J),J=1,10)
10     CONTINUE
```

will output the elements of the array A in row-wise order as five rows and ten columns. For use of nested DO-implied lists and more sophisticated FORMAT statements, the reader is referred to Ellis (1982).

1.11.2   Outputting to a file

A file is opened for writing in the same way as for reading and then the unit number associated with the file replaces * in the WRITE statement. Again, the permissible range of unit numbers is implementation dependent. No carriage control characters should be written to a file and so the 'additional' 1X can be omitted from the format specifications.

To write elements of a matrix A in row-wise order to a file OUTF, first open the file:

```
       OPEN (9,FILE='OUTF')
```

and then quote the unit number in the WRITE statement:

```
       DO 10, I=1,5
         WRITE (9,2050) (A(I,J),J=1,10)
10     CONTINUE
2050   FORMAT (10F7.2)
```

As a final point, note that output to a file can be unformatted. This is appropriate when the data output need not be in a form intelligible to a human reader but is intended solely for subsequent input by a program. To output an array A in unformatted form to a file opened as unit 9 use the statement

```
       WRITE (9) A
```

To input the array subsequently via unit 9, use the statement

```
       READ (9) A
```

As for input, it is good practice to close an output file explicitly.

1.12   Functions and subroutines

As mentioned in Section 1.1.1, a FORTRAN 77 program consists typically of a number of subprograms: one main subprogram and several function or subroutine subprograms. Each subroutine and function subprogram is given a name and concludes with the line END. Names and labels introduced within a subprogram are local to that subprogram.

Information may be passed between subprograms by arguments or COMMON blocks. The use of COMMON blocks restricts the portability of subprograms and can easily lead to error; consequently, we use only arguments. Those quoted in the subprogram heading and used within the subprogram are called **dummy** arguments and those supplied from the calling subprogram are called **actual** arguments.

The main differences between a function and a subroutine are as follows:

- A function should be responsible for computing one and only one value.
- The value computed by a function is returned to the calling subprogram via the function name and the values of the arguments should not be changed.
- A reference to a function produces a value and so constitutes an expression.
- A type is associated with a function name.
- A subroutine may be responsible for producing several values or possibly none at all (it may simply output some results).
- The values computed by a subroutine are returned to the calling subprogram via the arguments.
- A call to a subroutine initiates an action and so constitutes a statement.
- No type is associated with a subroutine name.

1.12.1   Function subprograms

In this book, all function subprograms will be of the following general form:

type FUNCTION *name* $(a_1, a_2, \ldots, a_n)$
type specifications
statements
name $= \ldots$
END

As an example, the following function subprogram counts the number of negative values within 20 values stored in an array A:

```
INTEGER FUNCTION NEGSIN (A)
INTEGER COUNT,I
```

```
      REAL    A(20)
      COUNT=0
      DO 10, I=1,20
         IF (A(I).LT.0) COUNT=COUNT+1
10    CONTINUE
      NEGSIN=COUNT
      END
```

Within some other subprogram, this function would be called in the usual way.
Given an INTEGER variable NEGS and a 20-element array X of type REAL, the
statement

```
      NEGS=NEGSIN(X)
```

will assign to NEGS the number of negative elements in X.

1.12.2 Subroutines

Subroutines have the general form

```
      SUBROUTINE name (a₁, a₂, . . . , aₙ)
      type specifications
      statements
      END
```

$$SUBROUTINE\ name\ (a_1, a_2, \ldots, a_n)$$

As a simple example, the following subroutine adds two 5×10 matrices:

```
      SUBROUTINE MATADD (A,B, C)
C        { forms C = A + B}
      INTEGER I,J
      REAL    A(5,10),B(5,10),C(5,10)
      DO 10, I=1,5
         DO 20, J=1,10
            C(I,J)=A(I,J)+B(I,J)
20       CONTINUE
10    CONTINUE
      END
```

We shall adopt the convention of including a space within the argument list to
separate **input arguments** (arguments whose values are supplied when the
subroutine is called) and **output arguments** (arguments whose values are
computed by the subroutine). When there are many arguments, input and output
arguments will be placed on separate lines.

1.12.3   Dynamic bounds

In the examples above, the size of each array argument is fixed. This constraint can be overcome by specifying dynamic bounds. When dynamic bounds are used, the array and the dynamic bounds must all be dummy arguments.

For example, the function NEGSIN can be made applicable to an array of any size:

```
      INTEGER FUNCTION NEGSIN (N,A)
      INTEGER COUNT,I,N
      REAL     A(N)
      COUNT=0
      DO 10, I=1,N
        IF (A(I).LT.0) COUNT=COUNT+1
10    CONTINUE
      NEGSIN=COUNT
      END
```

The situation is more complicated for an array with more than one dimension. To adapt the subroutine MATADD for arrays of any size, we might be tempted to produce the following version:

```
      SUBROUTINE MATADD (M,N,A,B, C)
C        { forms C = A + B}
      INTEGER I,J,M,N
      REAL     A(M,N),B(M,N),C(M,N)
      DO 10, I=1,M
        DO 20, J=1,N
          C(I,J)=A(I,J)+B(I,J)
20      CONTINUE
10    CONTINUE
      END
```

Unfortunately, this does not work! The subroutine will produce the correct results only if the value of M agrees with the value used for the first dimension of the actual arrays corresponding to A, B and C. This is a consequence of the column-wise storage of arrays referred to in Section 1.4; the array elements used within the subroutine will be the first *mn* elements of the actual arrays taken in column-wise order.

To be quite safe when using dynamic bounds with arrays of more than one dimension, we shall always supply as arguments the bounds used to dimension the actual arrays. A suitable version of the subroutine to perform matrix addition is as follows:

```
      SUBROUTINE MATADD (MSIZE,NSIZE,M,N,A,B, C)
C        { forms C = A + B}
      INTEGER I,J,M,MSIZE,N,NSIZE
      REAL     A(MSIZE,NSIZE),B(MSIZE,NSIZE),C(MSIZE,NSIZE)
```

```
      DO 10, I=1,M
        DO 20, J=1,N
          C(I,J)=A(I,J)+B(I,J)
20      CONTINUE
10    CONTINUE
      END
```

A further problem arises when a subprogram requires a local array with dynamic bounds. An array declared within a subprogram cannot be given dynamic bounds and so the array must be supplied as an argument. We shall always place such arguments at the end of the argument list, separated by a space from the preceding arguments. This is illustrated in the following subroutine which transposes a matrix A by first copying it to an array B and then copying back its transpose:

```
      SUBROUTINE MATTRA (NSIZE,N,A, B)
      INTEGER I,J,N,NSIZE
      REAL    A(NSIZE,NSIZE),B(NSIZE,NSIZE)
      DO 10, I=1,N
        DO 20, J=1,N
          B(I,J)=A(I,J)
20      CONTINUE
10    CONTINUE
      DO 30, I=1,N
        DO 40, J=1,N
          A(I,J)=B(J,I)
40      CONTINUE
30    CONTINUE
      END
```

To transpose a 10×10 matrix stored as the first 10 rows and columns of a 20×20 array X, we would introduce a workspace matrix the same size as X:

```
      REAL WORKM(20,20),X(20,20)
```

and use a subroutine call of the following form:

```
      CALL MATTRA (20,10,X, WORKM)
```

Of course, it is possible to write a subroutine that will transpose a matrix without using a second array; interested readers are invited to do this.

1.12.4   INTRINSIC statement

If the name of an intrinsic function is passed as an actual argument to a subprogram, it must be quoted in an INTRINSIC statement. For example, a program to list values of $\sin x$ for x (in degrees) taking values 0, 5, 10, . . . , 180 might use a subroutine with a call of the form

```
CALL LISTF (SIN,0,180,5)
```

The program must contain the line

```
INTRINSIC SIN
```

In accordance with our philosophy of specifying all names used in a subprogram, we shall quote in an INTRINSIC statement the names of *all* intrinsic functions it uses.

1.12.5   EXTERNAL **statement**

If a dummy argument in a subprogram represents a function subprogram, its name must appear within an EXTERNAL statement. For example, the subroutine LISTF mentioned above might have the following form:

```
SUBROUTINE LISTF (F,A,B,STEP)
REAL     A,B,F,STEP
EXTERNAL F
  ...
END
```

Also, if the name of a subroutine is passed as an actual argument to a subprogram, it must appear in an EXTERNAL statement.

In accordance with our philosophy of specifying all names used in a subprogram, we shall quote in an EXTERNAL statement the names of *all* other subprograms it uses.

Chapter 2
Program construction

2.1   Example 1   2.2   Example 2

Before a program can be used to solve a particular problem, its development involves three distinct phases:

(1)   A numerical algorithm must be developed.
(2)   This algorithm must be implemented as a computer program.
(3)   The program must be checked with test data.

In practice, it is likely that (1) will already have been done because a standard technique already exists and, in this case, (2) may also have been done partially in that a subroutine could be available in a software library. Under these circumstances it would be necessary only to write a main subprogram that calls this subroutine and performs input and output of values for the particular problem in hand – and, of course, to test the program (phase 3). Once the program is seen to perform satisfactorily for some test data, it can be supplied with the data for the actual problem.

There may be instances, however, when no suitable algorithm exists and we must carry out all three phases. The purpose of this chapter is to illustrate the whole process and we shall do this by considering two different examples. Subsequent chapters will concentrate on the first two phases (1 and 2) and will adopt the notation established here.

2.1 Example 1

Our main purpose here is to illustrate the technique of constructing a program and to introduce the style of programming to be adopted throughout the book. Consequently, we deliberately take a simple example, we ignore the existence of the SQRT function in FORTRAN 77 and write a program to compute the square root of a number.

2.1.1 Defining the algorithm

There are several numerical techniques that can produce the square root of a number (see Chapter 4) but, for this chapter, we develop an *ad hoc* algorithm. First, we state the problem in mathematical terms:

given a positive value v, determine a value u such that $u^2 = v$

Observe that, for any positive x (except $x = u$), x and v/x lie on opposite sides of u. That is,

if $x < u$ **then** $v/x > u$
if $x > u$ **then** $v/x < u$

Note also that the closer x is to u, the smaller is the difference between x and v/x.

This suggests that, if x is repeatedly replaced by the average of x and v/x, successive values should approach u, the square root of v. Accordingly, the mathematical algorithm is

Given v (> 0), *the value whose root is sought*
    and x_0 (> 0), *an initial approximation to the root*
Repeat (for $n = 0, 1, 2, \ldots$)
    $x_{n+1} = (x_n + v/x_n)/2$
Until converged

To illustrate this algorithm, we compute the square root of 10, taking 3 as the initial approximation (x_0) and working to seven decimal places. Substituting x_0 into

$x_1 = (x_0 + 10/x_0)/2$

gives

$x_1 = (3 + 10/3)/2$
    $= 3.166\ 666\ 7$ (from which $x_1^2 = 10.027\ 777\ 8$)

Computing

$x_2 = (x_1 + 10/x_1)/2$

EXAMPLE 1   31

gives

$$x_2 = (3.166\ 666\ 7 + 10/3.166\ 666\ 7)/2$$
$$= 3.162\ 280\ 7 \text{ (from which } x_2{}^2 = 10.000\ 019\ 2)$$

Now that $x^2 = 10$ to four decimal places, we could terminate the iteration and take $3.162\ 280\ 7$ to be the root. (In fact, this is correct to five decimal places.) Alternatively, we might decide to continue until two successive estimates of the root agree to seven decimal places. Using our iteration formula twice more gives

$$x_3 = (3.162\ 280\ 7 + 10/3.162\ 280\ 7)/2 = 3.162\ 277\ 7$$
$$x_4 = (3.162\ 277\ 7 + 10/3.162\ 277\ 7)/2 = 3.162\ 277\ 7$$

and, in fact, our estimate of the root is now correct to seven decimal places.

2.1.2 Bounding the number of iterations

In this hand-worked example, it was possible to continue until two successive estimates did not differ within the required number of decimal places. When an iterative algorithm is implemented on a computer it is not usually practical to expect successive estimates to agree to within the limits of machine accuracy; instead, it is sufficient to compute an answer to some specified accuracy. In the above example, two possibilities for the convergence test are:

$$|v - x_{n+1}{}^2| < tolerance$$
$$|x_{n+1} - x_n| < tolerance$$

for some chosen tolerance. The choice of convergence test does not affect the basic mathematical algorithm and so we have used the general term 'converged'.

In a program to implement this algorithm, we might choose one of these two possible convergence tests, but for several reasons convergence may not be achieved at all:

- We have performed no analysis of our numerical method and so we have no guarantee that it will converge.
- We may make a mistake in our program and, even if the method should give convergence, our program may not achieve it.
- If we specify a very small tolerance, convergence may take longer than we are prepared to allow the program to run – particularly if the tolerance is beyond the limits of machine accuracy.

Consequently, it is advisable to limit the number of loop iterations that may be performed and so our programs will contain a bound on the number permitted.

2.1.3 Planning the program

The overall structure of the program can be shown using a top-level **program plan**. Bearing in mind the comments from the previous section, this plan can take the following form.

(1)   *Define parameters*:
         tolerance, maximum number of iterations allowed

(2)   *Input*:
         v, x0

(3)   *Do*:
         square root process
            using (v, x0, tolerance, maximum number of iterations)
         to produce (either root, number of iterations used
                        or last approximation to root)

(4)   **if** *problem solved* **then**
         Print: *root, number of iterations used*
       if *limit on number of iterations reached without convergence* **then**
         Print: *last approximation to root*

We need some way of recording whether the iterative process has been successful or has reached the specified limit on the number of iterations without achieving convergence, and this is done as indicated in Section 1.9.2. We introduce an integer variable to record the *status* and a different value is associated with this variable for each possible outcome of the iteration process. In this case, there are two possible outcomes:

- problem solved (convergence achieved),
- limit on number of iterations reached without convergence.

We include the status variable and its possible values in step (1) of our program plan:

(1)   *Define parameters*:
         tolerance, maximum iterations allowed,
         status values (i.e. solved, limit)

and, because the status variable is assigned its value by the root-finding process, it is included in step (3):

(3)   *Do*:
         square root process
            using (v, x0, tolerance, maximum number of iterations)
         to produce (status and
                     either root, number of iterations used
                        or last approximation to root)

EXAMPLE 1   33

We now turn our attention to the production of the FORTRAN 77 program.

To associate meaningful names with the possible values of the status variable, we define them as named constants within a PARAMETER declaration. For this example, we use

```
PARAMETER (SOLVED=0,LIMIT=1)
```

Steps (1) and (2) are straightforward:

```
INTEGER   LIMIT,MAXITS,SOLVED
REAL      NUMBER,TOL,X0
PARAMETER (MAXITS=25,TOL=5E-7)
PARAMETER (SOLVED=0,LIMIT=1)

PRINT *,'Give a positive number whose square root you seek'
READ *, NUMBER
PRINT *,'Give an initial approximation to the square root'
READ *, X0
```

We have presented the four named integer constants in two separate PARAMETER statements and we shall retain this convention to stress the two different roles. Two are numeric constants whose values are important; the other two represent states of the iteration, and their actual values are arbitrary.

For the moment, we shall ignore step (3) except to note that it must give a value to the status variable. The program fragment for step (4) tests the value of the status variable. Because this can be only one of two possible values, an IF-THEN-ELSE-ENDIF construct could be used, but the program is made more readable if we test for each possible value explicitly:

```
IF (STATUS.EQ.SOLVED) WRITE(*,2000) ROOT,NOOFIT
IF (STATUS.EQ.LIMIT)  WRITE(*,2010) MAXITS,LASTX
```

The type information associated with the four new variables is

```
INTEGER NOOFIT,STATUS
REAL    LASTX,ROOT
```

Now consider step (3). It is possible to produce a program plan for this step, translate this plan into FORTRAN and then include the code produced, at the appropriate place in the main subprogram. For the relatively simple process of finding a square root, few statements are necessary and the resulting program should be easily readable. For more complicated processes, however, this is not the case and it is much better to incorporate a subroutine (or function) subprogram. Some benefits are as follows:

• Apart from the use of some values computed earlier and the production of some values to be used later, the process is logically distinct from the main subprogram and the use of a separate subprogram emphasizes this.

●   The main subprogram is significantly shorter than it would be if it contained all the coding for the whole program and, consequently, is easier to read.

●   Variables introduced simply for holding temporary values computed during the process are local to the subprogram implementing the process. (This makes for increased readability and reduces the possibility of making mistakes.)

●   By specifying the arguments used by a subprogram, the programmer is identifying the information used by a process and the information produced by a process. (This further aids program clarity.)

●   A process implemented as a separate subprogram can easily be incorporated into different programs (at different times and by different people – this is the basis of software libraries). The user need not know how the process is implemented or even what the names of the dummy arguments are in the subprogram; only the number, order and types of the arguments need be known.

Throughout this book we shall concentrate on the development of separate subprograms to implement numerical methods. To illustrate this, we shall adopt the same approach here and implement our root-finding process as a subroutine. Accordingly, step (3) can now be implemented as a subroutine call. As its arguments, it uses the *actual* names used in the main subprogram:

```
CALL SQROOT (NUMBER,X0,TOL,MAXITS,
*            STATUS,ROOT,NOOFIT,LASTX)
```

As in the program plan, we have placed the arguments on two lines to stress their differing roles. Those on the first line are *input* arguments used to *supply values* to the subroutine; those on the second line are *output* arguments and are the names of *variables* used to *record values returned from* the subroutine. The writing of the subroutine is described in the next section.

We achieve the full form of the main subprogram by collecting together the type information, specifying the subroutine SQROOT as EXTERNAL, providing suitable FORMAT statements and supplying a STOP statement, a PROGRAM line and an END. This has been done in Figure 2.1.

2.1.4 Writing the subroutine

Now we turn our attention to the subroutine that is to compute the square root. As for the main subprogram, we produce a program plan before the actual FORTRAN 77 statements are considered. This follows from the algorithm

EXAMPLE 1   35

```
      PROGRAM SQMAIN

      INTEGER   LIMIT,MAXITS,NOOFIT,SOLVED,STATUS
      REAL      LASTX,NUMBER,ROOT,TOL,X0
      PARAMETER (SOLVED=0,LIMIT=1)
      PARAMETER (TOL=5E-7,MAXITS=25)
      EXTERNAL  SQROOT

      PRINT  *,'Give a positive number whose square root you seek'
      READ *, NUMBER
      PRINT  *,'Give an initial approximation to the square root'
      READ *, X0

      CALL SQROOT (NUMBER,X0,TOL,MAXITS,
     *             STATUS,ROOT,NOOFIT,LASTX)

      IF (STATUS.EQ.SOLVED) WRITE(*,2000) ROOT,NOOFIT
      IF (STATUS.EQ.LIMIT)  WRITE(*,2010) MAXITS,LASTX

2000  FORMAT(1X,'Root = ',F10.6
     *       /1X,'- converged after ',I2,' iterations')
2010  FORMAT(1X,'Not converged after ',I2,' iterations'
     *       /1X,'- current estimate is ',F10.6)
      END
```

Figure 2.1 Main subprogram for square root.

developed earlier but with the added constraint that the number of iterations must not exceed a specified maximum. Note that the program need not record all values of x generated. If the convergence test involves x_{n+1} and x_n, only two values (the current value and the previous value) need be recorded; if the test involves x_{n+1} and v, only the current value of x need be recorded. In the latter case the body of the repeat-loop would be

Set: $x = (x + v/x)/2$

and the loop would be preceded by

Set: $x = x0$

However, we shall choose the former case and so computation of a new x will take the form

Set: $newx = (oldx + v/oldx)/2$

where *oldx* is the value that was *newx* the previous time round the loop. The obvious point at which to update *oldx* is immediately prior to computing *newx*:

Set: $oldx = newx$
$newx = (oldx + v/oldx)/2$

This implies that, upon entry to the loop, *newx* must be defined and, in particular, its value must be the initial approximation.

The program plan for the subroutine is as follows:

Given: *v*, *x0*, *tolerance*, *maximum number of iterations*

(1)   Set: $newx = x0$

(2)   **repeat**
    Set: $oldx = newx$
        $newx = (oldx + v/oldx)/2$
    if $|newx - oldx| \le tolerance$ **then**
        Note: 'solved'
    until 'solved' (or limit on number of iterations reached)

(3)   **if** 'solved' **then**
        Record: root, number of iterations used
    if 'limit' **then**
        Record: lastx

This must be implemented in FORTRAN 77. Step (1) is simply an assignment:

```
NEWX=X0
```

The repeat-loop of step (2) describes a common situation: a process must be repeated until convergence is achieved or, failing convergence, the number of iterations used reaches some specified limit:

repeat

    ⋮

if . . . { *converged* } **then**
    Note: 'solved'
until 'solved' (or limit on iterations reached)

To implement this in FORTRAN 77, we shall use a DO loop to bound the number of iterations and, should convergence be achieved, we shall update the value of STATUS accordingly and exit the loop prematurely. If the limit on the number of iterations is reached before convergence is achieved, we must give STATUS the value LIMIT and this is done with an assignment statement immediately following the DO loop (that is, immediately following the CONTINUE that marks the end of the loop):

EXAMPLE 1   37

```
      DO 10, COUNT=1,MAXITS
        ⋮

      IF (...) {converged} THEN
        STATUS=SOLVED
        GO TO 11
      END IF

10    CONTINUE
      STATUS=LIMIT

11    ...
```

Note that, as explained in Section 1.9.2, the point that we jump to upon premature exit from the loop is marked with a label 1 greater than that used by the DO loop. We can now produce the FORTRAN 77 implementation of step (2):

```
      DO 10, COUNT=1,MAXITS
      OLDX=NEWX
      NEWX=(OLDX+V/OLDX)/2

      IF (ABS(NEWX-OLDX).LE.TOL) THEN
        STATUS=SOLVED
        GO TO 11
      END IF

10    CONTINUE
      STATUS=LIMIT

11    ...
```

Step (3) follows directly. As in the main subprogram, we could use an IF–THEN–ELSE–ENDIF construct but, once again, we use program readability to enhance two separate IF statements. To record a value that is to be returned to the calling subprogram, we assign it to the appropriate dummy argument:

```
11    IF (STATUS.EQ.SOLVED) THEN
        ROOT  =NEWX
        NOOFIT=COUNT
      END IF

      IF (STATUS.EQ.LIMIT) LASTX=NEWX
```

Now all the dummy arguments of the subroutine heading can be named. Their number and order are dictated by the CALL statement in the main subprogram but the names used for them are governed by the names chosen for use inside the subroutine:

```
SUBROUTINE SQROOT (V,X0,TOL,MAXITS,
                   STATUS,ROOT,NOOFIT,LASTX)
```

All that remains is to reproduce the status parameter declaration of the main subprogram, include full type information, specify ABS as INTRINSIC and supply the final END. The full subroutine is given in Figure 2.2.

2.1.5 Multi-exit loops

Sometimes, there will be more than one reason for exiting a loop prematurely and, hence, more than one test to make inside the loop. In such cases, the combination of a DO loop with a status variable is particularly convenient. Each test is programmed in a similar way to the convergence test in the example; if the test holds, the value of STATUS is updated and control is transferred directly to the forced exit point.

We can illustrate this by giving further consideration to the square root example. If the value of *oldx* is very small, the term $v/oldx$ becomes very large and there is a danger that overflow could result (see Section 3.1). We can check for this situation – here is a modified program plan for the subroutine:

> Given: *v*, *x0*, *tolerance*, *maximum number of iterations.*
> Define: *tiny (a very small positive number)*
> Set: *newx* = *x0*
> **repeat** (*at most* MAXITS *times*)
>   **if** $|newx| \leq tiny$ **then**
>   Note: 'overflow'
>   **else**
>   Set: *oldx* = *newx*
>   *newx* = (*oldx* + *v*/*oldx*)/2
>   **if** $|newx - oldx| \leq tolerance$ **then**
>   Note: 'solved'
> **until** 'solved' **or** 'overflow' (or limit reached)
> **if** 'solved' **then**
>   Record: root, number of iterations used
> **if** 'limit' **then**
>   Record: lastx
> **if** 'overflow' **then**
>   Record: lastx

To cater for this in the main subprogram, we introduce a further value (say OVFLOW) for STATUS:

EXAMPLE 1   39

```
      SUBROUTINE SQROOT (V,XO,TOL,MAXITS,
     *                   STATUS,ROOT,NOOFIT,LASTX)

      INTEGER   COUNT,LIMIT,MAXITS,NOOFIT,SOLVED,STATUS
      REAL      LASTX,NEWX,OLDX,ROOT,TOL,V,XO
      PARAMETER (SOLVED=0,LIMIT=1)
      INTRINSIC ABS

      NEWX=XO

      DO 10, COUNT=1,MAXITS
        OLDX=NEWX
        NEWX=(OLDX+V/OLDX)/2

        IF (ABS(NEWX-OLDX).LE.TOL) THEN
          STATUS=SOLVED
          GO TO 11
        END IF

10    CONTINUE
      STATUS=LIMIT

11    IF (STATUS.EQ.SOLVED) THEN
        ROOT  =NEWX
        NOOFIT=COUNT
      END IF

      IF (STATUS.EQ.LIMIT) LASTX=NEWX

      END
```

Figure 2.2 Subroutine for square root.

```
      PARAMETER (SOLVED=0,LIMIT=1,OVFLOW=2)
```

and, within the tests following the subroutine CALL, include a test for this value:

```
      IF (STATUS.EQ.OVFLOW) WRITE(*,2020) NEWXO

2020  FORMAT(1X,'Approximation to root is too small'
     *       /1X,'- current value is ',E10.4)
```

Inside the subroutine, we must define a small constant:

```
      PARAMETER (TINY=1E-10)
```

and, within the loop, compare the magnitude of NEWX with this constant. If the value of NEWX does not exceed TINY, we could set STATUS to OVFLOW and exit the loop immediately. This might be acceptable when there are only two reasons for exit from the loop but it is less acceptable when the number of reasons increases. Flow of control within a program becomes less apparent as more GO TO statements are used and so, in general, this is not an approach to be encouraged. In the case of a loop, we prefer to have only one possible point of forced exit – at the end of the loop body, as in Figure 2.2.

To retain a single point of forced exit, we introduce a further value for STATUS, to indicate that we have not yet noted any state giving cause for premature exit. This additional value therefore indicates that we are still iterating:

```
INTEGER   ITRATE
PARAMETER (ITRATE=-1,SOLVED=0,LIMIT=1,OVFLOW=2)
```

Prior to entry to the DO loop, we state that we are iterating:

```
STATUS=ITRATE
```

and, as the last action within the loop, we test to see if we are no longer iterating (because some other status has been noted) and, if appropriate, exit the loop:

```
IF (STATUS.NE.ITRATE) GO TO 11
```

There are no other GO TO statements within the loop. Each test simply notes the new status but does not exit the loop. Instead, an IF-THEN-ELSE-ENDIF construct is used to arrange for appropriate statements to be executed:

```
      STATUS=ITRATE
      DO 10, COUNT=1,MAXITS
        IF (ABS(NEWX).LE.TINY) THEN
          STATUS=OVFLOW
        ELSE
          OLDX=NEWX
          NEWX=(OLDX+V/OLDX)/2
          IF (ABS(NEWX-OLDX).LE.TOL) STATUS=SOLVED
        END IF

        IF (STATUS.NE.ITRATE) GO TO 11
10    CONTINUE
      STATUS=LIMIT
11    ...
```

Upon exit from the loop, there is an additional state for which we must check (overflow). As can be seen from the plan, the action to be carried out if overflow

EXAMPLE 1   41

```
      SUBROUTINE SQROOT (V,X0,TOL,MAXITS,
     *                   STATUS,ROOT,NOOFIT,LASTX)

      INTEGER   COUNT,ITRATE,LIMIT,MAXITS,NOOFIT,OVFLOW,SOLVED,STATUS
      REAL      LASTX,NEWX,OLDX,ROOT,TINY,TOL,X0,V
      PARAMETER (TINY=1E-10)
      PARAMETER (ITRATE=-1,SOLVED=0,LIMIT=1,OVFLOW=2)
      INTRINSIC ABS

      NEWX=X0

      STATUS=ITRATE
      DO 10, COUNT=1,MAXITS
        IF (ABS(NEWX).LE.TINY) THEN
          STATUS=OVFLOW
        ELSE
          OLDX=NEWX
          NEWX=(OLDX+V/OLDX)/2
          IF (ABS(NEWX-OLDX).LE.TOL) STATUS=SOLVED
        END IF

        IF (STATUS.NE.ITRATE) GO TO 11
10    CONTINUE
      STATUS=LIMIT

11    IF (STATUS.EQ.SOLVED) THEN
        ROOT  =NEWX
        NOOFIT=COUNT
      END IF

      IF (STATUS.EQ.LIMIT .OR. STATUS.EQ.OVFLOW) LASTX=NEWX

      END
```

Figure 2.3 Subroutine for square root.

is detected is that for the limit on the number of iterations being reached without convergence. Accordingly, these two tests can be combined:

```
      IF (STATUS.EQ.LIMIT .OR. STATUS.EQ.OVFLOW) LASTX=NEWX
```

The full subroutine is presented in Figure 2.3. Note that the calling subprogram (Figure 2.1) must be extended to include a check for STATUS taking the value OVFLOW.

2.1.6 Testing the program

To test the program we must run it and supply appropriate data. Our square root program requires two values: the number whose root we require and an initial approximation to the root. As an initial check, it is sensible to use a number whose root is known and to supply an initial approximation from which we would expect the process to converge without difficulty; for example, we might attempt to compute the square root of 9, using 2 as the initial approximation.

If the program produces a sensible answer after relatively few iterations, its performance can be checked with one or two other straightforward cases. If the program does not perform satisfactorily in these simple cases, we must find out why. If a close examination of the program text reveals no obvious mistake, the best approach is to modify the program to output suitable intermediate results. We would do this by by inserting temporary PRINT or WRITE statements in the subroutine. Sensible values to display are:

- the input arguments, immediately upon entry;
- the appropriate output arguments, immediately prior to exit;
- the iteration count, current approximation and status, each time round the loop.

In fact, for any but the simplest algorithms, it is sensible to produce some diagnostic output for a few sample runs to be sure that all is well.

The subroutine of Figure 2.4 is equivalent to that of Figure 2.3 but includes appropriate diagnostic output statements. For V=9 and X0=2, the output produced is shown in Figure 2.5.

Figure 2.4 Subroutine (with diagnostic output) for square root.

```
      SUBROUTINE SQROOT (V,X0,TOL,MAXITS,
     *                   STATUS,ROOT,NOOFIT,LASTX)

      INTEGER   COUNT,ITRATE,LIMIT,MAXITS,NOOFIT,OVFLOW,SOLVED,STATUS
      REAL      LASTX,NEWX,OLDX,ROOT,TINY,TOL,X0,V
      PARAMETER (TINY=1E-10)
      PARAMETER (ITRATE=-1,SOLVED=0,LIMIT=1,OVFLOW=2)
      INTRINSIC ABS

C        {diagnostic output}
      WRITE(*,3000) V,X0,TOL,MAXITS
3000  FORMAT(1X,'Upon entry to SQROOT :-'
     *       /1X,'  V    = ',F10.6/1X,'  X0    = ',F10.6
     *       /1X,'  TOL  = ',E10.2/1X,'  MAXITS = ',I2/)
      PRINT *, 'Iteration    NEWX    STATUS'
```

EXAMPLE 1   43

```
      NEWX=X0

      STATUS=ITRATE
      DO 10, COUNT=1,MAXITS
        IF (ABS(NEWX).LE.TINY) THEN
          STATUS=OVFLOW
        ELSE
          OLDX=NEWX
          NEWX=(OLDX+V/OLDX)/2
          IF (ABS(NEWX-OLDX).LE.TOL) STATUS=SOLVED
        END IF

C          {diagnostic output}
          WRITE(*,3010) COUNT,NEWX,STATUS

3010    FORMAT(1X,I5,4X,F10.6,4X,I2)
        IF (STATUS.NE.ITRATE) GO TO 11

10      CONTINUE
        STATUS=LIMIT

11      IF (STATUS.EQ.SOLVED) THEN
          ROOT  =NEWX
          NOOFIT=COUNT

C          {diagnostic output}
          WRITE(*,3020) STATUS,ROOT,NOOFIT
3020    FORMAT(/1X,'At exit from SQROOT :-'
       *          /1X,'  STATUS = ',I3
       *          /1X,'  ROOT   = ',F10.6
       *          /1X,'  NOOFIT = ',I3)
        END IF

        IF (STATUS.EQ.LIMIT .OR. STATUS.EQ.OVFLOW) THEN
          LASTX=NEWX

C          {diagnostic output}
          WRITE(*,3030) STATUS,LASTX
3030    FORMAT(/1X,'At exit from SQROOT :-'
       *          /1X,'  STATUS = ',I3
       *          /1X,'   LASTX = ',F10.6)
        END IF

      END
```

Figure 2.4 *cont.*

```
Upon entry to SQROOT :-
  V     = 9.000000
  X0    = 2.000000
  TOL   = 0.50E-06
  MAXITS = 25

Iteration    NEWX    STATUS
    1      3.250000    -1
    2      3.009615    -1
    3      3.000015    -1
    4      3.000000    -1
    5      3.000000     0

At exit from SQROOT :-
  STATUS =  0
  ROOT   =  3.000000
  NOOFIT =  5
```

Figure 2.5 Diagnostic output from the subroutine of Figure 2.4.

Having confirmed that the program produces the correct answers for some straightforward values, the programmer should ensure that it recognizes the two special cases it tests for – overflow imminent and limit on iterations reached without convergence. The overflow check is used to guard against a value of x being too small and can be activated by supplying a very small value for X0 (say, X0=1E-20).

Because we have applied no mathematical analysis to our algorithm, we have no way of knowing how many iterations to expect for any particular initial values. Consequently, we do not know what values to supply to check the test on the number of iterations. The simplest way to check this is to reduce the value of MAXITS in the main subprogram. If we use MAXITS=4 and then try V=1E6 and X0=1, we would not expect convergence before the maximum number of iterations have been performed.

Once the program has been checked and found to work in all these respects, MAXITS can be reinstated with a sensible value and all the diagnostic output statements removed. If it is likely that the program will be modified subsequently, it is wise to suppress the diagnostic output rather than remove it. This way, it can be reactivated easily if it should ever be required again. To achieve this, we introduce a LOGICAL constant:

```
LOGICAL   DGNSTC
PARAMETER (DGNSTC=.FALSE.)
```

and the diagnostic output statements are bracketed with

EXAMPLE 1   45

```
IF (DGNSTC) THEN
   ...
END IF
```

To obtain diagnostic output, the logical constant is simply redefined:

```
PARAMETER (DGNSTC=.TRUE.)
```

2.2 Example 2

Many of the numerical methods discussed in this book involve vectors and matrices and, correspondingly, the subroutines implementing them utilize arrays. To illustrate the use of arrays, this example involves writing a program to perform matrix–vector multiplication. Given an $n \times n$ matrix A and a column vector v of n elements, the vector $u = Av$ will be produced.

Rather than use a single main subprogram to input the appropriate values and perform the multiplication, we shall write separate subprograms to perform each distinct operation required. For our simple example, the operations required are:

- Vector input
- Matrix input
- Matrix–vector product
- Vector output

2.2.1 The main subprogram

The plan for the main subprogram is straightforward:

(1) *Define parameters*:
  maximum permitted value of n

(2) *Dimension variables*:
  u, v (1:*maxn*)
  A (1:*maxn*, 1:*maxn*)

(3) *Input*:
  n, A, v

(4) *Do*:
  matrix–vector product
    using (maxn, n, A, v)
    to produce (u)

(5)   *Do*:
>>   *vector display*
>>   *using* (*n*, *u*)

Because we intend to use subroutines for matrix operations, we must pass as arguments both the value of *n*, indicating what proportion of each array is to be used, and also the value used to dimension the actual argument. The reasons for this were given in Section 1.12.3.

This program plan maps directly into FORTRAN 77 and the resulting main subprogram is given in Figure 2.6. Note that we have assumed that the supplied value of N does not exceed the value MAXN; in practice, the program should check this.

2.2.2 The subroutines

Each subroutine is so straightforward that program plans are probably unnecessary. We start with the subroutine for matrix–vector multiplication. To form $w = Ax$, we must compute w_i as the dot product of the *i*th row vector of A with the column vector x.

```
      SUBROUTINE MATVEC (SIZE,M,A,X,  AX)
C        {The array AX receives the vector resulting from the
C         postmultiplication of the matrix A by the vector x }

      INTEGER I,J,M,SIZE
      REAL    DPROD
      REAL    A(SIZE,SIZE),AX(M),X(M)

      DO 10, I=1,M
        DPROD=0
        DO 20, J=1,M
          DPROD=DPROD+A(I,J)*X(J)
20      CONTINUE
        AX(I)=DPROD
10    CONTINUE

      END
```

The other subroutines are as follows:

```
      SUBROUTINE VECIN (M, V)
      INTEGER I,M
      REAL    V(M)
      READ *, (V(I),I=1,M)
      END
```

EXAMPLE 2   47

```
PROGRAM MVPROD

INTEGER   MAXN,N
PARAMETER (MAXN=10)
REAL      A(MAXN,MAXN),U(MAXN),V(MAXN)
EXTERNAL  MATIN,MATVEC,VECIN,VECOUT

PRINT  *,'What is the value of n?'
READ *, N
PRINT  *,'Please supply the matrix A, row-wise'
CALL MATIN (MAXN,N, A)
PRINT  *,'and now the vector v'
CALL VECIN (N, V)
CALL MATVEC (MAXN,N,A,V, U)
CALL VECOUT (N,U)

END
```

Figure 2.6 Main subprogram for matrix–vector multiplication.

```
      SUBROUTINE MATIN (SIZE,M, A)
      INTEGER I,J,M,SIZE
      REAL    A(SIZE,SIZE)
      READ *, ((A(I,J),J=1,M),I=1,M)
      END

      SUBROUTINE VECOUT (M,X)
      INTEGER I,M
      REAL    X(M)
      WRITE(1,2000) (X(I),I=1,M)
2000  FORMAT (1X,F8.2)
      END
```

2.2.3 Use of files

Whenever vectors and matrices are involved, it is usually unrealistic to supply all data values from the keyboard and to display all results only on the screen. One would usually set up a file (or files) containing the data and, possibly, send a copy of the results to a file for subsequent printing.

   If we were to apply this approach in the present context, we would remove all the prompts from the main subprogram and modify the READ statement to take its data from a file. Each subroutine that reads data must be modified to take its data from this input file. The subroutine to display a vector could send a copy to an output file and, so that any output statement added subsequently to any subprogram uses the same file, we would open this file in the main subprogram. In particular, the calling subprogram might print a title in the output file before activating a subprogram that outputs to the file. Note that when output is to a file, we do not need a control character at the start of each output record. Figure 2.7 shows the complete program, with all these modifications.

Figure 2.7 Matrix–vector multiplication using files.

```
PROGRAM MVPROD

INTEGER   MAXN,N
PARAMETER (MAXN=10)
REAL      A(MAXN,MAXN),U(MAXN),V(MAXN)
EXTERNAL  MATIN,MATVEC,VECIN,VECOUT

OPEN( 9,FILE='MVDATA')
OPEN(10,FILE='MVOUT')
READ(9,*) N
CALL MATIN (MAXN,N, A)
CALL VECIN (N, V)
CALL MATVEC (MAXN,N,A,V, U)
PRINT(10,*) 'Vector resulting from matrix-vector product'
CALL VECOUT (N,U)

END

      SUBROUTINE MATVEC (SIZE,M,A,X, AX)
C        {The array AX receives the vector resulting from the
C           postmultiplication of the matrix A by the vector x}

INTEGER I,J,M,SIZE
REAL    DOTPRD
REAL    A(SIZE,SIZE),AX(M),X(M)

DO 10, I=1,M
  DOTPRD=0
  DO 20, J=1,M
    DOTPRD=DOTPRD+A(I,J)*X(J)
20     CONTINUE
  AX(I)=DOTPRD
10    CONTINUE
END

      SUBROUTINE VECIN (M, V)
      INTEGER I,M
      REAL    V(M)
      READ(9,*) (V(I),I=1,M)
      END
```

EXAMPLE 2   49

```
      SUBROUTINE MATIN (SIZE,M, A)
      INTEGER I,J,M,SIZE
      REAL    A(SIZE,SIZE)
      READ(9,*) ((A(I,J),J=1,M),I=1,M)
      END

      SUBROUTINE VECOUT (M,X)
      INTEGER I,M
      REAL    X(M)
      WRITE(10,2000) (X(I),I=1,M)
2000  FORMAT (F8.2)
      END
```

Figure 2.7   *cont.*

The information in the output file would be more comprehensible if it included the original matrix and vector; appropriate modification of the program to achieve this is left as an exercise for the interested reader.

Chapter 3
Rounding errors, conditioning and stability

3.1 Round-off errors

3.2 Conditioning and stability

A feature of numerical methods is that they usually provide only approximate solutions; a *deliberate* error may be made (the truncation of a series, perhaps) so that the problem can be reformulated as one suitable for computer solution. In subsequent chapters the occurrence of this deliberate error will be noted and its effect discussed. In this chapter we consider a separate type of error which is classified under the general heading of **round-off error**. Round-off errors arise when numbers are not represented to their full precision; for example, when the fraction 1/3 is represented as the decimal number 0.3333. This is a direct consequence of computer arithmetic.

3.1   Round-off errors

The arithmetic in a machine involves numbers with a finite number of digits and so errors automatically occur when values are combined through an arithmetic operation. Numbers are stored in the computer as a sequence of binary (base 2) digits, or **bits**. Throughout this chapter, to simplify the analysis of the effects of round-off errors, a hypothetical decimal computer will be used, in which numbers are represented in the *normalized decimal floating point* form:

$$\pm 0.d_1 d_2 \ldots d_k \times 10^n \tag{3.1}$$

where

$$1 \leqslant d_1 \leqslant 9 \quad \text{and} \quad 0 \leqslant d_i \leqslant 9 \quad \text{for } i = 2, 3, \ldots, k$$

The sequence of digits $d_1 d_2 \ldots$ in Expression (3.1) is known as the **mantissa** and the power, n, as the **exponent**. As an example, $-5/8$ has the form

$$-0.625 \times 10^0$$

and $25/4$ has the form

$$+0.625 \times 10^1$$

The finite size of the computer implies that there is a maximum number, k say, of digits with which a value can be represented; that is, the mantissa must contain only k digits. The value of k will vary for different computers and compilers. Any real number, x, can be represented in the form

$$x = \pm 0.d_1 d_2 \ldots d_k d_{k+1} \ldots \times 10^n$$

The floating point form (3.1), which can be denoted by $fl(x)$, is obtained by terminating the mantissa of x after k digits. There are two common ways of doing this. One is known as **chopping** or **truncating**: the digits $d_{k+1}, d_{k+2}, \ldots$ are chopped from the mantissa to give

$$fl(x) = \pm 0.d_1 d_2 \ldots d_k \times 10^n$$

The second method is known as **rounding**. In this case, if x is positive, $5 \times 10^{n-(k+1)}$ is added to the number which is then chopped to give

$$fl(x) = \pm 0.D_1 D_2 \ldots D_k \times 10^n$$

If x is negative, $5 \times 10^{n-(k+1)}$ is subtracted from the number before it is chopped. For example, if $k = 4$ and rounding is used, $1.234\,56$ and $-6.543\,21$ are represented as $+0.1235 \times 10^1$ and -0.6543×10^1 respectively. If $k = 4$

and chopping is used, the representations are $+0.1234 \times 10^1$ and -0.6543×10^1. The term 'round-off error' will be used to describe the difference between the exact representation of a number and the chopped or rounded machine representation. For the examples discussed above, the round-off errors are, for rounding,

$$1.234\ 56\ -\quad 0.1235 \times 10^1 \ = -0.44 \times 10^{-3}$$
$$-6.543\ 21\ -\ (-0.6543 \times 10^1) = -0.21 \times 10^{-3}$$

and, for chopping,

$$1.234\ 56\ -\quad 0.1234 \times 10^1 \ = \quad 0.56 \times 10^{-3}$$
$$-6.543\ 21\ -\ (-0.6543 \times 10^1) = -0.21 \times 10^{-3}$$

There are also limitations on the size of the exponent; n must satisfy the inequality

$$-m \leqslant n \leqslant M$$

where M and m are positive integers, which may differ for different machines. If n becomes larger than M the number has become too large to be represented in the machine and is said to have **overflowed**. Overflow usually occurs when an attempt is made to divide by a very small number, possibly zero, and the programmer should be on the lookout for situations where this is likely to occur. The effect of an overflow varies for different computers and compilers. Some FORTRAN 77 implementations will stop the execution of the program with a suitable error message. Others may replace the overflowed number by a special constant which will not be changed in subsequent computations, and so flag the overflow in the output from the program. **Underflow** occurs when n becomes smaller than $-m$. In this case some computers reset the value of the number to zero and continue the calculation; others give an error message.

During a computation, the accumulation of round-off errors can completely swamp the solution and so it is essential to identify those operations that can lead to large round-off errors. Two measures are usually used to quantify these errors.

Definition 3.1

If x^* is an approximation to x, the **absolute error** is given by $|x - x^*|$.

Thus the floating-point representation of x has absolute error

$$|x - fl(x)|$$

For example, when rounding to four decimal digits, the absolute error in the floating-point representation of $1.234\ 56$ is 0.44×10^{-3}.

Definition 3.2

The two numbers x and x^* are said to agree to s decimal places if s is the largest non-negative integer for which

$$|x - x^*| < 0.5 \times 10^{-s}$$

For example, 1.234 46 and 1.234 65 agree to three decimal places because

$$|1.234\ 46 - 1.234\ 65| = 0.000\ 19$$

and

$$0.5 \times 10^{-4} < 0.000\ 19 < 0.5 \times 10^{-3}$$

Similarly, 0.001 234 46 and 0.001 234 65 agree to six decimal places. Note that two numbers that agree to s decimal places according to Definition 3.2 are not necessarily equal when *rounded* to s decimal places. From this example we can see that the magnitude of the numbers has had an effect on our perception of their 'closeness'; 0.001 234 46 and 0.001 234 65 appear 'closer' than do 1.234 46 and 1.234 65 although the non-zero digits are the same.

There are several situations where the dependence on the magnitude of the numbers is a disadvantage. One occurs in the discussion of rounding errors and so the rest of this section concentrates on the concept of relative error.

Definition 3.3

If x^* is an approximation to x, the **relative error** is given by

$$\frac{|x - x^*|}{|x|}$$

provided that x is not zero.

The floating point representation of x has a relative error

$$\frac{|x - fl(x)|}{|x|}$$

If k decimal digits are available, a relative error bound of 10^{-k+1} is found for chopping and 5×10^{-k} for rounding.

Definition 3.4

The numbers x and x^* are said to agree to s *significant* digits (or figures) if s is the largest non-negative integer for which

$$\frac{|x - x^*|}{|x|} < 5 \times 10^{-s}$$

For example, the two numbers 123.45 and 124.35 agree to two significant figures, as do 0.012 345 and 0.012 435. The concept of two numbers agreeing to a certain number of significant figures is particularly useful whenever the numbers are large or small. When they are large the number of decimal places of agreement is probably not important. When they are small the number of leading zero decimal places is not helpful in deciding whether the numbers are 'close'. For this reason, a relative error is normally used to define the closeness of numbers; its implementation will be discussed after the next section.

3.1.1 Computer arithmetic

What happens to round-off errors when numbers are combined? This is not an easy question to answer because the analysis can be complicated and can vary from machine to machine. An indication of some of the problems that can arise can be obtained by looking at specific examples. Readers interested in a detailed analysis of round-off errors should consult Wilkinson (1963). Assume that $fl(x)$ and $fl(y)$ are the floating point representations of x and y and that $\oplus$, $\ominus$, $\otimes$ and $\oslash$ represent the machine operations of addition, subtraction, multiplication and division. These operations can be defined as follows:

$$x \oplus y = fl(fl(x) + fl(y))$$
$$x \ominus y = fl(fl(x) - fl(y))$$
$$x \otimes y = fl(fl(x) \times fl(y))$$
$$x \oslash y = fl(fl(x)/fl(y))$$

and we are interested, for example, in the difference between $x + y$ and $x \oplus y$. Before starting this discussion we note that computers usually perform arithmetic in registers that can hold twice as many digits as the floating-point representation of numbers. This $2k$-digit number is most often chopped, as opposed to rounded, to give a k-digit representation, and, in our examples we will do this. We shall illustrate the effect of the different operations in the case $k = 4$.

Consider each of the operations in turn, starting with $x \oplus y$. Now

$$x \oplus y = fl(fl(x) + fl(y))$$

and the error in $x \oplus y$ has two sources; the error in representing x and y, and the error in representing the sum $fl(x) + fl(y)$. For example, if $x = 4/3$ then, on a four-digit machine, $fl(x) = 0.1333 \times 10^1$ and if $y = 2/9$ then $fl(y) = 0.2222 \times 10^0$. Thus

$$fl(x) + fl(y) = 0.1333 \times 10^1 + 0.2222 \times 10^0$$

However, numbers that are to be added together must have the same exponent and so this sum is rewritten as

$$fl(x) + fl(y) = 0.1333 \times 10^1 + 0.022\ 22 \times 10^1$$
$$= 0.155\ 52 \times 10^1$$

from which

$$fl(fl(x) + fl(y)) = 0.1555 \times 10^1$$

and an additional error has occurred.

The effect of these errors can be more noticeable when a sequence of numbers is being added. For example, the order in which the numbers are added may affect the round-off error and, as a consequence, the sum. Consider the sum

$$x \oplus z \oplus z \oplus z \oplus z$$

where $x = 0.1333 \times 10^1$ and $z = 0.3000 \times 10^{-4}$. Now

$$x + z = 0.1333 \times 10^1 + 0.000\ 03 \times 10^1 = 0.133\ 33 \times 10^1$$

and

$$fl(x + z) = 0.1333 \times 10^1 = x$$

Continuing in this way,

$$fl(x + z + z + z + z) = 0.1333 \times 10^1 = x$$

Now reverse the order of the addition and form

$$z \oplus z \oplus z \oplus z \oplus x$$

instead. The first addition is

$$z + z = 0.3000 \times 10^{-4} + 0.3000 \times 10^{-4}$$
$$= 0.6000 \times 10^{-4}$$

and

$$fl(z + z) = 0.6000 \times 10^{-4}$$

Similarly,

$$fl(z + z + z + z) = 0.1200 \times 10^{-3}$$

and

$$fl(z + z + z + z + x) = fl(0.1200 \times 10^{-3} + 0.1333 \times 10^{1})$$
$$= fl(0.133\ 42 \times 10^{1})$$
$$= 0.1334 \times 10^{1}$$

which is the correctly rounded result. Ideally, when summing numbers of the same sign, they should be added in order of increasing magnitude.

Next consider the calculation of

$$x \ominus y = fl(fl(x) - fl(y))$$

A problem that can occur with this computation is illustrated by choosing $x = 3/11$ and $y = 8/29$; $fl(x) = 0.2727 \times 10^{0}$ and $fl(y) = 0.2759 \times 10^{0}$ and so

$$fl(fl(x) - fl(y)) = fl(-0.0032 \times 10^{0})$$
$$= -0.3200 \times 10^{-2} \qquad \qquad \textbf{(3.2)}$$

But

$$fl(x - y) = fl(-1/319) = -0.3134 \times 10^{-2}$$

The problem is that the zeros in Equation (3.2) do not represent useful information; they are there to fill in the floating-point representation of the result of the computation. There has been a loss of significant figures or of **precision**. This type of error is frequently called **cancellation error** and can be an important source of further error in numerical computation. If possible, calculations should be reorganized to avoid such cancellation error and an example of such a reorganization is given later in this section.

The operation

$$x \otimes y = fl(fl(x) \times fl(y))$$

presents few problems apart from possible overflow or underflow. For example, the product

$$(0.1234 \times 10^{M}) \otimes (0.4321 \times 10^{M})$$

cannot be represented on a machine with maximum exponent M. Similarly

$$(0.1234 \times 10^{-m}) \otimes (0.4321 \times 10^{-m})$$

is too small to be represented using minimum exponent $-m$. The predominant error present when $x \otimes y$ is formed is that of representing $x \times y$ in floating-point form. To illustrate this, consider the product of $x = 5/6$ and $y = 1/11$:

$$fl(x) = 0.8333 \times 10^0 \quad \text{and} \quad fl(y) = 0.9091 \times 10^{-1}$$

giving

$$fl(x) \times fl(y) = 0.757\ 553\ 03 \times 10^{-1}$$

and

$$fl(fl(x) \times fl(y)) = x \otimes y = 0.7575 \times 10^{-1}$$

The correct value of $x \times y$, to eight significant figures, is

$$x \times y = 0.757\ 575\ 75 \times 10^{-1}$$

and is 'significantly' different from $fl(x) \times fl(y)$. When chopped to four significant figures, $x \times y$ is

$$x \times y = 0.7575 \times 10^{-1}$$

and the floating point calculation has given the correctly chopped result. In a similar way the operation

$$x \oslash y = fl(fl(x)/fl(y))$$

presents few problems other than division by a number close to zero. The effect of this is to magnify the error that resulted from representing x in floating-point form. For example, if $x = 5/9$ is divided by $y = 1/9876$,

$$fl(x) = 0.5556 \times 10^0$$
$$fl(y) = 0.1013 \times 10^{-5}$$
$$fl(x)/fl(y) = 0.548\ 469\ 89 \times 10^4$$

and so

$$fl(fl(x)/fl(y)) = x \oslash y = 0.5484 \times 10^4$$

But

$$x/y = 0.548\ 666\ 67 \times 10^4$$

giving

$$fl(x/y) = 0.5486 \times 10^4$$

```
      REAL FUNCTION DTPROD (U,V,N)

      INTEGER  I,N
      REAL     U(N),V(N)
      DOUBLE PRECISION SUM
      INTRINSIC DPROD

      SUM=0
      DO 10, I=1,N
        SUM=SUM+DPROD(U(I),V(I))
10    CONTINUE
      DTPROD=SUM

      END
```

Figure 3.1   Function subprogram for sum of products.

and the earlier rounding errors have been magnified.

We illustrate two techniques for avoiding the accumulation of rounding errors. The first concerns the sum of a sequence of products:

$$z = u_1v_1 + u_2v_2 + \cdots + u_nv_n$$

Sums of this type occur frequently in matrix–vector calculations. One example of such a sum was given in Chapter 2 where the product of a matrix and a vector was formed; this involves the product of a row of the matrix with the vector giving a sum of the above form. In FORTRAN 77, one way of avoiding the accumulation of errors is to accumulate the sum, product by product, in a **double precision** variable. The specification

```
      DOUBLE PRECISION SUM
```

is included in the subprogram, and the sum is formed using the loop

```
      SUM=0
      DO 10, I=1,N
        { sum=sum+next term }
10    CONTINUE
```

The 'next term' in this loop consists of the double precision product of two values. This can be achieved using the FORTRAN intrinsic function DPROD; for example, the value given by the function DPROD(X,Y) is the double precision product of X and Y. A possible version of a function subprogram, DTPROD, is given in Figure 3.1.

This subprogram cannot be applied directly to the multiplication of a vector by a matrix because, in FORTRAN 77, there is no natural way of representing a row of a matrix as a vector. However, the same principle of accumulating a double precision sum could have been used within the program of Figure 2.7.

As an illustration of the technique of reordering arithmetic to avoid the loss of significant figures, consider the problem of determining the zeros of the polynomial

$$p(x) = x^2 - 50.02x + 1$$

using a machine carrying only four digits. We will use the well known formula

$$x = \frac{-b \pm (b^2 - 4ac)^{1/2}}{2a}$$

for the roots of the quadratic equation

$$ax^2 + bx + c = 0$$

Assuming that $b^2 - 4ac > 0$ and $b < 0$, as in this example, the smaller (in modulus) of the two roots is given by

$$x_s = \frac{-b - (b^2 - 4ac)^{1/2}}{2a} \qquad \textbf{(3.3)}$$

Now if $4ac$ is small compared with b^2 the value $(b^2 - 4ac)^{1/2}$ will be approximately equal to $|b|$ and the numerator in Equation (3.3) will involve the subtraction of nearly equal quantities. To see the effect of this, we calculate

$$b \otimes b \ominus 4 \otimes a \otimes c$$

as follows:

$$b \otimes b = fl(fl(0.5002 \times 10^2) \times fl(0.5002 \times 10^2)) = 0.2502 \times 10^4$$
$$4 \otimes a \otimes c = 0.4000 \times 10^1$$
$$b \otimes b \ominus 4 \otimes a \otimes c = fl(0.2502 \times 10^4 - 0.4000 \times 10^1)$$
$$= fl(0.250\,160\,00 \times 10^4)$$
$$= 0.2501 \times 10^4$$

Forming the square root in floating-point arithmetic gives

$$fl((b \otimes b \ominus 4 \otimes a \otimes c)^{1/2}) = 0.5000 \times 10^2$$

and so the smaller root is given by

$$x_s = fl((-(-0.5002 \times 10^2) - 0.5000 \times 10^2)/2) = 0.1000 \times 10^{-3}$$

whereas the correct value is $x_s = 0.2000 \times 10^{-1}$. This error can be avoided by calculating the larger root first, using the formula

$$x_1 = \frac{-b + (b^2 - 4ac)^{1/2}}{2a}$$

In this case the value of x_1 is 0.5001×10^2. The value of x_s can be found from the equality

$$x_s = \frac{c}{x_1 a} = fl(1/(0.5001 \times 10^2 \times 1)) = 0.1999 \times 10^{-2}$$

Now, despite round-off errors, both the zeros are found satisfactorily.

3.1.2 Relative error test

We now consider the implementation of the relative error test. Usually we will use it when we want to check for the convergence of a sequence of iterates; for example, to determine whether x_{n+1} and x_n are 'close', we test

$$\frac{|x_{n+1} - x_n|}{|x_n|} \leq tolerance$$

for some value of *tolerance* specified beforehand. This test can be implemented in the form

$$|x_{n+1} - x_n| \leq |x_n| \cdot tolerance$$

to avoid problems that may arise if x_n is close to zero. However, this approach presents a problem if the limit of the sequence is close to zero because $|x_n| \cdot tolerance$ can then be very small, possibly too small to be represented on the computer. To overcome this, we can use a number, usually called the **machine epsilon**, which is measure of the precision with which calculations can be performed on a particular machine.

Definition 3.5

The machine epsilon, ε_m, is the smallest positive number such that

$$1 + \varepsilon_m > 1$$

The machine epsilon will vary for different computers but, for any particular computer, its value can easily be determined. For our four-digit machine, using decimal arithmetic, $\varepsilon_m = 0.1000 \times 10^{-2}$ because

$$1 + \varepsilon_m = 0.1000 \times 10^1 + 0.1000 \times 10^{-2} = 0.1001 \times 10^1$$

It is clear that a difference $|x_{n+1} - x_n|$ smaller than ε_m cannot be represented, and so testing the relative error using a right-hand side

$$|x_n| \cdot tolerance \leqslant \varepsilon_m$$

is useless. Thus it is usual to test whether $|x_n| \cdot tolerance$ is less than a small multiple, 4 (say), of the machine epsilon. If this is the case, the error test takes the form

$$|x_{n+1} - x_n| \leqslant 4\varepsilon_m$$

The following fragment from a FORTRAN 77 subprogram indicates how such a test could be applied.

```
REAL     LOCTOL,MEPSX4,TOL,XN,XNP1
PARAMETER (TOL=...,MEPSX4=...)
       :
       :
LOCTOL=ABS(XN)*TOL
IF (LOCTOL.LT.MEPSX4) LOCTOL=MEPSX4
IF (ABS(XNP1 - XN).LE.LOCTOL) THEN
       :
       :
```

This modification is not included in the subprograms in later chapters because it is more important to present a clear explanation of the programming of the mathematical algorithms. The necessary modification of the subprograms is left to the interested reader.

3.2 Conditioning and stability

The **condition** of a function is a measure of the sensitivity of that function to small changes in its parameters. A function is **well-conditioned** if small changes in the parameters induce only a small change in the behaviour of the function and is **ill-conditioned** otherwise. The concept of conditioning is considered in more detail in Chapter 5 with reference to the solution of a system of linear algebraic equations. Here, ill-conditioning is illustrated by considering the classical problem, discussed by Wilkinson (1959), of finding the zeros of the polynomial:

$$p(x) = (x - 1)(x - 2) \ldots (x - 19)(x - 20)$$

of degree 20 with zeros at $x = 1, 2, \ldots, 20$. If the factors of this polynomial are multiplied out, giving

$$p(x) = x^{20} - 210x^{19} + \cdots + 20!$$

and the coefficient of the power x^{19} is changed by approximately 10^{-7} the behaviour of the polynomial changes radically. Now the polynomial has five pairs of complex roots and, using very accurate computations, Wilkinson has calculated the roots to be

1.000 000 000	2.000 000 000
3.000 000 000	4.000 000 000
4.999 999 928	6.000 006 944
6.999 697 234	8.007 267 603
8.917 250 249	20.846 908 101
10.095 266 145 ±	0.643 500 904i
11.793 633 881 ±	1.652 329 728i
13.992 358 137 ±	2.518 830 070i
16.730 737 466 ±	2.812 624 894i
19.562 439 400 ±	1.940 330 347i

The **stability** of a numerical process is related to its conditioning. A numerical method is said to be **stable** if small changes, including round-off errors, in the data induce only small changes in the solution of the process; the process is **unstable** otherwise. It is obviously desirable to use stable numerical methods in which the error in the numerical values does not grow, out of control.

If the error, E_n, at the nth stage of a numerical process has the form $|E_n| \propto n$, the growth in the error is said to be **linear**. If $|E_n| \propto k^n$, for some $k > 1$, the growth of the error is said to be **exponential**; if $k < 1$ the error decreases exponentially.

Normally it is difficult to avoid linear error growth; a convergent iterative process, such as that outlined in Section 2.1, is one of the few in which there is built-in control of the error. For $k > 1$, k^n grows quickly, even for quite small values of n, and so exponential error growth should be avoided. A method with linear error growth is usually deemed to be stable and one with exponential error growth unstable. The following is an example of an unstable numerical process.

Consider the sequence $1, 1/6, 1/36, 1/216, \ldots, 1/(6)^n, \ldots$ generated by defining $x_0 = 1$, $x_1 = 1/6$ and using the relation

$$x_n = 37x_{n-1}/6 - x_{n-2} \tag{3.4}$$

for $n = 2, 3, \ldots$. This equation is a difference relation and it can be shown that its general solution is

$$x_n = c_1(1/6)^n + c_2(6)^n \tag{3.5}$$

Table 3.1

n	x_n	$1/6^n$
0	1.0000	1.0000
1	0.1667	0.1667
2	0.0280	0.0278
3	0.0060	0.0046
4	0.0090	0.0008
5	0.0495	0.0001

In order for x_0 to be 1 and x_1 to be $1/6$, c_1 must take the value 1 and c_2 the value 0. Thus the correct value of x_n is $1/6^n$. The values in Table 3.1 were calculated using four-digit arithmetic with rounding and, as can be seen, the errors are increasing rapidly; by the stage $n = 4$ the solution, x_4, bears little resemblance to the correct answer.

The computer has not been able to reproduce the solution (3.5) because four-digit representations are being used. In this hypothetical machine $x_0 = 0.1000 \times 10^1$ and $x_1 = 0.1667 \times 10^0$ and so $c_1 = 0.1000 \times 10^1$ and $c_2 = 0.5556 \times 10^{-5}$. Consequently x_n now has the form

$$x_n = 0.1000 \times 10^1 \times (0.1667 \times 10^0)^n + 0.5556 \times 10^{-5} \times (0.6000 \times 10^1)^n$$

so that an error $0.5556 \times 10^{-5} \times (0.6000 \times 10^1)^n$ is being made at every stage. This is exponential error growth.

Even by using multiple-precision arithmetic, mentioned earlier, it is possible only to delay the moment when error growth swamps the solution. Thus it is important to choose numerical methods that are not susceptible to this problem.

Chapter 4
Non-linear algebraic equations

4.1	Methods without derivatives	4.2	Methods with derivatives
		4.3	Polynomial equations

A problem that occurs frequently is that of finding a value α which is a root of an equation of the form

$$f(x) = 0$$

and hence a zero of the function $f(x)$. For example, whenever the maximum of a function $F(x)$ is sought, a necessary condition that must be satisfied at the maximum is that the derivative of $F(x)$ should be zero. In practice, this condition is used as an aid to finding the maximum. The techniques described in this chapter, along with those for solving systems of linear algebraic equations, underpin many of the numerical methods used to solve applied mathematical problems.

The fastest methods for determining a zero of a function involve the evaluation of derivatives but these derivatives are sometimes difficult or even impossible to obtain, or are expensive to evaluate. Hence, we first consider methods that do not make use of derivatives. We shall assume throughout that $f(x)$ is continuous in the interval of interest and is sufficiently differentiable for the methods to be meaningful.

Where appropriate, the methods are illustrated by applying them to the test function

$$f(x) = x - e^{1/x}$$

This function has only one zero and, to six decimal places, it is 1.763 223.

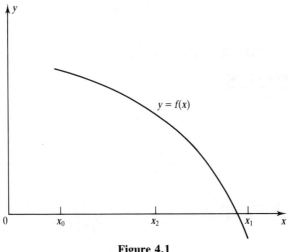

Figure 4.1

4.1 Methods without derivatives

Throughout this section it is assumed that an interval containing precisely one root has been established. This could have been obtained, for example, by sketching a rough graph of the function.

4.1.1 Bisection method

In the method of bisection, an interval containing the root is halved successively until the size of the interval reaches some specified tolerance. For the purposes of this discussion, it is assumed that the root does not coincide with an end-point of any interval constructed.

Starting with an interval $[x_0,x_1]$ containing the root, the mid-point, x_2, is determined from

$$x_2 = \frac{x_0 + x_1}{2}$$

and $f(x_2)$ is calculated. If $f(x_0)$ and $f(x_2)$ have opposite signs, the root must lie in the interval $[x_0,x_2]$. However, if $f(x_0)$ and $f(x_2)$ have the same sign, as in Figure 4.1, the root must lie in the interval $[x_2,x_1]$. In either case the size of the interval containing the root has been halved. A further bisection can be carried out on the new smaller interval and the procedure repeated as required.

Clearly, after n steps of bisection, the interval will have size

$$\frac{x_1 - x_0}{2^n}$$

Given $f(x)$, x_0, x_1
Repeat
  Set $x_2 = (x_0 + x_1)/2$
  If $f(x_0)$ *and* $f(x_2)$ *have opposite signs Then*
    { *root in left interval* }
    Set $x_1 = x_2$
  Otherwise
    { *root in right interval* }
    Set $x_0 = x_2$
Until converged

Figure 4.2 Algorithm for bisection method.

When this does not exceed some value t, any value within this interval differs from the root by no more than t. In particular, its mid-point differs from the root by no more than $t/2$ and so this value is taken as our estimate. By specifying a tolerance, t, we are imposing a limit $(t/2)$ on the acceptable error in this estimate.

An algorithm for the bisection method is given in Figure 4.2. To apply this algorithm to our test function, we can take $[x_0,x_1] = [1,2]$ as the initial interval because, using the notation $f_i = f(x_i)$, f_0 is negative (-1.7183) and f_1 is positive (0.3513). The first mid-point is

$$x_2 = (1 + 2)/2 = 1.5$$

and, working to four decimal places,

$$f_2 = 1.5 - e^{1/1.5} = -0.4477$$

Here, f_2 has the same sign as f_0 and so the root must lie in the right half-interval $[1.5,2]$. Thus we set $x_0 = x_2$ ($= 1.5$) and perform the next bisection step. The new x_2 is

$$x_2 = (1.5 + 2)/2 = 1.75$$

and

$$f_2 = -0.0208$$

Again, the values f_0 and f_2 have the same sign and so we set $x_0 = x_2$ ($= 1.75$). After the third step ($x_2 = 1.875$, $f_2 = 0.1704$), f_0 and f_2 have opposite signs indicating that the root is in the left half-interval $[1.75,1.875]$ and so we set $x_1 = x_2$ ($= 1.875$). Keeping track of the ends of the different intervals constructed is simplified if we tabulate the results as in Table 4.1. At each stage, the updated end-point, x_i, is the one for which $f(x_i)$ has the same sign as $f(x_2)$.

Table 4.1   Solution to the test equation using the bisection method.

x_0 ($f_0 < 0$)	x_2		x_1 ($f_1 > 0$)
1			2
	1.5	($f_2 < 0$)	
1.5			2
	1.75	($f_2 < 0$)	
1.75			2
	1.875	($f_2 > 0$)	
1.75			1.875
	1.825	($f_2 > 0$)	
1.75			1.825
	1.7813	($f_2 > 0$)	
1.75			1.7813
	1.7657	($f_2 > 0$)	

The procedure is continued until the root has been obtained to the required accuracy. Remember that the error in any approximation is always less than or equal to half the size of the last interval bisected. Thus, for example, the error in the last approximation (1.7657) displayed in Table 4.1 is less than or equal to $(1.7813 - 1.75)/2 = 0.015\,65$.

Program construction

Because the bisection method is the first presented, we discuss the program construction in more detail than will usually be the case in subsequent chapters.

As a first step, the main features to be incorporated are noted in a very general manner:

- Define: necessary parameters
- Input: initial approximations
- Do: bisection for a given function
- Print: results

Now we consider any special precautions that need to be built into the program. At the start of the bisection process, we shall check that the initial approximations do, in fact, bracket the root. Theoretically, the bisection alogrithm is guaranteed to converge. Nevertheless, we shall impose an upper bound on the number of iterations to be executed in case the tolerance specified for an acceptable solution is beyond the capabilities of the machine in use. If the bound on the number of iterations is reached before convergence is achieved, we

---

(1)   *Define parameters:*
    tolerance, maximum number of iterations,
    status values (i.e. solved, limit on number of iterations reached, no bracket)

(2)   *Input:*
    x0,x1

(3)   *Do:*
    bisection
        using (f(x),x0,x1,tolerance, maximum number of iterations)
    to produce (status and
            either root, residual, number of iterations used
            or end-points of current interval)

(4)   **if** *solved* **then**
    Print: root, residual, number of iterations used
    if *limit on iterations reached* **then**
    Print: maximum number of iterations, end-points of current interval
    if *no bracket* **then**
    Print: suitable message

Figure 4.3 Plan of main subprogram for bisection method.

---

shall output the end-points of the current interval. If the iteration does converge, we shall output the number of iterations used, the final estimate of the root and the corresponding value of $f(x)$; this last value is known as the **residual error**. With these points in mind, the expanded program plan is produced (see Figure 4.3).

This expanded plan can gradually be replaced by appropriate FORTRAN statements. Named constants are used to represent the tolerance, the maximum number of iterations permitted and the possible values of STATUS:

```
PARAMETER (TOL=1E-6,MAXITS=25)
PARAMETER (SOLVED=0,LIMIT=1,NOBRAC=2)
```

As in Chapter 2, we use separate PARAMETER declarations to emphasize the different roles. Following our policy of declaring all names used in programs, the above declarations will be preceded by

```
INTEGER LIMIT,MAXITS,NOBRAC,SOLVED,STATUS
REAL    TOL
```

Step (2) is straightforward; a prompt is issued and two values are read:

```
PRINT *,'Give two initial values that bracket the root'
READ *, X0,X1
```

```
      PROGRAM BIPROG

      INTEGER   LIMIT,MAXITS,NOBRAC,NOOFIT,SOLVED,STATUS
      REAL      F,LASTXO,LASTX1,RESID,ROOT,TOL,XO,X1
      PARAMETER (TOL=1E-6,MAXITS=25)
      PARAMETER (SOLVED=0,LIMIT=1,NOBRAC=2)
      EXTERNAL  BISECT,F

      PRINT *,'Give two initial values that bracket the root'
      READ *, XO,X1
      CALL BISECT (F,XO,X1,TOL,MAXITS,
     *            STATUS,ROOT,RESID,NOOFIT,LASTXO,LASTX1)

      IF (STATUS.EQ.SOLVED) WRITE(*,2000) ROOT,RESID,NOOFIT
      IF (STATUS.EQ.LIMIT)  WRITE(*,2010) MAXITS,LASTXO,LASTX1
      IF (STATUS.EQ.NOBRAC) WRITE(*,2020) XO,X1

2000  FORMAT(1X,'Root = ',F10.6,' at which f(x) = ',F8.6
     *      /1X,'Converged after ',I2,' iterations')
2010  FORMAT(1X,'Not converged after ',I2,' iterations'
     *      /1X,'Current interval is ',F10.6,' to ',F10.6)
2020  FORMAT(1X,'Initial approximations, ',F10.6,' and ',F10.6,
     *          ', are on the same side of the root')

      END
```

Figure 4.4 Main subprogram for bisection method.

Note that X0 and X1 will have to be added to the REAL declaration.

Step (3) will be done in a subroutine named BISECT. Thus a CALL statement is needed to supply the values that the subroutine uses and to return those that the subroutine produces:

```
      CALL BISECT (F,XO,X1,TOL,MAXITS,
     *            STATUS,ROOT,RESID,NOOFIT,LASTXO,LASTX1)
```

It is assumed that the function is supplied in a separate function subprogram called F. The type declarations will have to be extended to

```
      INTEGER LIMIT,MAXITS,NOBRAC,NOOFIT,SOLVED,STATUS
      REAL    F,LASTXO,LASTX1,RESID,ROOT,TOL,XO,X1
```

Furthermore, because the function F is named as an actual argument in the subroutine call, it must be declared as EXTERNAL. As in Chapter 2, the subroutine

Given: $f(x), x0, x1, tolerance, maximum$ *number of iterations*
Set: $f0 = f(x0)$
      $f1 = f(x1)$
if $f0 \cdot f1 > 0$ **then**
   Note: '*no bracket*'
else
   repeat (*not exceeding max iterations*)
      Set: $xmid = (x0+x1)/2$
            $fmid = f(xmid)$
      if $f0 \cdot fmid < 0$ **then**
         Set: $x1 = xmid$
      else
         Set: $x0 = xmid$
               $f0 = fmid$
      if $|x1-x0| \leq tolerance$ **then**
         Note: '*solved*'
   until '*solved*' (*or limit on number of iterations reached*)
   if '*solved*' **then**
      Record: *root, residual, number of iterations used*
   if '*limit*' **then**
      Record: *end-points of current interval*

Figure 4.5 Plan of subroutine for bisection method.

name is also included in the `EXTERNAL` statement

```
EXTERNAL BISECT,F
```

Step (4) follows directly:

```
IF (STATUS.EQ.SOLVED) WRITE(*,2000) ROOT,RESID,NOOFIT
IF (STATUS.EQ.LIMIT)  WRITE(*,2010) MAXITS,LASTX0,LASTX1
IF (STATUS.EQ.NOBRAC) WRITE(*,2020) X0,X1
```
              with appropriate Format statements

Thus, adding the initial and closing statements, the main subprogram takes the form shown in Figure 4.4.

Now consider the subroutine for step (3). Note that differing signs in f_i and f_j can be detected by examining the sign of the product $f_i f_j$. The subroutine plan of Figure 4.5 is produced from the mathematical algorithm of Figure 4.2

The first line of the subroutine follows from the `CALL` statement of the main subprogram:

```
SUBROUTINE BISECT (F,INX0,INX1,TOL,MAXITS,
*                   STATUS,ROOT,RESID,NOOFIT,LASTX0,LASTX1)
```

and incorporates the first line of the subroutine plan. In order to conform to the mathematical notation, we wish to use X0 and X1 inside the subroutine to represent the current interval. However, if X0 and X1 were used as the dummy arguments in the subroutine heading, any assignment to X0 or X1 within the subroutine would change our record of the initial interval. This is undesirable and we avoid it by using INX0 and INX1 as the two dummy arguments. We now specify the types of the variables that appear in the argument list.

```
INTEGER MAXITS,NOOFIT,STATUS
REAL    F,INX0,INX1,LASTX0,LASTX1,RESID,ROOT,TOL
```

We reproduce the PARAMETER declaration for the possible values of STATUS:

```
PARAMETER (SOLVED=0,LIMIT=1,NOBRAC=2)
```

noting that these values must be specified to be INTEGER. Then X0 and X1 are initialized:

```
X0=INX0
X1=INX1
```

The next five lines of the subroutine plan become

```
    FO=F(X0)
    F1=F(X1)

    IF (F0*F1.GT.0) THEN
C       { x0,x1 do not bracket the root}
        STATUS=NOBRAC
    ELSE
        ⋮
    END IF
```

As in Chapter 2, the repeat-loop limiting the number of iterations performed is implemented using a DO loop:

```
    DO 10, COUNT=1,MAXITS
        ⋮
    IF...{ converged } THEN
        STATUS=SOLVED
        GO TO 11
    END IF
10  CONTINUE
    STATUS=LIMIT
11      ...
```

The convergence test follows directly from the subroutine plan:

```
IF (ABS(X1-X0).LE.TOL) THEN
  STATUS=SOLVED
  GO TO 11
END IF
```

and so does the main body of the repeat-loop:

```
XMID=(X0+X1)/2
FMID=F(XMID)

IF (F0*FMID.LT.0) THEN
  X1=XMID
ELSE
  X0=XMID
  F0=FMID
END IF
```

If convergence to the specified accuracy has been achieved, we return an approximation to the root, together with the residual and a count of the number of iterations used. If the limit on the number of iterations has been reached without convergence, we return the positions of the ends of the current interval:

```
11   IF (STATUS.EQ.SOLVED) THEN
       ROOT  =(X0+X1)/2
       RESID =F(ROOT)
       NOOFIT=COUNT
     END IF
     IF (STATUS.EQ.LIMIT) THEN
       LASTX0=X0
       LASTX1=X1
     END IF
```

To complete our subroutine, we extend the type declarations to include all the variables, specify ABS to be INTRINSIC and F to be EXTERNAL, and add the closing END. The full subroutine is given in Figure 4.6.

To run the program a function subprogram must be supplied and, for the test example, it is

```
REAL FUNCTION F(X)
REAL X
INTRINSIC EXP
  F=X-EXP(1/X)
END
```

Note that the subroutine takes no special action should the root coincide either

```fortran
      SUBROUTINE BISECT (F,INX0,INX1,TOL,MAXITS,
     *                   STATUS,ROOT,RESID,NOOFIT,LASTX0,LASTX1)

      INTEGER   COUNT,LIMIT,MAXITS,NOBRAC,NOOFIT,SOLVED,STATUS
      REAL      F,F0,F1,FMID,INX0,INX1,LASTX0,LASTX1,
     *          RESID,ROOT,TOL,X0,X1,XMID
      PARAMETER (SOLVED=0,LIMIT=1,NOBRAC=2)
      INTRINSIC ABS
      EXTERNAL  F

      X0=INX0
      X1=INX1
      F0=F(X0)
      F1=F(X1)

      IF (F0*F1.GT.0) THEN
C       { x0,x1 do not bracket the root }
        STATUS=NOBRAC
      ELSE
C       { do bisection }
        DO 10, COUNT=1,MAXITS
          XMID=(X0+X1)/2
          FMID=F(XMID)

          IF (F0*FMID.LT.0) THEN
            X1=XMID
          ELSE
            X0=XMID
            F0=FMID
          END IF

          IF (ABS(X1-X0).LE.TOL) THEN
            STATUS=SOLVED
            GO TO 11
          END IF
10      CONTINUE
        STATUS=LIMIT

11      IF (STATUS.EQ.SOLVED) THEN
          ROOT  =(X0+X1)/2
          RESID =F(ROOT)
          NOOFIT=COUNT
        END IF
        IF (STATUS.EQ.LIMIT) THEN
          LASTX0=X0
          LASTX1=X1
        END IF
      END IF

      END
```

Figure 4.6 Subroutine for bisection method.

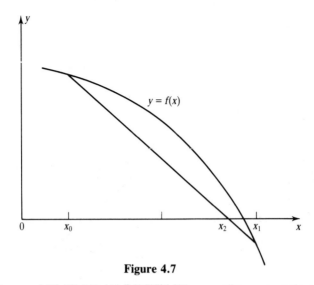

Figure 4.7

with one of the initial approximations or with the mid-point of any interval constructed. It is left as an exercise for the reader to modify the program along the lines suggested in Exercise 4.11.

4.1.2 Regula falsi

Although the bisection method is guaranteed to converge, it may do so only slowly. It is also inefficient in the sense that it is not using all the available information; it takes note of the signs of f_0, f_1 and f_2 but not of their values.

The regula falsi method, sometimes known as the method of false position, takes the function values into account. Let x_2 be the point of intersection of the x-axis with the straight line joining the points (x_0, f_0) and (x_1, f_1). For the function illustrated in Figure 4.7, the point x_2 is clearly a better approximation to the zero than is the mid-point of $[x_0, x_1]$.

To determine x_2, the equation of the line joining (x_0, f_0) and (x_1, f_1) is required. This can be written in the form

$$y = \frac{(x - x_1)f_0}{x_0 - x_1} + \frac{(x - x_0)f_1}{x_1 - x_0}$$

$$= \frac{x(f_1 - f_0) - x_0 f_1 + x_1 f_0}{x_1 - x_0}$$

When $y = 0$, and thus $x = x_2$, we have

$$x_2(f_1 - f_0) - x_0 f_1 - x_1 f_0 = 0$$

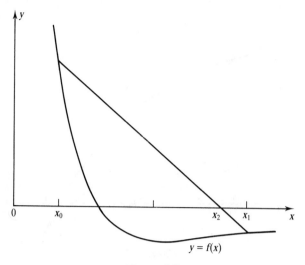

Figure 4.8

from which

$$x_2 = \frac{x_0 f_1 - x_1 f_0}{f_1 - f_0} \qquad (4.1)$$

This formula can be rewritten as

$$x_2 = x_1 - \frac{(x_1 - x_0) f_1}{f_1 - f_0} \qquad (4.2)$$

and this form is more appealing because it shows that x_2 is obtained by applying a correction to x_1.

Having calculated x_2, the process is repeated on the new interval containing the root, as in the bisection method. The algorithm for the regula falsi method can be obtained from Figure 4.2 by simply redefining x_2 in line 3. Similarly, a subroutine for this method is easily obtained from Figure 4.6.

The regula falsi method suffers from two main disadvantages. Firstly, it is not always the case that x_2 is a better estimate than the mid-point; Figure 4.8 shows a function for which the size of the interval in the regula falsi method will decrease more slowly than that in the bisection method.

Secondly, the size of the interval containing the root does not, in general, tend to zero. This is because, in the neighbourhood of the root, most functions are strictly concave or convex and this results in one of the end-points approaching the root whilst the other remains fixed. Consequently, the size of the interval is of little use as a bound on the error in the approximation or as a tolerance for the termination of the iteration. The secant method, a modification of the regula falsi method, overcomes this drawback.

4.1.3 Secant method

The secant method removes the restriction that successive iterates must bracket the root. Successive function values may now have the same sign and a consequence of this is that the iteration process becomes more sensitive to rounding errors. However, the effects of this are less when Formula (4.2) is used in preference to Formula (4.1).

An algorithm for the secant method is shown in Figure 4.9. We apply this algorithm to our test function

$$f(x) = x - e^{1/x}$$

with $x_0 = 1$, $f_0 = -1.7183$ and $x_1 = 2$, $f_1 = 0.3513$. Thus

$$
\begin{aligned}
x_2 &= x_1 - \frac{(x_1 - x_0)f_1}{(f_1 - f_0)} \\
&= 2 - \frac{(2 - 1)(0.3513)}{(0.3513 - (-1.7183))} \\
&= 1.8303
\end{aligned}
$$

from which $f_2 = 0.1033$. The next iterate is

$$
\begin{aligned}
x_3 &= x_2 - \frac{(x_2 - x_1)f_2}{(f_2 - f_1)} \\
&= 1.8303 - \frac{(1.8303 - 2)(0.1033)}{(0.1033 - 0.3513)} \\
&= 1.7595
\end{aligned}
$$

from which $f_3 = -0.0057$. Similarly,

$$
\begin{aligned}
x_4 &= 1.7595 - \frac{(1.7595 - 1.8303)(-0.0057)}{(-0.0057 - 0.1033)} \\
&= 1.7633
\end{aligned}
$$

and $f_4 = 0.0001$. At this point, note that an estimate of the absolute error is

$$|x_4 - x_3| = |1.7633 - 1.7595| = 0.0038 < 0.5 \times 10^{-2}$$

giving agreement to two decimal places, and an estimate of the relative error is

$$\frac{|x_4 - x_3|}{|x_3|} = 0.0022 < 5 \times 10^{-3}$$

giving agreement to three significant figures. If the root were required only to this accuracy, we could stop the iteration and take the value 1.76 as the approximation to the root.

Given $f(x), x_0, x_1$
Repeat (*for* $n = 1, 2, \ldots$)

$$\text{Set } x_{n-1} = x_n - \frac{(x_n - x_{n-1})}{(f_n - f_{n-1})} f_n$$

Until converged

Figure 4.9 Algorithm for secant method.

For the reasons outlined in Chapter 3, we will generally use the relative error test although, in the bisection algorithm, we used an absolute test because we considered it to be more appropriate for a 'bracketing' method. We implement the relative error test in the form presented in Chapter 3.

The values in Table 4.2 are the first five iterates, quoted to six decimal places, produced by the bisection and secant methods when applied to the test function with initial interval [1,2]. Already the secant method appears to have converged to seven significant figures whereas the bisection method has attained only two significant figures. Unfortunately, in certain circumstances, the secant method may not converge at all and this possibility will be covered in Section 4.2 when Newton's method is discussed.

Program construction

When a program is written to implement the algorithm of Figure 4.9 it must be remembered that, unlike the bisection method, the secant method does not require that the initial approximations bracket the root and so it is not necessary for the secant program to test for this. However, the secant algorithm can break down if the denominator of Equation (4.2) becomes very small. This may occur if the curve has a flat spot in the neighbourhood of any approximation to the root. It is therefore essential that the program tests for a possible flat spot at the start of *each* iteration and terminates the calculation with a suitable message if a flat spot is detected. We begin by writing a general program plan and this is reproduced in Figure 4.10.

Table 4.2 Bisection and secant iterates for the test equation.

Iteration	Bisection	Secant
1	1.500 000	1.830 264
2	1.750 000	1.759 564
3	1.875 000	1.763 285
4	1.812 500	1.763 223
5	1.781 250	1.763 223

(1)   *Define parameters*:
         tolerance, maximum number of iterations
         status values (i.e. solved, limit on number of iterations reached,
                         flat spot)

(2)   *Input*:
         x0,x1

(3)   *Do*:
         Secant algorithm
             using (*f(x),x0,x1,tolerance, maximum number of iterations*)
         to produce (*status and*
                         either root, residual, number of iterations used
                         or last two approximations to root)

(4)   **if** *solved* **then**
         Print: root, residual, number of iterations used
         if *limit on iterations reached* **then**
         Print: maximum number of iterations,
                 last two approximations to root
         if *flat spot* **then**
         Print: last two approximations to root

Figure 4.10   Plan of main subprogram for secant method.

The main subprogram takes a form similar to that for the bisection algorithm and so only the SECANT subroutine will be considered in detail. A plan of this subroutine, based on the algorithm of Figure 4.9, is given in Figure 4.11.

The first line of the subroutine follows immediately from step (3) of the main subprogram plan.

```
SUBROUTINE BISECT (F,INX0,INX1,TOL,MAXITS,
*                  STATUS,ROOT,RESID,NOOFIT,LASTX0,LASTX1)
```

Although we intend to use X0 and X1 inside the subroutine, note that we have used INX0 and INX1 as the dummy arguments to input the initial approximations so that the actual arguments will not be corrupted within the subroutine. Now we specify the types of variables that appear in the argument list.

```
INTEGER MAXITS,NOOFIT,STATUS
REAL    F,INX0,INX1,LASTX0,LASTX1,RESID,ROOT,TOL,X0,X1
```

We define a small number to use when testing for a flat spot:

```
PARAMETER (TINY=1E-10)
```

In this program there will be two possible reasons ('flat spot' or 'solved') why control may exit from the loop before the maximum number of iterations has

---

Given: $f(x), x0, x1, tolerance, maximum$ *number of iterations*
Set: $f0 = f(x0)$
    $f1 = f(x1)$
repeat (*not exceeding max iterations*)
    if $|f1 - f0| \leq$ *small number* **then**
       Note: '*flat spot*'
    else
       Set: $x2 = x1 - (x1 - x0) \cdot f1 / (f1 - f0)$
       if $|x2 - x1| \leq |x1| \cdot tolerance$ **then**
          Note: '*solved*'
       else
          Set: $x0 = x1$
             $x1 = x2$
             $f0 = f1$
             $f1 = f(x1)$
until '*solved*' **or** '*flat spot*'
          (*or limit on number of iterations reached*)
if '*solved*' **then**
    Record: root, residual, number of iterations used
if '*limit*' **then**
    Record: last two approximations to root
if '*flat spot*' **then**
    Record: last two approximations to root

Figure 4.11   Plan of subroutine for secant method.

been performed. Following the recommendations of Chapter 2, we begin by setting the variable STATUS equal to some initial value, say ITRATE, before entering the loop. Later, if appropriate, STATUS will be changed to FLAT or SOLVED and we shall exit the loop prematurely because STATUS is no longer equal to ITRATE. Thus

```
PARAMETER (ITRATE=-1,SOLVED=0,LIMIT=1,FLAT=2)
```

is required. It is necessary to initialize X0 and X1:

```
X0=INX0
X1=INX1
```

The next two lines of the subroutine follow immediately from Figure 4.11:

```
F0=F(X0)
F1=F(X1)
```

The repeat-loop is implemented by

```
STATUS=ITRATE
DO 10, COUNT=1,MAXITS
```

```
         ⋮
         IF (STATUS.NE.ITRATE) GO TO 11
10       CONTINUE
         STATUS=LIMIT
11       ...
```

The main body of the loop could follow immediately from Figure 4.11, but we note that x_2 is obtained by adding a correction to x_1. Consequently, this correction is evaluated separately so that we can use it in the convergence test.

```
         IF (ABS(F1-F0).LE.TINY) THEN
C          { flat spot }
           STATUS=FLAT
         ELSE
C          { perform secant algorithm }
           DX=-(X1-X0)*F1/(F1-F0)
           X2=X1+DX

           IF (ABS(DX).LE.ABS(X1)*TOL) THEN
             STATUS=SOLVED
           ELSE
             X0=X1
             X1=X2
             F0=F1
             F1=F(X1)
           END IF
         END IF
```

If convergence to the specified accuracy has been achieved, we return the last approximation to the root together with the residual and a count of the number of iterations used. If a flat spot is encountered or the limit on the number of iterations is reached without convergence, we return the last two approximations to the root.

```
11       IF (STATUS.EQ.SOLVED) THEN
           ROOT  =X2
           RESID =F(ROOT)
           NOOFIT=COUNT
         END IF
         IF (STATUS.EQ.LIMIT .OR. STATUS.EQ.FLAT) THEN
           LASTX0=X0
           LASTX1=X1
         END IF
```

It remains only to extend the type declarations so that they include all the variables, specify ABS to be INTRINSIC and F to be EXTERNAL, and add the closing END. The full subroutine is shown in Figure 4.12.

Figure 4.12 Subroutine for secant method.

```
      SUBROUTINE SECANT (F,INX0,INX1,TOL,MAXITS,
     *                   STATUS,ROOT,RESID,NOOFIT,LASTX0,LASTX1)

      INTEGER   COUNT,FLAT,ITRATE,LIMIT,MAXITS,NOOFIT,SOLVED,STATUS
      REAL      DX,F,F0,F1,INX0,INX1,LASTX0,LASTX1,
     *          RESID,ROOT,TINY,TOL,X0,X1,X2
      PARAMETER (TINY=1E-10)
      PARAMETER (ITRATE=-1,SOLVED=0,LIMIT=1,FLAT=2)
      INTRINSIC ABS
      EXTERNAL  F

      X0=INX0
      X1=INX1
      F0=F(X0)
      F1=F(X1)

      STATUS=ITRATE
      DO 10, COUNT=1,MAXITS

        IF (ABS(F1-F0).LE.TINY) THEN
C         { flat spot }
          STATUS=FLAT
        ELSE
C         { perform secant alogrithm }
          DX=-(X1-X0)*F1/(F1-F0)
          X2=X1+DX

          IF (ABS(DX).LE.ABS(X1)*TOL) THEN
            STATUS=SOLVED
          ELSE
            X0=X1
            X1=X2
            F0=F1
            F1=F(X1)
          END IF
        END IF

        IF (STATUS.NE.ITRATE) GO TO 11
10    CONTINUE
      STATUS=LIMIT

11    IF (STATUS.EQ.SOLVED) THEN
        ROOT  =X2
        RESID =F(ROOT)
        NOOFIT=COUNT
      END IF
```

```
IF (STATUS.EQ.LIMIT .OR. STATUS.EQ.FLAT) THEN
   LASTX0=X0
   LASTX1=X1
END IF

END
```

Figure 4.12   *cont.*

The main subprogram associated with this subroutine can be obtained easily from Figure 4.4. Apart from the obvious change of name in the subroutine call and the EXTERNAL statement, it is necessary merely to replace NOBRAC by FLAT and modify the last WRITE and FORMAT statements accordingly.

4.1.4   Successive substitution

This method, also known as the **fixed point method,** makes use of the form of the function to devise an iterative formula. To find a root α of

$$f(x) = 0 \tag{4.3}$$

the equation is manipulated into the form

$$x = g(x) \tag{4.4}$$

with an x on the left-hand side. Clearly α is also a root of Equation (4.4). The new equation acts as a basis for the iteration

$$x_{n+1} = g(x_n) \qquad n = 0,1,2, \ldots \tag{4.5}$$

where x_0 is an initial approximation to the required root. It will be shown later that, under suitable conditions, the sequence $x_1, x_2, \ldots$ obtained from Equation (4.5) converges to the root.

For example, the test equation

$$x - \exp(1/x) = 0$$

can be rearranged to give

$$x = \exp(1/x) \tag{4.6}$$

This is in the required form of Equation (4.4) where

$$g(x) = \exp(1/x) \tag{4.7}$$

Given $g(x), x_0$
Repeat (for $n = 0, 1, \ldots$)
   Set $x_{n+1} = g(x_n)$
Until converged

Figure 4.13   Algorithm for method of successive substitution.

and gives the iterative formula

$$x_{n+1} = \exp(1/x_n)$$

An algorithm for the method of successive substitution is given in Figure 4.13. Applying it to the test example, starting with $x_0 = 1.5$ and working to four decimal places, gives

$$
\begin{aligned}
x_1 &= \exp(1/x_0) = \exp(1/1.5) = 1.9477 \\
x_2 &= \exp(1/1.9477) = 1.6710 \\
x_3 &= 1.8193 \\
x_4 &= 1.7327 \\
x_5 &= 1.7809 \\
&\vdots \\
x_{12} &= 1.7629 \\
x_{13} &= 1.7634
\end{aligned}
$$

The last two approximations agree to four significant figures and, in fact, give an estimate of α which is correct to this accuracy.

An alternative method could have been obtained by taking logarithms of both sides of Equation (4.6) giving

$$\ln(x) = 1/x$$

from which

$$x = 1/\ln(x)$$

This equation is also of the form of Equation (4.4) with

$$g(x) = 1/\ln(x) \tag{4.8}$$

leading to the iterative formula

$$x_{n+1} = 1/\ln(x_n)$$

However, using $x_0 = 1.5$ as before, this scheme produces

$$x_1 = 1/\ln(x_0) = 1/\ln(1.5) = 2.4663$$
$$x_2 = 1/\ln(2.4663) = 1.1078$$
$$x_3 = 9.7711$$
$$\vdots$$

and these iterates do not appear to be converging to the required root.

Another (but less obvious) form of $g(x)$ can be obtained by adding x to each side of Equation (4.6) and then dividing by 2. This leads to

$$g(x) = \frac{x + \exp(1/x)}{2} \tag{4.9}$$

from which

$$x_{n+1} = \frac{x_n + \exp(1/x_n)}{2}$$

Taking $x_0 = 1.5$ gives

$$x_1 = (x_0 + \exp(1/x_0))/2 = (1.5 + \exp(1/1.5))/2 = 1.7239$$
$$x_2 = (1.7239 + \exp(1/1.7239))/2 = 1.7550$$
$$x_3 = 1.7615$$
$$x_4 = 1.7628$$
$$x_5 = 1.7631$$
$$\vdots$$

It is clear that these iterates are converging very rapidly and, in fact, x_4 and x_5 agree to four significant figures.

Table 4.3   Solutions to the test equation using the successive substitution method.

Iteration	(4.7)	(4.8)	(4.9)
1	1.947 734	2.466 304	1.723 867
2	1.670 991	1.107 763	1.755 034
3	1.819 291	9.771 132	1.761 464
4	1.732 671	0.438 706	1.762 843
5	1.780 944	−1.213 701	1.763 140
6	1.753 300	—	1.763 205
Convergence	25	—	9

For comparison purposes, Table 4.3 records the first few iterates produced by Equations (4.7), (4.8) and (4.9) and also shows, for the first and last cases, the number of steps required for convergence using a tolerance of 5E−7. Only five iterations are obtained with Equation (4.8) because, if a sixth were attempted, the logarithmic function would take a negative argument and so the calculations would break down.

From these examples it is obvious that the choice of $g(x)$ is very important and that a test is needed to determine whether or not a particular iteration will converge. A basic result concerning this is given in Theorem 4.1.

Theorem 4.1

Let α be a root of Equation (4.4)

$$x = g(x)$$

and let I be an interval centred on α and containing an initial approximation, x_0, to this root. Then, if $g(x)$ is continuous on I, the sequence

$$x_{n+1} = g(x_n)$$

converges to α as $n \to \infty$ provided that, for all x in I,

$$|g'(x)| \leqslant K < 1$$

where K is a constant.

Proof

By definition, α is a root of Equation (4.4) and so

$$\alpha = g(\alpha) \tag{4.10}$$

Subtracting Equation (4.10) from Equation (4.5) gives

$$x_{n+1} - \alpha = g(x_n) - g(\alpha) \tag{4.11}$$

By the Mean Value Theorem (see Appendix A), there is at least one point, $x = \xi_n$ (say), lying between x_n and α such that

$$g'(\xi_n) = \frac{g(x_n) - g(\alpha)}{x_n - \alpha}$$

and so

$$g(x_n) - g(\alpha) = g'(\xi_n)(x_n - \alpha)$$

Using this equation to replace the right-hand side of Equation (4.11) gives

$$x_{n+1} - \alpha = g'(\xi_n)(x_n - \alpha) \qquad (4.12)$$

Now, using ε_k to represent the error $(x_k - \alpha)$ in the kth iterate, Equation (4.12) becomes

$$\varepsilon_{n+1} = g'(\xi_n)\,\varepsilon_n \qquad (4.13)$$

from which

$$|\varepsilon_{n+1}| = |g'(\xi_n)||\varepsilon_n| \qquad (4.14)$$

For convergence we require that $|\varepsilon_n| \to 0$ as $n \to \infty$. Now, from Equation (4.14),

$$|\varepsilon_1| = |g'(\xi_0)||\varepsilon_0|$$

where ε_0 is the error in the initial approximation to the root. Because x_0 and α are in I, so is ξ_0; hence

$$|g'(\xi_0)| \leq K$$

giving

$$|\varepsilon_1| \leq K|\varepsilon_0| \qquad (4.15)$$

This shows that x_1 is closer to the root than is x_0 and so both x_1 and ξ_1 must be in I. It follows that

$$|\varepsilon_2| = |g'(\xi_1)||\varepsilon_1| \leq K|\varepsilon_1|$$

and using Equation (4.15) we have

$$|\varepsilon_2| \leq K{\cdot}K|\varepsilon_0| = K^2|\varepsilon_0|$$

Thus, in general,

$$|\varepsilon_n| \leq K^n|\varepsilon_0|$$

But $K < 1$ and so $K^n \to 0$ as $n \to \infty$ giving

$$|\varepsilon_n| \to 0 \text{ as } n \to \infty$$

This completes the proof.   ∎

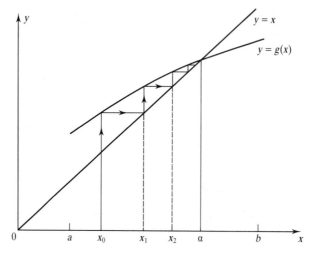

Figure 4.14 Converging iterates.

Figure 4.14 illustrates a sequence of iterates evaluated using a function for which $|g'(x)| < 1$ throughout the interval $[a,b]$. For the function of Figure 4.15, $|g'(x)| > 1$ throughout the interval $[a,b]$ and the sequence diverges.

Now we consider the application of Theorem 4.1 to our test example. Ideally, we should locate a small interval I containing the root and devise a form of $g(x)$ such that $|g'(x)| < 1$ for all x in I. Then we would choose x_0 to be within I and start the iteration with confidence. However, this procedure is rather cumbersome and, provided that x_0 is a good approximation to the root, it is sufficient for most examples to set up a form of $g(x)$ such that $|g'(x_0)| < 1$.

To illustrate this simpler procedure, consider again the three different forms of $g(x)$ devised earlier for the test equation

$$x - \exp(1/x) = 0$$

(1)   The rearrangement (4.7),

$$g(x) = \exp(1/x)$$

gives

$$g'(x) = \frac{-\exp(1/x)}{x^2}$$

and so

$$g'(x_0) = g'(1.5) = -0.8657$$

Thus $|g'(x_0)| < 1$ and, as we have already seen, the iterates do converge.

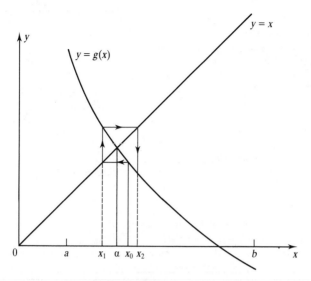

Figure 4.15   Diverging iterates.

(2)   For Equation (4.8),

$$g(x) = 1/\ln(x)$$

so

$$g'(x) = \frac{-1}{x(\ln(x))^2}$$

and

$$g'(x_0) = g'(1.5) = -4.0551$$

In this case $|g'(x_0)| > 1$ and so the iterates are not expected to converge; this is confirmed by the numerical results.

(3)   For Equation (4.9),

$$g(x) = \frac{x + \exp(1/x)}{2}$$

so

$$g'(x) = \frac{1}{2} - \frac{\exp(1/x)}{2x^2}$$

and

$$g'(x_0) = g'(1.5) = 0.0672$$

Here $|g'(x_0)| < 1$, indicating likely convergence.

(1)   *Define parameters:*
       tolerance, maximum number of iterations,
       status values (i.e. solved, limit on number of iterations reached)

(2)   *Input:*
       x0

(3)   *Do:*
       successive substitution
               using (g(x),x0,tolerance, maximum number of iterations)
       to produce (status and
                       either root, number of iterations used
                           or last approximation to root)

(4)   **if** *solved* **then**
       Print: root, number of iterations used
       if *limit on iterations reached* **then**
       Print: maximum number of iterations, last approximation to root

Figure 4.16   Plan of the main subprogram for successive substitution.

Given: g(x),x0,tolerance,maximum number of iterations
Set: newx = x0
repeat *(not exceeding max iterations)*
   Set: oldx = newx
        newx = g(oldx)
   if $|newx - oldx| \leq |oldx| \cdot tolerance$ **then**
     Note: 'solved'
until *'solved' (or limit on number of iterations reached)*
if *'solved'* **then**
   Record: root,number of iterations used
if *'limit'* **then**
   Record: last approximation to root

Figure 4.17   Plan of subroutine for successive substitution.

It is clear from Equation (4.14) that the smaller the magnitude of $g'(x)$ near the root the more rapid the rate of convergence. For this reason, the iteration based on Equation (4.9) would be expected to converge more rapidly than that derived from Equation (4.7) and this is indeed the case. Thus the convergence test also indicates the comparative rate of convergence of different iterative formulae.

Program construction

In general, we recommend that the theory is used to ensure that an iterative formula is convergent before starting the iterations, rather than simply adopting an arbitrary form of $g(x)$ and hoping for the best. However, when we write the program for this method, we shall take the precaution of imposing the usual

```
      SUBROUTINE SUCSUB (G,X0,TOL,MAXITS,
     *                    STATUS,ROOT,NOOFIT,LASTX)

      INTEGER   COUNT,LIMIT,MAXITS,NOOFIT,SOLVED,STATUS
      REAL      G,LASTX,NEWX,OLDX,ROOT,TOL,X0
      PARAMETER (SOLVED=0,LIMIT=1)
      INTRINSIC ABS
      EXTERNAL  G

      NEWX=X0

      DO 10, COUNT=1,MAXITS
        OLDX=NEWX
        NEWX=G(OLDX)

        IF (ABS(NEWX-OLDX).LE.ABS(OLDX)*TOL) THEN
          STATUS=SOLVED
          GO TO 11
        END IF

10    CONTINUE
      STATUS=LIMIT

11    IF (STATUS.EQ.SOLVED) THEN
        NOOFIT=COUNT
        ROOT =NEWX
      END IF

      IF (STATUS.EQ.LIMIT) THEN
        LASTX=NEWX
      END IF

      END
```

Figure 4.18   Subroutine for successive substitution.

bound on the number of iterations permitted. In addition, we note that, because the method of successive substitution does not use the original function $f(x)$ explicitly, the residual error will not be immediately available. A general program plan written with these points in mind is shown in Figure 4.16.

A detailed plan of the subroutine for step (3) is given in Figure 4.17. This is based on the mathematical algorithm of Figure 4.13. Adopting the conventions established for the bisection and secant algorithms, the subroutine is straightforward and is given in Figure 4.18. Note that, in this case, X0 can be used in the dummy argument list without fear of corrupting the X0 in the main subprogram because X0 does not appear on the left-hand side of any assignment statement in the subroutine.

4.1.5 Successive substitution with bisection

If $g(x)$ is such that

$$-1 < g'(x) < 0 \tag{4.16}$$

for values of x in the neighbourhood of a root then, from the theory, an iterative scheme based on this $g(x)$ will converge to the root because $|g'(x)| < 1$. However, in such a case, it follows from Equation (4.13) that the errors in any two consecutive approximations to the root will have opposite signs and so these approximations bracket the root. Therefore it may be possible to accelerate the rate of convergence by alternating between successive substitution and bisection. To illustrate this procedure, consider once more the solution of the equation

$$x - \exp(1/x) = 0$$

using the iterative scheme

$$x_{n+1} = \exp(1/x_n)$$

for which, to four decimal places, $g'(1.5) = -0.8657$.
Starting with

$$x_0 = 1.5$$

we calculate

$$x_1 = \exp(1/1.5) = 1.9477$$

and then bisect the interval $[1.5, 1.9477]$ to give

$$x_2 = (1.5 + 1.9477)/2 = 1.7239$$

The next substitution gives

$$x_3 = \exp(1/1.7239) = 1.7862$$

and a further bisection produces

$$x_4 = (1.7239 + 1.7862)/2 = 1.7551$$

Proceeding in this manner, the required root is obtained correct to four significant figures after only 8 iterations rather than the 12 needed by the method of successive substitution alone. In other words, the rate of convergence of the iterations has been accelerated. In practice acceleration techniques are often applied to slowly converging iterates although, clearly, the one used here is restricted to those forms of $g(x)$ that satisfy inequality (4.16). Now we consider a superior acceleration device which is of more general application.

4.1.6 Aitken's Δ^2 process

It has been shown in Section 4.1.4 that the method of successive substitution can be used to produce a sequence of iterates, $x_1, x_2, \ldots$, which converge to a root α of the equation $f(x) = 0$. Aitken's Δ^2 process is an acceleration technique which, basically, attempts to predict the value of α from any three consecutive iterates x_n, x_{n+1} and x_{n+2}.

From Equation (4.13),

$$\varepsilon_{n+1} = g'(\xi_n)\varepsilon_n$$

where ξ_n lies between x_n and α. For a converging sequence, x_n tends to α as n tends to infinity and so ξ_n must also tend to α. Hence, when the iterations have progressed sufficiently, Equation (4.13) provides the approximation

$$\varepsilon_{n+1} \simeq g'(\alpha)\varepsilon_n$$

or

$$\frac{\varepsilon_{n+1}}{\varepsilon_n} \simeq g'(\alpha)$$

Similarly,

$$\frac{\varepsilon_{n+2}}{\varepsilon_{n+1}} \simeq g'(\alpha)$$

so that

$$\frac{\varepsilon_{n+2}}{\varepsilon_{n+1}} \simeq \frac{\varepsilon_{n+1}}{\varepsilon_n}$$

or

$$\frac{x_{n+2} - \alpha}{x_{n+1} - \alpha} \simeq \frac{x_{n+1} - \alpha}{x_n - \alpha}$$

Rearranging gives

$$\alpha \simeq x_n - \frac{(x_{n+1} - x_n)^2}{x_{n+2} - 2x_{n+1} + x_n}$$

This formula predicts the value of α from x_n, x_{n+1} and x_{n+2} and hence provides a good approximation to α which can be used as the next iterate. Thus x_{n+3} is defined by

$$x_{n+3} = x_n - \frac{(x_{n+1} - x_n)^2}{x_{n+2} - 2x_{n+1} + x_n} \tag{4.17a}$$

or in the notation of finite differences

$$x_{n+3} = x_n - \frac{(\Delta x_n)^2}{\Delta^2 x_n}$$

whence the name of the method.

An alternative rearrangement leads to the formula

$$x_{n+3} = x_{n+2} - \frac{(x_{n+2} - x_{n+1})^2}{x_{n+2} - 2x_{n+1} + x_n} \tag{4.17b}$$

which gives the new value x_{n+3} in terms of a correction to the latest value x_{n+2}.

The process can continue by calculating two further iterates x_{n+4} and x_{n+5} using successive substitution and then applying a further Aitken Δ^2 step to evaluate x_{n+6} and so on.

In practice, for all values of n, the x_{n+3} calculated from Equation (4.17) is usually a more accurate approximation to α than is the value obtained from

$$x_{n+3} = g(x_{n+2})$$

Hence Aitken's formula is generally used to obtain the iterates $x_3, x_6, x_9, \ldots$ as shown in the mathematical algorithm of Figure 4.19.

For the test equation, values of x_1 and x_2 (1.9477 and 1.6710 respectively) have been obtained already using the method of successive substitution with $g(x_{n+1}) = \exp(1/x_n)$. Therefore Aitken's method can be used immediately to evaluate x_3 giving

$$x_3 = x_0 - \frac{(x_1 - x_0)^2}{(x_2 - 2x_1 + x_0)}$$

$$= 1.5 - \frac{(1.9477 - 1.5)^2}{(1.6710 - 2(1.9477) + 1.5)}$$

$$= 1.7767$$

from which

$$f(x_3) = 0.0210$$

The method of successive substitution gave $x_3 = 1.8193$ and $f(x_3) = 0.0866$. Clearly, the value produced using Aitken's method is already significantly better.

Given $g(x), x_0$
Repeat (*for* $n = 0, 3, 6 \ldots$)
  Set $x_{n+1} = g(x_n)$
    $x_{n+2} = g(x_{n+1})$
    $$x_{n+3} = x_n - \frac{(x_{n+1} - x_n)^2}{(x_{n+2} - 2x_{n+1} + x_n)}$$
Until converged

Figure 4.19 Algorithm for Aitken's method.

To confirm this improvement, we perform another Aitken cycle

$$x_4 = g(x_3) = \exp(1/1.7767) = 1.7557$$

and

$$x_5 = g(x_4) = 1.7675$$

from which

$$x_6 = x_3 - \frac{(x_4 - x_3)^2}{(x_5 - 2x_4 + x_3)}$$

$$= 1.7767 - \frac{(1.7577 - 1.7767)^2}{(1.7675 - 2(1.7577) + 1.7767)}$$

$$= 1.7633$$

and, rounded to four decimal places, $f(x_6) = 0.0001$. For this particular form of $g(x)$, the value of x_6 produced using the method of successive substitution alone is

$$x_6 = g(1.7809) = \exp(1/1.7809) = 1.7533$$

with

$$f(x_6) = -0.0156$$

and, again, the Aitken iterate is seen to be much more accurate.

Table 4.4 presents results, quoted to six decimal places, obtained by applying Aitken's Δ^2 process to both iteration (4.7) and iteration (4.9). Comparison with Table 4.3 shows that the effect of the Aitken acceleration is more pronounced with iteration (4.7) than with iteration (4.9). This happens because iteration (4.7) displays relatively slow convergence in comparison with (4.9).

Table 4.4 Solution to the test equation
using Aitken's Δ^2 method.

Iteration	(4.7)	(4.9)
1	1.947 734	1.723 867
2	1.670 991	1.755 034
3	1.776 704	1.760 075
4	1.755 651	1.762 543
5	1.767 541	1.763 076
6	1.763 249	1.763 222
Convergence	10	7

Program construction

A general program plan for Aitken's method can be obtained immediately from
Figure 4.16 simply by replacing the words 'successive substitution' in step (3)
by 'Aitken's algorithm'. A subroutine plan based on the algorithm of
Figure 4.19 is a little complicated because there are three separate iterations
inside the main repeat-loop and, after each one, it is necessary to test for
convergence and exit the loop prematurely if appropriate. However, if the
mathematical algorithm is rewritten in the form

Given $g(x), x_0$
Repeat (*for* $n = 0,1,2, \ldots$)
  If $n = 0,3,6, \ldots$
    Set $x_{n+1} = g(x_n)$
  If $n = 1,4,7, \ldots$
    Set $x_{n+1} = g(x_n)$
  If $n = 2,5,8, \ldots$

$$\text{Set } x_{n+1} = x_{n-2} - \frac{(x_{n-1} - x_{n-2})^2}{(x_n - 2x_{n-1} - x_{n-2})}$$

Until converged

there is effectively only one iteration inside the repeat-loop. The subroutine plan
based on this alternative form of the algorithm is straightforward and is given in
Figure 4.20.

To determine which of the three iterations inside the repeat-loop is to be
used at each stage, we divide the iteration count by three and examine the
remainder.

```
NEXT=MOD(COUNT,3)
IF (NEXT.EQ.1) THEN
   ⋮
```

Given: $g(x), x0, tolerance, maximum$ *number of iterations*
Set: $newx = x0$
repeat (*not exceeding max iterations*)
  Set: $oldx = newx$
  if *iteration count* = 1,4,7 . . . **then**
    Set: $x1 = g(x0)$
        $newx = x1$
  if *iteration count* = 2,5,8 . . . **then**
    Set: $x2 = g(x1)$
        $newx = x2$
  if *iteration count* = 3,6,9 . . . **then**
    Set: $x0 = x0 - (x1 - x0)(x1 - x0)/(x2 - 2x1 + x0)$
        $newx = x0$
  if $|newx - oldx| \leq |oldx| \cdot tolerance$ **then**
    Note: '*solved*'
until '*solved*' (*or limit on number of iterations reached*)
if '*solved*' **then**
  Record: root, number of iterations used
if '*limit*' **then**
  Record: last approximation to root

Figure 4.20 Plan of subroutine for Aitken's method.

```
      ELSE IF (NEXT.EQ.2) THEN
      :
      ELSE
C     {NEXT=0}
      :
      END IF
```

The complete subroutine is given in Figure 4.21.

4.2 Methods with derivatives

4.2.1 Newton's method

When the derivative $f'(x)$ is available, Newton's method, sometimes known as the Newton–Raphson method, usually provides a very efficient procedure for evaluating a root of the equation $f(x) = 0$. The iteration is derived as follows.

Let x_n be an approximation to α. Then, using Taylor's series (see Appendix A), $f(\alpha)$ can be expanded about the point x_n giving

$$f(\alpha) = f(x_n) + (\alpha - x_n)f'(x_n) + \frac{(\alpha - x_n)^2}{2!}f''(x_n) + \cdots$$

```
      SUBROUTINE AITKEN (G,INX0,TOL,MAXITS,
     *                   STATUS,ROOT,NOOFIT,LASTX)

      INTEGER   COUNT,LIMIT,MAXITS,NEXT,NOOFIT,SOLVED,STATUS
      REAL      G,INX0,LASTX,NEWX,OLDX,ROOT,TOL,X0,X1,X2
      PARAMETER (SOLVED=0,LIMIT=1)
      INTRINSIC ABS,MOD
      EXTERNAL  G

      X0=INX0
      NEWX=X0

      DO 10, COUNT=1,MAXITS
        OLDX=NEWX
        NEXT=MOD(COUNT,3)

        IF (NEXT.EQ.1) THEN
          X1  =G(X0)
          NEWX=X1
        ELSE IF (NEXT.EQ.2) THEN
          X2  =G(X1)
          NEWX=X2
        ELSE
          X0  =X0-(X1-X0)*(X1-X0)/(X2-2*X1+X0)
          NEWX=X0
        END IF

        IF (ABS(NEWX-OLDX).LE.ABS(OLDX)*TOL) THEN
          STATUS=SOLVED
          GO TO 11
        END IF

 10   CONTINUE
      STATUS=LIMIT

 11   IF (STATUS.EQ.SOLVED) THEN
        NOOFIT=COUNT
        ROOT  =NEWX
      END IF

      IF (STATUS.EQ.LIMIT) THEN
        LASTX=NEWX
      END IF

      END
```

Figure 4.21 Subroutine for Aitken's method.

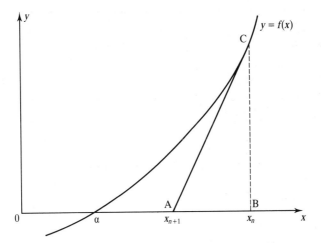

Figure 4.22

If x_n is close to α, then $(\alpha - x_n)$ is small and terms of order $(\alpha - x_n)^2$ and higher can be ignored. Thus

$$f(\alpha) \simeq f(x_n) + (\alpha - x_n) f'(x_n)$$

But $f(\alpha) = 0$ so

$$f(x_n) + (\alpha - x_n) f'(x_n) \simeq 0$$

from which

$$\alpha \simeq x_n - \frac{f(x_n)}{f'(x_n)}$$

This is the basis of the iteration

$$x_{n+1} = x_n - \frac{f(x_n)}{f'(x_n)} \qquad (4.18)$$

which is known as the Newton iteration.

Alternatively, Equation (4.18) can be derived geometrically and this approach gives some feeling for the way that the method works. Consider Figure 4.22, in which the graph of a function $f(x)$ is drawn. A root, α, of the function is indicated and the existing estimate, x_n, of the root is represented by OB. BC is the value $f(x_n)$ and the next iterate, x_{n+1}, is chosen to be the point at which the tangent to $f(x)$ at x_n cuts the x-axis. This tangent is represented by AC

Given $f(x), f'(x), x_0$
Repeat (*for* $n = 0, 1, \ldots$)
   Set $x_{n+1} = x_n - f(x_n)/f'(x_n)$
Until converged

Figure 4.23   Algorithm for Newton's method.

and so x_{n+1} is OA and is a better estimate than x_n. Now

$$OA = OB - AB$$

and

$$AB = \frac{BC}{\tan{(BAC)}}$$

where $\tan{(BAC)}$ is the gradient of the tangent at C and is given by $f'(x_n)$. Hence

$$\begin{aligned}
x_{n+1} = OA &= OB - AB \\
&= OB - \frac{BC}{\tan{(BAC)}} \\
&= x_n - f(x_n)/f'(x_n)
\end{aligned}$$

as before.

The algorithm for Newton's method is given in Figure 4.23. Applying it to the test example,

$$f(x) = x - \exp{(1/x)}$$

we require

$$f'(x) = 1 + \frac{\exp{(1/x)}}{x^2}$$

Then, using $x_0 = 1.5$ gives $f(x_0) = -0.4477$, $f'(x_0) = 1.8657$ and so the first Newton iterate is

$$\begin{aligned}
x_1 = x_0 &- \frac{f(x_0)}{f'(x_0)} \\
&= 1.5 - (-0.4477)/1.8657 \\
&= 1.7400
\end{aligned}$$

Hence $f(x_1) = -0.0366$, $f'(x_1) = 1.5868$ and the second iterate is

Table 4.5 Solution to the test
equation using
Newton's method.

Iteration	Newton
1	1.739 987
2	1.763 077
3	1.763 223
4	1.763 223
Convergence	4

$$x_2 = x_1 - f(x_1)/f'(x_1)$$
$$= 1.7400 - (-0.0366)/1.5868$$
$$= 1.7631$$

Similarly, the third iterate is

$$x_3 = 1.7632$$

and already there are two iterates, x_3 and x_2, agreeing to four significant figures. In fact, x_3 is the correct value of the root to five significant figures.

Table 4.5 presents values, quoted to six decimal places, obtained by applying Newton's method to the test equation with a starting value of 1.5 and a convergence tolerance of 5E−7. A comparison with the earlier tables shows how much more quickly Newton's method converges.

Although Newton's method generally gives extremely rapid convergence, it suffers from the disadvantage that knowledge of the first derivative of $f(x)$ is required. In certain cases, the calculation of this derivative can be extremely time consuming. In this situation the secant method should be considered because it is, in effect, Newton's method with the derivative of $f(x)$ approximated by the slope of the line joining the points $(x_{n-1}, f(x_{n-1}))$ and $(x_n, f(x_n))$, namely

$$f'(x_n) \simeq \frac{f(x_n) - f(x_{n-1})}{x_n - x_{n-1}}$$

Substituting this replacement into Equation (4.18), formula (4.2) is obtained. The relative rates of convergence of the secant and Newton methods are compared in Section 4.2.2.

As in the secant method, we would expect problems to arise with Newton's iteration if there were a flat spot in the neighbourhood of the root. There are three possibilities to consider:
(1)   If $f'(x_n) = 0$, attempted computation of x_{n+1} from Equation (4.18) would cause arithmetic overflow. This can often be avoided by choosing a different initial approximation.
(2)   If $f'(\alpha) = 0$, indicating a multiple root at $x = \alpha$, then, rather

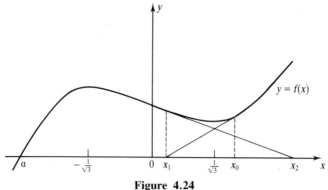

Figure 4.24

Given: $f(x), f'(x), x0, tolerance,$
      maximum number of iterations
Set: $newx = x0$
repeat (*not exceeding max iterations*)
  Set: $f dx = f'(newx)$
  if $|f dx| \leq$ *small number* **then**
    Note: '*flat spot*'
  else
    Set: $oldx = newx$
        $fx = f(oldx)$
        $newx = oldx - fx/f dx$
  if $|newx - oldx| \leq |oldx| \cdot tolerance$ **then**
    Note: '*solved*'
until '*solved*' **or** '*flat spot*'
      (*or limit on number of iterations reached*)
if '*solved*' **then**
  Record: *root,residual,number of iterations used*
if '*limit*' **then**
  Record: *last approximation to root*
if '*flat spot*' **then**
  Record: *last approximation to root*

Figure 4.25 Plan of subroutine for Newton's method.

surprisingly, the iteration will still converge although the rate of convergence will be impaired; this will be discussed in the next section.

(3)   If $f'(\alpha \pm \varepsilon) = 0$ for some small ε, indicating that $f(x)$ has a local maximum or minimum near to α, then the iteration may oscillate or converge to a different root. The former possibility is illustrated in Figure 4.24, using the graph of $f(x) = x^3 - x + 1$. An initial guess $x_0 > -1/\sqrt{3}$ will give iterates that oscillate around $x = 1/\sqrt{3}$, a local

minimum of $f(x)$. The method will converge only if a subsequent iterate takes a value less than $-1/\sqrt{3}$. The problem of maxima or minima near to a root can be overcome by sketching the function in order to obtain a better initial estimate. This is particularly important if almost coincident roots are suspected (see Exercises 4.6 and 4.14).

Program construction

The general program plan for Newton's method can be obtained immediately from Figure 4.10 by replacing the word 'secant' in step (3) by 'Newton'. The subroutine plan follows from the mathematical algorithm of Figure 4.23 and is given in Figure 4.25. Note that a test for a flat spot has been included.

Using this plan and assuming that the functions $f(x)$ and $f'(x)$ are supplied in separate function subprograms called F and FDASH respectively, we produce the subroutine given in Figure 4.26.

4.2.2 The order of an iterative method

Definition 4.1

Suppose that x_n, $\{n = 0,1,2, \ldots\}$, is a sequence that converges to α and let $\varepsilon_n = x_n - \alpha$ for each n. If positive constants c and p exist with

$$\lim_{n\to\infty} \frac{|\varepsilon_{n+1}|}{|\varepsilon_n|^p} = c$$

then the sequence of iterates, x_n, is said to converge to α with order p and asymptotic error constant c.

In other words, if an iterative formula is producing a converging sequence of iterates and the error in x_{n+1} is proportional to the pth power of the error in x_n, then the iterative formula is said to be of order p. Clearly, the higher the order of the iteration, the more rapid is the rate of convergence. The following can be shown (see Ralston and Rabinowitz 1978):

(1) In general, the secant method is of order $(1 + \sqrt{5})/2 \simeq 1.62$.

(2) The method of successive substitution is of order at least 1. However, in practice, the *ad hoc* rearrangement of the equation $f(x) = 0$ into the form $x = g(x)$ usually results in a first-order formula (i.e. with order 1).

(3) When used in conjunction with a first-order iterative method, Aitken's Δ^2 process gives second-order convergence unless α is a multiple root, in which case the order of convergence remains 1.

```
      SUBROUTINE NEWTON (F,FDASH,X0,TOL,MAXITS,
     *                     STATUS,ROOT,RESID,NOOFIT,LASTX)

      INTEGER   COUNT,FLAT,ITRATE,LIMIT,MAXITS,NOOFIT,SOLVED,STATUS
      REAL      DX,F,FDASH,FX,FDX,LASTX,NEWX,OLDX,X0,
     *          RESID,ROOT,TINY,TOL
      PARAMETER (TINY=1E-10)
      PARAMETER (ITRATE=-1,SOLVED=0,LIMIT=1,FLAT=2)
      INTRINSIC ABS
      EXTERNAL  F,FDASH

      NEWX=X0

      STATUS=ITRATE
      DO 10, COUNT=1,MAXITS
        FDX=FDASH(NEWX)

        IF (ABS(FDX).LE.TINY) THEN
C         { flat spot }
          STATUS=FLAT
        ELSE
C         { perform Newton algorithm }
          OLDX=NEWX
          FX  =F(OLDX)
          DX  =-FX/FDX
          NEWX=OLDX+DX
          IF (ABS(DX).LE.ABS(OLDX)*TOL) STATUS=SOLVED
        END IF

        IF (STATUS.NE.ITRATE) GO TO 11
10      CONTINUE
        STATUS=LIMIT

11    IF (STATUS.EQ.SOLVED) THEN
        NOOFIT=COUNT
        ROOT  =NEWX
        RESID =F(ROOT)
      END IF

      IF (STATUS.EQ.LIMIT .OR. STATUS.EQ.FLAT) THEN
        LASTX=NEWX
      END IF

      END
```

Figure 4.26 Subroutine for Newton's method.

(4)   Newton's method is of order 2 unless α is a multiple root, in which case the order of convergence is again only 1. However, modifications of Newton's method are available (see Exercise 4.8) which exhibit second-order convergence in this special case.

If derivatives of higher order are available, formulae of higher order can be derived and these produce very rapidly converging iterates. For example, appending a correction term to Newton's formula provides the general third-order procedure

$$x_{n+1} = x_n - \frac{f(x_n)}{f'(x_n)} - \frac{[f(x_n)]^2 f''(x_n)}{2[f'(x_n)]^3}$$

When applied to the test example with $x_0 = 1.5$, this iteration gives an estimate of the root which is correct to four significant figures after only one iteration. However, higher-order formulae involve higher-order derivates of $f(x)$ and these are frequently difficult to compute. The formulae are also more complicated and, in practice, are seldom used because the advantage of faster convergence is usually outweighed by the extra computational effort.

4.3   Polynomial equations

The problem of finding some or all of the zeros of a polynomial is one that occurs frequently. Great care must be taken when an attempt is made to solve such a problem. As has been seen in Chapter 3, difficulties can arise even when polynomials of degree 2 are involved. These difficulties multiply when polynomials of higher degree are considered.

Our usual notation for a polynomial of degree n is

$$p(x) = a_n x^n + a_{n-1} x^{n-1} + \cdots + a_1 x + a_0$$

In this chapter, however, it is convenient to adopt the alternative notation

$$p(x) = a_0 x^n + a_1 x^{n-1} + \cdots + a_{n-1} x + a_n \qquad (4.19)$$

Obviously all the methods described so far can be used to find a zero of a polynomial but the special structure of the function in this case makes it worthwhile to consider polynomials in more detail. Firstly, it is known exactly how many zeros a polynomial has and also, given that the coefficients a_i in polynomial (4.19) are real, it is known that the zeros are real or occur in complex conjugate pairs. Further information about the number of real roots can often be obtained very quickly from Descartes' rule of signs (see Appendix A). Secondly, polynomials can be evaluated extremely efficiently on a computer by using a technique called nested multiplication. This requires n additions and n multiplications whereas direct evaluation of polynomial (4.19) by forming x^n, multiplying by a_0 and then forming x^{n-1}, etc., would involve n additions and $n(n+1)/2$ multiplications. Even if x^n were formed as $x(x^{n-1})$, starting with $n = 2$, n additions and $2n - 1$ multiplications would be required. Nested multiplication simply involves rewriting the polynomial (4.19) in the form

$$p(x) = (. . . ((a_0x + a_1)x + a_2)x + \cdots + a_{n-1})x + a_n$$

Then, for a particular value of x, say $x = z$, it is evaluated from the innermost bracket outwards; i.e. the following sequence is formed

$$
\begin{aligned}
t_0 &= a_0 \\
t_1 &= t_0z + a_1 \\
t_2 &= t_1z + a_2 \\
&\;\;\vdots \\
t_n &= t_{n-1}z + a_n
\end{aligned}
$$

(4.20)

whence $p(z) = t_n$. To illustrate the use of this procedure, we evaluate the polynomial

$$p(x) = x^3 - 2x^2 - x - 6$$

at the point $x = 2$. The coefficients of the polynomial are $a_0 = 1$, $a_1 = -2$, $a_2 = -1$ and $a_3 = -6$. Hence, from relationships (4.20),

$$
\begin{aligned}
t_0 &= a_0 = 1 \\
t_1 &= t_0(2) + a_1 = 1(2) + (-2) = 0 \\
t_2 &= t_1(2) + a_2 = 0(2) + (-1) = -1 \\
t_3 &= t_2(2) + a_3 = -1(2) + (-6) = -8
\end{aligned}
$$

and so

$$p(2) = -8$$

The function subprogram of Figure 4.27 will evaluate the polynomial $p(x)$ using the relationships (4.20).

4.3.1 Real zeros and Newton's method

The derivatives of a polynomial $p(x)$ are obtained easily and so Newton's method is usually used to locate the zeros of $p(x)$. Given a suitable initial approximation,

```
REAL FUNCTION POLY (N,A,Z)

INTEGER I,N
REAL    Z
DOUBLE PRECISION T
REAL    A(0:N)

T=A(0)
DO 10, I=1,N
   T=T*Z+A(I)
10    CONTINUE
POLY=T

END
```

Figure 4.27   Function subprogram for nested multiplication.

x_0, it is necessary to calculate

$$x_{m+1} = x_m - \frac{p(x_m)}{p'(x_m)}$$

for $m = 0,1,2, \ldots$. Note that we have used m instead of n as the iteration count because, now, n represents the degree of $p(x)$. Of course, both $p(x_m)$ and $p'(x_m)$ can be evaluated very efficiently using the technique of nested multiplication described above. However, there is an even more efficient procedure available, which allows us to evaluate both $p(x_m)$ and $p'(x_m)$ without having to differentiate $p(x)$ explicitly.

The recurrence relation (4.20) can be derived in a different way using a technique known as **synthetic division**. If we divide $p(x)$ by $(x - z)$, where z is an arbitrary constant, we obtain

$$\frac{p(x)}{(x - z)} = q(x) + \frac{r}{(x - z)}$$

where $q(x)$ is the quotient polynomial, whose degree is one less than that of $p(x)$, and r is the constant remainder. Hence we may write

$$p(x) = (x - z) q(x) + r \tag{4.21}$$

Obviously

$$p(z) = r$$

and so $p(z)$ can be evaluated by finding the remainder when $p(x)$ is divided by $(x - z)$. It is possible to accomplish this without actually performing the division – hence the name **synthetic** division. Because $q(x)$ is of degree $(n - 1)$, we may write

$$q(x) = b_0 x^{n-1} + b_1 x^{n-2} + \cdots + b_{n-2} x + b_{n-1} \tag{4.22}$$

where the b values are constants. Substituting Equation (4.22) into Equation (4.21) and comparing coefficients of powers of x with those of Equation (4.19) gives

$$a_0 = b_0$$
$$a_1 = b_1 - b_0 z$$
$$a_2 = b_2 - b_1 z$$
$$\vdots$$
$$a_{n-1} = b_{n-1} - b_{n-2} z$$
$$a_n = r - b_{n-1} z$$

Now, rearranging these equations so that the unknown b values appear on the left-hand side,

$$b_0 = a_0$$
$$b_1 = b_0 z + a_1$$
$$b_2 = b_1 z + a_2$$
$$\vdots$$
$$b_{n-1} = b_{n-2} z + a_{n-1}$$

and

$$r = b_{n-1} z + a_n$$

If r is replaced by b_n, then $p(z)$ is b_n, the last value obtained from the recurrence relation

$$b_i = b_{i-1} z + a_i \tag{4.23}$$

where $i = 1, 2, \ldots , n$ and $b_0 = a_0$. Note that the b values produced by this recurrence relation are identical to the t values of Equation (4.20) and so synthetic division and nested multiplication are equivalent.

To obtain a similar formula for $p'(z)$, Equation (4.21) is differentiated to give

$$p'(x) = (x - z) q'(x) + q(x)$$

from which

$$p'(z) = q(z)$$

To evaluate $q(z)$, we apply the process of synthetic division to $q(x)$. Then, corresponding to Equation (4.21), we obtain an equation of the form

$$q(x) = (x - z)(c_0 x^{n-2} + c_1 x^{n-3} + \cdots + c_{n-3}x + c_{n-2}) + s \qquad (4.24)$$

Hence $q(z)$ is the remainder when $q(x)$ is divided by $(x - z)$. Comparing the coefficients of powers of x in Equation (4.24) with those in Equation (4.22) and rearranging the resulting equations gives

$$c_0 = b_0$$
$$c_1 = c_0 z + b_1$$
$$\vdots$$
$$c_{n-2} = c_{n-3}z + b_{n-2}$$

and

$$s = c_{n-2}z + b_{n-1}$$

If s is replaced by c_{n-1}, then $p'(z)$ is c_{n-1}, the last value obtained from the recurrence relation

$$c_i = c_{i-1}z + b_i \qquad (4.25)$$

where $i = 1, 2, \ldots, n - 1$ and $c_0 = b_0$.

Hence Newton's method for finding a *real* zero of a polynomial is

$$x_{m+1} = x_m - p(x_m)/p'(x_m)$$
$$= x_m - b_n/c_{n-1}$$

where $m = 1, 2, \ldots$ and b_n and c_{n-1} are obtained from Equations (4.23) and (4.25) respectively with z replaced by x_m.

To illustrate the use of the procedure, suppose that we wish to evaluate the root near $x = 1/2$ of the equation

$$x^3 + x - 1 = 0$$

We first calculate

$$b_0 = a_0 = 1$$
$$b_1 = b_0 z + a_1 = 1(1/2) + 0 = 1/2$$

$$b_2 = b_1 z + a_2 = (1/2)(1/2) + 1 = 5/4$$
$$b_3 = b_2 z + a_3 = (5/4)(1/2) - 1 = -3/8$$

$$c_0 = b_0 = 1$$
$$c_1 = c_0 z + b_1 = 1(1/2) + 1/2 = 1$$
$$c_2 = c_1 z + b_2 = 1(1/2) + 5/4 = 7/4$$

Then the next approximation to the root is

$$x_1 = 1/2 - \frac{-3/8}{7/4}$$
$$= 0.7143$$

Once a zero of $p(x)$ has been evaluated, the remainder in Equation (4.21) is zero and so

$$p(x) = (x - z)\, q(x)$$

Therefore, the remaining zeros of $p(x)$ are the zeros of $q(x)$. This means that $q(x)$ can be used to determine the other zeros of $p(x)$. This process is known as **deflation**. When a zero of $q(x)$ has been determined, a further deflation can take place and the process can be repeated (assuming that all the roots of $p(x)$ are real) until only a linear or quadratic factor remains. This must be done with care however, because any zero of $p(x)$, found using Newton's method, can be only approximate. Hence the coefficients of $q(x)$ will be slightly in error and any computed zero of $q(x)$ even more so. For this reason no subprogram to perform deflation is presented here and the interested reader should consult carefully a text that gives more detail – see, for example, Burden and Faires (1985) or Atkinson and Harley (1983).

Program construction

When the subprogram to evaluate $p(z)$ using the recurrence relation (4.23) is written, the b values must be recorded because these will be required later for the evaluation of $p'(z)$ using Equation (4.25). Therefore a subroutine must be used to evaluate $p'(z)$ because, now, the subprogram is producing more than one value of interest. This is in contrast to Figure 4.27 where a function subprogram was appropriate. It is convenient to include the evaluation of $p'(z)$ within the subroutine and this is done in EVPOLY of Figure 4.28. Note that there is no reason to store the c values and so a single real variable, C, is used rather than an array in the coding for relation (4.25). The subroutine also incorporates the STATUS parameter, allowing evaluation of $p(z)$ without evaluating $p'(z)$ – a feature that will be used to obtain the residual error when z has converged to a zero of $p(x)$. The array B is included in the argument list so that it can be dimensioned dynamically, as described in Section 1.12.3.

```
       SUBROUTINE EVPOLY (N,A,Z,STATUS, B,PZ,PDASHZ)

       INTEGER    I,ITRATE,N,STATUS
       REAL       PDASHZ,PZ,Z
       DOUBLE PRECISION C
       PARAMETER (ITRATE=-1)
       REAL       A(0:N),B(0:N)

C          { Calculate the b values and p(z) }
       B(0)=A(0)
       DO 10, I=1,N
         B(I)=B(I-1)*Z+A(I)
10     CONTINUE
       PZ=B(N)

       IF (STATUS.EQ.ITRATE) THEN
C          { Calculate the c values and p'(z) }
         C=B(0)
         DO 20, I=1,N-1
           C=C*Z+B(I)
20       CONTINUE
         PDASHZ=C
       END IF

       END
```

Figure 4.28 Subroutine for polynomial evaluation by synthetic division.

The subroutine, NEWPOL, of Figure 4.29 is modelled on the earlier Newton subroutine of Figure 4.26, but, in this case, the function parameters F and FDASH are not required. The coefficients of the polynomial are supplied as elements 0 through N of a one-dimensional array A. The array B, which is used locally within NEWPOL, is included in the argument list so that it may be dimensioned dynamically.

4.3.2 Complex zeros and Bairstow's method

It cannot be emphasized too much that trying to find zeros of polynomials is an extremely difficult process; a small change to one of the coefficients in $p(x)$ can alter the zeros of the polynomial completely. This was illustrated in Chapter 3 using a polynomial of degree 20. Computing complex zeros of polynomials is even more involved. The subroutine NEWPOL can be modified to use complex arithmetic and, using a complex initial guess, find a complex root of the polynomial. This approach has the disadvantage that, on computers, complex arithmetic is usually much slower than real arithmetic. Recall, however, that

```
      SUBROUTINE NEWPOL (N,A,B,X0,TOL,MAXITS,
     *                   STATUS,ROOT,RESID,NOOFIT,LASTX)

      INTEGER   COUNT,FLAT,ITRATE,LIMIT,MAXITS,N,NOOFIT,SOLVED,STATUS
      REAL      DX,LASTX,NEWX,OLDX,PDASHX,PDASHZ,PX,
     *          RESID,ROOT,TINY,TOL,X0
      PARAMETER (TINY=1E-10)
      PARAMETER (ITRATE=-1,SOLVED=0,LIMIT=1,FLAT=2)
      REAL      A(0:N),B(0:N)
      INTRINSIC ABS
      EXTERNAL  EVPOLY

      NEWX=X0

      STATUS=ITRATE
      DO 10, COUNT=1,MAXITS
        CALL EVPOLY (N,A,NEWX,ITRATE, B,PX,PDASHX)
C          { to calculate p(x) & p'(x) }

        IF (ABS(PDASHX).LE.TINY) THEN
C            { flat spot }
          STATUS=FLAT
        ELSE
C            { perform Newton algorithm }
          OLDX=NEWX
          DX  =-PX/PDASHX
          NEWX=OLDX+DX
          IF (ABS(DX).LE.ABS(OLDX)*TOL) STATUS=SOLVED
        END IF

        IF (STATUS.NE.ITRATE) GO TO 11
10    CONTINUE
      STATUS=LIMIT

11    IF (STATUS.EQ.SOLVED) THEN
        NOOFIT=COUNT
        ROOT  =NEWX
        CALL EVPOLY (N,A,NEWX,SOLVED, B,RESID,PDASHZ)
C          { to obtain residual }
      END IF

      IF (STATUS.EQ.LIMIT .OR. STATUS.EQ.FLAT) THEN
        LASTX=NEWX
      END IF

      END
```

Figure 4.29 Subroutine for Newton's method applied to a polynomial.

complex roots of polynomials with real coefficients occur in conjugate pairs. This suggests that we should seek a quadratic, rather than a linear, factor of the polynomial. This is the basis for the method known as Bairstow's method.

Let $(x^2 + ux + v)$ be an approximate quadratic factor of $p(x)$. Then

$$\frac{p(x)}{(x^2 + ux + v)} = q(x) + \frac{rx + t}{(x^2 + ux + v)} \tag{4.26}$$

where $q(x)$ is the quotient polynomial of degree $(n - 2)$ and $rx + t$ is the remainder. Equation (4.26) can be rewritten as

$$p(x) = (x^2 + ux + v)\, q(x) + rx + t$$

For reasons that will become apparent later, it is convenient to write this equation in the equivalent form

$$p(x) = (x^2 + ux + v)\, q(x) + r(x + u) + s \tag{4.27}$$

where $s = t - ru$. Note that r, s and $q(x)$ will depend on u and v. Thus, in order to obtain an exact quadratic factor, we have to find increments δu and δv which, when added to u and v respectively, will make r and s zero. In other words, given u and v, we have to solve the equations

$$r(u + \delta u, v + \delta v) = 0$$
$$s(u + \delta u, v + \delta v) = 0$$

for δu and δv. Unfortunately, these equations are non-linear, so Taylor's theorem for functions of two variables (see Appendix A) is used to approximate them by the linear relations

$$r + (r)_u \delta u + (r)_v \delta v \simeq 0$$
$$s + (s)_u \delta u + (s)_v \delta v \simeq 0$$

where, for example, $(r)_u$ is the first partial derivative of $r(u,v)$, with respect to u, evaluated at the point (u,v). Isolating δu and δv in these approximations gives

$$\delta u \simeq [s(r)_v - r(s)_v]/\det(J)$$
$$\delta v \simeq [r(s)_u - s(r)_u]/\det(J) \tag{4.28}$$

where

$$J = \begin{bmatrix} (r)_u & (r)_v \\ (s)_u & (s)_v \end{bmatrix}$$

and is known as the **Jacobian** matrix of the pair of functions $r(u,v)$ and $s(u,v)$

with respect to u and v. Relations (4.28) give δu and δv only approximately and so they form the basis of an iterative scheme to find an exact quadratic factor of $p(x)$. To set up this iteration, equations for r, s, $(r)_u$, $(r)_v$, $(s)_u$ and $(s)_v$ are required.

To find r and s, let

$$q(x) = b_0 x^{n-2} + b_1 x^{n-3} + \cdots + b_{n-3}x + b_{n-2}$$

Substituting this into Equation (4.27) and comparing coefficients of powers of x with those of Equation (4.19) gives

$$a_0 = b_0$$
$$a_1 = b_1 + b_0 u$$
$$a_2 = b_2 + b_1 u + b_0 v$$
$$\vdots$$
$$a_{n-2} = b_{n-2} + b_{n-3}u + b_{n-4}v$$
$$a_{n-1} = r + b_{n-2}u + b_{n-3}v$$
$$a_n = s + ru + b_{n-2}v$$

These equations can be rewritten in the form

$$b_0 = a_0$$
$$b_1 = a_1 - b_0 u$$
$$b_2 = a_2 - b_1 u - b_0 v$$
$$\vdots$$
$$b_{n-2} = a_{n-2} - b_{n-3}u - b_{n-4}v$$
$$r = a_{n-1} - b_{n-2}u - b_{n-3}v$$
$$s = a_n - ru - b_{n-2}v$$

If r is replaced by b_{n-1} and s by b_n, then r and s are given by the last two values obtained from the recurrence relation

$$b_i = a_i - b_{i-1}u - b_{i-2}v \tag{4.29}$$

where $i = 1, 2, \ldots n$, $b_0 = a_0$ and $b_{-1} = 0$. This justifies the form adopted for the remainder in Equation (4.27).

To find $(r)_u$ and $(s)_u$, Equations (4.29) are differentiated with respect to u.

$$(b_0)_u = 0$$
$$(b_1)_u = -b_0$$
$$(b_2)_u = -b_1 - (b_1)_u u$$
$$(b_3)_u = -b_2 - (b_2)_u u - (b_1)_u v$$
$$\vdots$$

Given n, the coefficients of $p(x), u_0, v_0$
Repeat (for $j = 0,1, \ldots$)
    Evaluate b_i, $i = 0,1, \ldots, n$ using (4.29)
    Evaluate c_i, $i = 0,1, \ldots, n$ using (4.30)
    Set $\det(J) = c_{n-1}^2 - c_n c_{n-2}$
      $\delta u = (b_n c_{n-2} - b_{n-1} c_{n-1})/\det(J)$
      $\delta v = (b_{n-1} c_n - b_n c_{n-1})/\det(J)$
      $u_{j+1} = u_j + \delta u$
      $v_{j+1} = v_j + \delta v$
Until converged

Figure 4.30 Algorithm for Bairstow's method.

$$(b_{n-1})_u = -b_{n-2} - (b_{n-2})_u u - (b_{n-3})_u v$$
$$(b_n)_u = -b_{n-1} - (b_{n-1})_u u - (b_{n-2})_u v$$

If we define $c_i = (b_i)_u$, then $(r)_u = c_{n-1}$ and $(s)_u = c_n$ and these are given by the last two equations of the recurrence relation

$$c_i = -b_{i-1} - c_{i-1}u - c_{i-2}v \qquad (4.30)$$

where $i = 1,2, \ldots, n$ and $c_0 = c_{-1} = 0$.

To find $(r)_v$ and $(s)_v$, we differentiate Equations (4.29) with respect to v and proceed in a similar manner. If we define $d_i = (b_{i+1})_v$, so that $(r)_v = d_{n-2}$ and $(s)_v = d_{n-1}$, we obtain the recurrence relation

$$d_i = -b_{i-1} - d_{i-1}u - d_{i-2}v \qquad (4.31)$$

where $i = 1,2, \ldots, n - 1$, and $d_0 = d_{-1} = 0$. Clearly the d values of (4.31) are identical to the c values of (4.30). Hence, $(r)_v = c_{n-2}$, $(s)_v = c_{n-1}$ and the last recurrence relation, (4.31), is redundant.

Thus, from (4.28), estimates of δu and δv are given by

$$\delta u \simeq (b_n c_{n-2} - b_{n-1} c_{n-1})/\det(J)$$
$$\delta v \simeq (b_{n-1} c_n - b_n c_{n-1})/\det(J)$$

where

$$J = \begin{bmatrix} c_{n-1} & c_{n-2} \\ c_n & c_{n-1} \end{bmatrix}$$

An algorithm for Bairstow's method is presented in Figure 4.30.

In practice, the last three terms of $p(x)$ are often used, after dividing through by a_{n-2}, as an initial approximation to a quadratic factor. Thus, for example, to obtain a quadratic factor of the polynomial

$$p(x) = 2x^4 + x^3 + 2x^2 + x + 2$$

we could take $(x^2 + x/2 + 1)$ as the initial approximation. Then $u = 1/2$ and $v = 1$ so that

$$b_0 = a_0 = 2$$
$$b_1 = a_1 - b_0 u = 1 - 2(1/2) = 0$$
$$b_2 = a_2 - b_1 u - b_0 v = 2 - 0(1/2) - 2(1) = 0$$
$$b_3 = a_3 - b_2 u - b_1 v = 1 - 0(1/2) - 0(1) = 1$$
$$b_4 = a_4 - b_3 u - b_2 v = 2 - 1(1/2) - 0(1) = 3/2$$

$$c_1 = -b_0 = -2$$
$$c_2 = -b_1 - c_1 u = 0 - (-2)(1/2) = 1$$
$$c_3 = -b_2 - c_2 u - c_1 v = 0 - 1(1/2) - (-2)1 = 3/2$$
$$c_4 = -b_3 - c_3 u - c_2 v = -1 - (3/2)(1/2) - 1(1) = -11/4$$

from which

$$\delta u = \frac{b_4 c_2 - b_3 c_3}{c_3^2 - c_4 c_2} = \frac{(3/2)(1) - 1(3/2)}{(3/2)(3/2) - (-11/4)1} = \frac{0}{5} = 0$$

$$\delta v = \frac{b_3 c_4 - b_4 c_3}{c_3^2 - c_4 c_2} = \frac{1(-11/4) - (3/2)(3/2)}{(3/2)(3/2) - (-11/4)1} = \frac{-5}{5} = -1$$

The next approximations to u and v are then

$$u_1 = u_0 + \delta u = 1/2 + 0 = 1/2$$
$$v_1 = v_0 + \delta v = 1 + (-1) = 0$$

Continuing in this manner until u and v have converged to seven significant figures, the values $u = 1.280\ 776$ and $v = 1.000\ 000$ are obtained after eight iterations. Thus

$$(x^2 + 1.280\ 776x + 1)$$

may be taken as the quadratic factor. It is then a trivial matter to compute the complex zeros and these are

$$x = -0.640\ 389 \pm 0.768\ 051i$$

Program construction

If the Jacobian matrix is singular, then $\det(J) = 0$ and problems will arise with Bairstow's method. Therefore, the program plan of Figure 4.31, which is based

Given: *n,the coefficients of* $p(x),u_0,v_0,tolerance,*
          maximum number of iterations
Set: *newu* = u_0
      newv = v_0
      b_0 = a_0
      c_0 = 0
      c_1 = $-b_0$
repeat (*not exceeding max iterations*)
   Set: $b_1 = a_1 - b_0 newu$
   for $i = 2,3, \ldots ,n$
      Set: $b_i = a_i - b_{i-1} newu - b_{i-2} newv$
   for $i = 2,3, \ldots ,n$
      Set: $c_i = -b_{i-1} - c_{i-1} newu - c_{n-2} newv$
   Set: $\det(J) = c_{n-1}^2 - c_n c_{n-2}$
   if $|\det(J)| \leq$ *small number* **then**
      Note: '*J sing*'
   else
      oldu = *newu*
      oldv = *newv*
      du   = $(b_n c_{n-2} - b_{n-1} c_{n-1})/\det(J)$
      dv   = $(b_{n-1} c_n - b_n c_{n-1})/\det(J)$
      newu = *oldu* + *du*
      newv = *oldv* + *dv*
      if $|du| \leq |oldu| \cdot tolerance$ **and** $|dv| \leq |oldv| \cdot tolerance$ **then**
         Note: '*solved*'
until '*solved*' **or** '*J sing*'
         (*or limit on number of iterations reached*)
if '*solved*' **then**
   Record: *u,v,number of iterations used*
if '*limit*' **then**
   Record: *Last approximations to u and v*
if '*J sing*' **then**
   Record: *last approximations to u and v*

Figure 4.31   Plan of subroutine for Bairstow's method.

on the algorithm of Figure 4.30, tests for this possibility and stops the calculations if $\det(J)$ becomes small. The subroutine of Figure 4.32 follows directly from the program plan of Figure 4.31 and sets STATUS to JSING if the matrix J becomes singular.

Figure 4.32 Subroutine for Bairstow's method.

```
      SUBROUTINE BRSTOW (N,A,B,C,U0,V0,TOL,MAXITS,
     *                   STATUS,U,V,NOOFIT,LASTU,LASTV)

      INTEGER   COUNT,I,ITRATE,JSING,LIMIT,MAXITS,N,NOOFIT,SOLVED,STATUS
      REAL      DETJ,DU,DV,LASTU,LASTV,NEWU,NEWV,OLDU,OLDV,
     *          TINY,TOL,U,U0,V,V0
      PARAMETER (TINY=1E-10)
      PARAMETER (ITRATE=-1,SOLVED=0,LIMIT=1,JSING=2)
      REAL      A(0:N),B(0:N),C(0:N)
      INTRINSIC ABS

      NEWU=U0
      NEWV=V0
      B(0)=A(0)
      C(0)=0
      C(1)=-B(0)

      STATUS=ITRATE
      DO 10, COUNT=1,MAXITS
        B(1)=A(1)-B(0)*NEWU
        DO 20 I=2,N
          B(I)=A(I)-B(I-1)*NEWU-B(I-2)*NEWV
20      CONTINUE

        DO 30, I=2,N
          C(I)=-B(I-1)-C(I-1)*NEWU-C(I-2)*NEWV
30      CONTINUE
        DETJ=C(N-1)*C(N-1)-C(N)*C(N-2)

        IF (ABS(DETJ).LE.TINY) THEN
          STATUS=JSING
        ELSE
          OLDU=NEWU
          OLDV=NEWV
          DU  =(B(N)*C(N-2)-B(N-1)*C(N-1))/DETJ
          DV  =(B(N-1)*C(N)-B(N)*C(N-1))/DETJ
          NEWU=OLDU+DU
          NEWV=OLDV+DV
          IF (ABS(DU).LE.ABS(OLDU)*TOL .AND.
     *        ABS(DV).LE.ABS(OLDV)*TOL) STATUS=SOLVED
        END IF

        IF (STATUS.NE.ITRATE) GO TO 11
10    CONTINUE
      STATUS=LIMIT
```

```
11     IF (STATUS.EQ.SOLVED) THEN
          NOOFIT=COUNT
          U=NEWU
          V=NEWV
       END IF

       IF (STATUS.EQ.LIMIT .OR. STATUS.EQ.JSING) THEN
          LASTU=NEWU
          LASTV=NEWV
       END IF

       END
```

Figure 4.32 *cont.*

EXERCISES

4.1 Use the bisection, regula falsi and secant methods to determine the zero of the function

$$f(x) = xe^x - 5$$

Take [0,2] as the starting interval and work throughout correct to three decimal places.

4.2 Compare the performance of the bisection, regula falsi and secant methods on the function

$$f(x) = x^3 - x + 1$$

of Figure 4.24 using a variety of starting intervals.

4.3 The equation

$$x^2 + 2x \sin x - 1 = 0$$

has a root in the interval [0,1]. Derive several rearrangements of this equation for use in the method of successive substitution. Check whether the iterations based on these rearrangements are convergent by applying the result of Theorem 4.1. Verify your conclusions by attempting to find the root of the equation using each iterative formula.

4.4 Apply Aitken's Δ^2 process to the sequences of iterates produced in Exercise 4.3.

4.5 Use Newton's method to determine the zeros of the functions in Exercises 4.1 and 4.2. Work throughout using four decimal place arithmetic.

4.6 Use Newton's method to determine all the real zeros of the function

$$f(x) = x^3 + x^2 - 1.0001x - 0.9999$$

Work throughout using four decimal place arithmetic.

4.7 Use Newton's method to determine a zero of the function

$$f(x) = x^{20} - 1$$

taking first 0.5 and then 1.5 as starting values. Comment on any differences in the progress of the iterations. Use four decimal place arithmetic throughout.

4.8 Newton's method may be modified so that second-order convergence can be obtained for functions that have multiple roots. The function $H(x) = f(x)/f'(x)$ replaces $f(x)$ in Newton's formula giving the iteration

$$x_{n+1} = x_n - H(x_n)/H'(x_n)$$

Compare the performance of Newton's method and its modification on the function

$$f(x) = 32x^3 - 150x + 125$$

taking $x_0 = 1.0$ as the starting value. Work throughout using four decimal place arithmetic.

4.9 Using the method of synthetic division, find all the real roots of the equations

(a) $x^3 + 3x - 7 = 0$
(b) $x^4 + 2x - 1 = 0$

working correct to four decimal places. (*Hint*: use Descartes' rule of signs to help determine the number of real roots in each case.)

4.10 Given that $x^2 + 2x + 2$ is an approximate quadratic factor of the polynomial

$$x^4 - 3x^3 + 20x^2 + 44x + 54$$

perform one iteration of Bairstow's method to improve this approximation.

Programming exercises

4.11 Modify the bisection subprogram of Figure 4.6 to take appropriate action if the mid-point or an end-point of an interval considered happens to be the zero. Check your program by testing it on the polynomial

$$p(x) = 2x^2 - 7x + 3$$

using first the interval [2,3] and then [0,1].

4.12 Write a subroutine to perform the regula falsi iteration. Examine the performance of the subroutine when applied to finding a zero of the function

$$f(x) = xe^x - 5$$

in the interval [0,2]. Print out clearly the result of each iteration.

4.13 Write a program that calls the subroutine AITKEN of Figure 4.21 to apply Aitken's Δ^2 process to each of the rearrangements, convergent or divergent, derived in Exercise 4.3. Comment on the results.

4.14 Apply the subroutines NEWPOL and EVPOL of Figures 4.29 and 4.28, respectively, to the problem of determining all the zeros of the polynomial

$$p(x) = 2x^4 + 16x^3 + x^2 - 74x + 56$$

All the zeros lie in the interval [−10,10]. Continue each iteration until successive estimates of the zero agree to six significant figures.

4.15 Write a program to apply the third-order method, described in Section 4.2.2, to the function of Exercise 4.1. Compare the results with those produced by a program that uses Newton's method.

4.16 (a) Write a program that uses Bairstow's method to find a quadratic factor of a polynomial and run it for

$$p(x) = x^5 + 14x^2 + 12x + 12$$

using $u_0 = 1$ and $v_0 = 1$ as initial estimates of u and v.

(b) Extend the program to include a subroutine that calculates the roots of the quadratic factor, given the values of u and v. Use the program to find a pair of zeros of the above polynomial.

Chapter 5
Linear algebraic equations

5.1   Direct methods   5.2   Iterative methods

This chapter is concerned with the problem of determining the values $x_1, x_2, \ldots, x_n$ which satisfy the following system of n linear equations:

$$
\begin{aligned}
a_{11}x_1 + a_{12}x_2 + \cdots + a_{1n}x_n &= b_1 \\
a_{21}x_1 + a_{22}x_2 + \cdots + a_{2n}x_n &= b_2 \\
&\;\;\vdots \\
a_{n1}x_1 + a_{n2}x_2 + \cdots + a_{nn}x_n &= b_n
\end{aligned}
\tag{5.1}
$$

Equations (5.1) can be written in the form

$$
A\boldsymbol{x} = \boldsymbol{b} \tag{5.2}
$$

where A is an $n \times n$ matrix whose (i,j)th element, a_{ij}, is the jth coefficient in the ith equation of (5.1). Chapter 4 gave an example of this type of problem in which it was necessary to solve two linear equations in two unknowns to obtain the corrections in Bairstow's method. In that case n had the value 2 and writing down the solution was simple.

It is assumed throughout this chapter that the reader is familiar with basic linear algebra, including the result that the solution to Equation (5.2) is unique provided that the matrix A is non-singular, i.e. the determinant of A is non-zero. It will normally be assumed that this is the case, but various tests will be included to detect possible singularity. Readers are referred to McKeown and Rayward-Smith (1982) as a general background text.

This chapter is divided into two sections. The first discusses some *direct* methods; these reduce the given equations to a form from which the solution can be obtained simply. The second presents several *iterative* methods; in these an initial approximation is successively refined until it is acceptably close to the exact solution. There will also be a brief discussion of some of the possible effects of ill-conditioning, a topic already mentioned in Chapter 3.

5.1   Direct methods

If the matrix in Equation (5.2) is diagonal (i.e. $a_{ij} = 0$ for $i \neq j$; $a_{ii} \neq 0$ for $i = 1,2, \ldots ,n$) the solution can be written down immediately:

$$x_i = b_i/a_{ii} \qquad \text{for } i = 1,2, \ldots ,n$$

The solution can be obtained almost as easily if A is triangular. For example, if the system of equations is upper triangular, that is of the form

$$
\begin{aligned}
a_{11}x_1 + a_{12}x_2 + & \quad \cdots \quad + a_{1n}x_n && = b_1 \\
a_{22}x_2 + & \quad \cdots \quad + a_{2n}x_n && = b_2 \\
& \quad \ddots \\
a_{n-1n-1}x_{n-1} + & a_{n-1n}x_n && = b_{n-1} \\
& a_{nn}x_n && = b_n
\end{aligned}
$$

$$(5.3)$$

and no diagonal element, a_{ii}, is zero then x_n, the nth element of the solution vector, is immediately determined from the nth equation of (5.3), namely

$$x_n = b_n/a_{nn}$$

Once x_n has been determined, x_{n-1} is the only unknown in the $(n - 1)$th equation and can be obtained directly by rewriting this equation in the form

$$x_{n-1} = \frac{b_{n-1} - a_{n-1n}x_n}{a_{n-1n-1}}$$

In general,

$$x_i = \frac{b_i - a_{ii+1}x_{i+1} - \cdots - a_{in}x_n}{a_{ii}} \qquad \text{for } i = n - 1, n - 2, \ldots ,1 \qquad (5.4)$$

*Given n, upper triangular A, **b***
Set $x_n = b_n/a_{nn}$
For $i = n - 1, n - 2, \ldots, 1$

$$\text{Set } x_i = \left(b_i - \sum_{j=i+1}^{n} a_{ij}x_j \right) \bigg/ a_{ii}$$

Figure 5.1   Algorithm for back-substitution.

Thus x_n is immediately available and all the other x_i, $i = n - 1, \ldots, 1$, can be determined by this *back-substitution* process. The mathematical algorithm is given in Figure 5.1.

As an illustration, this algorithm is applied to the following system of three equations:

$$2x_1 + x_2 + 3x_3 = 11$$
$$x_2 + 4x_3 = 6$$
$$2x_3 = 2$$

to obtain

$$x_3 = b_3/a_{33} = 2/2 = 1$$
$$x_2 = (b_2 - a_{23}x_3)/a_{22} = (6 - 4 \times 1)/1 = 2$$
$$x_1 = (b_1 - a_{12}x_2 - a_{13}x_3)/a_{11} = (11 - 1 \times 2 - 3 \times 1)/2 = 3$$

Thus the solution is

$$x = \begin{bmatrix} 3 \\ 2 \\ 1 \end{bmatrix}$$

A subprogram plan for back-substitution follows directly from the mathematical algorithm of Figure 5.1 and is given in Figure 5.2.

Given: $n, A, \boldsymbol{b}$
Set: $x_n = b_n/a_{nn}$
for $i = n - 1, n - 2, \ldots, 1$
  Set: $sum = b_i$
  for $j = i + 1, \ldots, n$
    Set: $sum = sum - a_{ij} * x_j$
  Set: $x_i = sum/a_{ii}$

Figure 5.2   Plan of program fragment for back-substitution.

```
      X(N)=B(N)/A(N,N)
      DO 10, I=N-1,1,-1
        SUM=B(I)
        DO 20, J=I+1,N
         SUM=SUM-DPROD(A(I,J),X(J))
20      CONTINUE
        X(I)=SUM/A(I,I)
10    CONTINUE
```

Figure 5.3 Program fragment for back-substitution.

We wish to make use of the back-substitution algorithm in the next section and so we now produce a program fragment corresponding to the plan of Figure 5.2. Implementing each **for** loop directly as a DO loop, we obtain the fragment of program given in Figure 5.3. Recalling the comments made in Chapter 3 concerning the accumulation of sums, the variable SUM must be DOUBLE PRECISION in order to minimize the effects of rounding errors.

A process for reducing a general system of linear equations to upper triangular form will now be discussed.

5.1.1 Gaussian elimination

The method of Gaussian elimination comprises two stages. First, a process of **elimination** is used systematically to reduce a non-singular system of equations of the form of (5.1) to the upper triangular form of (5.3). The new system is then solved by the back-substitution process described in Figure 5.1.

The elimination procedure involves the subtraction of a multiple of one equation from another. The proof of the following theorem is left as an exercise for the reader.

Theorem 5.1

Let $Ax = b$ be a given linear system and suppose that the system is subjected to a sequence of operations of the following kind:

(1) multiplication of one equation by a non-zero constant,

(2) addition (subtraction) of a multiple of one equation to (from) another,

(3) interchange of two equations.

If this sequence of operations produces the new system $A^*x = b^*$, then the systems $Ax = b$ and $A^*x = b^*$ are equivalent and, in particular, have the same solution.

The Gaussian elimination method will be described by considering an example. Suppose that the solution to the three equations

$$2x_1 + x_2 + 3x_3 = 11$$
$$4x_1 + 3x_2 + 10x_3 = 28 \qquad\qquad (5.5)$$
$$2x_1 + 4x_2 + 17x_3 = 31$$

is required. The first step in the 'triangularization' of this system of equations is to eliminate x_1 from the second and third equations of (5.5). This can be achieved by subtracting suitable multiples of the first equation from the other two. During this process, the first equation is called the **pivotal** equation and its first coefficient (2) is called the **pivot**. To eliminate x_1 from the second equation the **multiplier** must be $4/2 = 2$, and to eliminate x_1 from the third equation the multiplier must be $2/2 = 1$. This elimination gives the reduced set of equations

$$2x_1 + x_2 + 3x_3 = 11$$
2 $\qquad\qquad x_2 + 4x_3 = 6$
1 $\qquad\qquad 3x_2 + 14x_3 = 20$

The two multipliers have been recorded, to the left of the equations. This system is reduced to triangular form by eliminating x_2 from the third equation. The second equation now becomes the pivotal equation and its diagonal element (1), the coefficient of x_2, becomes the pivot. The multiplier $3/1$ is formed and this multiple of the second equation is subtracted from the third to give

$$2x_1 + x_2 + 3x_3 = 11$$
2 $\qquad\qquad x_2 + 4x_3 = 6 \qquad\qquad (5.6)$
1   3 $\qquad\qquad\qquad 2x_3 = 2$

and, again, the multiplier has been recorded. As we have seen already the process of back-substitution applied to this triangular system produces the solution

$$x = \begin{bmatrix} 3 \\ 2 \\ 1 \end{bmatrix}$$

In practice, hand computations for reducing a matrix to triangular form are best done in tabular form as shown in Table 5.1 in which the pivots have been underlined. This table incorporates a very simple but effective check on arithmetic accuracy.

In the first three rows the coefficient matrix and right-hand-side constants of the original system of equations are entered under appropriate headings. The numbers appearing in each row are then added and the result is recorded in the column headed *Sum*. The numbers in rows [4] and [9], including those in the *Sum* column, are obtained as a result of the operations described in the *Explanation*

Table 5.1 Tabular form for Gaussian elimination.

Row	Multiplier	x_1	x_2	x_3	b	Sum	Explanation
[1]		2̲	1	3	11	17	first equation
[2]		4	3	10	28	45	second equation
[3]		2	4	17	31	54	third equation
[4]		2	1	3	11	17	[1]
[5]	2		1̲	4	6	11	[2] − 2[1]
[6]	1		3	14	20	37	[3] − 1[1]
[7]		2	1	3	11	17	[1]
[8]			1	4	6	11	[5]
[9]	3			2	2	4	[6] − 3[5]

column. After each operation on a row, the numbers entered under the x and b headings in that row are added and their total compared with that in the *Sum* column. Any discrepancy here (apart from possible rounding error) indicates that an arithmetic error has occurred and this would, of course, have to be located and corrected before proceeding to the next operation. The required triangular system of equations appears in rows [7] to [9] although, after a little practice, rows [4], [7] and [8] can be omitted because they merely duplicate previous rows.

As a final check, the left-hand sides of the original equations in rows [1], [2] and [3] are summed, giving

$$8x_1 + 8x_2 + 30x_3$$

Substituting the computed values of x_1, x_2 and x_3 gives

$$8(3) + 8(2) + 30(1) = 70$$

This value is compared with the sum of the right-hand-side values:

$$11 + 28 + 31 = 70$$

If these two values do not agree (to within the effect of rounding error), an arithmetic error has been committed in the back-substitution and must be corrected. Note that close agreement of the two numbers does not guarantee that the answer is correct; this possibility will be discussed later under ill-conditioning.

To see how the elimination can be written down for a general matrix, A, assume that the process is partially completed and has reached the ith stage where the system of equations has the form

*Given n, A, **b***
For i = 1,2, . . . ,n − 1
  For k = i + 1, . . . ,n
    Set $m_{ki} = a_{ki}/a_{ii}$
    For j = i + 1, . . . ,n
      Set $a_{kj} = a_{kj} - m_{ki} * a_{ij}$
    Set $b_k = b_k - m_{ki} * b_i$

Figure 5.4 Algorithm for Gaussian elimination.

$$
\begin{aligned}
a_{11}x_1 + a_{12}x_2 + &\cdots + a_{1n}x_n = b_1 \\
a_{22}x_2 + &\cdots + a_{2n}x_n = b_2 \\
&\vdots \\
a_{ii}x_i + \cdots + a_{in}x_n &= b_i \\
a_{i+1,i}x_i + \cdots + a_{i+1,n}x_n &= b_{i+1} \\
&\vdots \\
a_{ni}x_i + \cdots + a_{nn}x_n &= b_n
\end{aligned}
\tag{5.7}
$$

Thus the elimination has been carried out on the first $i - 1$ columns of A and now it is the turn of the ith column. It should be noted that only the coefficients in the first equation correspond to those of the original system, all the others having been modified during the elimination. The process will be the same for each row k $\{k = i + 1, . . . ,n\}$; first, the multiplier a_{ki}/a_{ii} is formed and then that multiple of row i is subtracted from row k so that the following steps are taken for each value $k = i + 1, . . . ,n$

(1)   form the multiplier

$$m_{ki} = \frac{a_{ki}}{a_{ii}}$$

(2)   for each value of $j = i + 1, . . . ,n$ form the new value

$$a_{kj} = a_{kj} - m_{ki} * a_{ij}$$

(3)   form the new value

$$b_k = b_k - m_{ki} * b_i$$

A mathematical algorithm for the elimination process is given in Figure 5.4.

Burden and Faires (1985) perform an operation count and show that the total number of multiplications and divisions used in the elimination and back substitution is

$$\frac{n^3 + 3n^2 - n}{3}$$

(1)   *Define parameter*:
        maximum permitted value of n

(2)   *Input*:
        n, *A*, *b*

(3)   *Do*:
        Gaussian elimination
                using (*maxn*, *n*, *A*, *b*)
            to produce (*x*)

(4)   *Print*:
        Results

Figure 5.5 Plan of main subprogram for Gaussian elimination.

Program construction

Before we write down the subroutine plan, we discuss the structure of the program that will call the Gaussian elimination subroutine. The program plan is illustrated in Figure 5.5 and is very similar in structure to that given in Chapter 4 for the bisection process.

As before, this plan is expanded using appropriate FORTRAN statements. Following the practice established in Chapter 2, a constant is used to represent the maximum value for the dimension of the system of equations, i.e. the size of the actual array A dimensioned in the main subprogram.

```
INTEGER    MAXN
PARAMETER (MAXN=10)
```

The right-hand-side vector *b* and the solution vector *x* will be represented by one-dimensional arrays B and X, respectively, and the matrix *A* will be represented by the two-dimensional array A. These are declared as follows:

```
REAL A(MAXN,MAXN),B(MAXN),X(MAXN)
```

Step (2) is straightforward; the main program fragment of Figure 2.6 is adapted:

```
PRINT *,'What is the value of n?'
READ *,N
PRINT *,'Please supply the matrix A, row-wise'
CALL MATIN (MAXN,N, A)
PRINT *,'and now the vector b'
CALL VECIN (N, B)
```

Note that the subroutines MATIN and VECIN must be EXTERNAL. Step (3) will

```
PROGRAM LINEQN

INTEGER   MAXN,N
PARAMETER (MAXN=10)
REAL      A(MAXN,MAXN),B(MAXN),X(MAXN)
EXTERNAL  GAUSS,MATIN,VECIN,VECOUT

PRINT *,'What is the value of n?'
READ *,N
PRINT *,'Please supply the matrix A, row-wise'
CALL MATIN (MAXN,N, A)
PRINT *,'and now the vector b'
CALL VECIN (N, B)

CALL GAUSS (MAXN,N,A,B, X)

CALL VECOUT (N,X)

END
```

Figure 5.6   Main subprogram for Gaussian elimination.

take the form of a call of a subroutine GAUSS:

```
CALL GAUSS (MAXN,N,A,B, X)
```

Finally, step (4) will take the form of a call to a subroutine that will print out the results of the computation along with suitable messages.

```
CALL VECOUT (N,X)
```

Collecting these statements together and declaring the necessary variables gives the main subprogram of Figure 5.6.

The subroutine plan for Gaussian elimination is a straightforward expansion of the mathematical algorithm and is given in Figure 5.7. So that the subroutine plan represents the whole of the solution process, a comment is included to indicate the stage at which the back-substitution program fragment of Figure 5.3 should be inserted. Note that, because there is no need to store the value of the multiplier m_{ki}, any reference to the subscripted variable m_{ki} is replaced by a reference to the scalar variable *multiplier*.

A subroutine for Gaussian elimination can now be constructed using the plan of Figure 5.7. The subroutine heading follows directly from the call in the main subprogram plan with MAXN replaced by SIZE:

```
SUBROUTINE GAUSS (SIZE,N,A,B, X)
```

Given: n, A, b
for $i = 1, 2, \ldots, n - 1$
  for $k = i + 1, \ldots, n$
    Set: *multiplier* $= a_{ki}/a_{ii}$
    for $j = i + 1, \ldots, n$
      Set: $a_{kj} = a_{kj} - $ *multiplier* $* a_{ij}$
    Set: $b_k = b_k - $ *multiplier* $* b_i$

{ *now do back-substitution* }

Record: *solution* x

Figure 5.7 Plan of subroutine for Gaussian elimination.

and the description of the arguments is similar to that used in Chapter 2:

```
INTEGER N,SIZE
REAL    A(SIZE,SIZE),B(N),X(N)
```

In exactly the same way as for the back-substitution process, we implement for-loops by DO loops because we know precisely how many times each operation is to be performed. Thus the heart of the Gaussian elimination subprogram can be written as

```
      DO 10, I=1,N-1
        PIVOT=A(I,I)
        DO 20, K=I+1,N
          MULT=A(K,I)/PIVOT
          DO 30, J=I+1,N
            A(K,J)=A(K,J)-MULT*A(I,J)
30        CONTINUE
          B(K)=B(K)-MULT*B(I)
20      CONTINUE
10    CONTINUE
```

Note that, to minimize references to the doubly subscripted variable A(I,I), a variable PIVOT is used and so PIVOT (and also MULT) must be declared as being of type REAL. If the back-substitution fragment from Figure 5.3 is now incorporated and all necessary variables are declared, the subroutine presented in Figure 5.8 is obtained.

Clearly, problems will arise if a zero pivot is encountered and so Figure 5.9 presents a modified subroutine which checks for small pivots. In this version, an integer variable STATUS is used, in the same way as in Chapter 4, to indicate whether such a pivot has been found. If the absolute value of a pivot is less than a small value TINY, STATUS is set to PTINY and control leaves the procedure immediately. This is achieved with a GO TO statement to a label (999 in

```
SUBROUTINE GAUSS (SIZE,N,A,B, X)

INTEGER    I,J,K,N,SIZE
REAL       MULT,PIVOT
DOUBLE PRECISION SUM
REAL       A(SIZE,SIZE),B(N),X(N)
INTRINSIC DPROD

DO 10, I=1,N-1
  PIVOT=A(I,I)
  DO 20, K=I+1,N
    MULT=A(K,I)/PIVOT
    DO 30, J=I+1,N
      A(K,J)=A(K,J)-MULT*A(I,J)
30    CONTINUE
    B(K)=B(K)-MULT*B(I)
20  CONTINUE
10 CONTINUE

X(N)=B(N)/A(N,N)
DO 40, I=N-1,1,-1
  SUM=B(I)
  DO 50, J=I+1,N
    SUM=SUM-DPROD(A(I,J),X(J))
50  CONTINUE
  X(I)=SUM/A(I,I)
40 CONTINUE

END
```

Figure 5.8 Subroutine for Gaussian elimination.

this case). The main subprogram of Figure 5.5 would have to be modified to include an error message indicating the occurrence of a small pivot. It is also possible for the value of A(N,N) to become zero without any of the pivots failing the test and so, before the back-substitution, it too is compared with TINY. In addition, the modified subroutine avoids row subtraction for small multipliers; there is little point in performing the row subtraction if the multiplier is effectively zero.

5.1.2 Pivoting strategy

The subroutine of Figure 5.9 abandons computation if a zero pivot is encountered. However, a system of equations can have a zero on the diagonal and yet have a perfectly well defined solution. For example, the system of

```
      SUBROUTINE GAUSS2 (SIZE,N,A,B, STATUS,X)

      INTEGER   I,J,K,N,PTINY,SIZE,SOLVED,STATUS
      REAL      MULT,PIVOT,TINY
      DOUBLE PRECISION SUM
      PARAMETER (TINY=1E-10)
      PARAMETER (SOLVED=0,PTINY=1)
      REAL      A(SIZE,SIZE),B(N),X(N)
      INTRINSIC ABS,DPROD

      DO 10, I=1,N-1
        PIVOT=A(I,I)
        IF (ABS(PIVOT).LE.TINY) THEN
          STATUS=PTINY
          GO TO 999
        END IF

        DO 20, K=I+1,N
          MULT=A(K,I)/PIVOT
          IF (ABS(MULT).GT.TINY) THEN
            DO 30, J=I+1,N
              A(K,J)=A(K,J)-MULT*A(I,J)
30          CONTINUE
            B(K)=B(K)-MULT*B(I)
          ELSE
            A(K,I)=0
          END IF
20      CONTINUE
10    CONTINUE

      IF (ABS(A(N,N)).GT.TINY) THEN
        STATUS=SOLVED

        X(N)=B(N)/A(N,N)
        DO 40, I=N-1,1,-1
          SUM=B(I)
          DO 50, J=I+1,N
            SUM=SUM-DPROD(A(I,J),X(J))
50        CONTINUE
          X(I)=SUM/A(I,I)
40      CONTINUE

      ELSE
        STATUS=PTINY
      END IF

999   END
```

Figure 5.9 Subroutine for Gaussian elimination (checking pivots).

equations

$$x_2 = 1$$
$$x_1 + x_2 = 2$$

has a zero on the diagonal but the solution, $x_1 = 1$ and $x_2 = 1$, is well defined. The problem can be resolved by reordering the equations to give

$$x_1 + x_2 = 2$$
$$x_2 = 1$$

which can be solved using back-substitution because the system is now upper triangular. Thus it appears that the problem of a zero pivot can be overcome, for example, by looking down the pivotal column until a non-zero element is met and then interchanging this row with the existing pivotal row. This will work, but there is one further consideration. Because problems arise if a pivot is zero, it seems reasonable to assume that they may also arise if the pivot is small compared to the other elements of the matrix. In this event, the small pivot could lead to a large multiplier and then any rounding errors in the coefficients of the pivotal equation would be magnified in the next stage of the elimination. Obviously it is undesirable that this should happen and its occurrence can be avoided by choosing the pivot so that the multiplier is as small as possible. Hence, rather than accept the first non-zero element in the pivotal column, the whole column, below the pivot, should be scanned to determine the element of maximum modulus and then, if necessary, the rows interchanged so that this element becomes the pivot. Any calculation involving Gaussian elimination should involve this process, which is known as **partial pivoting**.

There is a process of **complete pivoting**, in which the element of greatest modulus in the submatrix, a_{kj} for $k,j \geqslant i$ in Equation (5.7), is located, whereupon row *and* column interchanges are performed to move this element to the pivotal position. Computationally, this is extremely costly and rarely necessary in practice; partial pivoting is usually adequate. If no non-zero element can be found in the pivotal column, the matrix is singular and this gives a check for singularity.

The process of partial pivoting can be illustrated by considering the solution of Equations (5.5) discussed earlier. The coefficients of x_1 in each row are 2, 4 and 2, respectively, so that the multipliers are 2 and 1. To make the pivot as large as possible and thus reduce the size of the multipliers, the first and second rows are interchanged. This produces the system

$$4x_1 + 3x_2 + 10x_3 = 28$$
$$2x_1 + x_2 + 3x_3 = 11$$
$$2x_1 + 4x_2 + 17x_3 = 31$$

with 0.5 as the multiplier for both rows 2 and 3. However, if the system of equations is very large, the process of interchanging rows is extremely time consuming.

Table 5.2   Tabular form for Gaussian elimination with partial pivoting.

Row	Multiplier	x_1	x_2	x_3	b	Sum	Explanation
[1]		2	1	3	11	17	first equation
[2]		4	3	10	28	45	second equation
[3]		2	4	17	31	54	third equation
[4]	0.5		−0.5	−2	−3	−5.5	[1]−0.5[2]
[5]		4	3	10	28	45	[2]
[6]	0.5		2.5	12	17	31.5	[3]−0.5[2]
[7]	−0.2			0.4	0.4	0.8	[4]−(−0.2)[6]
[8]		4	3	10	28	45	[2]
[9]			2.5	12	17	31.5	[6]

During hand-calculation it is simpler, using the tabular form of Table 5.1, merely to mark the pivot and so produce the modified table of Table 5.2.

The upper triangular matrix, used for the back-substitution, consists of rows [8], [9] and [7]. From [7]

$$x_3 = 0.4/0.4 = 1$$

from [9]

$$x_2 = (17 - 12(1))/2.5 = 2$$

and from [8]

$$x_1 = (28 - 3(2) - 10(1))/4 = 3$$

as before.

In a subroutine to implement partial pivoting, row interchanges are avoided by maintaining a record of the *order* in which rows are to be considered and the ordering is updated as successive pivotal rows are chosen. In the ensuing example, the permutation of the rows is indicated by three pointers p_1, p_2 and p_3, where row p_1 should be taken to mean the row currently pointed to by p_1, and similarly for rows p_2 and p_3. Initially p_1, p_2 and p_3 point to rows 1, 2 and 3 respectively.

		A			b
p_1	$\longrightarrow$	2	1	3	11
p_2	$\longrightarrow$	4	3	10	28
p_3	$\longrightarrow$	2	4	17	31

To determine the first pivot, the element of maximum modulus in the first column is sought. It is located in row p_2 (row 2) so we wish to interchange rows p_1 (row 1) and p_2 (row 2). Rather than interchange the rows themselves, we merely interchange the destinations of the two pointers:

		A		b
p_1	2	1	3	11
p_2	4	3	10	28
p_3	2	4	17	31

(with p_1 and p_2 destinations crossed)

Now x_1 is eliminated from all the rows 'below' the pivotal row by subtracting suitable multiples (0.5 in each case) of row p_1 (row 2) from rows p_2 (row 1) and p_3 (row 3).

		A		b
p_1	0	-0.5	-2	-3
p_2	4	3	10	28
p_3	0	2.5	12	17

(with p_1 and p_2 destinations crossed)

Henceforth, p_1 is ignored and subsequent processing involves rows p_2 (row 1) and p_3 (row 3). The second column of these two rows is scanned to determine the pivot. This turns out to be 2.5 in row p_3 (row 3) so now rows p_2 (row 1) and p_3 (row 3) must be interchanged. Accordingly, the destinations of the two pointers are interchanged:

		A		b
p_1	0	-0.5	-2	-3
p_2	4	3	10	28
p_3	0	2.5	12	17

(with p_2 and p_3 destinations crossed)

Row p_2 (row 3) will remain unchanged and the multiplier for row p_3 (row 1) is

$$\frac{-0.5}{2.5} = -0.2$$

producing the upper triangular form

		A		b
p_1	0	0	0.4	0.4
p_2	4	3	10	28
p_3	0	2.5	12	17

(with p_2 and p_3 destinations crossed)

The first row is p_1 (row 2), the second is p_2 (row 3) and the third is p_3 (row 1).

The back-substitution is performed as before, this time working through the rows in the order indicated by the pointers: p_3, p_2, p_1. From row p_3 (row 1),

$$x_3 = \frac{0.4}{0.4} = 1$$

From row p_2 (row 3),

$$x_2 = \frac{17 - 12x_3}{2.5} = 2$$

From row p_1 (row 2),

$$x_1 = \frac{28 - 3x_2 - 10x_3}{4} = 3$$

As will be seen in Section 5.1.4, the multipliers serve a useful purpose and should be recorded. In practice, within a program, the multipliers would overwrite the unwanted coefficients and so the final form of the coefficient matrix would be as follows:

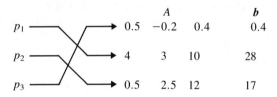

	A			b
p_1	0.5	−0.2	0.4	0.4
p_2	4	3	10	28
p_3	0.5	2.5	12	17

Program construction

Within a FORTRAN program the idea of pointers can be implemented using an array P of integers. Each component of P will 'point' to one of the rows of the array A. Initially, P(1) will be 1 indicating that it is pointing to row 1 of A, P(2) will be 2, P(3) will be 3, etc. To indicate the interchange of rows 3 and 7, P(3) would be changed to 7 and P(7) to 3. In this way P(I) is always pointing to the Ith row of the permuted array. Figure 5.10 shows the values stored in P before and after the elimination performed above.

Before	After
P(1)=1	P(1)=2
P(2)=2	P(2)=3
P(3)=3	P(3)=1

Figure 5.10   Use of an array of pointers.

Because P is an array of integers, the value P(I), say, can be used as a subscript in a reference to an element of A; for example, A(P(I),J) is the element in position J of the row pointed to by P(I). Using the final values of P from Figure 5.10, the element A(P(2),1) is the array element A(3,1). Thus, to implement partial pivoting, any references to A(I,J) in Figure 5.9 are replaced by references to A(P(I),J). The only other modification required is the inclusion of a fragment to determine the pivot. The complete subroutine is given in Figure 5.11. Note that INTEGER variables PI and PK have been used to avoid multiple references to P(I) and P(K).

5.1.3 Scaling

In partial pivoting, the choice of pivot may be changed if one of the equations is multiplied by a large constant. For example, given the system of equations

$$
\begin{aligned}
x_1 + \quad x_2 &= 2 \\
0.0001x_1 + 0.1x_2 &= 1
\end{aligned}
\tag{5.8}
$$

the multiplier is 0.0001. However, if the second equation is multiplied through by 100 000 to give

$$
\begin{aligned}
x_1 + \quad\quad x_2 &= \quad 2 \\
10x_1 + 10\ 000x_2 &= 100\ 000
\end{aligned}
$$

then the rows should be interchanged and the multiplier would become 0.1 instead. This multiplication does not change the theoretical solution of the system of equations but could have some effect on the numerical solution; the calculations performed during the elimination would be changed giving a different accumulation of rounding errors. This is clearly an undesirable state of affairs and so it is usual to scale the system of equations in some standard manner. As yet, there is no agreement about a single 'best' way of scaling a system of equations to reduce the accumulation of rounding errors, but one popular method is that of 'equilibration'. In this technique, the equations are scaled so that the maximum elements in the rows and columns of the matrix A have roughly the same magnitude, usually unity. An 'equilibration' of Equations (5.8) gives

$$
\begin{aligned}
x_1 + x_2 &= \quad 2 \\
0.001x_1 + x_2 &= 10
\end{aligned}
$$

It is recommended that the equations be scaled before an elimination process is applied and equilibration is suggested as the technique to use for the first attempt to solve any system. For a more detailed discussion of scaling see Wilkinson (1965).

Figure 5.11   Subroutine for Gaussian elimination with partial pivoting.

```
         SUBROUTINE GAUSSP (SIZE,N,A,B, STATUS,X,P)

         INTEGER   I,J,K,N,PI,PK,PTINY,SIZE,SOLVED,STATUS
         REAL      MAX,MULT,PIVOT,TINY
         DOUBLE PRECISION SUM
         PARAMETER (TINY=1E-10)
         PARAMETER (SOLVED=0,PTINY=1)
         INTEGER   P(N)
         REAL      A(SIZE,SIZE),B(N),X(N)
         INTRINSIC ABS, DPROD

C        { Give P its initial values }

         DO 10, I=1,N
           P(I)=I
10       CONTINUE

         DO 20, I=1,N-1

C          { Find the pivot }

         MAX=0
         PI =P(I)
         DO 30, J=I,N
           IF (ABS(A(P(J),I)).GT.MAX) THEN
             MAX=ABS(A(P(J),I))
             K  =J
           END IF
30         CONTINUE

C          { Signal if pivot is too small }

         IF (MAX.LE.TINY) THEN
           STATUS=PTINY
           GO TO 999
         END IF

C          { Otherwise swap elements in P if necessary }

         IF (K.NE.I) THEN
           P(I)=P(K)
           P(K)=PI
           PI  =P(I)
         END IF

C          { Now do the elimination }
```

```
        PIVOT=A(PI,I)
        DO 40, K=I+1,N
          PK  =P(K)
          MULT=A(PK,I)/PIVOT
          IF (ABS(MULT).GT.TINY) THEN
            A[PK,I]=MULT
            DO 50, J=I+1,N
              A(PK,J)=A(PK,J)-MULT*A(PI,J)
50          CONTINUE
            B(PK)=B(PK)-MULT*B(PI)
          ELSE
            A(PK,I)=0
          END IF
40        CONTINUE

20    CONTINUE

C     {Perform the back-substitution}

      IF (ABS(A(P(N))).GT.TINY) THEN
        STATUS=SOLVED

        X(N)=B(P(N))/A(P(N),N)
        DO 60, I=N-1,1,-1
          PI =P(I)
          SUM=B(PI)
          DO 70, J=I+1,N
            SUM=SUM-DPROD(A(PI,J),X(J))
70        CONTINUE
          X(I)=SUM/A(PI,I)
60      CONTINUE

      ELSE
        STATUS=PTINY
      END IF

999   END
```

Figure 5.11   *cont.*

5.1.4 *LU* decomposition

In this method we first factorize (or decompose) the matrix A into the product of two matrices, L and U, where L is lower triangular and U is upper triangular. Thus Equation (5.2) becomes

$$LUx = b \tag{5.9}$$

where

$$L = \begin{bmatrix} l_{11} & 0 & 0 & \cdots & 0 \\ l_{21} & l_{22} & 0 & \cdots & 0 \\ \vdots & \vdots & \vdots & \vdots & \vdots \\ l_{n1} & l_{n2} & \cdot & \cdots & l_{nn} \end{bmatrix}$$

and

$$U = \begin{bmatrix} u_{11} & u_{12} & u_{13} & \cdots & u_{1n} \\ 0 & u_{22} & u_{23} & \cdots & u_{2n} \\ \vdots & \vdots & \vdots & \vdots & \vdots \\ 0 & 0 & 0 & \cdots & u_{nn} \end{bmatrix}$$

A new column vector $y = Ux$ is then introduced so that Equation (5.9) can be replaced by the two equations

$$Ly = b \tag{5.10a}$$

and

$$Ux = y \tag{5.10b}$$

These two systems of equations are easy to solve because of their triangular form. The solution of Equation (5.10a) gives the column vector y and this provides the right-hand-side constants for the second system which is then solved to find the solution x of system (5.1).

The straightforward way to factorize the matrix A is to multiply together the general forms of L and U and compare the elements of the product matrix with those of A. This process produces a system of n^2 equations in the $n^2 + n$ unknowns l_{ij} and u_{ij} and so the factorization of A is not unique; arbitrary values can be assigned to n of the unknowns. Conventionally, to produce unique factors, the diagonal elements of L or U are usually constrained in a pre-specified manner. In *Doolittle's* algorithm, the elements on the leading diagonal of L are restricted to be unity; in *Crout's* algorithm, this restriction is applied to the elements on the leading diagonal of U.

The general principle can be illustrated by applying the Doolittle algorithm to Equations (5.5), giving

$$\begin{bmatrix} 1 & 0 & 0 \\ l_{21} & 1 & 0 \\ l_{31} & l_{32} & 1 \end{bmatrix} \begin{bmatrix} u_{11} & u_{12} & u_{13} \\ 0 & u_{22} & u_{23} \\ 0 & 0 & u_{33} \end{bmatrix} = \begin{bmatrix} 2 & 1 & 3 \\ 4 & 3 & 10 \\ 2 & 4 & 17 \end{bmatrix}$$

from which

$$u_{11} = 2$$
$$u_{12} = 1$$
$$u_{13} = 3$$

$$l_{21}u_{11} = 4 \Rightarrow l_{21} = 4/u_{11} = 4/2 = 2$$
$$l_{21}u_{12} + u_{22} = 3 \Rightarrow u_{22} = 3 - l_{21}u_{12} = 3 - 2 \times 1 = 1$$
$$l_{21}u_{13} + u_{23} = 10 \Rightarrow u_{23} = 10 - l_{21}u_{13} = 10 - 2 \times 3 = 4$$

$$l_{31}u_{11} = 2 \Rightarrow l_{31} = 2/u_{11} = 2/2 = 1$$
$$l_{31}u_{12} + l_{32}u_{22} = 4 \Rightarrow l_{32} = (4 - l_{31}u_{12})/u_{22}$$
$$= (4 - 1 \times 1)/1 = 3$$
$$l_{31}u_{13} + l_{32}u_{23} + u_{33} = 17 \Rightarrow u_{33} = 17 - l_{31}u_{13} - l_{32}u_{23}$$
$$= 17 - 1 \times 3 - 3 \times 4 = 2$$

Hence

$$L = \begin{bmatrix} 1 & 0 & 0 \\ 2 & 1 & 0 \\ 1 & 3 & 1 \end{bmatrix} \quad \text{and} \quad U = \begin{bmatrix} 2 & 1 & 3 \\ 0 & 1 & 4 \\ 0 & 0 & 2 \end{bmatrix} \tag{5.11}$$

Thus, from Equation (5.10a),

$$y_1 = 11$$
$$2y_1 + y_2 = 28 \Rightarrow y_2 = 28 - 2y_1 = 28 - 2 \times 11 = 6$$
$$y_1 + 3y_2 + y_3 = 31 \Rightarrow y_3 = 31 - y_1 - 3y_2$$
$$= 31 - 11 - 3 \times 6 = 2$$

and, from Equation (5.10b),

$$\begin{aligned} 2x_1 + x_2 + 3x_3 &= 11 \\ x_2 + 4x_2 &= 6 \\ 2x_3 &= 2 \end{aligned} \tag{5.12}$$

Equations (5.12) are solved using back-substitution to obtain

$$x = \begin{bmatrix} 3 \\ 2 \\ 1 \end{bmatrix}$$

the solution previously calculated.

An algorithm for the solution of a system of linear equations using the *LU* factors is given in Figure 5.12.

Note that Equations (5.12) are identical to Equations (5.6) obtained using Gaussian elimination and, furthermore, that l_{21}, l_{31} and l_{32} are the multipliers from that calculation. We now examine the reasons for this.

*Given n, L, U, **b***

Set $y_1 = b_1$
For $i = 2, \ldots, n$

$$\text{Set } sum = b_i - \sum_{j=1}^{i-1} l_{ij} y_j$$

Set $y_i = sum$

Set $x_n = y_n / u_{nn}$
For $i = n - 1, \ldots, 1$

$$\text{Set } sum = y_i - \sum_{j=i+1}^{n} u_{ij} x_j$$

Set $x_i = sum / u_{ii}$

Figure 5.12 Algorithm for *LU* solution.

It is instructive to rewrite the elimination phase of Gaussian elimination in terms of matrices. We shall start by assuming that pivoting is not necessary for the algorithm to proceed and, later, discuss the effect of its inclusion.

The first stage of the elimination process is to introduce zeros below the diagonal of the first column of A to produce a matrix A_1. This is achieved by subtracting multiples

$$m_{k1} = a_{k1} / a_{11}$$

of the first row from the kth $\{k = 2, 3, \ldots, n\}$ and can be written as the product

$$A_1 = L_1 A_0$$

where $A_0 = A$ and L_1 is the unit lower triangular matrix

$$
\begin{bmatrix}
1 & 0 & \ldots & 0 \\
-m_{21} & 1 & \ldots & 0 \\
\vdots & \vdots & \vdots & \vdots \\
-m_{n1} & 0 & \ldots & 1
\end{bmatrix}
$$

For example, considering the matrix from Equations (5.5):

$$
A_0 = \begin{bmatrix}
2 & 1 & 3 \\
4 & 3 & 10 \\
2 & 4 & 17
\end{bmatrix}
$$

then

$$m_{21} = 4/2 = 2 \qquad m_{31} = 2/2 = 1$$

and so

$$L_1 = \begin{bmatrix} 1 & 0 & 0 \\ -2 & 1 & 0 \\ -1 & 0 & 1 \end{bmatrix}.$$

Thus

$$A_1 = L_1 A_0 = \begin{bmatrix} 2 & 1 & 3 \\ 0 & 1 & 4 \\ 0 & 3 & 14 \end{bmatrix}$$

The algorithm proceeds by forming the product

$$A_2 = L_2 A_1$$

where L_2 is the lower triangular matrix

$$\begin{bmatrix} 1 & 0 & 0 & \ldots & 0 \\ 0 & 1 & 0 & \ldots & 0 \\ 0 & -m_{32} & 1 & \ldots & 0 \\ \vdots & \vdots & \vdots & \vdots & \vdots \\ 0 & -m_{n2} & 0 & \ldots & 1 \end{bmatrix}$$

and the m_{k2} $\{k = 3,4, \ldots ,n\}$ are the multipliers required to introduce zeros below the diagonal of the second column of A_1. Thus, for the present example,

$$m_{32} = 3/1 = 3$$

and so

$$L_2 = \begin{bmatrix} 1 & 0 & 0 \\ 0 & 1 & 0 \\ 0 & -3 & 1 \end{bmatrix}$$

giving

$$A_2 = L_2 A_1 = L_2(L_1 A_0)$$

$$= \begin{bmatrix} 2 & 1 & 3 \\ 0 & 1 & 4 \\ 0 & 0 & 2 \end{bmatrix}$$

which is the upper triangular matrix from Equations (5.6). In general, multiplying A_{i-1} by the matrix

$$
L_i = \begin{bmatrix}
1 & 0 & \cdots & & 0 & & \cdots & 0 \\
0 & 1 & \cdots & & 0 & & \cdots & 0 \\
\vdots & \vdots & \vdots & & \vdots & & & \vdots \\
0 & 0 & \cdots & & 1 & & \cdots & 0 \\
0 & 0 & \cdots & & -m_{i+1\,i} & & \cdots & 0 \\
\vdots & \vdots & \vdots & & \vdots & & & \vdots \\
0 & 0 & \cdots & & -m_{ni} & & \cdots & 1
\end{bmatrix}
$$

to form the product

$$A_i = L_i A_{i-1} \qquad \text{for } i = 1, 2, \ldots, n-1$$

introduces zeros below the diagonal of the ith column of A_{i-1}. Thus

$$A_{n-1} = L_{n-1} L_{n-2} \ldots L_2 L_1 A_0 \tag{5.13}$$

and A_{n-1} is an upper triangular matrix which we shall rename U.

Each of the matrices L_i $\{i = 1, 2, \ldots, n-1\}$ has the property that its inverse is L_i with the signs of the m_{ki} $\{k = i+1, \ldots, n\}$ reversed. Thus

$$
L_i^{-1} = \begin{bmatrix}
1 & 0 & \cdots & 0 & & \cdots & 0 \\
0 & 1 & \cdots & 0 & & \cdots & 0 \\
\vdots & \vdots & \vdots & \vdots & & & \vdots \\
0 & 0 & \cdots & 1 & & \cdots & 0 \\
0 & 0 & \cdots & m_{i+1\,i} & & \cdots & 0 \\
\vdots & \vdots & \vdots & \vdots & & & \vdots \\
0 & 0 & \cdots & m_{ni} & & \cdots & 1
\end{bmatrix}
$$

The verification of this result is left as an exercise for the reader. For the example above

$$
L_1^{-1} = \begin{bmatrix} 1 & 0 & 0 \\ 2 & 1 & 0 \\ 1 & 0 & 1 \end{bmatrix} \qquad \text{and} \qquad L_2^{-1} = \begin{bmatrix} 1 & 0 & 0 \\ 0 & 1 & 0 \\ 0 & 3 & 1 \end{bmatrix}
$$

Equation (5.13) can now be rewritten as

$$A_0 = L_1^{-1} L_2^{-1} \ldots L_{n-2}^{-1} L_{n-1}^{-1} U$$

and, in Exercise 5.6, the reader is asked to show that the matrix

$$L = L_1^{-1}L_2^{-1} \ldots L_{n-2}^{-1}L_{n-1}^{-1}$$

takes the form

$$L = \begin{bmatrix} 1 & 0 & \cdots & 0 & \cdots & 0 \\ m_1 & 1 & \cdots & 0 & \cdots & 0 \\ \vdots & \vdots & & \vdots & \vdots & & \vdots \\ m_{i1} & m_{i2} & \cdots & 1 & \cdots & 0 \\ m_{i+11} & m_{i+12} & \cdots & m_{i+1i} & \cdots & 0 \\ \vdots & \vdots & & \vdots & \vdots & & \vdots \\ m_{n1} & m_{n2} & \cdots & m_{ni} & \cdots & 1 \end{bmatrix}$$

Now, because $A_0 = A$,

$$A = LU \tag{5.14}$$

In the example,

$$L = L_1^{-1}L_2^{-1}$$

$$= \begin{bmatrix} 1 & 0 & 0 \\ 2 & 1 & 0 \\ 1 & 0 & 1 \end{bmatrix}\begin{bmatrix} 1 & 0 & 0 \\ 0 & 1 & 0 \\ 0 & 3 & 1 \end{bmatrix} = \begin{bmatrix} 1 & 0 & 0 \\ 2 & 1 & 0 \\ 1 & 3 & 1 \end{bmatrix}$$

Note that L is merely the identity matrix augmented by the strictly lower triangular matrix

$$\begin{bmatrix} 0 & 0 & 0 \\ 2 & 0 & 0 \\ 1 & 3 & 0 \end{bmatrix}$$

of multipliers given in Equations (5.6).

A mathematical algorithm for the LU decomposition is given in Figure 5.13.

Definition 5.1

The $n \times n$ matrix A is said to be **weakly diagonally dominant** if

$$|a_{ii}| \geq \sum_{\substack{j=1 \\ j \neq i}}^{n} |a_{ij}| \qquad \text{for } i = 1, 2, \ldots, n$$

with strict inequality holding for at least one value of i. A is **strictly diagonally dominant** if strict inequality holds for all values of i.

Given n, A
For $i = 1,2, \ldots, n - 1$
  For $k = i + 1, \ldots, n$
    Set $m_{ki} = a_{ki}/a_{ii}$
      $l_{ki} = m_{ki}$
      For $j = i + 1, \ldots, n$
        Set $a_{kj} = a_{kj} - m_{ki}a_{ij}$
      For $j = i, \ldots, n$
        Set $u_{ij} = a_{ij}$
Set $u_{nn} = a_{nn}$

Figure 5.13   Algorithm for LU decomposition.

The proofs of the following theorems are outlined in Burden and Faires (3rd edn, 1985 Ex 6.6.16 and Ex 6.6.12).

Theorem 5.2

If A is strictly diagonally dominant, it is non-singular and Gaussian elimination can be performed on any system

$$Ax = b$$

to obtain its unique solution without pivoting being necessary to control the growth of rounding errors.

Theorem 5.3

If Gaussian elimination, without pivoting, can be performed on the system of equations

$$Ax = b$$

then A can be **factorized** or **decomposed** into the product

$$A = LU$$

of a lower triangular matrix L with unit diagonal and an upper triangular matrix U.

The *LU* decomposition takes a special form when *A* is symmetric and satisfies certain restrictions.

Definition 5.2

A **symmetric** $n \times n$ matrix *A* is said to be **positive definite** if

$$x^T A x > 0$$

for every *n*-vector $x \neq 0$. This condition is satisfied if *all* the eigenvalues of *A* are strictly positive.

To reflect the symmetry of *A*, it is usual to obtain a **symmetric** factorization and the following theorem shows that this is possible.

Theorem 5.4

If *A* is a positive definite $n \times n$ matrix, it has a factorization of the form

$$A = LL^T$$

where *L* is a lower triangular matrix.

A proof of this theorem can be found in Burden and Faires.

This factorization, known as the *Choleski* factorization, can be obtained in the same way as the *LU* decomposition except that, instead of enforcing $l_{ii} = 1$ $\{i = 1,2,. . .,n\}$, the condition $l_{ii} = u_{ii}$ $\{i = 1,2,. . .,n\}$ is imposed. Furthermore, if symmetry is fully taken into account, the factorization requires about half as many multiplications and divisions ($[n^3 + 9n^2 + 2n]/6$).

Program construction

The *LU* decomposition is particularly useful if the same matrix *A* appears in conjunction with many, different, right-hand-side vectors *b*. Once *L* and *U* have been determined, *A* can be discarded and the system

$$LUx = b$$

solved for each different *b*. This, of course, is much faster than performing a full Gaussian elimination each time. Consequently, two subroutines will be produced; one to decompose *A* into *L* and *U* and the other to solve a system of equations given *L*, *U* and a right-hand-side vector *b*.

Given: n, A
for $i = 1, 2, \ldots, n - 1$
   if $|a_{ii}| >$ *small number* **then**
      for $k = i + 1, \ldots, n$
         if $|a_{ki}| >$ *small number* **then**
            Set: $m_{ki} = a_{ki}/a_{ii}$
                 $a_{ki} = m_{ki}$
            for $j = i + 1, \ldots, n$
               Set: $a_{kj} = a_{kj} - m_{ki} * a_{ij}$
         else
            Set: $a_{ki} = 0$
   else
      Note: *'small pivot' and abandon calculation*

Figure 5.14   Plan of subroutine for *LU* decomposition.

Because all the diagonal elements of L are unity they need not be stored and so both L and U can be stored in the space originally occupied by A. For example, the two matrices (5.11) can be stored as the one matrix

$$\begin{bmatrix} 2 & 1 & 3 \\ 2 & 1 & 4 \\ 1 & 3 & 2 \end{bmatrix}$$

and, furthermore, the elements of A can be overwritten as the calculation proceeds. A check for a possible zero multiplier is included, and computation abandoned if a small multiplier is encountered. The subroutine plan is given in Figure 5.14.

A subroutine based on Figure 5.14 must be supplied with the dimensions SIZE and N, and the two-dimensional array A. It will produce the factors L and U, overwriting A, and a STATUS argument which will indicate the outcome of the factorization. Thus the subroutine heading takes the form

```
SUBROUTINE LUDEC (SIZE,N,A, STATUS)
```

with the declarations

```
INTEGER N,SIZE,STATUS
REAL    A(SIZE,SIZE)
```

The factorization will fail only if a small pivot is discovered and to check for this we use a small number, TINY. If the factorization is successful, we give the STATUS argument the value FACTRD; otherwise it is given the value PTINY. The

```
      SUBROUTINE LUDEC (SIZE,N,A, STATUS)

      INTEGER  FACTRD,I,J,K,N,PTINY,SIZE,STATUS
      READ     MULT,PIVOT,TINY
      PARAMETER (FACTRD=0,PTINY=1)
      PARAMETER (TINY=1E-10)
      REAL     A(SIZE,SIZE)
      INTRINSIC ABS

      DO 10, I=1,N-1
        PIVOT=A(I,I)
        IF (ABS(PIVOT).GT.TINY) THEN
          DO 20, K=I+1,N
            IF (ABS(A(K,I)).GT.TINY) THEN
              MULT=A(K,I)/PIVOT
              A(K,I)=MULT
              DO 30, J=I+1,N
              A(K,J)=A(K,J)-MULT*A(I,J)
30            CONTINUE
            ELSE
              A(K,I)=0
            END IF
20        CONTINUE
        ELSE
          STATUS=PTINY
          GO TO 999
        END IF
10    CONTINUE
      STATUS=FACTRD

999   END
```

Figure 5.15 Subroutine for *LU* decomposition.

necessary variables are declared as

```
      INTEGER  FACTRD,PTINY
      REAL     TINY
      PARAMETER (TINY=1E-10)
      PARAMETER (FACTRD=0,PTINY=1)
```

Note that the calling subprogram must include a suitable declaration of `FACTRD` and must store the multipliers. It is now a simple task to produce the subroutine given in Figure 5.15.

A subroutine is now constructed to take the *LU* decomposition stored in A and a right-hand-side vector b, stored in B, and produce the solution x in X. The program plan for this step is simple and is, in effect, adequately described in the earlier section on Gaussian elimination. Consequently we proceed directly to the subroutine given in Figure 5.16, noting the addition of the work vector Y to the argument list.

The storage requirements in this subroutine can be reduced because the elements of B are used only once, in the forward substitution. The extra array Y is not needed because the intermediate results of the forward substitution can be stored in B. The forward substitution fragment of the subroutine then takes the form

```
      DO 10, I=2,N
        SUM=B(I)
        DO 20, J=1,I-1
          SUM=SUM-DPROD(A(I,J),B(J))
20      CONTINUE
        B(I)=SUM
10    CONTINUE
```

The modification of the back-substitution fragment is left as an exercise for the reader.

Permuted *LU* factorization

Unfortunately, not all matrices have an *LU* factorization. For example, the matrix

$$A = \begin{bmatrix} 0 & 1 \\ 1 & 1 \end{bmatrix} \tag{5.15}$$

does not have an *LU* factorization. It has already been shown that Gaussian elimination can be used to solve systems involving matrices of this type by exchanging (or permuting) rows of the matrix. This was given the name partial pivoting and, in effect, corresponds to the premultiplication of the matrix A by a *permutation* matrix, P. Permutation matrices have the same form as the identity matrix except that the order of the rows is different. For example, premultiplication of a 3×3 matrix by the permutation matrix

$$P = \begin{bmatrix} 0 & 1 & 0 \\ 1 & 0 & 0 \\ 0 & 0 & 1 \end{bmatrix}$$

```
      SUBROUTINE LUSOL (SIZE,N,A,B, STATUS,X, Y)

      INTEGER   I,J,N,PTINY,SIZE,SOLVED,STATUS
      REAL      TINY
      DOUBLE PRECISION SUM
      PARAMETER (SOLVED=0,PTINY=1)
      PARAMETER (TINY=1E-10)
      REAL      A(SIZE,SIZE),B(N),X(N),Y(N)
      INTRINSIC ABS,DPROD

C     { check for singular matrix }

      IF (ABS(A(N,N).GT.TINY) THEN
        STATUS=SOLVED

C     { forward substitution }

      Y(1)=B(1)
      DO 10, I=2,N
        SUM=B(I)
        DO 20, J=1,I-1
          SUM=SUM-DPROD(A(I,J),Y(J))
20        CONTINUE
        Y(I)=SUM
10      CONTINUE

C     { back substitution }

      X(N)=Y(N)/A(N,N)
      DO 30, I=N-1,1,-1
        SUM=Y(I)
        DO 40, J=I+1,N
          SUM=SUM-DPROD(A(I,J),X(J))
40        CONTINUE
        X(I)=SUM/A(I,I)
30      CONTINUE

      ELSE
        STATUS=PTINY
      END IF

      END
```

Figure 5.16 Subroutine for *LU* solution.

would interchange its first two rows. Returning to Equation (5.15), premultiplication of A by the matrix

$$P = \begin{bmatrix} 0 & 1 \\ 1 & 0 \end{bmatrix} \qquad \text{gives} \qquad PA = \begin{bmatrix} 1 & 1 \\ 0 & 1 \end{bmatrix}$$

which *does* have an LU factorization. Application of the elimination phase of Gaussian elimination with partial pivoting is equivalent to LU decomposition of a permuted version of the coefficient matrix. The interested reader is invited to modify the subroutine GAUSSP of Figure 5.11 simply to provide the permuted LU decomposition. This entails removing the back substitution phase and, optionally, the now redundant argument X. Premultiplication of the system

$$Ax = b$$

by the permutation matrix P gives

$$PAx = Pb = c$$

and so the solution vector x can be found by forming the LU decomposition of PA and solving

$$LUx = c$$

by the standard technique.

Program construction

Mention must be made of storing the factorized matrix. If partial pivoting has been employed, the rows of the LU matrix will be in some permuted order and this order must be recorded. It will be assumed that the LU representation has been filed in the original row order (i.e. in non-permuted form) together with a permutation vector indicating the order in which the rows are to be processed. This vector is a compressed form of the permutation matrix; its elements are integers recording the order in which rows of the identity matrix occur within the permutation matrix. The example in Section 5.1.2 shows that this vector performs the same function as a vector of pointers, an example of which is given in Figure 5.10.

The subroutine of Figure 5.17 is based on that of Figure 5.16 but is modified to take a non-permuted LU decomposition, stored in an array A, and a permutation vector P. To reduce the number of array references, multiple references to P(I) are replaced by PI, as in Figure 5.11.

```
      SUBROUTINE LUPSOL (SIZE,N,A,B,P, STATUS,X)


      INTEGER   I,J,N,PI,PTINY,SIZE,SOLVED,STATUS
      REAL      TINY
      DOUBLE PRECISION SUM
      PARAMETER (SOLVED=0,PTINY=1)
      PARAMETER (TINY=1E-10)
      INTEGER   P(N)
      REAL      A(SIZE,SIZE),B(N),X(N)
      INTRINSIC ABS,DPROD


C        { L and U are assumed to be stored in unpermuted }
C        { form in A and P is assumed to hold the permutations }

      IF (ABS(A(P(N),N)).GT.TINY) THEN
        STATUS=SOLVED

        DO 10, I=2,N
          PI =P(I)
          SUM=B(PI)
          DO 20, J=1,I-1
            SUM=SUM-DPROD(A(PI,J),B(P(J)))
20        CONTINUE
          B(PI)=SUM
10      CONTINUE

        X(N)=B(P(N))/A(P(N(,N)
        DO 30, I=N-1,1,-1
          PI =P(I)
          SUM=B(PI)
          DO 40, J=I+1,N
            SUM=SUM-DPROD(A(PI,J),X(J))
40        CONTINUE
          X(I)=SUM/A(PI,I)
30      CONIIN'

      ELSE
        STATUS=PTINY
      END IF


      END
```

Figure 5.17   Subroutine for permuted *LU* solution.

5.1.5 The inverse matrix

The **inverse** of a real $n \times n$ matrix A is the $n \times n$ matrix A^{-1} with the property that

$$A^{-1}A = AA^{-1} = I \tag{5.16}$$

where I is the $n \times n$ identity matrix. The LU factorization, described in Section 5.1.4, can be used to evaluate the inverse matrix efficiently. From Equation (5.16),

$$AA^{-1} = I$$

and so the product of A with the first column of A^{-1} gives the first column, e_1, of the identity matrix. If the first column of A^{-1} is denoted by the vector x_1, it can be obtained as the solution of the system of equations

$$Ax_1 = e_1$$

In general, if x_j is the jth column of A^{-1} and e_j is the jth column of the identity matrix, they satisfy the equation

$$Ax_j = e_j \quad \text{for } j = 1,2, \ldots ,n \tag{5.17}$$

Now Equation (5.17) represents a situation in which the same matrix, A, appears with many right-hand sides, e_j, so the solution vectors, x_j, can be obtained easily using the LU factorization of A. Hence, by solving the system

$$Ax_j = LUx_j = e_j \quad \text{for } j = 1,2, \ldots ,n$$

the inverse matrix is built up column by column to give

$$A^{-1} = [x_1 ,x_2, \ldots ,x_n]$$

Consequently, a program to calculate A^{-1} comprises two steps; firstly the LU factors of the matrix A are calculated and secondly the n systems of equations, represented by Equation (5.17), are solved using this factorization. Burden and Faires calculate that the number of multiplications and divisions necessary to compute the inverse is

$$\frac{4n^3 - n}{3}$$

Some words of warning are necessary here. Unless *exact* arithmetic has been used, the calculated inverse should *never* be used to solve the system of equations

$$Ax = b$$

by forming

$$x = A^{-1}b$$

because it would involve an unnecessary amount of computational effort and thus lead to increased rounding errors. Solution of the system

$$Ax = b$$

using LU decomposition involves only one LU factorization, one forward-substitution and one back-substitution. The construction of A^{-1} would involve the same LU factorization plus n forward-substitutions and n back-substitutions and finally, to obtain x, a matrix–vector multiplication would be necessary. Because of the extra work involved, further rounding errors would be accumulated and so the solution obtained using the matrix inverse would, in general, be less accurate than that calculated using the LU decomposition.

5.1.6 Tri-diagonal systems

Strictly diagonally dominant (or positive definite) tri-diagonal systems of linear equations occur frequently in the solution of differential equations. As is usual in numerical analysis, it is desirable to take advantage of all the available information and, in this case, the structure of the matrix A is too specialized to be ignored.

Consider the following tri-diagonal system of n equations:

$$\begin{aligned}
d_1x_1 + c_1x_2 &= b_1 \\
a_2x_1 + d_2x_2 + c_2x_3 &= b_2 \\
a_3x_2 + d_3x_3 + c_3x_4 &= b_3
\end{aligned}$$

(5.18)

$$\begin{aligned}
a_{n-1}x_{n-2} + d_{n-1}x_{n-1} + c_{n-1}x_n &= b_{n-1} \\
a_nx_{n-1} + d_nx_n &= b_n
\end{aligned}$$

A saving in storage on the computer can be made by storing only the sub-, super- and main diagonals. Obviously, when n is large, this saving is significant. The next point to notice is that, in each column, there is only one non-zero element to be eliminated and so the computational effort can be reduced.

If $d_1 \neq 0$ in Equations (5.18), x_1 can be eliminated from the second equation by forming the multiplier

$$m_1 = \frac{a_2}{d_1}$$

and producing the new equation

$$d_2' x_2 + c_2 x_3 = b_2'$$

where

$$d_2' = d_2 - m_1 c_1$$
$$b_2' = b_2 - m_1 b_1$$

Similarly, if $d_2' \neq 0$, x_2 can be eliminated from the third equation to give as the new third equation

$$d_3' x_3 + c_3 x_4 = b_3'$$

where

$$d_3' = d_3 - m_2 c_2$$
$$b_3' = b_3 - m_2 b_2'$$

and

$$m_2 = \frac{a_3}{d_2'}$$

Continuing in this way, at the ith stage, x_i can be eliminated from equation $i + 1$ (assuming $d_i' \neq 0$) to give the new equation

$$d_{i+1}' x_{i+1} + c_{i+1} x_{i+2} = b_{i+1}' \tag{5.19}$$

where

$$d_{i+1}' = d_{i+1} - m_i c_i \tag{5.20}$$
$$b_{i+1}' = b_{i+1} - m_i b_i' \tag{5.21}$$

and

$$m_i = \frac{a_{i+1}}{d_i'} \tag{5.22}$$

If the sequence of Equations (5.20), (5.21) and (5.22), resulting in Equation (5.19), is repeated for $i = 1, 2, \ldots, n - 1$, the original system (5.18) is transformed to upper triangular form and so the solution can be obtained using a modified version of the back-substitution discussed earlier. Assuming $d_n' \neq 0$,

$$x_n = \frac{b_n'}{d_n'}$$

Given n, coefficients **a,d,c,b**
Set $d_1' = d_1$
     $b_1' = b_1$
For $i = 1,2,\ldots,n-1$
   Set $m_i = a_{i+1}/d_i'$
       $d_{i+1}' = d_{i+1} - m_i c_i$
       $b_{i+1}' = b_{i+1} - m_i b_i'$
Set $x_n = b_n'/d_n'$
For $i = n-1, n-2, \ldots, 1$
   Set $x_i = (b_i' - c_i x_{i+1})/d_i'$

Figure 5.18   Algorithm for solving a tri-diagonal system of equations.

and then, for $i = n-1, n-2, \ldots, 1$,

$$x_i = \frac{b_i' - c_i x_{i+1}}{d_i'}$$

Collecting these equations leads to the mathematical algorithm of Figure 5.18. As an illustration, this algorithm is applied to the system of equations

$$\begin{bmatrix} -4 & 1 & 0 & 0 \\ 1 & -4 & 1 & 0 \\ 0 & 1 & -4 & 1 \\ 0 & 0 & 1 & -3 \end{bmatrix} \begin{bmatrix} x_1 \\ x_2 \\ x_3 \\ x_4 \end{bmatrix} = \begin{bmatrix} -1 \\ 0 \\ 0 \\ 0 \end{bmatrix}$$

for which

$a_2 = a_3 = a_4 = 1$
$d_1 = d_2 = d_3 = -4, \qquad d_4 = -3$
$c_1 = c_2 = c_3 = 1$
$b_1 = -1, \qquad b_2 = b_3 = b_4 = 0$

Thus, from the algorithm,

$d_1' = d_1 = -4, \qquad b_1' = b_1 = -1$
$m_1 = a_2/d_1' = 1/-4 = -1/4$
$d_2' = d_2 - m_1 c_1 = (-4) - (-1/4)(1) = -15/4$
$b_2' = b_2 - m_1 b_1' = (0) - 1/4$

$m_2 = a_3/d_2' = 1/(-15/4) = -4/15$
$d_3' = d_3 - m_2 c_2 = (-4) - (-4/15)(1) = -56/15$
$b_3' = b_3 - m_2 b_2' = (0) - (-4/15)(-1/4) = -1/15$

$m_3 = a_4/d_3' = 1/(-56/15) = -15/56$
$d_4' = d_4 - m_3 c_3 = (-3) - (-15/56)(1) = -153/56$
$b_4' = b_4 - m_3 b_3' = (0) - (-15/56)(-1/15) = -1/56$

and so

$$x_4 = b_4'/d_4' = (-1/56)/(-153/56) = 1/153$$

$$x_3 = (b_3' - c_3 x_4)/d_3'$$
$$= ((-1/15) - (1)(1/153))/(-56/15) = 1/51$$

$$x_2 = (b_2' - c_2 x_3)/d_2'$$
$$= ((-1/4) - (1)(1/51))/(-15/4) = 11/153$$

$$x_1 = (b_1' - c_1 x_2)/d_1'$$
$$= ((-1) - (1)(11/153))/(-4) = 41/153$$

giving the solution

$$x = \begin{bmatrix} 41/153 \\ 11/153 \\ 1/51 \\ 1/153 \end{bmatrix}$$

The tri-diagonal structure of the equations will be lost if any form of pivoting is used. Pivoting is unnecessary if the coefficient matrix has a unique LU factorization and, as the following theorem shows, this is the case for the class of matrices considered here.

Theorem 5.5

If a matrix A is strictly diagonally dominant (or positive definite) and tri-diagonal, it has a unique LU factorization in which both L and U have only two diagonals: L the main and first subdiagonal and U the main and first superdiagonal.

Proof

From Theorem 5.3, A has a unique LU decomposition. The remainder of the proof is straightforward and is left as an exercise for the reader.   ∎

Program construction

The subroutine plan, given in Figure 5.19, is a simple translation from the mathematical algorithm of Figure 5.18 in which the new d and b values overwrite the old values.

The subroutine plan is implemented in Figure 5.20. The tri-diagonal matrix is stored in three one-dimensional arrays; the subdiagonal in A, the diagonal in D and the superdiagonal in C. The right-hand-side vector is stored in B. Checks are included to identify small pivots or small multipliers.

Given: n, a, d, c, b
for $i = 1, 2, \ldots, n - 1$
  if $|d_i| >$ *small number* **then**
    Set: $m_i = a_{i+1}/d_i$
        $d_{i+1} = d_{i+1} - m_i c_i$
        $b_{i+1} = b_{i+1} - m_i b_i$

  else
    Note: 'small pivot' and abandon calculation

  if $|d_n| >$ *small number* **then**
    Set: $x_n = b_n/d_n$
    for $i = n - 1, n - 2, \ldots, 1$
      Set: $x_i = (b_i - c_i x_{i+1})/d_i$
  else
    Note: 'small pivot'

Figure 5.19   Plan of subroutine for tri-diagonal solver.

In practice, it is likely that system (5.18) will need to be solved for many right-hand sides so this subroutine stores the multipliers m_k in the vector that originally contained the a_k.

In later chapters, it will be necessary to solve tri-diagonal systems of equations for which the range of subscripts does not start at 1 or where the actual array supplied to hold the solution vector is not the same size as those holding the coefficient vectors. A specific version of TRISOL could be produced in each case but instead Figure 5.21 gives a generalized version which caters for both.

5.1.7   Iterative refinement

All the methods discussed so far have been direct methods; only one estimate of the solution is produced. This has the slight disadvantage that there is no indication how close the numerical solution is to the exact solution. The technique of **iterative refinement** can be used to check and, if necessary, to improve an existing estimate of the solution. Suppose that the *LU* decomposition has been used to solve system (5.2):

$$Ax = b$$

to obtain the numerical solution $x^{(1)}$. Because of the effects of rounding errors this solution will not be exact and we define e to be the difference between the computed and exact solutions. Thus

$$e = x^{(1)} - x$$

```
      SUBROUTINE TRISOL (N,A,D,C,B, STATUS,X)

      INTEGER   I,N,PTINY,SOLVED,STATUS
      REAL      MULT,PIVOT,TINY
      PARAMETER (SOLVED=0,PTINY=1)
      PARAMETER (TINY=1E-10)
      REAL      A(N),B(N),C(N),D(N),X(N)
      INTRINSIC ABS

C     { first the elimination stage }

      DO 10, I=1,N-1
        PIVOT=D(I)
        IF (ABS(PIVOT).GT.TINY) THEN
          MULT=A(I+1)/PIVOT
          IF (ABS(MULT).GT.TINY) THEN
            A(I+1)=MULT
            D(I+1)=D(I+1)-MULT*C(I)
            B(I+1)=B(I+1)-MULT*B(I)
          ELSE
            A(I+1)=0
          END IF
        ELSE
          STATUS=PTINY
          GOTO 999
        END IF
10    CONTINUE

C     { now the back-substitution }

      IF (ABS(D(N)).GT.TINY) THEN
        STATUS=SOLVED
        X(N)  =B(N)/D(N)
        DO 20, I=N-1,1,-1
          X(I)=(B(I)-C(I)*X(I+1))/D(I)
20      CONTINUE
      ELSE
        STATUS=PTINY
      END IF

999   END
```

Figure 5.20   Subroutine for tri-diagonal system of equations.

```
SUBROUTINE TRISL2 (LB,UB,LBX,UBX,A,D,C,B, STATUS,X)

INTEGER   I,LB,LBX,PTINY,SOLVED,STATUS,UB,UBX
REAL      MULT,PIVOT,TINY
PARAMETER (SOLVED=0,PTINY=1)
PARAMETER (TINY=1E-10)
REAL      A(LB:UB),B(LB:UB),C(LB:UB),D(LB:UB),X(LBX:UBX)
INTRINSIC ABS

C       { first the elimination stage }

DO 10, I=LB,UB-1
  PIVOT=D(I)
  IF (ABS(PIVOT).GT.TINY) THEN
    MULT=A(I+1)/PIVOT
    IF (ABS(MULT).GT.TINY) THEN
      A(I+1)=MULT
      D(I+1)=D(I+1)-MULT*C(I)
      B(I+1)=B(I+1)-MULT*B(I)
    ELSE
      A(I+1)-0
    END IF
  ELSE
    STATUS=PTINY
    GOTO 999
  END IF
10    CONTINUE

C       { now the back-substitution }

IF (ABS(D(UB)).GT.TINY) THEN
  STATUS=SOLVED
  X(UB)=B(UB)/D(UB)
  DO 20, I=UB-1,LB,-1
    X(I)=(B(I)-C(I)*X(I+1))/D(I)
20    CONTINUE
ELSE
  STATUS=PTINY
END IF

999   END
```

Figure 5.21 Modified subroutine for tri-diagonal system of equations.

Now

$$Ae = A(x^{(1)} - x) = Ax^{(1)} - b$$

If we define

$$r^{(1)} = Ax^{(1)} - b$$

then

$$Ae = r^{(1)} \qquad\qquad\qquad \textbf{(5.23)}$$

and we can obtain an *estimate*, $e^{(1)}$, of e by solving Equation (5.23) using the *LU* factors of A. We then set

$$x^{(2)} = x^{(1)} - e^{(1)}$$

and $x^{(2)}$ should approximate x more closely than does $x^{(1)}$. This process is repeated by calculating

$$r^{(2)} = Ax^{(2)} - b$$

and then solving the system

$$Ae = r^{(2)}$$

to obtain $e^{(2)}$, a correction to $x^{(2)}$, and so on.

   In iterative refinement, the residual vector $r^{(k)}$ must be calculated using double precision arithmetic before being rounded to single precision and substituted in the right-hand side of Equation (5.23). The solution of Equation (5.23) can be obtained easily using the subroutine of Figure 5.17. Normally, the elements of successive corrections, $e^{(k)}$, become smaller and only a few iterations are required before they become small enough for the iteration to be terminated.

   The technique of iterative refinement can be illustrated using a simple example. The equations

$$\begin{aligned} 2004x_1 + 22x_2 &= 225.28 \\ 22x_1 + 2001x_2 &= 442.64 \end{aligned}$$

have the exact solution $x_1 = 0.11$ and $x_2 = 0.22$. We use the four-digit chopping computer, introduced in Chapter 3, to solve these equations. In this computer these equations are represented as

$$\begin{aligned} 0.2004 \times 10^4 x_1 + 0.2200 \times 10^2 x_2 &= 0.2252 \times 10^3 \\ 0.2200 \times 10^2 x_1 + 0.2001 \times 10^4 x_2 &= 0.4426 \times 10^3 \end{aligned}$$

and so the equations have already been affected by rounding error. The reader can verify that the LU factors of the matrix involved in the equations are

$$L = \begin{bmatrix} 0.1000 \times 10^1 & 0.0000 \times 10^0 \\ 0.1097 \times 10^{-1} & 0.1000 \times 10^1 \end{bmatrix}$$

$$U = \begin{bmatrix} 0.2004 \times 10^4 & 0.2200 \times 10^2 \\ 0.0000 \times 10^0 & 0.2000 \times 10^4 \end{bmatrix}$$

and these lead to the computed solution

$$x_1^{(1)} = 0.1099 \times 10^0$$
$$x_2^{(1)} = 0.2200 \times 10^0$$

which is close to the exact solution. Using double precision arithmetic, the residuals are

$$r_1^{(1)} = 0.2004 \times 10^4(0.1099 \times 10^0) + 0.2200 \times 10^2(0.2200 \times 10^0)$$
$$- 0.2252 \times 10^3$$
$$= -0.120\,400\,012 \times 10^0$$

$$r_2^{(1)} = 0.2200 \times 10^2(0.1099 \times 10^0) + 0.2001 \times 10^4(0.2200 \times 10^0)$$
$$- 0.4426 \times 10^3$$
$$= 0.377\,998\,352 \times 10^{-1}$$

which are chopped to give

$$r_1^{(1)} = -0.1204 \times 10^0$$
$$r_2^{(1)} = 0.3779 \times 10^{-1}$$

These residuals are small relative to the size of the coefficients of the equations. Equation (5.23) can now be solved to obtain the result

$$e_1^{(1)} = -0.6027 \times 10^{-4}$$
$$e_2^{(1)} = 0.1955 \times 10^{-4}$$

These corrections are small, indicating that the calculated solution is indeed close to the correct solution. The new estimates of the solution are

$$x_1^{(2)} = x_1^{(1)} - e_1^{(1)} = 0.1099 \times 10^0$$
$$x_2^{(2)} = x_2^{(1)} - e_2^{(1)} = 0.2200 \times 10^0$$

and so the corrections, on this computer, have had no effect on the computed solution. The iteration can be terminated and $x^{(2)}$ taken as the estimate of the solution.

5.1.8   Ill-conditioning

In Chapter 3 we introduced the concept of an *ill-conditioned* problem citing as an example the calculation of the zeros of the polynomial

$$p(x) = (x - 1)(x - 2) \ldots (x - 20)$$

Recall that an ill-conditioned problem is one in which a small change in one of the parameters results in a large change in the solution. In the case of a system of linear equations this phenomenon can be illustrated with a very simple example. The equations

$$x_1 + x_2 = 1$$
$$1.0001x_1 + x_2 = 2$$

have the solution

$$x_1 = 10\ 000$$
$$x_2 = -9999$$

However, if the coefficient of x_1 in the second equation is changed from 1.0001 to 0.9999, the new system has the solution

$$x_1 = -10\ 000$$
$$x_2 = 10\ 001$$

In this example it is easy to account for the dramatic change in the solution because the original system of equations represents two almost parallel lines which converge in the fourth quadrant at a large distance from the origin. The perturbation introduced into the second equation has the effect of changing the gradient of one of the lines so that the point of intersection is moved to the second quadrant, again at a large distance from the origin.

Clearly, rounding errors can produce disastrous results if the equations to be solved are ill-conditioned and so it will be useful to have some way of determining whether this is the case. The technique of iterative refinement, introduced in Section 5.1.7, can give some indication that a problem is ill-conditioned. Normally, the elements of successive corrections, $e^{(k)}$, become smaller as the iteration proceeds; however, if the equations are ill-conditioned, the elements of $e^{(k)}$ do not necessarily become smaller and this can be used as an indicator of possible conditioning problems. The following simple example illustrates this. The equations

$$2004x_1 + 2002x_2 = 660.88$$
$$2002x_1 + 2001x_2 = 660.44$$

have the solution

$$x_1 = 0.11$$
$$x_2 = 0.22$$

We use the four-digit chopping computer, as in the previous section, to solve these equations. In this computer the equations are represented as

$$0.2004 \times 10^4 x_1 + 0.2002 \times 10^4 x_2 = 0.6608 \times 10^3$$
$$0.2002 \times 10^4 x_1 + 0.2001 \times 10^4 x_2 = 0.6604 \times 10^3$$

and so the equations have already been affected by rounding errors. The LU factors of the matrix involved in the equations are

$$L = \begin{bmatrix} 0.1000 \times 10^1 & 0.0000 \times 10^0 \\ 0.9990 \times 10^0 & 0.1000 \times 10^1 \end{bmatrix}$$

$$U = \begin{bmatrix} 0.2004 \times 10^4 & 0.2002 \times 10^4 \\ 0.0000 \times 10^0 & 0.2000 \times 10^1 \end{bmatrix}$$

from which the computed solution is

$$x_1^{(1)} = 0.1798 \times 10^0$$
$$x_2^{(1)} = 0.1500 \times 10^0$$

These are not good estimates of the solution. A relative change of the order of $0.04/600.44 = 0.67 \times 10^{-5}$ and $0.08/660.88 = 0.12 \times 10^{-3}$ has resulted in relative errors in the solution of $-0.69 \times 10^{-1}/0.11 = -0.6345$ in x_1 and $-0.69 \times 10^{-1}/0.22 = -0.3136$ in x_2; i.e. approximately 63% and 31% respectively. The residuals, calculated in double precision, are

$$\begin{aligned} r_1^{(1)} &= 0.2004 \times 10^4 (0.1798 \times 10^0) + 0.2002 \times 10^4 (0.1500 \times 10^0) \\ &\quad - 0.6608 \times 10^3 \\ &= 0.360\,319\,2 \times 10^3 + 0.300\,300\,00 \times 10^3 - 0.6608 \times 10^3 \\ &= -0.180\,799\,961 \times 10^0 \end{aligned}$$

$$\begin{aligned} r_2^{(1)} &= 0.2002 \times 10^4 (0.1798 \times 10^0) + 0.2001 \times 10^4 (0.1500 \times 10^0) \\ &\quad - 0.6604 \times 10^3 \\ &= 0.359\,959\,6 \times 10^3 + 0.300\,150\,0 \times 10^3 - 0.6604 \times 10^3 \\ &= -0.290\,400\,028 \times 10^0 \end{aligned}$$

which, when chopped to four figures, are

$$r_1^{(1)} = -0.1807 \times 10^0$$
$$r_2^{(1)} = -0.2904 \times 10^0$$

It must be emphasized, in passing, that these residuals are small compared with the magnitude of the coefficients of the problem. Thus small residuals are not always an indicator of a 'good' solution.

Solving Equation (5.23) gives the result

$$e_1^{(1)} = \quad 0.5479 \times 10^{-1}$$
$$e_2^{(1)} = -0.5495 \times 10^{-1}$$

from which

$$e_1^{(1)}/x_1^{(1)} = \quad 0.5479 \times 10^{-1}/0.1798 \times 10^0 = \quad 0.3047 \times 10^0$$
$$e_2^{(1)}/x_2^{(1)} = -0.5495 \times 10^{-1}/0.1500 \times 10^0 = -0.3663 \times 10^0$$

giving relative corrections of about 30% and 37% respectively. These relative corrections are large and so indicate possible conditioning problems. Further iterations make these problems apparent. Evaluating

$$\begin{aligned} x_1^{(2)} &= x_1^{(1)} - e_1^{(1)} \\ &= 0.1798 \times 10^0 - 0.5479 \times 10^{-1} \\ &= 0.1250 \times 10^0 \end{aligned}$$

$$\begin{aligned} x_2^{(2)} &= x_2^{(1)} - e_2^{(1)} \\ &= 0.1500 \times 10^0 - (-0.5495 \times 10^{-1}) \\ &= 0.2049 \times 10^0 \end{aligned}$$

gives better approximations to the exact solution. The residuals are

$$r_1^{(2)} = -0.9019 \times 10^{-1}$$
$$r_2^{(2)} = -0.1451 \times 10^0$$

Note that they have decreased in modulus. Solving Equation (5.23), we obtain

$$e_1^{(2)} = \quad 0.2742 \times 10^{-1}$$
$$e_2^{(2)} = -0.2750 \times 10^{-1}$$

giving

$$x_1^{(3)} = 0.9758 \times 10^{-1}$$
$$x_2^{(3)} = 0.2324 \times 10^0$$

which show further improvement. However, a further calculation gives

$$r_1^{(3)} = \quad 0.1512 \times 10^{-1}$$
$$r_2^{(3)} = -0.1243 \times 10^{-1}$$

and

$$e_1^{(3)} = 0.1374 \times 10^{-1}$$
$$e_2^{(3)} = -0.1376 \times 10^{-1}$$

Thus

$$x_1^{(4)} = 0.8384 \times 10^{-1}$$
$$x_2^{(4)} = 0.2461 \times 10^{0}$$

showing a deterioration.

5.2 Iterative methods

Iterative methods are particularly useful when the system of equations is large and most of the coefficients are zero. Systems of this type occur frequently in the solution of problems involving partial differential equations and it is the need for such solutions that has prompted much of the research into these methods. Throughout this section we will assume that the matrix A is strictly diagonally dominant (see Definition 5.1) because this ensures the convergence of the methods that follow. In some cases a coefficient matrix of this form can be obtained simply by reordering the equations.

The basic idea behind the methods is essentially the same as that for those of Section 4.1.4 in which the equation

$$f(x) = 0$$

was rearranged to give an iteration formula of the form

$$x_{k+1} = g(x_k) \qquad \text{for } k = 0,1,2, \ldots$$

for finding a zero of $f(x)$.

5.2.1 Jacobi's method

As an example of such a rearrangement consider the system of equations

$$10x_1 + 3x_2 + x_3 = 19$$
$$3x_1 + 10x_2 + 2x_3 = 29$$
$$x_1 + 2x_2 + 10x_3 = 35$$

The first equation can be rearranged to give

$$x_1 = (19 - 3x_2 - x_3)/10$$

which provides the basis for the iterative formula

$$x_1^{(k+1)} = (19 - 3x_2^{(k)} - x_3^{(k)})/10$$

where k is the iteration number.

Similarly, from the second equation, an iterative formula for x_2 can be obtained:

$$x_2^{(k+1)} = (29 - 3x_1^{(k)} - 2x_3^{(k)})/10$$

and, from the third, one for x_3:

$$x_3^{(k+1)} = (35 - x_1^{(k)} - 2x_2^{(k)})/10$$

These equations form the *Jacobi* iteration for finding the solution of the system of equations. We could choose $x^{(0)} = (0,0,0)^T$ as an initial estimate of the solution and this would lead to $x^{(1)} = (19/10, 29/10, 35/10)^T$, that is

$$x_i^{(1)} = b_i/a_{ii} \qquad \text{for } i = 1, 2, \ldots, n$$

However, rather than perform an extra iteration to obtain these values, we shall begin with $x^{(0)} = (1.9, 2.9, 3.5)^T$. Thus

$$
\begin{aligned}
x_1^{(1)} &= (19 - 3(2.9) - (3.5))/10 &= 0.68 \\
x_2^{(1)} &= (29 - 3(1.9) - 2(3.5))/10 &= 1.63 \\
x_3^{(1)} &= (35 - (1.9) - 2(2.9))/10 &= 2.73
\end{aligned}
$$

and so

$$x^{(1)} = (0.68, 1.63, 2.73)^T$$

Similarly,

$$
\begin{aligned}
x^{(2)} &= (1.138, 2.150, 3.106)^T \\
x^{(3)} &= (0.9444, 1.9374, 2.9562)^T \\
x^{(4)} &= (1.0232, 2.0254, 3.0181)^T \\
&\vdots \\
x^{(20)} &= (1.0000, 2.0000, 3.0000)^T \\
x^{(21)} &= (1.0000, 2.0000, 3.0000)^T
\end{aligned}
$$

and successive iterates appear to be converging to the exact answer

$$x = (1,2,3)^{\mathrm{T}}$$

It must be emphasized that the convergence test must be applied to *every* component of successive iterates because, in general, the components do not converge at the same rate.

For the general system of n equations in n unknowns

$$
\begin{aligned}
a_{11}x_1 + a_{12}x_2 + \cdots + a_{1n}x_n &= b_1 \\
a_{21}x_1 + a_{22}x_2 + \cdots + a_{2n}x_n &= b_2 \\
\vdots \qquad \vdots \qquad\qquad \vdots \quad \vdots \\
a_{n1}x_1 + a_{n2}x_2 + \cdots + a_{nn}x_n &= b_n
\end{aligned}
\tag{5.24}
$$

the first equation is used in exactly the same way to give an iterative formula for x_1. Thus

$$x_1 = \frac{b_1 - a_{12}x_2 - a_{13}x_3 - \cdots - a_{1n}x_n}{a_{11}}$$

and this leads to the iteration

$$x_1^{(k+1)} = \frac{b_1 - a_{12}x_2^{(k)} - \cdots - a_{1n}x_n^{(k)}}{a_{11}}$$

Similarly the second equation can be rearranged to give an iteration for x_2 and, in general, an iteration for x_i can be obtained from the ith equation giving

$$x_i^{(k+1)} = \frac{b_i - a_{i1}x_1^{(k)} - \cdots - a_{ii-1}x_{i-1}^{(k)} - a_{ii+1}x_{i+1}^{(k)} - \cdots - a_{in}x_n^{(k)}}{a_{ii}}
\tag{5.25}$$

This is Jacobi's method for a general system of equations. The mathematical algorithm is given in Figure 5.22. A discussion of the convergence properties of this method is deferred until Section 5.2.4.

Program construction

Figure 5.23 shows a subroutine plan derived from the algorithm of Figure 5.22. Current estimates of x are computed in an array X, while those of the previous iteration are held in OLDX. Note that the convergence test is applied to each element X(I) immediately it has been computed: a (logical) variable 'tolerance exceeded' is set .FALSE. prior to each iteration and is subsequently set .TRUE. if the absolute difference between two elements X(I) and OLDX(I) exceeds the

Given n, A, b
For $i = 1,2, \ldots ,n$
  Set $x_i^{(0)} = b_i/a_{ii}$
Repeat (for $k = 0,1,2, \ldots$)
  For $i = 1,2, \ldots ,n$

$$\text{Set } x_i^{(k+1)} = \frac{b_i - a_{i1}x_1^{(k)} - \cdots - a_{ii-1}x_{i-1}^{(k)} - a_{ii+1}x_{i+1}^{(k)} - \cdots - a_{in}x_n^{(k)}}{a_{ii}}$$

Until converged

Figure 5.22 Algorithm for Jacobi's method.

Given: $n,A,b,tolerance,maximum$ number of iterations
for $i = 1,2, \ldots ,n$
  Set: $x_i^{(0)} = b_i/a_{ii}$
repeat (*not exceeding max iterations*)
  Set vector: $oldx = x$
        Set: tolerance exceeded = .FALSE.
  for $i = 1,2, \ldots ,n$
    Set: $sum - b_i$
    for $j = 1,2, \ldots ,i - 1,i + 1, \ldots ,n$
    Set: $sum = sum - a_{ij}oldx_j$
    Set: $x_j = sum/a_{ii}$

    if $|x_i - oldx_i| > |oldx_i| \cdot tolerance$ **then**
      Set: tolerance exceeded = .TRUE.

  if not *tolerance exceeded* **then**
    Note: 'solved'

until *'solved' (or limit on number of iterations reached)*

if *'solved'* **then**
  Record: solution, number of iterations used
if *'limit'* **then**
  Record: last approximation to solution

Figure 5.23 Plan of subroutine for Jacobi's method.

specified tolerance. If the variable 'tolerance exceeded' retains the value .FALSE. after all the elements of X have been computed, the iteration sequence has converged. Note that the convergence test for an element X(I) can be avoided if a previous element has failed to converge. This has been done in the subroutine of Figure 5.24.

Figure 5.24 Subroutine for Jacobi's method.

```
      SUBROUTINE JACOBI (SIZE,N,A,B,TOL,MAXITS,
     *                   STATUS,X,NOOFIT, OLDX)

      INTEGER   COUNT,I,J,LIMIT,MAXITS,N,NOOFIT,
     *          SIZE,SOLVED,STATUS
      REAL      TOL
      DOUBLE PRECISION SUM
      LOGICAL   TOLEX
      PARAMETER (SOLVED=0,LIMIT=1)
      REAL      A(SIZE,SIZE),B(N),OLDX(N),X(N)
      INTRINSIC ABS,DPROD

C     { Set up starting values }

      DO 10, I=1,N
        X(I)=B(I)/A(I,I)
10    CONTINUE

C     { Now start the iteration }

      DO 20, COUNT=1,MAXITS
        DO 30, I=1,N
          OLDX(I)=X(I)
30      CONTINUE

        TOLEX=.FALSE.
        DO 40, I=1,N
          SUM=B(I)
          DO 50, J=1,I-1
            SUM=SUM-DPROD(A(I,J),OLDX(J))
50        CONTINUE
          DO 60, J=I+1,N
            SUM=SUM-DPROD(A(I,J),OLDX(J))
60        CONTINUE
          SUM=SUM/A(I,I)
          X(I)=SUM

          IF (.NOT. TOLEX) THEN
            IF (ABS(SUM-OLDX(I)).GT.ABS(OLDX(I))*TOL) TOLEX=.TRUE.
          END IF
40      CONTINUE

        IF (.NOT. TOLEX) THEN
          STATUS=SOLVED
          GO TO 21
        END IF
```

```
20    CONTINUE
      STATUS=LIMIT

21    IF (STATUS.EQ.SOLVED) NOOFIT=COUNT

      END
```

Figure 5.24   *cont.*

5.2.2   The Gauss–Seidel method

In the Jacobi method, we begin with initial approximations

$$x_1^{(0)}, x_2^{(0)}, \ldots, x_n^{(0)}$$

and use these to calculate better approximations

$$x_1^{(1)}, x_2^{(1)}, \ldots, x_n^{(1)}$$

However, in the calculation of $x_2^{(1)}$, it seems pointless to use the initial estimate $x_1^{(0)}$ of x_1 when a better approximation $x_1^{(1)}$ has just been obtained. For the same reason, when calculating $x_3^{(1)}$, it would be sensible to make use of the new values $x_1^{(1)}$ and $x_2^{(1)}$ along with the values $x_4^{(0)}, \ldots, x_n^{(0)}$ obtained from the previous iteration. This idea can be applied to each component of the solution vector and gives the *Gauss–Seidel* method, a modification of Jacobi's method in which the most recent approximations are used at all times. The Gauss–Seidel iteration is thus given by

$$x_i^{(k+1)} = \frac{b_i - a_{i1}x_1^{(k+1)} - \cdots - a_{ii-1}x_{i-1}^{(k+1)} - a_{ii+1}x_{i+1}^{(k)} - \cdots - a_{in}x_n^{(k)}}{a_{ii}} \qquad (5.26)$$

When $i = 1$ the right-hand side includes terms with superscript (k) only, and when $i = n$ terms with superscript $(k + 1)$ only. In general, the Gauss–Seidel iterates converge more rapidly than do those of Jacobi's method although, for certain examples, the initial convergence of Jacobi's method can be faster.

For the system of equations

$$\begin{aligned} 10x_1 + 3x_2 + x_3 &= 19 \\ 3x_1 + 10x_2 + 2x_3 &= 29 \\ x_1 + 2x_2 + 10x_3 &= 35 \end{aligned}$$

which has been solved already using Jacobi's method, the Gauss–Seidel equations are

$$x_1^{(k+1)} = (19 - 3x_2^{(k)} - x_3^{(k)})/10$$
$$x_2^{(k+1)} = (29 - 3x_1^{(k+1)} - 2x_3^{(k)})/10$$
$$x_3^{(k+1)} = (35 - x_1^{(k+1)} - 2x_2^{(k+1)})/10$$

Using the same initial estimate, $x^{(0)} = (1.9, 2.9, 3.5)^T$, as for Jacobi's method, the Gauss–Seidel method gives

$$x_1^{(1)} = (19 - 3(2.9) - (3.5))/10 = 0.68$$

as before. However, in forming $x_2^{(1)}$ this new estimate of $x_1^{(1)}$ is used immediately to give

$$x_2^{(1)} = (29 - 3(0.68) - 2(3.5))/10 = 1.996$$

compared with $x_2^{(1)} = 1.63$ obtained from Jacobi's method – a significant improvement. Similarly the latest values of x_1 and x_2 are used to compute the new x_3:

$$x_3^{(1)} = (35 - (0.68) - 2(1.996))/10 = 3.0328$$

again a significant improvement. Thus

$$x^{(1)} = (0.68, 1.996, 3.0328)^T$$

Continuing in a similar manner we obtain

$$x^{(2)} = (0.9979, 1.9941, 3.0014)^T$$
$$x^{(3)} = (1.0016, 1.9992, 3.0000)^T$$

and

$$x^{(4)} = (1.0002, 1.9999, 3.0000)^T$$

Hence, after only four iterations, the solution is obtained correct to four significant figures. A discussion of rate of convergence is given in Section 5.2.4.

Program construction

The subroutine to perform the Gauss–Seidel iteration is a simple modification of that for Jacobi's method. Some saving in storage can be achieved by noting that, once a new value $x_i^{(k+1)}$ has been calculated and compared with $x_i^{(k)}$, the old value $x_i^{(k)}$ is no longer needed and can be overwritten. This means that it is not necessary to have two arrays X and OLDX to store both current and previous estimates; each value can be overwritten as soon as the convergence test has been applied, and so only one array, X, is required. A subroutine that performs the Gauss–Seidel iteration is given in Figure 5.25.

5.2.3 Successive over-relaxation

Numerical analysts have attempted to increase the rate of convergence of the Jacobi and Gauss–Seidel iterations. It is possible, for example, to use Aitken's Δ^2 process to try to speed up the progress of the iteration. One of the best known methods, and the only one considered here, is that of **successive over-relaxation**, commonly known as SOR. This method is based on the idea that having produced a new value $\bar{x}_i^{(k+1)}$, using the Gauss–Seidel method, an even better value may result by forming a weighted average of the old and new values. Hence, the 'final' value, $x_i^{(k+1)}$, is given by

$$x_i^{(k+1)} = \omega \bar{x}_i^{(k+1)} + (1 - \omega)x_i^{(k)} \tag{5.27}$$

where ω (> 0) is an arbitrary parameter independent of k and i. Notice that, if $\omega = 1$, then $x_i^{(k+1)}$ is the value given by the Gauss–Seidel method. If $\omega > 1$ then Equation (5.27) defines the method of successive over-relaxation and, for a large class of matrices, it can be shown that the optimum value of ω lies between 1 and 2 (see Theorems 5.8 and 5.9). This optimum ω is difficult to determine and, usually, an educated guess must suffice (but see Theorem 5.8 for a special case).

The effect of SOR can be demonstrated with the system

$$A = \begin{bmatrix} 10 & -8 & 0 \\ -8 & 10 & -1 \\ 0 & -1 & 10 \end{bmatrix} \quad b = \begin{bmatrix} -6 \\ 9 \\ 28 \end{bmatrix}$$

which has solution (1,2,3). Using the initial approximation $x_i = b_i/a_{ii}$, $\{i = 1,2,3\}$, and a tolerance of 5E−7, the Jacobi iterates converge after 65 cycles and the Gauss–Seidel iterates after 33. For this coefficient matrix, the optimum value of ω can be calculated and, to four decimal places, it is 1.2566. Using this value, and with the same initial approximation and tolerance, the SOR iterates converge after only 14 iterations.

5.2.4 Convergence

The three methods discussed so far are examples of the general iterative scheme

$$x^{(k+1)} = Bx^{(k)} + c \tag{5.28}$$

```
      SUBROUTINE GSEIDL (SIZE,N,A,B,TOL,MAXITS,
     *                   STATUS,X,NOOFIT)

      INTEGER   COUNT,I,J,LIMIT,MAXITS,N,NOOFIT,
     *          SIZE,SOLVED,STATUS
      REAL      TOL
      DOUBLE PRECISION SUM
      LOGICAL   TOLEX
      PARAMETER (SOLVED=0,LIMIT=1)
      REAL      A(SIZE,SIZE),B(N),X(N)
      INTRINSIC ABS,DPROD

C        { Set up starting values }

      DO 10, I=1,N
        X(I)=B(I)/A(I,I)
10    CONTINUE

C        { Now start the iteration }

      DO 20, COUNT=1,MAXITS

        TOLEX=.FALSE.
        DO 30, I=1,N
          SUM=B(I)
          DO 40, J=1,I-1
            SUM=SUM-DPROD(A(I,J),X(J))
40        CONTINUE
          DO 50, J=I+1,N
            SUM=SUM-DPROD(A(I,J),X(J))
50        CONTINUE
          SUM=SUM/A(I,I)

          IF (.NOT. TOLEX) THEN
            IF (ABS(SUM-X(I)).GT.ABS(X(I))*TOL) TOLEX=.TRUE.
          END IF
          X(I)=SUM
30      CONTINUE

        IF (.NOT. TOLEX) THEN
          STATUS=SOLVED
          GO TO 21
        END IF
20    CONTINUE
      STATUS=LIMIT

21    IF (STATUS.EQ.SOLVED) NOOFIT=COUNT

      END
```

Figure 5.25   Subroutine for the Gauss–Seidel method.

The matrix A can be written in the form

$$A = L + D + U$$

where D is a non-zero diagonal matrix, L is strictly lower triangular and U is strictly upper triangular. If A is non-singular then such a D can always be found by reordering the rows and columns of A. Using this notation the Jacobi iteration matrix is

$$B_J = -D^{-1}(L + U)$$

and

$$c_J = D^{-1}b$$

The Gauss–Seidel iteration matrix is

$$B_{GS} = -(D + L)^{-1}U$$

with

$$c_{GS} = (D + L)^{-1}b$$

For the SOR method

$$B_{SOR} = (D + \omega L)^{-1}((1 - \omega)D - \omega U)$$

with

$$c_{SOR} = (D + \omega L)^{-1}b$$

The verification of these results is left as an exercise for the reader.

Definition 5.3

The iterates produced using Equation (5.28) are said to converge to the vector x as k tends to infinity if

$$\lim_{k \to \infty} x^{(k)} = x$$

or, equivalently,

$$\lim_{k \to \infty} (x^{(k)} - x) = 0$$

Definition 5.4

The maximum modulus eigenvalue of a matrix A is called the **spectral radius** of A and is denoted by $\rho(A)$. If λ_1, λ_2, . . . , λ_n are the eigenvalues of A (see Chapter 6) then

$$|\lambda_i| \leq \rho(A) \qquad \text{for } i = 1,2, . . . ,n$$

Theorem 5.6

The iteration

$$x^{(k+1)} = Bx^{(k)} + c$$

will converge if

$$\rho(B) \leq \beta < 1$$

where β is a constant.

We shall not give a rigorous proof of this result but merely indicate why it is reasonable that it should be true. The exact solution x satisfies Equation (5.28) and so

$$x = Bx + c$$

Subtracting Equation (5.28) from this equation gives

$$x - x^{(k+1)} = B(x - x^{(k)})$$

which, by defining $e^{(k+1)} = x - x^{(k+1)}$, can be rewritten as

$$e^{(k+1)} = Be^{(k)}$$

Hence

$$e^{(k+1)} = B^2 e^{(k-1)} = \cdots = B^{k+1} e^{(0)} \tag{5.29}$$

Now, making the (rather large) assumption that B has a set of linearly independent eigenvectors x_i $\{i = 1,2, . . . ,n\}$, we may write

$$e^{(0)} = \sum_{i=1}^{n} \alpha_i x_i$$

where α_i $\{i = 1,2, . . . ,n\}$ are constants, not all zero.

Substituting this into Equation (5.29) gives

$$
\begin{aligned}
e^{(k+1)} &= B^{k+1} \sum_{i=1}^{n} \alpha_i x_i \\
&= \sum_{i=1}^{n} \alpha_i B^{k+1} x_i \\
&= \sum_{i=1}^{n} \alpha_i \lambda_i^{k+1} x_i
\end{aligned}
$$

where λ_i is the eigenvalue of B corresponding to the eigenvector x_i. By the statement of the theorem, each λ_i is less than or equal to β and so, for each component $e_j^{(k+1)}$,

$$
\begin{aligned}
|e_j^{(k+1)}| &\leq \sum_{i=1}^{n} |\alpha_i \lambda_i^{k+1} x_{ij}| \\
&\leq \beta^{k+1} \sum_{i=1}^{n} |\alpha_i x_{ij}|
\end{aligned}
$$

But, because $\beta < 1$, β^{k+1} tends to zero as k tends to infinity and so the components of the error vector $e^{(k+1)}$ must also tend to zero.

The following theorem concerns the convergence of the Jacobi and Gauss–Seidel methods.

Theorem 5.7

When A has non-negative elements, one of the following conditions holds:

(1) $\rho(B_J) = \rho(B_{GS}) = 0$
(2) $\rho(B_J) = \rho(B_{GS}) = 1$
(3) $0 < \rho(B_{GS}) < \rho(B_J) < 1$
(4) $1 < \rho(B_J) < \rho(B_{GS})$

A proof of this theorem, known as the Stein–Rosenberg theorem, can be found in Young (1971).

Following Theorem 5.7 the Jacobi and Gauss–Seidel iterations both converge or both diverge, and when they both converge the Gauss–Seidel method converges faster (except in the trivial case, (1)). Theorems 5.8 and 5.9 concern the SOR iteration.

Theorem 5.8

$\rho(B_{SOR}) < 1$ only if $0 < \omega < 2$.

Theorem 5.9

If A is positive definite then

$$\rho(B_{GS}) = (\rho(B_J))^2 < 1$$

and the optimal SOR parameter, ω, is given by

$$\omega_{opt} = \frac{2}{1 + (1 - (\rho(B_J)^2)^{1/2}}$$

and, with this choice, $\rho(B_{SOR}) = \omega_{opt} - 1$.

The calculation of the spectral radii of the iteration matrices, to check convergence, is not simple and so it is desirable to have a convergence test that is more easily verified. If the matrix A is strictly diagonally dominant, it is possible to prove that the iteration matrices are convergent. To give some justification for this statement consider the Jacobi iteration; the (i,j)th element of B_J is

$$(B_J)_{ij} = \begin{cases} a_{ij}/a_{ii} & i \neq j \\ 0 & i = j \end{cases}$$

In Chapter 6 we discuss Gershgorin's circle theorem (Theorem 6.6) which gives bounds on the positions of the eigenvalues of a matrix. In effect, for the matrix B_J, the theorem indicates that *all* of the eigenvalues lie in a disc, based on the origin and with radius

$$r = \sum_{\substack{j=1 \\ j \neq i}}^{n} \frac{|a_{ij}|}{|a_{ii}|}$$

But A is strictly diagonally dominant and so the sum on the right of this equation is strictly less than one. Thus all the eigenvalues of B_J have modulus less than 1; in particular $\rho(B_J)$ must be less than one and, by Theorem 5.6, the Jacobi iteration matrix must be convergent.

The situation is more complicated for the Gauss–Seidel matrix but a similar result can be proved. Testing for diagonal dominance is more restrictive than checking the spectral radius with the result that both methods may still converge for matrices that are not diagonally dominant.

EXERCISES

5.1 Prove the result quoted in Theorem 5.1 and complete the proof of Theorem 5.5.

5.2   Use the method of Gaussian elimination to solve the following systems of equations:

(a)
$$\begin{aligned}
x_1 + x_2 + x_3 + x_4 &= 0 \\
x_1 + 2x_2 + 2x_3 + 2x_4 &= 1 \\
x_1 + 2x_2 + 3x_3 + 3x_4 &= 1 \\
x_1 + 2x_2 + 3x_3 + 4x_4 &= 0
\end{aligned}$$

(b)
$$\begin{aligned}
x_1 + x_2 + x_3 + x_4 + x_5 &= 1 \\
x_1 + 2x_2 + 3x_3 + 4x_4 + 5x_5 &= 0 \\
x_1 + 3x_2 + 6x_3 + 10x_4 + 15x_5 &= 0 \\
x_1 + 4x_2 + 10x_3 + 20x_4 + 35x_5 &= 0 \\
x_1 + 5x_2 + 15x_3 + 35x_4 + 70x_5 &= 0
\end{aligned}$$

5.3   Use the method of Gaussian elimination to solve the equations

$$\frac{1}{9}x_1 + \frac{4}{5}x_2 + \frac{3}{4}x_3 = 7$$

$$\frac{1}{7}x_1 + x_2 + x_3 - 10$$

$$\frac{1}{6}x_1 - x_2 + 4x_3 = 89$$

working

(a)   with exact arithmetic,

(b)   to four significant figures but without pivoting,

(c)   to four significant figures and with partial pivoting.

Compare the three solutions and discuss any discrepancies.

5.4   (a)   The system of equations

$$\begin{aligned}
2x_1 + 3x_2 + x_3 &= 2 \\
x_1 + x_2 + 2x_3 &= 4 \\
3x_1 + 4x_2 + 3x_3 &= 6
\end{aligned}$$

is singular. Verify that this is the case by attempting to solve the system using Gaussian elimination with partial pivoting.

(b)   Verify that the system of equations

$$\begin{aligned}
2x_1 + 3x_2 + x_3 &= 2 \\
x_1 + x_2 + 2x_3 &= 4 \\
3x_1 + 4x_2 + 3x_3 &= 7
\end{aligned}$$

does not have a solution by attempting to solve the system using Gaussian elimination with partial pivoting.

5.5   Use Doolittle's method to solve the following systems of equations:

(a) $\begin{aligned} 2x_1 + \quad\quad\quad x_3 &= 25 \\ 4x_1 + \quad x_2 + 13x_3 &= 108 \\ 6x_1 + 4x_2 + 42x_3 &= 292 \end{aligned}$

(b) $\begin{aligned} 2x_1 + \quad 4x_2 + \quad 2x_3 + \quad 5x_4 &= 59 \\ 4x_1 + \quad 9x_2 + \quad 2x_3 + 11x_4 &= 118 \\ 2x_1 + \quad\quad\quad\quad\ 2x_3 + \quad 3x_4 &= 33 \\ 8x_1 + 17x_2 - 10x_3 + 26x_4 &= 191 \end{aligned}$

5.6 Verify that the inverse of the matrix

$$L_i = \begin{bmatrix} 1 & 0 & \cdots & 0 & & \cdots & 0 \\ 0 & 1 & \cdots & 0 & & \cdots & 0 \\ \vdots & \vdots & \vdots & \vdots & & \vdots & \vdots \\ 0 & 0 & \cdots & 1 & & \cdots & 0 \\ 0 & 0 & \cdots & -m_{i+1\,i} & & \cdots & 0 \\ \vdots & \vdots & \vdots & \vdots & & \vdots & \vdots \\ 0 & 0 & \cdots & -m_{ni} & & \cdots & 1 \end{bmatrix}$$

is

$$L_i^{-1} = \begin{bmatrix} 1 & 0 & \cdots & 0 & & \cdots & 0 \\ 0 & 1 & \cdots & 0 & & \cdots & 0 \\ \vdots & \vdots & \vdots & \vdots & & \vdots & \vdots \\ 0 & 0 & \cdots & 1 & & \cdots & 0 \\ 0 & 0 & \cdots & m_{i+1\,i} & & \cdots & 0 \\ \vdots & \vdots & \vdots & \vdots & & \vdots & \vdots \\ 0 & 0 & \cdots & m_{ni} & & \cdots & 1 \end{bmatrix}$$

for $i = 1, 2, \ldots, n$.

5.7 Verify that the product

$$L_1^{-1} L_2^{-1} \cdots L_{n-2}^{-1} L_{n-1}^{-1}$$

takes the form

$$L = \begin{bmatrix} 1 & 0 & \cdots & 0 & & \cdots & 0 \\ m_{21} & 1 & \cdots & 0 & & \cdots & 0 \\ \vdots & \vdots & \vdots & \vdots & & \vdots & \vdots \\ m_{i1} & m_{i2} & \cdots & 1 & & \cdots & 0 \\ m_{i+1\,1} & m_{i+1\,2} & \cdots & m_{i+1\,i} & & \cdots & 0 \\ \vdots & \vdots & \vdots & \vdots & & \vdots & \vdots \\ m_{n1} & m_{n2} & \cdots & m_{ni} & & \cdots & 1 \end{bmatrix}$$

5.8 Solve the system of equations in Exercise 5.2a using the permuted version of the *LU* decomposition. Use the *LU* factors obtained to find the solution for the new right-hand-side vector $\mathbf{b} = (10,19,26,30)^{T}$.

5.9 Use the tri-diagonal algorithm to solve the system

$$
\begin{array}{rcl}
2x_1 + x_2 & = & 25 \\
2x_1 + 4x_2 + 3x_3 & = & 61 \\
3x_2 + 6x_3 + 2x_4 & = & 57 \\
3x_3 + 8x_4 + 4x_5 & = & 43 \\
3x_4 + 10x_5 & = & 19
\end{array}
$$

5.10 Show that a permutation matrix, *P*, is its own inverse. Hence describe how the permuted *LU* decomposition technique can be used to find the inverse of a matrix *A*. Thus determine the inverse of the matrix

$$
A = \begin{bmatrix} 1 & 4 & 4 \\ 2 & 9 & 3 \\ 6 & 27 & 10 \end{bmatrix}
$$

5.11 Working correct to three significant figures, solve the following system of equations:

$$
\begin{array}{rcl}
3x_1 - 2x_2 & = & 5 \\
-x_1 + 2x_2 - x_3 & = & 0 \\
- 2x_2 + 3x_3 & = & -1
\end{array}
$$

using the method of

(a)   Jacobi,
(b)   Gauss–Seidel,
(c)   SOR with $\omega = 1.32$.

Programming exercises

5.12 Write a program that uses the subroutine GAUSS of Figure 5.8 to solve the systems of equations in Exercise 5.2 and hence obtain the solutions.

5.13 Write a program that uses the subroutine GAUSSP of Figure 5.11 to solve the systems of equations in Exercise 5.2 and compare the solutions obtained with those from Exercise 5.2.

5.14 Write a program that uses the Doolittle algorithm of Section 5.1.4 to find the *L* and *U* factors of a matrix *A*. Apply the program to find the *L* and *U* factors of the matrix

$$
A = \begin{bmatrix} 2 & 1 & 3 \\ 4 & 3 & 10 \\ 2 & 4 & 17 \end{bmatrix}
$$

Note: *L* and *U* are given in Equation (5.11).

5.15 Use the subroutine TRISOL of Figure 5.20 to solve the following system of equations:

$$
\begin{bmatrix}
4 & -1 & 0 & 0 & 0 \\
-1 & 4 & -1 & 0 & 0 \\
0 & -1 & 4 & -1 & 0 \\
0 & 0 & -1 & 4 & -1 \\
0 & 0 & 0 & -1 & 4
\end{bmatrix} x =
\begin{bmatrix}
100 \\
200 \\
200 \\
200 \\
100
\end{bmatrix}
$$

This system of equations is typical of those encountered in the numerical solution of differential equations.

5.16 The *Hilbert* matrix

$$
H = \begin{bmatrix}
1 & \dfrac{1}{2} & \cdots & \dfrac{1}{n} \\
\dfrac{1}{2} & \dfrac{1}{3} & \cdots & \dfrac{1}{n+1} \\
\vdots & \vdots & \vdots & \vdots \\
\dfrac{1}{n} & \dfrac{1}{n+1} & \cdots & \dfrac{1}{2n-1}
\end{bmatrix}
$$

is classically ill-conditioned. The 4×4 Hilbert matrix is

$$
H_4 = \begin{bmatrix}
1 & 1/2 & 1/3 & 1/4 \\
1/2 & 1/3 & 1/4 & 1/5 \\
1/3 & 1/4 & 1/5 & 1/6 \\
1/4 & 1/5 & 1/6 & 1/7
\end{bmatrix}
$$

Use the subroutines

(a)   GAUSS of Figure 5.8 and

(b)   GAUSSP of Figure 5.11

to solve the system $H_4 x = b$, with $b = (4, 163/60, 21/10, 241/140)^T$ and compare your answers with the exact solution $x = (1,2,3,4)^T$.

5.17 Scale the system of equations given in Exercise 5.16 and solve the scaled system using the subroutine GAUSSP. Compare your solution with that of Exercise 5.16.

5.18 Calculate the inverse of the 4×4 Hilbert matrix and hence solve the system in Exercise 5.16, again comparing your solution with those of Exercises 5.16 and 5.17.

5.19 Use the subroutines JACOBI (Figure 5.24) and GSEIDL (Figure 5.25) to solve the weakly diagonally dominant system of equations

$$
\begin{aligned}
-5x_1 + 2x_2 + 2x_3 &= -8 \\
3x_1 - 7x_2 + 2x_3 &= -7 \\
3x_1 + 4x_2 - 7x_3 &= -11
\end{aligned}
$$

correct to four significant figures.

5.20 Write a subroutine that applies the method of successive over-relaxation, for any specified value of ω, to solve a system of equations $Ax = b$. Write a program that uses this subroutine to solve the system of equations

$$
\begin{aligned}
4x_1 + 3x_2 \qquad &= 24 \\
3x_1 + 4x_2 - x_3 &= 30 \\
-x_2 + 4x_3 &= -24
\end{aligned}
$$

correct to four significant figures. Run this program for a sequence of values of ω between 1 and 2. Sketch a rough graph of the number of iterations used against ω and hence estimate the optimum value of ω. Run your program again with this value.

Chapter 6
Eigenvalues and eigenvectors

Eigenvalues are very important in obtaining a full understanding of many physical systems. For example, the stability of aircraft in flight and the modes of vibration of a bridge are governed by eigenvalues. They are also important in the study of the growth of certain types of population. In a given population, the number of females of a certain age may be represented by the elements of a vector y. Assuming that the population is in the state of age stability, the vector y satisfies an equation of the form

$$Ay = \lambda y$$

where A is a square matrix and λ is a positive real number which determines whether or not the population increases. If $\lambda > 1$ the total population increases, if $\lambda = 1$ it remains the same, and if $\lambda < 1$ it decreases.

For a given matrix A there are, in fact, only a limited number of values of λ which lead to a non-trivial solution. These values are known as the **eigenvalues** of the matrix A and the corresponding solution vectors are known as the **eigenvectors** of A. Unless A is very small, numerical methods have to be used to evaluate its eigenvalues and eigenvectors. Before we can describe any of these methods, some elementary theory is required.

6.1 Basic theory

The system of equations above is a particular case of the general system of linear equations

$$
\begin{aligned}
a_{11}x_1 + a_{12}x_2 + \cdots + a_{1n}x_n &= \lambda x_1 \\
a_{21}x_1 + a_{22}x_2 + \cdots + a_{2n}x_n &= \lambda x_2 \\
&\vdots \\
a_{n1}x_1 + a_{n2}x_2 + \cdots + a_{nn}x_n &= \lambda x_n
\end{aligned}
$$

or

$$
Ax = \lambda x \tag{6.1}
$$

where λ is a constant. Note that Equation (6.1) will have a non-trivial solution only if

$$
p(\lambda) = \det(A - \lambda I) = 0 \tag{6.2}
$$

Equation (6.2) is a polynomial equation of degree n in λ and so it will have n roots $\lambda_1, \lambda_2, \ldots, \lambda_n$ which may be real or complex. These roots are known as the **eigenvalues** of the matrix A and the function $p(\lambda)$ is known as the **characteristic polynomial**. Any non-zero vector x that satisfies Equation (6.1) is known as an **eigenvector** of the matrix A corresponding to the eigenvalue λ.

For example, the eigenvalues of the matrix

$$
A = \begin{bmatrix} 1 & 2 \\ 2 & 1 \end{bmatrix}
$$

are the roots of the equation

$$
p(\lambda) = \begin{vmatrix} 1 - \lambda & 2 \\ 2 & 1 - \lambda \end{vmatrix} = 0
$$

Thus, in this case, the quadratic equation

$$
(1 - \lambda)^2 - 4 = 0
$$

can be solved to obtain the eigenvalues

$$
\lambda_1 = 3 \quad \text{and} \quad \lambda_2 = -1
$$

To find the eigenvector x_1 corresponding to the eigenvalue λ_1, let

$$
x_1 = \begin{bmatrix} \alpha \\ \beta \end{bmatrix}
$$

Then, from Equation (6.1),

$$A x_1 = \lambda_1 x_1$$

or

$$\begin{bmatrix} 1 & 2 \\ 2 & 1 \end{bmatrix} \begin{bmatrix} \alpha \\ \beta \end{bmatrix} = 3 \begin{bmatrix} \alpha \\ \beta \end{bmatrix}$$

Thus α and β must satisfy the equations

$$\alpha + 2\beta = 3\alpha$$
$$2\alpha + \beta = 3\beta$$

and both simplify to

$$\alpha = \beta$$

Hence x_1 can be represented by any vector of the form $(\alpha, \alpha)^{\mathrm{T}}$. Similarly, we can show that the eigenvector x_2, corresponding to the eigenvalue $\lambda_2 = -1$, is a vector of the form $(\alpha, -\alpha)^{\mathrm{T}}$.

This example shows that each eigenvector is unique only to within a constant multiplier. In fact, this is a general result because

$$A x = \lambda x$$

and so

$$A(\sigma x) = \lambda(\sigma x)$$

for any constant σ. Hence, to impose a unique form for an eigenvector, it is convenient to normalize it so that either

(1)   the element of largest modulus is unity, or
(2)   the square root of the sum of the squares of the elements is unity.

Using the first method, the eigenvectors in the above example would be written

$$x_1 = \begin{bmatrix} 1 \\ 1 \end{bmatrix} \quad \text{and} \quad x_2 = \begin{bmatrix} 1 \\ -1 \end{bmatrix}$$

but using the second method they would be written

$$x_1 = \begin{bmatrix} 1/\sqrt{2} \\ 1/\sqrt{2} \end{bmatrix} \quad \text{and} \quad x_2 = \begin{bmatrix} 1/\sqrt{2} \\ -1/\sqrt{2} \end{bmatrix}$$

Unfortunately, because of problems associated with the solution of high order polynomial equations, the direct method used above for calculating the eigenvalues of a 2×2 matrix is not suitable for obtaining those of large matrices. However, before discussing alternative methods, some theorems necessary for the study of eigenvalues will be given. Proofs can be found in any standard text on linear algebra, for example Gourlay and Watson (1973), Wilkinson (1965) or Golub and Van Loan (1983).

Definition 6.1

A set of vectors $\{y_1, y_2, \ldots, y_n\}$ is said to be **orthogonal** if

$$y_i^T y_j = 0$$

for all $i \neq j$. If, in addition, $y_i^T y_i = 1$, for all $i = 1, 2, \ldots, n$, then the set is said to be **orthonormal**.

Definition 6.2

An $n \times n$ matrix P is said to be orthogonal if

$$P^T P = I$$

Note that this implies

$$P^T = P^{-1}$$

and so the inverse of an orthogonal matrix is simply its own transpose.

Definition 6.3

Two $n \times n$ matrices, A and B, are said to be **similar** if there exists a non-singular matrix S such that

$$S^{-1} A S = B$$

Theorem 6.1

A symmetric $n \times n$ matrix with n distinct eigenvalues has n linearly independent eigenvectors.

Theorem 6.2

The number of linearly independent eigenvectors associated with an eigenvalue of multiplicity m is m or less.

Theorem 6.3

The eigenvalues of a symmetric matrix are real.

Theorem 6.4

If A is a symmetric matrix then there exists an orthogonal matrix, P, such that

$$P^{-1}AP = D$$

where D is a diagonal matrix consisting of the eigenvalues of A.

A direct result of this theorem is Corollary 6.1.

Corollary 6.1

If A is a symmetric matrix, then there exist n eigenvectors of A which form an orthonormal set.

Theorem 6.5

Let A and B be similar matrices such that $S^{-1}AS = B$ for some non-singular matrix S. Let λ be an eigenvalue of A and x be its associated eigenvector. Then λ is also an eigenvalue of B and the associated eigenvector is $S^{-1}x$.

Theorem 6.6   (Gershgorin's Circle Theorem)

Let A be an $n \times n$ matrix and let C_i be the disc in the complex plane with centre a_{ii} and radius

$$r_i = \sum_{\substack{j=1 \\ j \neq i}}^{n} |a_{ij}|$$

i.e. C_i consists of all points z such that

$$|z - a_{ii}| \leq \sum_{\substack{j=1 \\ j \neq i}}^{n} |a_{ij}|$$

Let D be the union of all the discs C_i $\{i = 1, 2, \ldots, n\}$; then all the eigenvalues of A lie within D.

Theorem 6.6 enables us to locate the eigenvalues of a matrix approximately. For example, consider the matrix

$$A = \begin{bmatrix} 1 & 2 & -1 \\ 2 & 7 & 0 \\ -1 & 0 & -5 \end{bmatrix}$$

This is a symmetric matrix and so, by Theorem 6.3, all its eigenvalues are real. For this matrix

C_1 is the disc with centre $(1,0)$ and radius 3
C_2 is the disc with centre $(7,0)$ and radius 2
C_3 is the disc with centre $(-5,0)$ and radius 1

and so any eigenvalue of A must be in one of the intervals

$[-2,4]$ $[5,9]$ or $[-6,-4]$

Thus all the eigenvalues are in the interval $[-6, 9]$; in fact, they are -5.1712, 0.5589 and 7.6123 when rounded to four decimal places.

Now we consider some numerical methods that enable us to calculate eigenvalues and eigenvectors without having to solve Equation (6.2). To simplify the analysis, we shall concentrate on symmetric matrices because, from Theorem 6.3, all their eigenvalues are real.

6.2 Methods for a single eigenvalue

It is frequently the case that we require only one eigenvalue or eigenvector of the matrix A, for example, in the section on the convergence of iterative methods in Chapter 5, we were interested in the size of the eigenvalue of maximum modulus. In this section we describe techniques to determine a single eigenvalue and we shall assume it to be simple. (For a discussion of multiple eigenvalues, see Gourlay and Watson, 1973, p. 40.)

6.2.1 The power method

The power method is an iterative technique for finding the *dominant* eigenvalue of a matrix A and so it is assumed that the eigenvalues are ordered by size such that

$$|\lambda_1| > |\lambda_2| \geqslant \cdots \geqslant |\lambda_n|$$

It is also assumed that the eigenvectors of A are linearly independent and that they are normalized so that their largest element is unity.

We begin by choosing a column vector $z^{(0)}$ whose largest element is unity (for example, if A is a 3×3 matrix we could choose $z^{(0)}$ to be $(0,1,0)^T$ or $(1,1,1)^T$ or even $(7/17,-9/123,1)^T$), then we calculate

$$y^{(k)} = Az^{(k-1)}$$
$$z^{(k)} = y^{(k)}/\mu_k$$

for $k = 1,2, \ldots$, where μ_k is the element of $y^{(k)}$ with largest modulus. We will show later that

$$z^{(k)} \rightarrow x_1$$

and

$$\mu_k \rightarrow \lambda_1$$

as $k \rightarrow \infty$, but first we will illustrate the technique by calculating the dominant eigenvalue and corresponding eigenvector of the matrix

$$A = \begin{bmatrix} -2 & 1 & 0 \\ 1 & -2 & 1 \\ 0 & 1 & -2 \end{bmatrix} \tag{6.3}$$

Starting with $z^{(0)} = (0,1,0)^T$, we obtain

$$y^{(1)} = Az^{(0)} = \begin{bmatrix} -2 & 1 & 0 \\ 1 & -2 & 1 \\ 0 & 1 & -2 \end{bmatrix}\begin{bmatrix} 0 \\ 1 \\ 0 \end{bmatrix} = \begin{bmatrix} 1 \\ -2 \\ 1 \end{bmatrix}$$

$$z^{(1)} = y^{(1)}/\mu_1 = \begin{bmatrix} 1 \\ -2 \\ 1 \end{bmatrix}/(-2) = \begin{bmatrix} -1/2 \\ 1 \\ -1/2 \end{bmatrix}$$

$$y^{(2)} = Az^{(1)} = (2,-3,2)^T$$
$$z^{(2)} = y^{(2)}/\mu_2 = (-2/3,1,-2/3)^T$$

and so on. It is convenient to set down the calculations in tabular form as shown in Table 6.1.

The final entry in this table shows that, to four significant figures, $\lambda_1 = -3.414$ and $x_1 = (-0.7071, 1, -0.7071)^T$. The mathematical algorithm for the power method is given in Figure 6.1.

Table 6.1 Power iterations for matrix (6.3).

k	$\mathbf{y}^{(k)^{\mathrm{T}}}$			μ_k	$\mathbf{z}^{(k)^{\mathrm{T}}}$		
0					0	1	0
1	1	-2	1	-2	$-1/2$	1	$-1/2$
2	2	-3	2	-3	$-2/3$	1	$-2/3$
3	7/3	$-10/3$	7/3	$-10/3$	-0.7000	1	-0.7000
4	2.4000	-3.4000	2.4000	-3.4000	-0.7059	1	-0.7059
5	2.4118	-3.4118	2.4118	-3.4118	-0.7069	1	-0.7069
6	2.4138	-3.4138	2.4138	-3.4138	-0.7071	1	-0.7071
7	2.4142	-3.4142	2.4142	-3.4142	-0.7071	1	-0.7071

Given A, $\mathbf{z}^{(0)}$
Repeat (*for* $k = 1.2, \ldots$)
  Set $\mathbf{y}^{(k)} = A\mathbf{z}^{(k-1)}$
  μ_k = *the element of* $\mathbf{y}^{(k)}$ *with maximum modulus*
  $\mathbf{z}^{(k)} = \mathbf{y}^{(k)}/\mu_k$
Until converged

Figure 6.1 Algorithm for the power method.

Analysis of the power method

It has been assumed that the eigenvectors of A are linearly independent and so the initial vector $\mathbf{z}^{(0)}$ may be expressed in the form

$$\mathbf{z}^{(0)} = \alpha_1 \mathbf{x}_1 + \alpha_2 \mathbf{x}_2 + \cdots + \alpha_n \mathbf{x}_n$$
$$= \sum_{i=1}^{n} \alpha_i \mathbf{x}_i$$

where the α_i $\{i = 1,2, \ldots ,n\}$ are constants, not all zero. Substituting this form for $\mathbf{z}^{(0)}$ into the iteration

$$\mathbf{y}^{(k)} = A\mathbf{z}^{(k-1)}$$

with $k = 1$ gives

$$\mathbf{y}^{(1)} = A\mathbf{z}^{(0)}$$
$$= A\alpha_1 \mathbf{x}_1 + A\alpha_2 \mathbf{x}_2 + \cdots + A\alpha_n \mathbf{x}_n$$
$$= \alpha_1 A\mathbf{x}_1 + \alpha_2 A\mathbf{x}_2 + \cdots + \alpha_n A\mathbf{x}_n$$

and, using Equation (6.1), this may be written

$$y^{(1)} = \alpha_1\lambda_1x_1 + \alpha_2\lambda_2x_2 + \cdots + \alpha_n\lambda_nx_n$$

Thus

$$z^{(1)} = \frac{y^{(1)}}{\mu_1} = \frac{\sum\limits_{i=1}^{n} \alpha_i\lambda_ix_i}{\mu_1}$$

Similarly

$$y^{(2)} = Az^{(1)} = \frac{\sum\limits_{i=1}^{n} \alpha_i\lambda_iAx_i}{\mu_1}$$

$$= \frac{\sum\limits_{i=1}^{n} \alpha_i\lambda_i^2x_i}{\mu_1}$$

from which

$$z^{(2)} = \frac{y^{(2)}}{\mu_2} = \frac{\sum\limits_{i=1}^{n} \alpha_i\lambda_i^2x_i}{\mu_1\mu_2}$$

and so on. In general,

$$z^{(k)} = \frac{\sum\limits_{i=1}^{n} \alpha_i\lambda_i^kx_i}{\mu_1\mu_2\cdots\mu_k}$$

$$= \frac{\lambda_1^k\left(\alpha_1x_1 + \alpha_2\left(\frac{\lambda_2}{\lambda_1}\right)^k x_2 + \cdots + \alpha_n\left(\frac{\lambda_n}{\lambda_1}\right)^k x_n\right)}{\mu_1\mu_2\cdots\mu_k} \tag{6.4}$$

Now $|\lambda_i|/|\lambda_1| < 1$ $\{i = 2,3, \ldots ,n\}$ and so it follows that, as k tends to infinity,

$$z^{(k)} \rightarrow \frac{\alpha_1\lambda_1^k}{\mu_1\mu_2\cdots\mu_k} x_1$$

However, since both $z^{(k)}$ and x_1 are normalized so that their largest element is unity,

$$z^{(k)} \rightarrow x_1 \qquad \text{as } k \rightarrow \infty$$

It also follows that

$$\frac{\alpha_1 \lambda_1^k}{\mu_1 \mu_2 \ldots \mu_k} \rightarrow 1 \qquad \text{as } k \rightarrow \infty$$

and this can be rewritten as

$$\mu_1 \mu_2 \ldots \mu_k \rightarrow \alpha_1 \lambda_1^k \qquad \text{as } k \rightarrow \infty. \tag{6.5}$$

Similarly,

$$\mu_1 \mu_2 \ldots \mu_k \mu_{k+1} \rightarrow \alpha_1 \lambda_1^{k+1} \qquad \text{as } k \rightarrow \infty \tag{6.6}$$

and dividing (6.6) by (6.5) gives the result that

$$\mu_{k+1} \rightarrow \lambda_1 \qquad \text{as } k \rightarrow \infty.$$

It is possible that the initial vector $z^{(0)}$ may be *deficient* in x_1 (i.e. $\alpha_1 = 0$). In this case, the result in (6.6) no longer holds and, if $\alpha_2 \neq 0$, successive values μ_k will tend to λ_2 instead. However, after many iterations, rounding errors can come to the rescue because they will introduce a small multiple of x_1 into the approximation and then subsequent approximations will converge to the dominant eigenvector as required. An example illustrating this phenomenon is given in the exercises at the end of this chapter.

Program construction

The power method is slightly different from the iterative procedures discussed in previous chapters in that it produces *two* items of interest – an eigenvalue and an eigenvector. Therefore we must decide to which of these our program should apply the convergence test.

If the eigenvector were used to detect convergence, the test would have to be applied to each element and would be similar to those for the iterative methods of Chapter 5. However, in most cases, it is the eigenvalue rather than the eigenvector which is of particular interest and so we shall test the eigenvalue. During the early stages of the iteration, there is a remote possibility that the elements of $y^{(k)}$ and $y^{(k+1)}$ with maximum modulus may have the *same* magnitude but be situated at *different* positions within the vector. In this event, the eigenvalue test would indicate convergence prematurely. The subroutine plan of Figure 6.2 makes allowance for this possibility by using *oldi* and *newi* to record and compare the position of the element of maximum modulus in any two consecutive approximations to the vector y.

Given: A, z, *tolerance*,
        maximum number of iterations
Set: *new*μ = 0
      newi = 0
repeat (*not exceeding max iterations*)

   Set vector: $y = A.z$

   Set: *old*μ = *new*μ
        oldi   = *newi*
        newμ = 0
   for i = 1,2, . . . ,n
     if $|y_i| > |new\mu|$ **then**
       Set: *new*μ = y_i
             newi = i

   for i = 1,2, . . . ,n
     Set: $z_i = y_i/new\mu$

   if $|new\mu - old\mu| \leq |old\mu|$ · *tolerance* **and** *newi* = *oldi* **then**
     Note: 'converged'
until 'converged' (*or limit on number of iterations reached*)

if 'converged' **then**
   Record: λ_1, x_1, *number of iterations used*
if 'limit' **then**
   Record: *last approximation to* λ_1 *and* x_1

Figure 6.2   Plan of subroutine for the power method.

The subroutine follows immediately from the plan and is given in Figure 6.3. Note that the array Y is included in the subroutine heading so that it can be dimensioned dynamically. The matrix–vector multiplication Az has been achieved by calling the subroutine MATVEC of Figure 2.7.

The analysis showed that the eigenvalue produced may not be the dominant one. It is therefore recommended that the program be run with more than one starting vector for a given matrix in case the first choice happens to be deficient in x_1.

6.2.2 Acceleration techniques

From the analysis of the power method, it can be seen that the rate of convergence is governed largely by the quantity $|\lambda_2|/|\lambda_1|$. Thus, if the magnitude of λ_2 is almost as great as that of λ_1, the procedure is likely to be slow to converge. For example, rounded to four significant figures, the eigenvalues of

Figure 6.3 Subroutine for the power method.

```
      SUBROUTINE POWER (SIZE,N,A,Z,TOL,MAXITS,
                        STATUS,LAMBDA,X,NOOFIT,LASTMU, Y)
      INTEGER   CONVGD,COUNT,I,LIMIT,MAXITS,N,
     *          NEWI,NOOFIT,OLDI,SIZE,STATUS
      REAL      LAMBDA,LASTMU,NEWMU,OLDMU,TOL
      PARAMETER (CONVGD=0,LIMIT=1)
      REAL      A(SIZE,SIZE),X(N),Y(N),Z(N)
      INTRINSIC ABS
      EXTERNAL  MATVEC

      NEWMU=0
      NEWI =0

      DO 10, COUNT=1, MAXITS

        CALL MATVEC (SIZE,N,A,Z, Y)

        OLDMU=NEWMU
        OLDI =NEWI
        NEWMU=0
        DO 20, I=1,N
          IF (ABS(Y(I)).GT.ABS(NEWMU)) THEN
            NEWMU=Y(I)
            NEWI =I
          END IF
20      CONTINUE

        DO 30, I=1,N
          Z(I)=Y(I)/NEWMU
30      CONTINUE

        IF ( (ABS(NEWMU-OLDMU) .LE. ABS(OLDMU)*TOL)
     *       .AND. (NEWI.EQ.OLDI) ) THEN
          STATUS=CONVGD
          GO TO 11
        END IF

10    CONTINUE
      STATUS=LIMIT

11    DO 40, I=1,N
        X(I)=Z(I)
40    CONTINUE
```

```
IF (STATUS.EQ.CONVGD) THEN
   LAMBDA=NEWMU
   NOOFIT=COUNT
END IF

IF (STATUS.EQ.LIMIT) THEN
   LASTMU=NEWMU
END IF

END
```

Figure 6.3 *cont.*

Table 6.2 Power iterations for matrix (6.7).

k	$y^{(k)^{\mathrm{T}}}$			μ_k	$z^{(k)^{\mathrm{T}}}$		
0					0	1	0
1	-6	3	4	-6	1	-0.5000	-0.6667
2	3.6667	-10.1667	5	-10.1667	-0.3607	1	-0.4918
3	-9.9016	3.1967	3.6721	-9.9016	1	-0.3228	-0.3709
4	4.0828	-8.4520	4.8212	-8.4520	-0.4831	1	-0.5704
5	-10.7843	3.6166	3.2960	-10.7843	1	-0.3354	-0.3056

the matrix

$$A = \begin{bmatrix} 4 & -6 & 5 \\ -6 & 3 & 4 \\ 5 & 4 & -3 \end{bmatrix} \tag{6.7}$$

are 9.622, -9.120 and 3.498 and so, in this case, the rate of convergence is governed by the factor $9.120/9.622 \simeq 0.95$. Thus, unless we were very fortunate in the choice of starting vector, many iterations of the power method would be required to evaluate λ_1 and x_1 accurately. Of course, in practice, this information is not available in advance although, after a few iterations such as those in Table 6.2, it soon becomes apparent that the iteration is likely to be slow to converge. In fact, if we continued these calculations until the results are obtained correct to four significant figures, we would have to perform 216 iterations!

Fortunately, various techniques are available to accelerate the rate of convergence of the power iterations. Those discussed below are illustrated using matrix (6.7); in each case we start the iteration from $(0,1,0)^{\mathrm{T}}$ and evaluate λ_1 and

x_1 correct to four significant figures. The subroutine of Figure 6.3 can be modified to incorporate any of the following acceleration techniques and this exercise is left for the reader.

Aitken's Δ^2 process

It can be shown that the power method is a first-order iterative procedure and so the Aitken formula of Chapter 4 can be applied to the elements of any three consecutive iterates $y^{(k)}$, $y^{(k+1)}$ and $y^{(k+2)}$. Thus, for example, if we apply Equation (4.17b) to the $y^{(1)}$, $y^{(2)}$ and $y^{(3)}$ of Table 6.2, we obtain a new vector, y^*, whose elements are given by

$$y_1^* = -9.9016 - \frac{(-9.9016 - 3.6667)^2}{-9.9016 - 2(3.6667) - 6} = -1.9783$$

$$y_2^* = 3.1967 - \frac{(3.1967 - (-10.1667))^2}{3.1967 - 2(-10.1667) + 3} = -3.5345$$

$$y_3^* = 3.6721 - \frac{(3.6721 - 5)^2}{3.6721 - 2(5) + 4} = 4.4296$$

We rename this vector $y^{(4)}$ and perform two further iterations of the power method, followed by another application of Aitken's method and so on. Some of these calculations are displayed in Table 6.3 in which the Aitken entries are marked with an asterisk. Using this acceleration technique we obtain the required results after only 43 iterations of the power method together with 21 applications of Aitken's formula. Thus, for our test example, the number of iterations required has been reduced by over 70%.

Alternatively, Aitken's formula could be applied to the z vectors instead of the y vectors. Note that, after a few iterations, the same element of $z^{(k)}$ will always be unity and so only the remaining $n - 1$ elements from this stage need be predicted.

The reader should be aware that, if the initial vector z_0 is deficient in x_1, this accelerating procedure may suppress the effects of rounding errors to such an extent that they are not able to introduce components of x_1 into the calculations. In this case, the power iteration will converge to the subdominant eigenvalue and its associated eigenvector. An example illustrating this phenomenon is given as an exercise at the end of this chapter.

Shift of origin

Rather than apply the power iteration to the matrix A, it can be applied to the related matrix

$$B = A - pI$$

Table 6.3 Power iterations with Aitken's formula for matrix (6.7).

k	$y^{(k)^T}$			μ_k	$z^{(k)^T}$		
0					0	1	0
1	−6	3	4	−6	1	−0.5000	−0.6667
2	3.6667	−10.1667	5.0000	−10.1667	−0.3607	1	−0.4918
3	−9.9016	3.1967	3.6721	−9.9016			
*4	−1.9783	−3.5345	4.4296	4.4296	−0.4466	−0.7979	1
5	8.0012	4.2858	−8.4248	−8.4248	−0.9497	−0.5087	1
6	4.2534	8.1722	−9.7835	−9.7835			
*7	5.2766	12.0114	−9.9441	12.0114	0.4393	1	−0.8279
8	−8.3822	−2.9474	8.6802	8.6802	−0.9657	−0.3396	1
9	3.1746	8.7754	−9.1866	−9.1866			
*10	−2.1221	3.6249	−0.4386	3.6249	−0.5854	1	−0.1210
⋮	⋮	⋮	⋮	⋮	⋮	⋮	⋮
*64	9.6220	−7.9338	1.2974	9.6220	1	−0.8246	0.1348
65	9.6215	−7.9343	1.2973	9.6215	1	−0.8246	0.1348

where p is a constant. Clearly the eigenvectors of the matrix B are the same as those of A because

$$Ax = \lambda x$$

and so

$$\begin{aligned} Bx &= (A - pI)x \\ &= Ax - px \\ &= \lambda x - px \\ &= (\lambda - p)x \end{aligned} \tag{6.8}$$

From Equation (6.8), the eigenvalues of B are $\lambda_i - p \{i = 1, 2, \ldots, n\}$. Thus, if we calculate the dominant eigenvalue and associated eigenvector of the matrix B, then we have x_1 immediately and can compute λ_1 very easily. The advantage of this approach is that there are likely to be values of p for which the power iteration will converge more rapidly for B than for A. For example, taking $p = -3$ with the test matrix (6.7) gives

$$B = A - (-3)I = \begin{bmatrix} 7 & -6 & 5 \\ -6 & 6 & 4 \\ 5 & 4 & 0 \end{bmatrix}$$

and the power iteration for B converges to the required accuracy after only 16

Table 6.4 Power iterations with shift of origin for matrix (6.7).

k	$y^{(k)^\mathrm{T}}$			μ_k	$z^{(k)^\mathrm{T}}$		
0					0	1	0
1	-6	6	4	-6	1	-1	-0.6667
2	9.6667	-14.6667	1	-14.6667	-0.6591	1	-0.0682
3	-10.9545	9.6818	0.7045	-10.9545	1	-0.8838	-0.0643
4	11.9813	-11.5602	1.4647	11.9813	1	-0.9648	0.1223
5	13.4003	-11.3001	1.1406	13.4003	1	-0.8433	0.0851
$\vdots$	$\vdots$	$\vdots$	$\vdots$	$\vdots$	$\vdots$	$\vdots$	$\vdots$
16	12.6219	-10.4092	1.7012	12.6219	1	-0.8247	0.1348
17	12.6221	-10.4090	1.7012	12.6221	1	-0.8247	0.1348

iterations. This compares with 216 iterations for A, representing a saving of over 93% in computational effort. Some of the computations are displayed in Table 6.4. The last entry in this table gives the required eigenvector $x_1 = (1,-0.8247,0.1348)^\mathrm{T}$ immediately and it is a simple matter to evaluate the eigenvalue

$$\lambda_1 = 12.622 + (-3) = 9.622$$

In this case, because we already know all the eigenvalues of A, we can see why this choice of p is so effective. The eigenvalues of the matrix B are 12.622, -6.120 and 6.498 and so the rate of convergence of the power iterations for the matrix B is governed by the ratio $6.498/12.622 \simeq 0.51$ whereas the factor for A is 0.95. In practice, it is usually possible to estimate a suitable value of p after just a few iterations of the power method. If necessary, the value can be adjusted as the iteration progresses.

Rayleigh quotient

When the eigenvalue alone is required, the formula

$$q^{(k+1)} = \frac{y^{(k+1)^\mathrm{T}} z^{(k)}}{z^{(k)^\mathrm{T}} z^{(k)}} \qquad k = 0, \ 1, \ 2, \ 3, \ \dots$$

can be used in conjunction with the power method to give a sequence of approximations $q^{(1)}, q^{(2)}, \dots$, which converges more rapidly to λ_1. This allows the power iteration to be terminated prematurely. For example, applying Rayleigh's formula to the entries in Table 6.2 gives

$$q^{(1)} = \frac{y^{(1)^\mathrm{T}} z^{(0)}}{z^{(0)^\mathrm{T}} z^{(0)}} = \frac{(-6,3,4)(0,1,0)^\mathrm{T}}{(0,1,0)(0,1,0)^\mathrm{T}} = 3$$

$$q^{(2)} = \frac{y^{(2)^T}z^{(1)}}{z^{(1)^T}z^{(1)}} = \frac{(3.6667,-10.1667,5)(1,-0.5,-0.6667)^T}{(1,-0.5,-0.6667)(1,-0.5,-0.6667)^T} = 3.1967$$

$$q^{(3)} = 3.6166$$

$$q^{(4)} = 4.0450$$

$$\vdots$$

Using this technique, the iterations started in Table 6.2 could be terminated after only 95 iterations if the eigenvalue alone was required.

6.2.3 Deflation

Having calculated good approximations to λ_1 and x_1, we may be interested in calculating the subdominant eigenvalue λ_2. Assuming that λ_2 is unique, this can be done by applying the power method to a matrix B which has been constructed to have eigenvalues $0, \lambda_2, \lambda_3, \ldots, \lambda_n$. The process of producing B from A is known as **deflation**. Various deflation techniques are available but only one will be described here.

Denoting the position of the unit element of x_1 by r and adopting the notation

$$a_r^T = (a_{r1}, a_{r2}, \ldots, a_{rn})$$

to represent row r of A, *Wielandt's* method produces the matrix

$$B = A - x_1 a_r^T$$

We illustrate the method by deflating matrix (6.3)

$$A = \begin{bmatrix} -2 & 1 & 0 \\ 1 & -2 & 1 \\ 0 & 1 & -2 \end{bmatrix}$$

for which $\lambda_1 = -3.4142$ and $x_1 = (-0.7071,1,-0.7071)^T$, when rounded to four decimal places. Note that a unit element occurs as the second component of x_1; hence, $r = 2$ and so the row of A to be used in the deflation process is

$$a_2^T = (1,-2,1)$$

Thus

$$B = \begin{bmatrix} -2 & 1 & 0 \\ 1 & -2 & 1 \\ 0 & 1 & -2 \end{bmatrix} - \begin{bmatrix} -0.7071 \\ 1 \\ -0.7071 \end{bmatrix} (1,-2,1)$$

$$= \begin{bmatrix} -2 & 1 & 0 \\ 1 & -2 & 1 \\ 0 & 1 & -2 \end{bmatrix} - \begin{bmatrix} -0.7071 & 1.4142 & -0.7071 \\ 1 & -2 & 1 \\ -0.7071 & 1.4142 & -0.7071 \end{bmatrix}$$

$$= \begin{bmatrix} -1.2929 & -0.4142 & 0.7071 \\ 0 & 0 & 0 \\ 0.7071 & -0.4142 & -1.2929 \end{bmatrix}$$

In this case symmetry of the matrix has been preserved, but this is not a general feature of this type of deflation; it occurs here because x_1 is symmetric.

Note that row r of B consists entirely of zeros; this is always the case with Wielandt's method. Consequently, if λ is a non-zero eigenvalue of B and the associated eigenvector is denoted by v, then the element in position r must be zero in order to satisfy the equation $Bv = \lambda v$. Thus, column r of B makes no contribution to the product Bv and so B can be replaced by the $(n - 1) \times (n - 1)$ matrix B^* obtained by deleting the rth row and column. B^* will have eigenvalues $\lambda_2, \lambda_3, \ldots, \lambda_n$.

In general, the power method would be applied to B^* to determine λ_2 but, in the above example,

$$B^* = \begin{bmatrix} -1.2929 & 0.7071 \\ 0.7071 & -1.2929 \end{bmatrix}$$

and, because this is only a 2×2 matrix, both of its eigenvalues can be obtained from the characteristic polynomial

$$p(\lambda) = (-1.2929 - \lambda)^2 - (0.7071)^2$$

This gives $\lambda_2 = -2$ and $\lambda_3 = -0.5858$. The eigenvectors of the original matrix A are related to those of the matrix B^* and can be obtained if required (see Burden and Faires, 1985).

In theory, deflation could be used in conjunction with the power method to evaluate all the eigenvalues and eigenvectors of a matrix but in practice this procedure is very prone to the accumulation of rounding errors. When all the eigenvalues and eigenvectors are required, methods that make use of similarity transformations are to be preferred. These will be the subject of Section 6.3.

6.2.4 The inverse power method

We have seen how the power method can be used to evaluate the dominant eigenvalue λ_1 and associated eigenvector x_1 of an $n \times n$ matrix A. If the eigenvalues of A are such that

$$|\lambda_1| \geq |\lambda_2| \geq \cdots |\lambda_{n-1}| > |\lambda_n|$$

then the same method can be used to evaluate the eigenvalue, λ_n, of *least* modulus together with its associated eigenvector x_n. From Equation (6.1),

$$Ax = \lambda x$$

If we multiply this equation through by A^{-1}, we obtain

$$x = \lambda A^{-1}x$$

from which

$$A^{-1}x = \frac{1}{\lambda}x$$

Hence, the matrix A^{-1} has the same eigenvectors as the matrix A but its eigenvalues are the *reciprocals* of those of A. In particular, the dominant eigenvalue of A^{-1} is $1/\lambda_n$. Thus, if we apply the power method to the inverse of A, we will obtain $1/\lambda_n$ and x_n; then it is a trivial matter to compute the required eigenvalue λ_n.

This idea can be extended to provide a scheme for finding that eigenvalue of A closest to a given value, p; we will denote this eigenvalue by λ^* and the associated eigenvector by x^* and will assume that λ^* is a simple eigenvalue. In section 6.2.1 we saw that the eigenvectors of the matrix

$$B = A - pI \quad (p \text{ constant})$$

are the same as those of A but that the eigenvalues are $\lambda_i - p$ $\{i = 1,2, \ldots ,n\}$. Hence, the eigenvectors of the matrix B^{-1} must also be the same as those of A but its eigenvalues are $1/(\lambda_i - p)$ $\{i = 1,2, \ldots ,n\}$. In particular, the dominant eigenvalue of B^{-1} is $1/(\lambda^* - p)$. Thus, if we apply the power method to the matrix

$$B^{-1} = (A - pI)^{-1} \tag{6.9}$$

we obtain the eigenvector x^* together with the value of $1/(\lambda^* - p)$; then it is a simple task to evaluate the required eigenvalue λ^*. Note that we can obtain λ_n and x_n by setting $p = 0$ in Equation (6.9).

In practice, the procedure is modified so that the inverse of the matrix B need not be determined. Rather than apply the power method directly to B^{-1} using the iterative procedure

$$y^{(k)} = B^{-1}z^{(k-1)}$$
$$z^{(k)} = y^{(k)}/\mu_k$$

Given A, p, z⁽⁰⁾

Set $B = A - pI$

Repeat (for $k = 1,2, \ldots$)

  Solve $By^{(k)} = z^{(k-1)}$

  Set μ_k = the element of $y^{(k)}$ with largest modulus

  $z^{(k)} = y^{(k)}/\mu_k$

Until converged

Figure 6.4 Algorithm for the inverse power method.

(for $k = 1,2 \ldots$), $y^{(k)}$ is computed by solving the equation

$$By^{(k)} = z^{(k-1)} \tag{6.10}$$

from which

$$z^{(k)} = y^{(k)}/\mu_k$$

as before. The modified algorithm is given in Figure 6.4.

Using this algorithm, Equation (6.10) will have to be solved many times (for $k = 1,2, \ldots$) and so LU decomposition provides a particularly suitable method of solution. For example, consider the matrix

$$A = \begin{bmatrix} 2 & -3 & 0 \\ -3 & 1 & 1 \\ 0 & 1 & 2 \end{bmatrix} \tag{6.11}$$

Using Theorem 6.6, it is easily shown that all the eigenvalues of A are in the interval $[-3,5]$. To illustrate the use of the inverse power method, we calculate the eigenvalue closest to -2 and its associated eigenvector. We begin by forming the matrix

$$B = A - (-2)I = \begin{bmatrix} 4 & -3 & 0 \\ -3 & 3 & 1 \\ 0 & 1 & 4 \end{bmatrix}$$

and, using the initial approximation $z^{(0)} = (1,1,1)^{\mathrm{T}}$, to solve the equation

$$By^{(1)} = (1,1,1)^{\mathrm{T}} \tag{6.12}$$

Factorizing B into the product of two triangular matrices L and U gives

$$B = LU = \begin{bmatrix} 1 & 0 & 0 \\ -3/4 & 1 & 0 \\ 0 & 4/3 & 1 \end{bmatrix} \begin{bmatrix} 4 & -3 & 0 \\ 0 & 3/4 & 1 \\ 0 & 0 & 8/3 \end{bmatrix}$$

Table 6.5 Inverse power iterations for matrix (6.11).

k	$y^{(k)^T}$			μ_k	$z^{(k)^T}$		
0					1	1	1
1	5/2	3	−1/2	3	5/6	1	−1/6
2	65/24	10/3	−7/8	3.3333	0.8125	1	−0.2625
3	2.7156	3.3500	−0.9031	3.3500	0.8106	1	−0.2696
4	2.7157	3.3507	−0.9051	3.3507	0.8105	1	−0.2701
5	2.7157	3.3508	−0.9052	3.3508	0.8105	1	−0.2701

and then Equation (6.12) becomes

$$LUy^{(1)} = (1,1,1)^T \tag{6.13}$$

Following the procedure described in Section 5.1.4, we define

$$Uy^{(1)} = v^{(1)} \tag{6.14}$$

Thus, Equation (6.13) becomes

$$Lv^{(1)} = (1,1,1)^T$$

from which we calculate

$$v^{(1)} = (1, 7/4, -4/3)^T$$

Substituting for $v^{(1)}$ in Equation (6.14) and solving for $y^{(1)}$,

$$y^{(1)} = (5/2, 3, -1/2)^T$$

Hence

$$\mu_1 = 3$$

and so

$$z^{(1)} = y^{(1)}/\mu_1$$
$$= (5/6, 1, -1/6)^T$$

Thus, after the first iteration of the inverse power method, $\mu_1 = 3$ and $z^{(1)} = (5/6, 1, -1/6)^T$. Using the same L and U obtained above, further iterations are performed until consecutive values of μ have converged to four significant figures. The results of these calculations are given in Table 6.5.

This table gives the eigenvector

$$x* = (0.8105, 1, -0.2701)^{\mathrm{T}}$$

The required eigenvalue $\lambda*$ is given by

$$\frac{1}{\lambda* - (-2)} = 3.3508$$

and so

$$\lambda* = -1.702$$

The inverse power method is a very efficient method. If it is applied to matrix (6.7) with $p = 10$, the dominant eigenvalue is obtained correct to four significant figures after only four iterations! This is extremely impressive when it is recalled that the standard power method requires 216 iterations for this calculation.

Program construction

A subroutine plan for the inverse power method would be very similar to that of Figure 6.2 for the power method and so we proceed directly to the subroutine in this case. The major difference between the two algorithms lies in the different methods used to evaluate the vector $y^{(k)}$; the power algorithm uses matrix–vector multiplication whereas the inverse power algorithm requires the solution of a set of linear equations. This is reflected in the subroutine INVPOW of Figure 6.5.

Figure 6.5   Subroutine for the inverse power method.

```
       SUBROUTINE INVPOW (SIZE,N,A,P,Z,TOL,MAXITS,
      *                    STATUS,LAMBDA,X,NOOFIT,LASTMU, Y,WORKV)
       INTEGER    CONVGD,COUNT,I,LIMIT,MAXITS,N,NEWI,
      *           NOOFIT,OLDI,PTINY,SIZE,STATUS
       REAL       LAMBDA,LASTMU,NEWMU,OLDMU,P,TOL
       PARAMETER (CONVGD=0,PTINY=1,LIMIT=2)
       REAL       A(SIZE,SIZE),WORKV(N),X(N),Y(N),Z(N)
       INTRINSIC ABS
       EXTERNAL  LUDEC,LUSOL

       DO 10, I=1,N
         A(I,I)=A(I,I)-P
10     CONTINUE
```

```
      CALL LUDEC (SIZE,N,A, STATUS)
      IF (STATUS.EQ.PTINY) GO TO 999
C        { Factorization successful }

      NEWMU=0
      NEWI =0
      DO 20, COUNT=1, MAXITS

         CALL LUSOL (SIZE,N,A,Z, STATUS,Y, WORKV)
         IF (STATUS.EQ.PTINY) GO TO 999
C           { Equations solved successfully }

         OLDMU=NEWMU
         OLDI =NEWI
         NEWMU=0
         DO 30, I=1,N
           IF (ABS(Y(I)).GT.ABS(NEWMU)) THEN
             NEWMU=Y(I)
             NEWI=I
           END IF
30       CONTINUE

         DO 40, I=1,N
           Z(I)=Y(I)/NEWMU
40       CONTINUE

         IF ( (ABS(NEWMU-OLDMU) .LE. ABS(OLDMU)*TOL)
     *        .AND. (NEWI.EQ.OLDI) ) THEN
           STATUS=CONVGD
           GO TO 21
         END IF

20    CONTINUE
      STATUS=LIMIT

21    DO 50, I=1,N
        X(I)=Z(I)
50    CONTINUE

      IF (STATUS.EQ.CONVGD) THEN
        LAMBDA=P+1/NEWMU
        NOOFIT=COUNT
      END IF

      IF (STATUS.EQ.LIMIT) THEN
        LASTMU=P+1/NEWMU
      END IF

999   END
```

Figure 6.5   *cont.*

Instead of calling the subroutine MATVEC as in Figure 6.3, we call the subroutines LUDEC (Figure 5.15) and LUSOL (Figure 5.16). Note that we must abort the process if either of these subroutines encounters a small pivot, and so we test the value of STATUS immediately after each subroutine call. The subroutines LUDEC and LUSOL both use the value 1 for PTINY and so we include PTINY=1 in the PARAMETER list of subroutine INVPOW. To reduce storage requirements, the elements of array A are overwritten by those of B.

6.3   Methods for the complete eigensystem

When all the eigenvalues of a matrix A are required, methods based on **similarity transformations** are usually employed. These make use of an orthogonal matrix P to transform A into a *similar* matrix B which is of simpler form. By Theorem 6.5, the similarity transformation

$$P^{-1}AP = B$$

preserves the eigenvalues of A. Because P is an orthogonal matrix, $P^{-1} = P^{T}$, and so the transformation may also be written

$$P^{T}AP = B$$

Here, only one transformation method, *Jacobi's method*, is described. For details of others, the reader is referred to more advanced texts such as Golub and Van Loan (1983).

6.3.1   Jacobi's method

If A is symmetric, then from Theorem 6.4 there is an orthogonal matrix P such that

$$P^{T}AP = D$$

where D is a diagonal matrix whose diagonal elements are the eigenvalues of A. Jacobi's method transforms A into diagonal form by annihilating its off-diagonal elements *one by one*. It makes use of *plane rotation* matrices $R(p,q)$ which are basically unit matrices except for the elements

$$
\begin{aligned}
r_{pp} &= \cos\theta & r_{pq} &= -\sin\theta \\
r_{qp} &= \sin\theta & r_{qq} &= \cos\theta
\end{aligned}
$$

for some chosen value θ. It is easily shown that $R(p,q)$ is an orthogonal matrix and so a transformation of the form

$$A^* = R^T A R \tag{6.15}$$

preserves the eigenvalues of A. The essence of the method is to choose θ so that the element of A^* in position (p,q) is reduced to zero. To determine θ we require the relationship between a^*_{pq} and the elements of A and R. Clearly, a^*_{pq} is the product of row p of $(R^T A)$ with column q of R. However, the latter is simply the null vector except for the elements r_{pq} and r_{qq} and so, to form the product we need only the elements in positions (p,p) and (p,q) of

$$R^T A = \begin{bmatrix} 1 & \cdots & 0 & \cdots & 0 & \cdots & 0 \\ \vdots & & \vdots & & \vdots & & \vdots \\ 0 & \cdots & c & \cdots & s & \cdots & 0 \\ \vdots & & \vdots & & \vdots & & \vdots \\ 0 & \cdots & -s & \cdots & c & \cdots & 0 \\ \vdots & & \vdots & & \vdots & & \vdots \\ 0 & \cdots & 0 & \cdots & 0 & \cdots & 1 \end{bmatrix} \begin{bmatrix} a_{11} & \cdots & a_{1p} & \cdots & a_{1q} & \cdots & a_{1n} \\ \vdots & & \vdots & & \vdots & & \vdots \\ a_{p1} & \cdots & a_{pp} & \cdots & a_{pq} & \cdots & a_{pn} \\ \vdots & & \vdots & & \vdots & & \vdots \\ a_{q1} & \cdots & a_{qp} & \cdots & a_{qq} & \cdots & a_{qn} \\ \vdots & & \vdots & & \vdots & & \vdots \\ a_{n1} & \cdots & a_{np} & \cdots & a_{nq} & \cdots & a_{nn} \end{bmatrix}$$

where $c = \cos\theta$ and $s = \sin\theta$. Clearly

$$(R^T A)_{pp} = c a_{pp} + s a_{qp}$$

and

$$(R^T A)_{pq} = c a_{pq} + s a_{qq}$$

and so

$$\begin{aligned} a^*_{pq} &= (c a_{pp} + s a_{qp})(-s) + (c a_{pq} + s a_{qq})c \\ &= -cs a_{pp} - s^2 a_{qp} + c^2 a_{pq} + cs a_{qq} \end{aligned}$$

Because A is symmetric, this expression reduces to

$$\begin{aligned} a^*_{pq} &= (c^2 - s^2) a_{pq} + cs(a_{qq} - a_{pp}) \\ &= \frac{1}{2}\sin 2\theta(a_{qq} - a_{pp}) + \cos 2\theta\, a_{pq} \end{aligned}$$

Hence, if

$$\theta = \begin{cases} \dfrac{1}{2}\tan^{-1}\left(\dfrac{2a_{pq}}{a_{pp} - a_{qq}}\right) & a_{pp} \neq a_{qq} \\[2ex] \pm \dfrac{\pi}{4} & a_{pp} = a_{qq} \end{cases} \tag{6.16}$$

Given A (symmetric)
Repeat
  Locate element a_{pq} ($p < q$) with maximum modulus

$$Set \; \theta = \begin{cases} \dfrac{1}{2} \tan^{-1}\left(\dfrac{2a_{pq}}{a_{pp} - a_{qq}}\right) & a_{pp} \ne a_{qq} \\[2ex] \text{sign}(a_{pq}) \dfrac{\pi}{4} & a_{pp} = a_{qq} \end{cases} \qquad -\frac{\pi}{4} \le \theta \le \frac{\pi}{4}$$

  Construct $R(p,q)$
  Set $A = R^{T}AR$
Until converged

Figure 6.6 Algorithm for Jacobi's transformation.

then the similarity transformation of (6.15) reduces a_{pq}^{*} to zero. Unfortunately, as the calculation progresses, subsequent transformations will probably change the values of elements previously reduced to zero. Thus the method becomes an iterative one in which we construct the sequence of matrices

$$A^{(k+1)} = R^{T}(p,q)A^{(k)}R(p,q) \qquad k = 0,1,2, \ldots \tag{6.17}$$

with $A^{(0)} = A$. For each value of k, we must decide which off-diagonal element a_{pq} is to be reduced to zero. It seems reasonable to choose the element of maximum modulus and this gives the standard Jacobi method. We constrain θ, satisfying Equation (6.16), to lie in the interval $[-\pi/4, \pi/4]$ and, if $a_{pp} = a_{qq}$, take its sign to be that of $a_{pq}^{(k)}$. These additional restrictions ensure that the iteration tends to a *fixed* diagonal matrix. The process is terminated when the modulus of each off-diagonal element does not exceed some specified tolerance. Note that, because of symmetry, only the elements above the diagonal need be considered. The Jacobi algorithm is given in Figure 6.6.

We illustrate the method by evaluating the eigenvalues of the matrix

$$A = \begin{bmatrix} 10 & 3 & 2 \\ 3 & 5 & 1 \\ 2 & 1 & 0 \end{bmatrix} \tag{6.18}$$

working correct to five decimal places and terminating the iteration when the magnitude of each off-diagonal element of $A^{(k)}$ does not exceed 0.0001. Throughout the computations, any elements with magnitude below this tolerance are set to zero.

The element of $A^{(0)}$ with maximum modulus and above the diagonal is in position (1,2). Hence, for the first transformation, we use the rotation matrix

$$R(1,2) = \begin{bmatrix} \cos\theta & -\sin\theta & 0 \\ \sin\theta & \cos\theta & 0 \\ 0 & 0 & 1 \end{bmatrix}$$

where

$$\begin{aligned} \theta &= \frac{1}{2}\tan^{-1}\left(\frac{2a_{12}}{a_{11} - a_{22}}\right) \\ &= \frac{1}{2}\tan^{-1}\left(\frac{2\times 3}{10 - 5}\right) \\ &= 0.438\ 03 \end{aligned}$$

from which $\sin\theta = 0.424\ 16$ and $\cos\theta = 0.905\ 59$. Now we calculate

$$\begin{aligned} R^{\mathrm{T}}A &= \begin{bmatrix} 0.905\ 59 & 0.424\ 16 & 0 \\ -0.424\ 16 & 0.905\ 59 & 0 \\ 0 & 0 & 1 \end{bmatrix}\begin{bmatrix} 10 & 3 & 2 \\ 3 & 5 & 1 \\ 2 & 1 & 0 \end{bmatrix} \\ &= \begin{bmatrix} 10.328\ 38 & 4.837\ 57 & 2.235\ 34 \\ -1.524\ 83 & 3.255\ 47 & 0.057\ 27 \\ 2 & 1 & 0 \end{bmatrix} \end{aligned}$$

and

$$\begin{aligned} A^{(1)} = R^{\mathrm{T}}AR &= \begin{bmatrix} 10.328\ 38 & 4.837\ 57 & 2.235\ 34 \\ -1.524\ 83 & 3.255\ 47 & 0.057\ 27 \\ 2 & 1 & 0 \end{bmatrix}\begin{bmatrix} 0.905\ 59 & -0.424\ 16 & 0 \\ 0.424\ 16 & 0.905\ 59 & 0 \\ 0 & 0 & 1 \end{bmatrix} \\ &= \begin{bmatrix} 11.405\ 18 & 0 & 2.235\ 34 \\ 0 & 3.594\ 89 & 0.057\ 27 \\ 2.235\ 34 & 0.057\ 27 & 0 \end{bmatrix} \end{aligned}$$

Next we rotate in the (1,3) plane using

$$R(1,3) = \begin{bmatrix} \cos\theta & 0 & -\sin\theta \\ 0 & 1 & 0 \\ \sin\theta & 0 & \cos\theta \end{bmatrix}$$

where

$$\begin{aligned} \theta &= \frac{1}{2}\tan^{-1}\left(\frac{2a_{13}}{a_{11} - a_{33}}\right) \\ &= \frac{1}{2}\tan^{-1}\left(\frac{2\times 2.235\ 34}{11.405\ 18 - 0}\right) \\ &= 0.186\ 79 \end{aligned}$$

and so

$$A^{(2)} = \begin{bmatrix} 11.827\ 77 & 0.010\ 64 & 0 \\ 0.010\ 64 & 3.594\ 89 & 0.056\ 27 \\ 0 & 0.056\ 27 & -0.422\ 46 \end{bmatrix}$$

Note that the second iteration has destroyed the zero elements in positions (1,2) and (2,1). The element with maximum modulus in the upper region of $A^{(2)}$ is in position (2,3) and so we use

$$R(2,3) = \begin{bmatrix} 1 & 0 & 0 \\ 0 & \cos\theta & -\sin\theta \\ 0 & \sin\theta & \cos\theta \end{bmatrix}$$

with

$$\theta = \frac{1}{2}\tan^{-1}\left(\frac{2 \times 0.056\ 27}{3.594\ 81 - (-0.422\ 46)}\right)$$
$$= 0.014\ 01$$

giving

$$A^{(3)} = \begin{bmatrix} 11.827\ 77 & 0.010\ 64 & 0 \\ 0.010\ 64 & 3.595\ 67 & 0 \\ 0 & 0 & -0.423\ 25 \end{bmatrix}$$

Finally, rotating again in the (1,2) plane with $\theta = 0.001\ 29$ gives

$$A^{(4)} = \begin{bmatrix} 11.827\ 80 & 0 & 0 \\ 0 & 3.595\ 67 & 0 \\ 0 & 0 & -0.423\ 25 \end{bmatrix}$$

from which the eigenvalues are obtained; rounded to four decimal places, these are

$$\lambda_1 = 11.8278 \qquad \lambda_2 = 3.5957 \qquad \text{and} \qquad \lambda_3 = -0.4233$$

If required, the eigenvectors of A can be computed from the rotation matrices used in the transformations because Equation (6.17) can be written

$$D = \hat{R}^{\mathrm{T}}A\hat{R} \tag{6.19}$$

where $\hat{R}$ is the product of successive rotation matrices and so is itself orthogonal. Thus $\hat{R}\hat{R}^{\mathrm{T}} = I$ and pre-multiplication of Equation (6.19) by $\hat{R}$ gives

$$A\hat{R} = \hat{R}D$$

from which it follows that the eigenvectors of A are the columns of $\hat{R}$. Hence, in this example, the eigenvectors are given by the columns of

$$\hat{R} = R(1,2)R(1,3)R(2,3)R(1,2)$$

$$= \begin{bmatrix} 0.905\ 59 & -0.424\ 16 & 0 \\ 0.424\ 16 & 0.905\ 59 & 0 \\ 0 & 0 & 1 \end{bmatrix} \begin{bmatrix} 0.982\ 61 & 0 & -0.185\ 71 \\ 0 & 1 & 0 \\ 0.185\ 71 & 0 & 0.982\ 61 \end{bmatrix} \times$$

$$\begin{bmatrix} 1 & 0 & 0 \\ 0 & 0.999\ 90 & -0.014\ 01 \\ 0 & 0.014\ 01 & 0.999\ 90 \end{bmatrix} \begin{bmatrix} 1 & -0.001\ 29 & 0 \\ 0.001\ 29 & 1 & 0 \\ 0 & 0 & 1 \end{bmatrix}$$

$$= \begin{bmatrix} 0.889\ 29 & -0.427\ 62 & -0.162\ 22 \\ 0.417\ 95 & 0.903\ 86 & -0.091\ 45 \\ 0.185\ 73 & 0.012\ 26 & 0.982\ 51 \end{bmatrix}$$

The computational effort can be reduced because it is not necessary to perform full matrix multiplication. Recalling the form of R, it is clear that:

(1)   pre-multiplication of a matrix by $R^{T}(p,q)$ affects only the elements in rows p and q of that matrix, and

(2)   post-multiplication of a matrix by R affects only the elements in columns p and q of that matrix.

Thus, the matrix

$$A^* = R^{T}AR$$

is identical to the matrix A except for the elements in rows p and q and those in columns p and q. We will derive formulae for the modified elements.

When A is pre-multiplied by R^{T}, the elements in row p become

$$ca_{pj} + sa_{qj} \qquad j = 1, \ldots, n$$

while those in row q become

$$-sa_{pj} + ca_{qj} \qquad j = 1, \ldots, n$$

Hence, the elements in A^* are given by

$$\left. \begin{aligned} a_{ip}^* &= a_{ip}c + a_{iq}s = a_{pi}^* \\ a_{iq}^* &= a_{ip}(-s) + a_{iq}c = a_{qi}^* \end{aligned} \right\} \quad i \neq p,q$$

$$\begin{aligned} a_{pp}^* &= (ca_{pp} + sa_{qp})c + (ca_{pq} + sa_{qq})s \\ &= c^2 a_{pp} + 2csa_{pq} + s^2 a_{qq} \end{aligned}$$

$$\begin{aligned} a_{qq}^* &= (-sa_{pp} + ca_{qp})(-s) + (-sa_{pq} + ca_{qq})c \\ &= s^2 a_{pp} - 2csa_{pq} + c^2 a_{qq} \end{aligned}$$

(6.20)

Given: A, *tolerance, maximum number of cycles*
repeat (*not exceeding max cycles*)
  Set: *tolerance exceeded* = .FALSE.
  for $i = 1, 2, \ldots, n - 1$
    for $j = i + 1, i + 2, \ldots, n$
      if $|a_{ij}| > tolerance$ **then**
        Set: *tolerance exceeded* = .TRUE.
        Do:
          Jacobi Transformation
              using (*matrix A, plane* (i,j))
            to produce (*transformed matrix* A* *in A*)
  if *tolerance not exceeded* **then**
    Note: '*converged*'
until '*converged*' (*or limit on number of cycles reached*)

if '*converged*' **then**
  Record: *eigenvalues, number of cycles used*
if '*limit*' **then**
  Record: *current elements of A*

Figure 6.7 Plan of subroutine for the cyclic Jacobi method.

$$a_{pq}^* = a_{qp}^* = 0$$
$$a_{ij}^* = a_{ij} \qquad i,j \neq p,q$$

An important feature of Jacobi's method is that it produces all the eigenvalues of a matrix directly although, because it is an iterative method, it can be expensive in computational effort. More recent methods such as those of Givens and Householder have the advantage that they require only a *finite* number of transformations. However, the final matrix produced by these methods is of tri-diagonal rather than diagonal form; another method such as the QR algorithm has to be used to obtain the eigenvalues of the tri-diagonal matrix. Nevertheless, this procedure is usually more efficient; details are given in Atkinson and Harley (1983).

Program construction

When implemented on a computer, Jacobi's method is rather time consuming because, at each stage, a complete search of the upper triangular region of $A^{(k)}$ is required to determine p and q. The *cyclic* Jacobi method is a modification of the classical method in which elements are annihilated in strict order. The ordering is usually row-wise, working from left to right along each row. If an element is small, the rotation for that element is omitted. Another variation, the *threshold* Jacobi method, makes a limited search to find an off-diagonal element whose modulus exceeds some threshold value. This element is annihilated and the

```
      SUBROUTINE JACCYC (SIZE,N,A,TOL,MAXCYC, STATUS,DIAG,NOOFIT)

      INTEGER    CONVGD,COUNT,I,J,LIMIT,MAXCYC,N,NOOFIT,SIZE,STATUS
      REAL       TOL
      LOGICAL    TOLEX
      PARAMETER (CONVGD=0,LIMIT=1)
      REAL       A(SIZE,SIZE),DIAG(N)
      EXTERNAL   JTRANS
      INTRINSIC  ABS

      DO 10, COUNT=1,MAXCYC
        TOLEX=.FALSE.

        DO 20, I=1,N-1
          DO 30, J=I+1,N
            IF (ABS(A(I,J)).GT.TOL) THEN
              TOLEX=.TRUE.
              CALL JTRANS (SIZE,N,A,I,J)
            END IF
30        CONTINUE
20      CONTINUE

        IF (.NOT.TOLEX) THEN
          STATUS=CONVGD
          GO TO 11
        END IF

10    CONTINUE
      STATUS=LIMIT

11    IF (STATUS.EQ.CONVGD) THEN
        NOOFIT=COUNT
        DO 40, I=1,N
          DIAG(I)=A(I,I)
40      CONTINUE
      END IF

      END
```

Figure 6.8 Subroutine for the cyclic Jacobi method.

search continued. The magnitude of the threshold is gradually reduced as the computation progresses until it does not exceed the tolerance prescribed for the off diagonal elements. Only a subroutine for the cyclic method is considered here, and a plan for this is given in Figure 6.7.

As in Figure 5.23, we set a (logical) variable *tolerance exceeded* to .FALSE. before each iteration and change it to .TRUE. if the modulus of any

Given: A, (p,q)
Define: small number
if $|a_{pp} - a_{qq}| >$ small number **then**
$\quad$ *Set*: $\theta = \dfrac{1}{2} \tan^{-1}\left(\dfrac{2a_{pq}}{a_{pp} - a_{qq}}\right)$
$\quad$ **if** $|\theta| > \pi/4$ **then**
$\quad\quad$ *Set*: $\theta = \theta - \text{sign}(\theta)\pi/2$
else
$\quad$ *Set*: $\theta = \text{sign}(a_{pq})\pi/4$

Set: $c = \cos\theta$
$\quad\quad s = \sin\theta$
$\quad\quad app = a_{pp}$
$\quad\quad a_{pp} = c^2app + 2csa_{pq} + s^2a_{qq}$
$\quad\quad a_{qq} = s^2app - 2csa_{pq} + c^2a_{qq}$
$\quad\quad a_{pq} = 0$
$\quad\quad a_{qp} = 0$

for $i = 1,2,\ldots,n$
$\quad$ **if** $i \neq p,q$ **then**
$\quad\quad$ *Set*: $aip = a_{ip}$
$\quad\quad\quad a_{ip} = caip + sa_{iq}$
$\quad\quad\quad a_{pi} = a_{ip}$
$\quad\quad\quad a_{iq} = -saip + ca_{iq}$
$\quad\quad\quad a_{qi} = a_{iq}$

Figure 6.9 Plan of subroutine for a single Jacobi transformation.

off-diagonal element is greater than the permitted tolerance. If the logical variable retains the value `.FALSE.` after a complete scan of the upper region of A, the iteration sequence has converged. The subroutine of Figure 6.8, which is based on this plan, calls another subroutine, JTRANS, to carry out the actual transformation.

A plan for the subroutine JTRANS is given in Figure 6.9. This plan uses formulae (6.20) to modify the appropriate elements of A. Note that it is essential to take copies of a_{pp} and a_{ip} before they are updated because the original values are used in later expressions.

A subroutine based on this plan is given in Figure 6.10. We have taken copies of a_{pq}, a_{qq} and a_{iq} to reduce the number of run-time references and have moved the copying of a_{pp} to the top of the subroutine for the same reason. Our use of the function ATAN to compute π gives this value to machine accuracy.

The subroutine JTRANS computes $\sin\theta$ and $\cos\theta$ in a straightforward manner. Atkinson and Harley (1983) describe a more efficient technique which obtains these values without evaluating θ explicitly.

```
SUBROUTINE JTRANS (SIZE,N,A,P,Q)

INTEGER   I,N,P,Q,SIZE
REAL      AIP,AIQ,APP,APQ,AQQ,C,CS,CSQ,PI,S,SSQ,TINY,THETA
PARAMETER (TINY=1E-10)
REAL      A(SIZE,SIZE)
INTRINSIC ABS,ATAN,COS,SIGN,SIN

PI=4*ATAN(1.0)
APP=A(P,P)
APQ=A(P,Q)
AQQ=A(Q,Q)
IF (ABS(APP-AQQ).GT.TINY) THEN
  THETA=ATAN(2*APQ/(APP-AQQ))/2
  IF (ABS(THETA).GT.PI/4) THETA=THETA-SIGN(PI/2,THETA)
ELSE
  THETA=SIGN(PI/4,THETA)
END IF

C=COS(THETA)
S=SIN(THETA)
CSQ=C*C
SSQ=S*S
CS=C*S
A(P,P)=CSQ*APP+2*CS*APQ+SSQ*AQQ
A(Q,Q)=SSQ*APP-2*CS*APQ+CSQ*AQQ
A(P,Q)=0
A(Q,P)=0

DO 10, I=1,N
  IF (I.NE.P .AND. I.NE.Q) THEN
    AIP=A(I,P)
    AIQ=A(I,Q)
    A(I,P)=C*AIP+S*AIQ
    A(P,I)=A(I,P)
    A(I,Q)=-S*AIP+C*AIQ
    A(Q,I)=A(I,Q)
  END IF
10  CONTINUE

END
```

Figure 6.10 Subroutine for a single Jacobi transformation.

EXERCISES

6.1 Evaluate all the eigenvalues of the matrix

$$A = \begin{bmatrix} 3 & 0 & 1 \\ 0 & 3 & 2 \\ 1 & 2 & 3 \end{bmatrix}$$

by locating the zeros of its characteristic polynomial. Hence determine the associated eigenvectors and normalize them so that their largest elements are unity. Give your answers correct to five decimal places.

6.2 Starting with $z^{(0)} = (0,0,1)^{\mathrm{T}}$, use the power method to evaluate the dominant eigenvalue λ_1 and associated eigenvector x_1 of the matrix given in Exercise 6.1. Give your answers correct to four decimal places and compare them with those obtained previously.

6.3 Repeat Exercise 6.2 using

(a)   Aitken's Δ^2 process

(b)   a shift of origin with $p = 1$

to accelerate the rate of convergence. [Note that the improvement will be marginal because A was chosen in such a way that the power iteration in Exercise 6.2 would converge fairly rapidly.]

6.4 Extend the calculations of Exercise 6.2 using the Rayleigh quotient to evaluate λ_1 correct to seven decimal places.

6.5 Using your estimate of x_1 obtained in Exercise 6.2, deflate the matrix A and hence calculate the remaining eigenvalues and eigenvectors directly. Compare your results with those obtained in Exercise 6.1.

6.6 Use the inverse power method to determine, correct to three decimal places, the smallest eigenvalue and associated eigenvector of matrix A above. Compare your answers with those obtained in Exercise 6.1.

6.7 Use the Jacobi method to determine all the eigenvalues of the matrix given in Exercise 6.1. Terminate the iteration when all the off-diagonal elements have modulus not exceeding 0.0001. Again compare your results with those obtained in Exercise 6.1.

6.8 Prove the results of Theorems 6.1 and 6.2.

Programming exercises

6.9 Using the subroutine of .Figure 6.3, write a program for the power method. Choosing a suitable starting vector and tolerance, run the program to determine the dominant eigenvalue of the matrix

$$B = \begin{bmatrix} -1 & 2 & 3 & 3 \\ 2 & -3 & 4 & 1 \\ 3 & 4 & -1 & 2 \\ 3 & 1 & 2 & -3 \end{bmatrix}$$

6.10 Modify your program of Exercise 6.9 so that it includes one of the acceleration techniques discussed in Section 6.2.1. Using the same starting vector and tolerance, run the program to determine the dominant eigenvalue of B and compare the performances of the two programs.

6.11 Using the subroutine of Figure 6.5, write a program for the inverse power method. Hence, for the matrix given in Exercise 6.9, determine the eigenvalue of least modulus and its associated eigenvector.

6.12 Using the subroutines of Figures 6.8 and 6.10, write a program for the cyclic Jacobi method and hence determine all the eigenvalues of the matrix of Exercise 6.9. Modify your program so that it also calculates the eigenvectors and compare the results with those obtained in Exercises 6.9 and 6.11.

6.13 Write a program for the threshold Jacobi method and use it, with the sequence of thresholds 1, 0.1, 0.01, 0.001 and 0.0001, to, determine the eigenvalues of the matrix of Exercise 6.9.

6.14 Modify your program for the power method (Exercise 6.9) so that it outputs the approximations μ_k and $z^{(k)}$ after each iteration. Apply the modified program to the matrix

$$\begin{bmatrix} 3.75 & -6.25 & 4.6 \\ -6.25 & 3.75 & 4.6 \\ 4.6 & 4.6 & -2.5 \end{bmatrix}$$

starting with

(a) $z_0 = (1,1,1)^T$
(b) $z_0 = (1,-1,0)^T$
(c) $z_0 = (0,1,0)^T$

Run the Jacobi program of Exercise 6.12 for this matrix and compare the results. Explain any peculiar features.

Chapter 7
Discrete function approximation

7.1   Polynomial interpolation   7.2   Data fitting

A problem that arises frequently is that of estimating the value of a function $f(x)$ at a point $\bar{x}$, given some information about the function. This chapter considers two examples of this problem in which the information takes the form of a set of function values f_i $\{i = 0,1, \ldots ,n\}$ given at a set of data points x_i $\{i = 0,1,\ldots,n\}$. In the first example, the data is exact except, perhaps, for the effect of rounding errors; in the second, the function values may be experimental readings and so subject to more significant errors. A different technique is used to estimate $f(\bar{x})$ in each case: **interpolation** when the data is exact and **data fitting** for values that include errors.

     In both cases a polynomial is used to approximate the function $f(x)$. There are other types of approximating function but polynomials are widely used because they are convenient to use and usually produce satisfactory results.

7.1 Polynomial interpolation

Polynomial interpolation is used when the data is exact. The principle is extremely simple: we determine a polynomial, $p(x)$, which passes through all the data points and then we take $p(\bar{x})$ as an estimate of $f(\bar{x})$. It is assumed that the discrete points $x_0, x_1, \ldots, x_n$ are ordered so that $x_0 < x_1 < \cdots < x_n$. Strictly, the process is known as interpolation only when the point $\bar{x}$ lies in the interval $[x_0, x_n]$; when $\bar{x}$ lies outside this interval, the process is the same but is known as **extrapolation**. Figure 7.1 illustrates a cubic interpolation polynomial.

Theorem 7.1

Let x_i $\{i = 0,1, \ldots ,n\}$ be $n + 1$ distinct points and let f_i $\{i = 0,1, \ldots ,n\}$ be any set of $n + 1$ real numbers. Then there exists a unique polynomial

$$p_n(x) \equiv a_n x^n + a_{n-1} x^{n-1} + \cdots + a_1 x + a_0 \qquad (7.1)$$

of degree at most n such that $p_n(x_i) = f_i$ $\{i = 0,1,\ldots,n\}$.

Proof

In Section 7.1.1 we shall prove the existence of such a polynomial by constructing it. It remains for us to prove that the polynomial is unique. This is done by assuming the converse and obtaining a contradiction.

Let there be two polynomials $p_n(x)$ and $q_n(x)$, of degree at most n, interpolating the data. We define the difference $d_n(x)$ by

$$d_n(x) \equiv p_n(x) - q_n(x)$$

Thus $d_n(x)$ is also a polynomial of degree at most n and so has at most n zeros. However, $d_n(x)$ is zero whenever $x = x_0, x_1, \ldots, x_n$ because, at each of these points, $p_n(x_i) = q_n(x_i) = f_i$. Thus $d_n(x)$ has at least $n + 1$ zeros and so there is a contradiction; this can be resolved only if $d_n(x)$ is identically zero everywhere. Thus

$$p_n(x) \equiv q_n(x)$$

and so the interpolation polynomial is unique.   ∎

Now we have to decide how to determine the form of the polynomial $p_n(x)$ or, at least, its value at $x = \bar{x}$. One method would be to substitute each x_i $\{i = 0,1, \ldots ,n\}$ in turn into Equation (7.1) and equate the resulting expression with the function value f_i. This would give $n + 1$ linear equations in the $n + 1$ unknowns $a_0, a_1, \ldots, a_n$ and these equations could be solved using Gaussian elimination, for example. However, the coefficient matrix of the

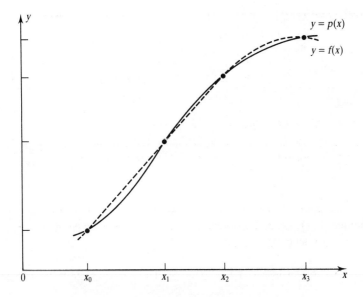

Figure 7.1 Cubic interpolation polynomial $p(x)$.

system of linear equations is related to the Hilbert matrix introduced in the exercises of Chapter 5 where it became apparent that it is ill-conditioned. For this reason, an alternative technique will be used to determine the interpolating polynomial.

7.1.1 Lagrangian interpolation

The Lagrange interpolation polynomial for the data values (x_i, f_i) $\{i = 0, 1, \ldots, n\}$ is written in the form

$$p_n(x) = f_0 l_0(x) + f_1 l_1(x) + \cdots + f_n l_n(x) \tag{7.2}$$

where each function $l_i(x)$ $\{i = 0, 1, \ldots, n\}$ is a polynomial of degree n and has the property that

$$l_i(x_j) = \delta_{ij} = \begin{cases} 0 & \text{if } i \neq j \\ 1 & \text{if } i = j \end{cases} \tag{7.3}$$

where δ_{ij} is the *Kronecker delta* function. Thus Equation (7.2) is the equation of a polynomial of degree n and, using the result of Equation (7.3), we have that

$$p_n(x_i) = f_j \qquad i = 0, 1, \ldots, n$$

so that $p_n(x)$ *is* the interpolation polynomial.

Given $n, \bar{x}, (x_i, f_i)$ $\{i = 0, 1, \ldots, n\}$
Repeat $\{$ *for* $i = 0, 1, \ldots, n\}$

$$\text{Set} \quad l_i = \frac{(\bar{x} - x_0)(\bar{x} - x_1) \ldots (\bar{x} - x_{i-1})(\bar{x} - x_{i+1}) \ldots (\bar{x} - x_n)}{(x_i - x_0)(x_i - x_1) \ldots (x_i - x_{i-1})(x_i - x_{i+1}) \ldots (x_i - x_n)}$$

Set $p_n(\bar{x}) = f_0 l_0 + f_1 l_1 + \cdots + f_n l_n$

Figure 7.2   Algorithm for Lagrangian interpolation.

Equation (7.3) can be used to derive the equation for each of the polynomials $l_i(x)$. Because $l_i(x)$ is required to be zero at the points x_j $\{i \neq j\}$, its equation must take the form

$$l_i(x) = K(x - x_0)(x - x_1) \ldots (x - x_{i-1})(x - x_{i+1}) \ldots (x - x_n)$$

where K is a constant still to be determined. We use the condition that $l_i(x_i) = 1$ to fix the value of K. Thus

$$1 = K(x_i - x_0)(x_i - x_1) \ldots (x_i - x_{i-1})(x_i - x_{i+1}) \ldots (x_i - x_n)$$

and so

$$K = \frac{1}{(x_i - x_0)(x_i - x_1) \ldots (x_i - x_{i-1})(x_i - x_{i+1}) \ldots (x_i - x_n)}$$

Thus each of the polynomials $l_i(x)$ has the form

$$l_i(x) = \frac{(x - x_0)(x - x_1) \ldots (x - x_{i-1})(x - x_{i+1}) \ldots (x - x_n)}{(x_i - x_0)(x_i - x_1) \ldots (x_i - x_{i-1})(x_i - x_{i+1}) \ldots (x_i - x_n)}$$

in which the numerator is the product of all the factors $(x - x_j)$ excluding the term $(x - x_i)$ (i.e. the one with the same subscript as $l_i(x)$) and the denominator is simply the numerator evaluated at $x = x_i$.

A mathematical algorithm for Lagrangian interpolation is given in Figure 7.2. We illustrate its use by estimating $f(0.14)$ from the values of $f(x) = e^x$ presented in Table 7.1.

First, each of the polynomials $l_i(x)$ is evaluated at the point $x = 0.14$:

$$l_0(0.14) = \frac{(0.14 - x_1)(0.14 - x_2)(0.14 - x_3)}{(x_0 - x_1)(x_0 - x_2)(x_0 - x_3)}$$

$$= \frac{(0.04)(-0.16)(-0.46)}{(-0.1)(-0.3)(-0.6)} = -0.163\ 556$$

Table 7.1   Values of $f(x) = e^x$.

i	0	1	2	3
x_i	0	0.1	0.3	0.6
$f(x_i)$	1.000 000	1.105 171	1.349 859	1.822 119

$$l_1(0.14) = \frac{(0.14 - x_0)(0.14 - x_2)(0.14 - x_3)}{(x_1 - x_0)(x_1 - x_2)(x_1 - x_3)} = 1.030\ 400$$

$$l_2(0.14) = \frac{(0.14 - x_0)(0.14 - x_1)(0.14 - x_3)}{(x_2 - x_0)(x_2 - x_1)(x_2 - x_3)} = 0.143\ 111$$

$$l_3(0.14) = \frac{(0.14 - x_0)(0.14 - x_1)(0.14 - x_2)}{(x_3 - x_0)(x_3 - x_1)(x_3 - x_2)} = -0.009\ 956$$

Hence

$$f(0.14) \simeq f_0 l_0(0.14) + f_1 l_1(0.14) + f_2 l_2(0.14) + f_3 l_3(0.14)$$
$$= (1.000\ 000)(-0.163\ 556) + (1.105\ 171)(1.030\ 400)$$
$$+ (1.349\ 859)(0.143\ 111) + (1.822\ 119)(-0.009\ 956)$$
$$= 1.150\ 251$$

To six decimal places, the correct value for $f(0.14) = e^{(0.14)}$ is 1.150 274.
Note that the sum of the numerical values of the polynomials $l_i(x)$ evaluated at $x = 0.14$ is

$$l_0(0.14) + l_1(0.14) + l_2(0.14) + l_3(0.14)$$
$$= (-0.163\ 556) + (1.030\ 400) + (0.143\ 111) + (-0.009\ 956)$$
$$= 0.999\ 996$$

which is approximately 1. This is a consequence of the fact that the interpolating polynomial must be able to reproduce exactly any function $f(x)$ which is a polynomial of degree n or less. In particular, if $f(x)$ is constant, equal to c everywhere, then

$$f(x) = c = \sum_{i=0}^{n} c l_i(x)$$

and so

$$\sum_{i=0}^{n} l_i(x) = 1$$

for all x. This result provides a useful arithmetic check during hand computation.

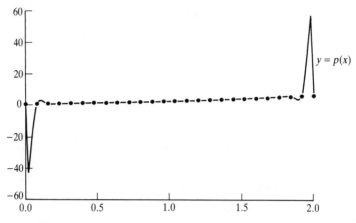

Figure 7.3   Interpolation polynomial of degree 20.

We introduce a word of caution here. When n is large, it is not advisable to use the full interpolation polynomial of degree n. For example, if $n = 20$, the full interpolation polynomial has degree 20 and could oscillate 19 times. As is shown in Figure 7.3 this oscillation property can lead to a poor approximation near the end-points. There is, of course, the further disadvantage that a large amount of computation would be needed to calculate each of the 21 individual Lagrange polynomial values $l_i(\bar{x})$. It is usually preferable to use an interpolating polynomial of low order based on points near $\bar{x}$. For reasons of accuracy, it is advisable to choose points on both sides of $\bar{x}$.

Program construction

The subprogram plan for Lagrange interpolation, given in Figure 7.4, closely follows the mathematical algorithm. The major difference is that the value of $p_n(x)$ is accumulated as the l_i are evaluated rather than formed explicitly as a separate step.

We consider the subprogram plan in some detail. This subprogram takes the array bound n, the value $\bar{x}$ and the (x_i, f_i) $\{i = 0, 1, \ldots, n\}$ and produces a single value, the value of the Lagrange interpolate. The natural form that such a subprogram takes is that of a FUNCTION and, in this case, a REAL FUNCTION.

The tabular values (x_i, f_i) $\{i = 0, 1, \ldots, n\}$ are best represented using two one-dimensional arrays, X and F. Given the array bound N, the declaration of these arrays is

```
REAL F(0:N),X(0:N)
```

Given: $n, \bar{x}, (x_i, f_i)$ $\{i = 0, 1, \ldots, n\}$
Set: *sum* $= 0$
repeat $\{for\ i = 0, 1, \ldots, n\}$

$$\text{Set}: li = \frac{(\bar{x} - x_0)(\bar{x} - x_1) \ldots (\bar{x} - x_{i-1})(\bar{x} - x_{i+1}) \ldots (\bar{x} - x_n)}{(x_i - x_0)(x_i - x_1) \ldots (x_i - x_{i-1})(x_i - x_{i+1}) \ldots (x_i - x_n)}$$

$sum = sum + f_i li$

Set: $p_n(\bar{x}) = sum$

Figure 7.4 Plan of subprogram for Lagrange interpolation.

Note that the lower subscript in each case is zero so that the natural indexing system can be used for each x_i and f_i. The value of each individual Lagrange polynomial $l_i(x)$ will be accumulated in the DOUBLE PRECISION variable LI. Using XBAR to represent $\bar{x}$, the evaluation of LI takes the form

```
      XI=X(I)
      LI=1
      DO 20, J=0,N
         IF (I.NE.J) THEN
            XJ=X(J)
            LI=LI*(XBAR-XJ)/(XI-XJ)
         END IF
20    CONTINUE
```

The variables XI and XJ have been used to hold the values of X(I) and X(J), thus reducing the number of subscript references. The complete function subprogram is given in Figure 7.5.

It is possible that this subprogram could be given an argument XBAR which is very close to a tabular value X(I) and, in this case, it is necessary to pass back only the function value F(I). The modification of the function of Figure 7.5 to take appropriate action is left as an exercise for the reader.

Interpolation error

There is no natural way of finding out how good an approximation to $f(\bar{x})$ is obtained. This contrasts, for example, with the situation of solving a system of linear equations; there, the residuals of the equations do give some information about the correctness of the solution. Thus, some method of estimating the error in the approximation is needed.

```
REAL FUNCTION LAGINT (N,XBAR,X,F)

INTEGER   I,J,N
REAL      XBAR,XI,XJ
DOUBLE PRECISION LI,SUM
REAL      F(0:N),X(0:N)

SUM=0
DO 10, I=0,N
  XI=X(I)
  LI=1
  DO 20, J=0,N
    IF (I.NE.J) THEN
      XJ=X(J)
      LI=LI*(XBAR-XJ)/(XI-XJ)
    END IF
20    CONTINUE
  SUM=SUM+F(I)*LI
10  CONTINUE
  LAGINT=SUM

END
```

Figure 7.5 Function subprogram for Lagrange interpolation.

Theorem 7.2

The error

$$E(x) = f(x) - p_n(x)$$

in Lagrangian interpolation is given by

$$E(x) = \frac{(x - x_0)(x - x_1) \ldots (x - x_n)}{(n + 1)!} f^{(n+1)}(\xi) \qquad (7.4)$$

where ξ is dependent on x and lies in the range $x_0 < \xi < x_n$.

A proof of this result can be found in Burden and Faires (1985, p. 87).

The form of Equation (7.4) means that the error cannot be evaluated exactly because the precise dependence of ξ on x is not known. However, if the function $f(x)$ is known, it may be possible to bound its derivatives and so give upper and lower bounds on the magnitude of $E(x)$

$$|E(x)| \leq \frac{|(x - x_0)(x - x_1) \ldots (x - x_n)|}{(n + 1)!} \max_{x_0 < x < x_n} |f^{(n+1)}(x)|$$

and

$$|E(x)| \geq \frac{|(x - x_0)(x - x_1) \ldots (x - x_n)|}{(n + 1)!} \min_{x_0 < x < x_n} |f^{(n+1)}(x)|$$

For the numerical example given above, the error formula is

$$E(x) = \frac{(x - x_0)(x - x_1)(x - x_2)(x - x_3)}{4!} f^{(4)}(\xi) \qquad x_0 < \xi < x_3$$

In this case $f(x)$ and each of its derivatives is e^x. Thus we can bound the error as follows:

$$|E(0.14)| \leq \frac{|(0.14 - 0.00)(0.14 - 0.10)(0.14 - 0.30)(0.14 - 0.60)|}{4!}$$
$$\times \max_{0.00 < x < 0.60} |e^x|$$
$$= 0.000\ 025$$

and

$$|E(0.14)| \geq \frac{|(0.14)(0.04)(-0.16)(-0.46)|}{24} \min_{0.00 < x < 0.60} |e^x|$$
$$= 0.000\ 017$$

We can see that the actual error, $1.150\ 274 - 1.150\ 251 = 0.000\ 023$, lies within the error bounds that we have calculated.

Of course, in many situations the function $f(x)$ or its derivatives will not be known and so the above analysis will be of theoretical interest only. In a few special cases, however, it may be possible to evaluate the derivatives and so estimate the error bounds.

If x lies outside the interval $[x_0, x_n]$, the extrapolated value can be inaccurate unless $\bar{x}$ is close to x_0 or x_n. This happens because the product of the terms $(x - x_i)$ in Equation (7.4) can become very large and the upper and lower bounds on the position of ξ expand to become

$$\min(\bar{x}, x_0, x_1, \ldots, x_n) \leq \xi \leq \max(\bar{x}, x_0, x_1, \ldots, x_n)$$

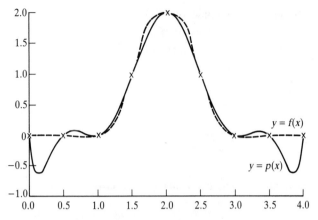

Figure 7.6 Interpolant of degree 8.

To illustrate the problem with extrapolation, we estimate $f(0.7)$ using the data of Table 7.1. The Lagrange polynomial values are

$$l_0 = -1.333\ 333$$
$$l_1 = 2.800\ 000$$
$$l_2 = -2.333\ 333$$
$$l_3 = 1.866\ 667$$

and, performing the usual check,

$$l_0 + l_1 + l_2 + l_3 = 1.000\ 001$$

The extrapolated value is

$$f(0.7) \simeq 2.012\ 765$$

while the value of $e^{0.7}$, rounded to six decimal places, is 2.013 753. Therefore, the error is $E(0.7) = 0.000\ 988$. The error bounds are

$$0.000\ 700 \leqslant |E(0.7)| \leqslant 0.001\ 410$$

and so the error and its bounds are significantly larger than those of the interpolated value at $x = 0.140$.

7.1.2 Cubic spline interpolation

One disadvantage of the Lagrange form of interpolation polynomial (there are other types) is that all the $l_i(x)$ have to be recalculated if an extra data point is

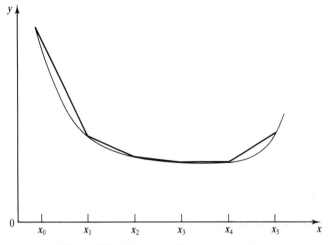

Figure 7.7 Piecewise-linear interpolation.

taken into account. There are modifications of the Lagrange polynomial which circumvent this problem and, for the case of equidistant data, extremely efficient methods exist to evaluate the polynomial (see Ralston and Rabinowitz, 1978, p. 56).

However, there are still problems with polynomial interpolation when the data displays relatively rapid changes in some part of the interval. In Figure 7.6, the data presented by the crosses was taken from the function represented by the dashed line. There are nine data points and these define a unique interpolation polynomial of degree 8. This polynomial is represented by the solid line. From the diagram it is clear that the interpolation polynomial is not a good representation of the function near the ends of the interval.

In general, a better technique is to divide the interval into a series of subintervals and use separate approximations in each. This is subject to the proviso that, at the common point of each pair of adjacent subintervals, consecutive approximations should match in some sense. The simplest form of this type of approximation is illustrated in Figure 7.7 where the function is approximated by a straight line in each subinterval; the function values at the ends of the subintervals coincide so that the overall approximation is continuous. This is the technique employed when using tables to evaluate logarithms at non-tabular points.

The process of approximation on subintervals is known, for obvious reasons, as **piecewise approximation.** Unfortunately, as can be seen from the diagram, this linear approximation to the function is not smooth ('smoothness' usually refers to the continuity of the derivatives) because, at the end-points (sometimes known as **nodes**) of each subinterval, the derivative of the approximation is discontinuous. It may be possible to make the approximation smoother by using piecewise-quadratic, rather than piecewise-linear, approxima-

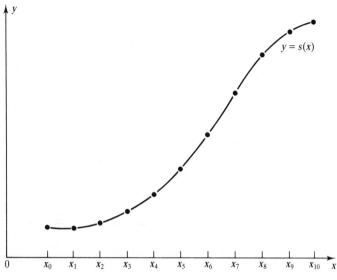

Figure 7.8 Cubic spline.

tion. A quadratic has three free parameters: two of these are determined by the function values at the ends of the subinterval leaving the third free to be used to smooth the approximation. Unfortunately, there are not enough free parameters to ensure smoothness over the whole interval: the approximation cannot match the derivatives of the function at the end-points of the interval. However, derivatives can be matched by using cubic polynomials in each subinterval and then the approximating polynomials are known as **cubic splines.** A cubic spline is illustrated in Figure 7.8; note that the overall approximation is smooth even though a different cubic is used in each interval.

A 'spline' is an instrument once used by draughtsmen to join points on a curve. It consists of a flexible wooden strip which is forced to match up with the data points and, because the spline takes up the shape that minimizes the potential energy, the resulting curve is smooth. (A jagged curve corresponds to a broken spline!) The cubic spline is the mathematical equivalent of the wooden spline; it has sufficient free parameters to ensure the continuity of first *and* second derivatives throughout the interval and to satisfy extra conditions at the ends of the interval. Note that the construction of a cubic spline does not assume that the derivatives of the interpolant agree with those of the function anywhere except, perhaps, at the ends of the interval.

The conditions which we will impose on the cubic spline, and which will be used to determine equations for the coefficients of the spline, are as follows. Given the set of function values $f_0, f_1, \ldots, f_n$ defined at the distinct points $x_0, x_1, \ldots, x_n$, our cubic spline interpolant $s(x)$ for the data will satisfy the following conditions:

(1)   In each interval $[x_i, x_{i+1}]$ $\{i = 0, 1, \ldots, n - 1\}$, $s(x)$ is a cubic polynomial (denoted by s_i).

(2)   At each point x_i $\{i = 0, 1, \ldots, n\}$, the spline must match the function value and so $s(x_i) = f_i$.

(3)   At the common point x_i of the two subintervals $[x_{i-1}, x_i]$ and $[x_i, x_{i+1}]$, we impose conditions that ensure the continuity and smoothness of the spline:

(a) $s_{i-1}(x_i) = s_i(x_i)$
(b) $s'_{i-1}(x_i) = s'_i(x_i)$
(c) $s''_{i-1}(x_i) = s''_i(x_i)$ for $i = 1, 2, \ldots, n - 1$

These conditions ensure that the spline and its first and second derivatives are continuous at the node.

Now we consider how to evaluate the spline for the given set of data. In each subinterval $[x_i, x_{i+1}]$ it is convenient to write the spline in the form

$$s_i(x) = a_i(x - x_i)^3 + b_i(x - x_i)^2 + c_i(x - x_i) + d_i$$
$$\text{for } i = 0, 1, \ldots, n - 1 \tag{7.5}$$

We have to determine values of a_i, b_i, c_i and d_i. To satisfy conditions 3(b) and 3(c) above, we will need the derivatives

$$s'_i(x) = 3a_i(x - x_i)^2 + 2b_i(x - x_i) + c_i \tag{7.6}$$

and

$$s''_i(x) = 6a_i(x - x_i) + 2b_i \tag{7.7}$$

To derive a numerically stable algorithm for determining the unknown coefficients, we set

$$\sigma_0 = s''_0(x_0)$$
$$\sigma_i = s''_{i-1}(x_i) = s''_i(x_i) \qquad i = 1, 2, \ldots, n - 1 \tag{7.8}$$
$$\sigma_n = s''_{n-1}(x_n)$$

and then express the coefficients in terms of σ_i $\{i = 0, 1, \ldots, n\}$. Substituting $x = x_i$ into Equations (7.5) and (7.7) gives

$$s_i(x_i) = f_i = d_i \qquad i = 0, 1, \ldots, n - 1 \tag{7.9}$$

and

$$\sigma_i = 2b_i \qquad i = 0, 1, \ldots, n - 1 \tag{7.10}$$

Substituting $x = x_{i+1}$ into Equations (7.5) and (7.7) gives

$$s_i(x_{i+1}) = f_{i+1} = a_i h_i^3 + b_i h_i^2 + c_i h_i + d_i \qquad i = 0,1, \ldots ,n - 1 \qquad \text{(7.11)}$$

and

$$\sigma_{i+1} = 6a_i h_i + 2b_i \qquad i = 0,1, \ldots ,n - 1 \qquad \text{(7.12)}$$

where $h_i = (x_{i+1} - x_i)$ $\{i = 0,1, \ldots ,n - 1\}$. From Equations (7.9), (7.10) and (7.12),

$$d_i = f_i \qquad \text{(7.13)}$$
$$b_i = \sigma_i/2 \qquad \text{(7.14)}$$

and

$$a_i = (\sigma_{i+1} - \sigma_i)/6h_i \qquad i = 0,1, \ldots ,n - 1 \qquad \text{(7.15)}$$

Substituting these into Equation (7.11) gives

$$f_{i+1} = \frac{(\sigma_{i+1} - \sigma_i)}{6} h_i^2 + \frac{\sigma_i}{2} h_i^2 + c_i h_i + f_i \qquad i = 0,1, \ldots ,n - 1$$

from which

$$c_i = \frac{(f_{i+1} - f_i)}{h_i} - \frac{(\sigma_{i+1} + 2\sigma_i)}{6} h_i \qquad i = 0,1, \ldots ,n - 1 \qquad \text{(7.16)}$$

Now we make use of condition 3(b) by equating the slopes of the cubics at the point x_i. From Equation (7.6), we have

$$s_{i-1}'(x_i) = 3a_{i-1} h_{i-1}^2 + 2b_{i-1} h_{i-1} + c_{i-1}$$

and

$$s_i'(x_i) = c_i$$

Hence

$$c_i = 3a_{i-1} h_{i-1}^2 + 2b_{i-1} h_{i-1} + c_{i-1}$$

and substituting for a_{i-1}, b_{i-1}, c_{i-1} and c_i from Equations (7.15), (7.14) and

(7.16) we obtain the equation

$$\sigma_{i-1}h_{i-1} + 2\sigma_i(h_{i-1} + h_i) + \sigma_{i+1}h_{i+1} = \frac{6}{h_i}(f_{i+1} - f_i) - \frac{6}{h_{i-1}}(f_i - f_{i-1})$$

$$i = 1,2, \ldots ,n - 1 \tag{7.17}$$

The only unknowns in Equation (7.17) are the values σ_{i-1}, σ_i and σ_{i+1} because the h_i values are predetermined by the x_i values. Thus there are $n - 1$ equations in the $n + 1$ unknown values σ_i $\{i = 0,1, \ldots ,n\}$. To obtain a unique cubic spline interpolate, we impose two extra conditions on the spline. These can take many different forms but only three are considered here. The simplest approach is to specify that

$$s''(x_0) = \sigma_0 = 0 \qquad s''(x_n) = \sigma_n = 0 \tag{7.18}$$

thus reducing the number of unknowns by two. Hence, the first and last equations in (7.17) become

$$2\sigma_1(h_0 + h_1) + \sigma_2 h_2$$
$$= \frac{6}{h_1}(f_2 - f_1) - \frac{6}{h_0}(f_1 - f_0) \tag{7.19a}$$

and

$$\sigma_{n-2}h_{n-2} + 2\sigma_{n-1}(h_{n-2} + h_{n-1})$$
$$= \frac{6}{h_{n-1}}(f_n - f_{n-1}) - \frac{6}{h_{n-2}}(f_{n-1} - f_{n-2}) \tag{7.19b}$$

giving $n - 1$ equations in $n - 1$ unknowns.

Another form of end-condition, based on the supposition that more information can be obtained about $f(x)$ and, specifically, its derivatives, is

$$s'(x_0) = f'_0 \qquad s'(x_n) = f'_n \tag{7.20}$$

This involves the first derivative of $f(x)$ at the end-points of the interval and so these conditions are rewritten in terms of the σ values. From Equation (7.6),

$$f'_0 = s'(x_0) = s'_0(x_0) = c_0$$

and substituting for c_0 from Equation (7.16) gives

$$f'_0 = \frac{(f_1 - f_0)}{h_0} - \frac{(\sigma_1 + 2\sigma_0)}{6}h_0$$

or

$$2\sigma_0 + \sigma_1 = \frac{6(f_1 - f_0)}{h_0^2} - \frac{6f_0'}{h_0} \tag{7.21a}$$

Similarly,

$$f_n' = s'(x_n) = s_{n-1}'(x_n) = 3a_{n-1}h_{n-1}^2 + 2b_{n-1}h_{n-1} + c_{n-1}$$

and so, using Equations (7.15), (7.14) and (7.16),

$$\sigma_{n-1} + 2\sigma_n = \frac{6f_n'}{h_{n-1}} - \frac{6(f_n - f_{n-1})}{h_{n-1}^2} \tag{7.21b}$$

Thus Equations (7.17) and (7.21) give the required $(n + 1)$ equations in the $(n + 1)$ unknowns σ_i $\{i = 0,1, \ldots ,n\}$. Note that, for either set of conditions, the system of linear equations is tri-diagonal.

The final form of condition requires no information about the function but assumes that the second derivative of the spline is linear in the first and last pair of subintervals. Thus it is assumed that

$$\frac{\sigma_1 - \sigma_0}{h_0} = \frac{\sigma_2 - \sigma_1}{h_1}$$

and

$$\frac{\sigma_{n-1} - \sigma_{n-2}}{h_{n-2}} = \frac{\sigma_n - \sigma_{n-1}}{h_{n-1}}$$

and, again, there are $n + 1$ equations in the $n + 1$ unknowns. Note that, in this case, the system of equations is no longer tri-diagonal. However, it is a simple matter to eliminate σ_0 from the first two equations and σ_n from the last two and thereby produce a tri-diagonal $(n - 1) \times (n - 1)$ system.

The equations can be simplified if the data is equally spaced. In this case, Equation (7.17) may be written

$$\sigma_{i-1} + 4\sigma_i + \sigma_{i+1} = \frac{6}{h^2}(f_{i-1} - 2f_i + f_{i+1}) \qquad i = 1,2, \ldots ,n - 1 \tag{7.22}$$

and the other equations can be modified in a similar manner. A mathematical algorithm for equally spaced data is given in Figure 7.9.

We illustrate the use of the algorithm by interpolating $f(0.22)$ from the equally spaced data of Table 7.2 and incorporating the boundary conditions $\sigma_0 = \sigma_5 = 0$.

Given $n, \bar{x}, (x_i, f_i)$ $\{i = 0, 1, \ldots, n\}$
Set up system of linear equations

$$\sigma_{i-1} + 4\sigma_i + \sigma_{i+1} = \frac{6}{h^2}(f_{i-1} - 2f_i + f_{i+1}) \qquad i = 1, 2, \ldots, n-1$$

Incorporate boundary conditions
Solve system for unknown values σ_i

Obtain the coefficients using the equations

$$a_i = (\sigma_{i+1} - \sigma_i)/6h$$
$$b_i = \sigma_i/2$$
$$c_i = \frac{(f_{i+1} - f_i)}{h} - \frac{(\sigma_{i+1} + 2\sigma_i)}{6}h$$
$$d_i = f_i \qquad\qquad\qquad i = 0, 1, \ldots, n-1$$

Evaluate the spline at $\bar{x}$

Figure 7.9 Algorithm for cubic spline interpolation.

From Equation (7.22), we obtain the equations

$$\begin{aligned}
4\sigma_1 + \sigma_2 &= 139.2000 \\
\sigma_1 + 4\sigma_2 + \sigma_3 &= 198.9600 \\
\sigma_2 + 4\sigma_3 + \sigma_4 &= 288.6000 \\
\sigma_3 + 4\sigma_4 &= 425.1600
\end{aligned}$$

These have the solution

$$\begin{aligned}
\sigma_1 &= 26.5074 \\
\sigma_2 &= 33.1704 \\
\sigma_3 &= 39.7706 \\
\sigma_4 &= 96.3472
\end{aligned}$$

Using these values we obtain the coefficients of Table 7.3.
     The value $\bar{x} = 0.22$ lies in the interval $[0.2, 0.3]$ and so the coefficients needed to evaluate the spline are those of column 3 in Table 7.3. Noting that $\bar{x} - 0.2 = 0.02$, we obtain

$$\begin{aligned}
s(\bar{x}) &= 11.0002(0.02)^3 + 16.5852(0.02)^2 + 10.2195(0.02) + 4.2207 \\
&= 4.4318
\end{aligned}$$

Rounded to four decimal places, the value of $f(0.22)$ is 4.4300 and so we have

Table 7.2   Values of $f(x) = \exp(1 + x)^2$

i	0	1	2	3	4	5
x_i	0.0	0.1	0.2	0.3	0.4	0.5
f_i	2.7183	3.3535	4.2207	5.4195	7.0993	9.4877

Table 7.3   Spline coefficients.

i	0	1	2	3	4
a_i	44.1791	11.1050	11.0002	94.2944	−160.5787
b_i	0.0000	13.2537	16.5852	19.8853	48.1736
c_i	5.9102	7.2356	10.2195	13.8665	20.6724
d_i	2.7183	3.3535	4.2207	5.4195	7.0993

obtained quite a good approximation. In the same way, we can estimate the value of $f'(0.22)$ ($= 10.8092$) using the derivative of the spline. To four decimal places, the spline derivative gives $s'(0.22) = 10.8961$ and this is close to the correct answer. The reader may care to compare these answers with those obtained using Lagrangian interpolation.

A modification of the technique described above, which removes the necessity to specify extra boundary conditions, is to choose only the internal points $x_1, x_2, \ldots, x_{n-1}$ as the spline nodes and to specify that

$$s(x_0) = f_0 \quad \text{and} \quad s(x_n) = f_n$$

This method works well in many cases where information about the derivatives of f is not available.

Program construction

The mathematical algorithm of Figure 7.9 comprises two parts; the first evaluates the unknown σ_i values and the second takes these and produces the coefficients of the spline and its value at a point $\bar{x}$. We will write a subroutine to evaluate the σ_i and a function subprogram that takes the σ_i and evaluates the spline at $\bar{x}$. It will be assumed that the data is equally spaced and that the boundary conditions

$$\sigma_0 = 0 \quad \text{and} \quad \sigma_n = 0$$

are used. The modifications necessitated by unequally spaced data or by the use of alternative boundary conditions are left as an exercise. A plan for a subroutine

Given: $n,(x_i,f_i)$ $\{i = 0,1, \ldots ,n\}$
    $\{$ *Form tri-diagonal system of equations* $\}$
for $i = 1,2, \ldots ,n - 1$
  Set: $d_i = 4$
      $b_i = 6(f_{i-1} - 2f_i + f_{i+1})/h^2$
for $i = 1,2, \ldots ,n - 2$
  Set: c_i $= 1$
    $a_{i+1} = 1$

  $\{$ *Now solve tri-diagonal system of equations* $\}$

Set: $\sigma_0 = 0$
    $\sigma_n = 0$

Figure 7.10 Plan of subroutine for cubic spline σ values.

that obtains the σ values is given in Figure 7.10. Note that the plan is written in the notation of Figure 5.19.

Implementation of the plan of Figure 7.10 is straightforward and the resulting subroutine is given in Figure 7.11. The tri-diagonal system of equations is solved by calling TRISL2 (of Figure 5.21) rather than TRISOL (of Figure 5.20) because the bounds of the array which records the solution (SIGMA) are not the same as the bounds of the arrays holding the coefficients (AT,BT,CT,DT). The system of equations is known to be strictly diagonally dominant and so the value of STATUS is not checked after the call of TRISL2.

A plan for a subprogram that evaluates $s(\bar{x})$ is given in Figure 7.12. Note that a form of nested multiplication is used to evaluate the spline. To determine the subinterval within which $\bar{x}$ lies, we take advantage of the fact that the data is equally spaced. If

$$x_j \leq \bar{x} \leq x_{j+1}$$

then j is the integer part of the expression

$$(\bar{x} - x_0)/h$$

and so, in the function, is evaluated using the statement

J=INT((XBAR-X0)/H)

where X0 replaces X(0) to reduce subscript references. The subprogram is implemented as a FUNCTION as given in Figure 7.13.

The analysis of the accuracy of cubic spline interpolation is beyond the scope of this book but Birkhoff and de Boor (1964) have shown that, under

```
      SUBROUTINE CSPLIN (N,X,F, SIGMA, AT,DT,CT,BT)

      REAL      H,HSQBY6
      INTEGER   I,N,NM1,STATUS
      REAL      AT(N-1),BT(N-1),CT(N-1),DT(N-1),F(0:N),
     *          SIGMA(0:N),X(0:N)
      EXTERNAL   TRISL2

      H      =(X(N)-X(0))/N
      HSQBY6=H*H/6
      NM1    =N-1
      DO 10, I=1,NM1
        DT(I)=4.0
        BT(I)=(F(I-1)-2*F(I)+F(I+1))/HSQBY6
10    CONTINUE

      DO 20, I=1,N-2
        CT(I)  =1
        AT(I+1)=1
20    CONTINUE

      CALL TRISL2 (1,NM1,0,N,AT,DT,CT,BT, STATUS,SIGMA)

      SIGMA(0)=0
      SIGMA(N)=0

      END
```

Figure 7.11 Subroutine for cubic spline σ values.

suitable circumstances,

$$\max_{x_0 \leqslant x \leqslant x_n} |f^{(k)}(x) - s^{(k)}(x)| \leqslant Ch^{4-k} \qquad \text{for } k = 0,1,2$$

as $h \to 0$, where $h = \max(h_i)$ and C is some constant independent of h. Consequently, the difference between the function and the cubic spline, at a fixed point x, behaves as h^4 as h tends to zero.

We meet splines again in Chapter 8 in the discussion of methods for evaluating derivatives of functions. Here, however, we continue by discussing methods for fitting data subject to (possibly experimental) error.

7.2 Data fitting

The situation considered here is illustrated by Figure 7.14. The data values, denoted by crosses, have been obtained from an experiment. The underlying

$Given: n,\bar{x},(x_i,f_i,\sigma_i)\ \{i = 0,1, \ldots ,n\}$
$Determine\ the\ subinterval\ [x_j,x_{j+1}]\ that\ contains\ \bar{x}$
$Set: \quad h = (x_n - x_0)/n$
$\qquad a_j = (\sigma_{j+1} - \sigma_j)/6h$
$\qquad b_j = \sigma_j/2$
$\qquad c_j = \dfrac{(f_{j+1} - f_j)}{h} - \dfrac{(\sigma_{j+1} + 2\sigma_j)}{6}\,h$
$\qquad d_j = f_j$

$Set: diff = \bar{x} - x_j$
$Set: s(x) = ((a_j diff + b_j)diff + c_j)diff + d_j$

Figure 7.12   Plan of subprogram to evaluate $s(\bar{x})$.

```
REAL FUNCTION SPLNEV (N,XBAR,X,F,SIGMA)

INTEGER   J,N
REAL      AJ,BJ,CJ,DIFF,DJ,H,X0,XBAR
REAL      F(0:N),SIGMA(0:N),X(0:N)
INTRINSIC INT

X0=X(0)
H =(X(N)-X(0))/N
J =INT((XBAR-X0)/H)

AJ=(SIGMA(J+1)-SIGMA(J))/(6*H)
BJ=SIGMA(J)/2
CJ=(F(J+1)-F(J))/H-(SIGMA(J+1)+2*SIGMA(J))*H/6
DJ=F(J)

DIFF =XBAR-X(J)
SPLNEV=((AJ*DIFF+BJ)*DIFF+CJ)*DIFF+DJ

END
```

Figure 7.13   Function subprogram to evaluate $s(\bar{x})$.

theory of the experiment suggests that there should be a linear relationship between the variables x and y such that

$$y = a_1 x + a_0$$

where a_0 and a_1 are constants. Because of experimental error, the points do *not* lie on a straight line. However, we have faith in our theory and want to know

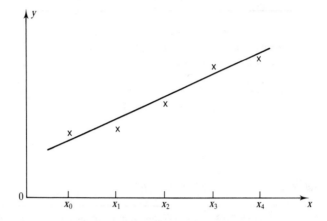

Figure 7.14   Experimental data.

which straight line 'best' fits the data obtained. There are two problems to solve: first, to decide what 'best' means and, having made that decision, to find a method of calculating this best fit.

In this section, we shall concentrate on finding best approximations to the data using polynomials. We address ourselves to the first question: 'What do we mean by best?' What we are seeking is some measure of the difference between the data and the values of the approximating polynomial. For example, if the data $(x_0, f_0), (x_1, f_1), \ldots, (x_m, f_m)$ is given and we want to use a polynomial of degree $n \ (<m)$

$$p_n(x) = a_n x^n + a_{n-1} x^{n-1} + \cdots + a_1 x + a_0$$

to fit this data, then we are interested in **residuals**:

$$f_i - p_n(x_i) \qquad \text{for } i = 0, 1, \ldots, m \tag{7.23}$$

Only one measure of the residuals is considered here: the **least squares** measure. This is widely used for fitting experimental data and is the basis of a solution technique that is computationally straightforward. Descriptions of other measures can be found in Atkinson and Harley (1983).

7.2.1   Least squares approximation

The least squares method determines values for the coefficients $a_0, a_1, \ldots, a_n$ which minimize the function

$$F_2 = \left[\sum_{i=0}^{m} \left(f_i - \sum_{j=0}^{n} a_j x_i^j \right)^2 \right]^{1/2} \tag{7.24}$$

In practice, we minimize F_2^2 (this function has a minimum at the same point as F_2) and thus avoid the need to calculate the square root. Now, F_2^2 is a continuous function of the unknowns and so its minimum can be identified by setting its first derivatives to zero. (F_2^2 can be made arbitrarily large by an appropriate choice of a_j $\{j = 0,1, \ldots ,n\}$ and so, because of the form of F_2^2, zero first derivatives are associated only with minima.) Differentiating F_2^2 with respect to an arbitrary coefficient a_k and setting the result equal to zero gives the equation

$$2 \sum_{i=0}^{m} \left[f_i - \sum_{j=0}^{n} a_j x_i^j \right] (-x_i^k) = 0$$

which can be rearranged to give

$$\sum_{j=0}^{n} a_j \sum_{i=0}^{m} x_i^{j+k} = \sum_{i=0}^{m} f_i x_i^k \tag{7.25}$$

Now, because the choice of the coefficient a_k was arbitrary, Equation (7.25) must hold for each $k = 0,1, \ldots ,n$, resulting in a system of $n + 1$ simultaneous linear equations in the $n + 1$ unknowns a_k $\{k = 0,1, \ldots ,n\}$. These equations are known as the **normal** equations and can be rewritten in the obvious matrix–vector form

$$Ca = b \tag{7.26}$$

where

$$c_{jk} = \sum_{i=0}^{m} x_i^{j+k} \qquad \text{for } j,k = 0,1, \ldots ,n$$

and

$$b_k = \sum_{i=0}^{m} f_i x_i^k$$

Equations (7.26) have a unique solution provided that the x_i are distinct. It appears that a solution can be obtained very easily by applying any of the methods of Section 5.1 and, in fact, this *is* the case when n, the degree of the polynomial, does not exceed 5 or 6, say. A mathematical algorithm for this polynomial least squares method is given in Figure 7.15.

We apply this algorithm to determine the least squares line $p_1(x) = a_1 x + a_0$ which fits the values given in Table 7.4. The elements of the matrix C of Equation (7.26) are

Given $m,(x_i, f_i)$ $\{i = 0,1, \ldots ,m\}$, n
For $k = 0,1, \ldots ,n$
  For $j = 0,1, \ldots ,n$

$$\text{Set } c_{jk} = \sum_{i=0}^{m} x_i^{j+k}$$

$$\text{Set } b_k = \sum_{i=0}^{m} f_i x_i^k$$

Solve system of linear equations using pivoted Gaussian elimination

Figure 7.15 Algorithm for finding the least squares polynomial.

Table 7.4 Values of $f(x) = e^x$.

x	-2	-1	0	1	2
$f(x)$	0.1353	0.3679	1.0000	2.7183	7.3891

$$c_{00} = \sum_{i=0}^{m} x_i^0 = \sum_{i=0}^{4} 1 = 5$$

$$c_{01} = c_{10} = \sum_{i=0}^{m} x_i^1 = \sum_{i=0}^{4} x_i = 0$$

$$c_{11} = \sum_{i=0}^{m} x_i^2 = \sum_{i=0}^{4} x_i^2 = 10$$

and so

$$C = \begin{bmatrix} 5 & 0 \\ 0 & 10 \end{bmatrix}$$

The elements of b are

$$b_0 = \sum_{i=0}^{m} f_i x_i^0 = \sum_{i=0}^{4} f_i = 11.6106$$

$$b_1 = \sum_{i=0}^{m} f_i x_i^1 = \sum_{i=0}^{4} f_i x_i = 16.8580$$

Thus the unknown coefficients a_0 and a_1 can be determined from the equations

$$\begin{bmatrix} 5 & 0 \\ 0 & 10 \end{bmatrix} \begin{bmatrix} a_0 \\ a_1 \end{bmatrix} = \begin{bmatrix} 11.6106 \\ 16.8580 \end{bmatrix}$$

Solving these equations gives $a_0 = 2.3221$ and $a_1 = 1.6858$.

For larger values of n, the least squares approximations obtained by solving Equation (7.26) become progressively worse, independently of the method of solution. This happens because the matrix C is closely related to the ill-conditioned Hilbert matrix, mentioned in Exercise 5.16. The difficulties associated with the solution of Equation (7.26) can be avoided by using a sequence of polynomials $P_j(x)$ of degree j ($j = 0, 1, \ldots$) which are **orthogonal** on the set of points $\{x_i\}$.

Definition 7.1

Two polynomials $P_k(x)$ and $P_l(x)$ are said to be orthogonal on the set of points $\{x_i, i = 0, 1, \ldots, m\}$ if

$$\sum_{i=0}^{m} P_k(x_i)P_l(x_i) \quad \begin{cases} = 0 & k \neq l \\ > 0 & k = l \end{cases}$$

Now, instead of using the polynomial

$$\sum_{j=0}^{n} a_j x^j$$

as the approximation, we use

$$\sum_{j=0}^{n} b_j P_j(x)$$

Theorem 7.3

If the polynomials $P_j(x)$ $\{j = 0, 1, \ldots, n\}$ of degree j are orthogonal on the set of points x_i $\{i = 0, 1, \ldots, m\}$, then the least squares approximation to $f(x)$, on the set of points $\{x_i\}$, by a polynomial of degree at most n is given by

$$p_n(x) = \sum_{j=0}^{n} b_j P_j(x)$$

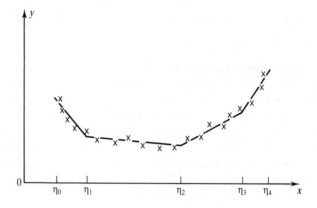

Figure 7.16   Piecewise-linear approximation.

where

$$b_j - \dfrac{\displaystyle\sum_{i=0}^{m} f_i P_j(x_i)}{\displaystyle\sum_{i=0}^{m} P_j^2(x_i)}$$

A proof of this result can be found in Atkinson and Harley (1983).

The use of orthogonal polynomials has the obvious advantage that the coefficients of the approximation can be written down immediately. However, a disadvantage of this approach is that whenever the points, x_i, are changed so are the equations of the orthogonal polynomials; in this sense they are similar to the Lagrange polynomials.

   Many of the advantages of the use of orthogonal polynomials are also associated with the use of piecewise polynomial approximations. Cubic splines, a form of piecewise polynomial, were used in Section 7.1.2 to interpolate data and it is also possible to use them to fit data in the least squares sense. However, a rather simpler problem will be considered here – that of using piecewise linear polynomials to fit data.

7.2.2   Piecewise polynomial approximation

In Figure 7.16, the crosses represent given data and the straight lines represent an approximation to this data using piecewise polynomials. The points $\eta_0, \eta_1, \ldots, \eta_n$, on the x-axis, are the *nodes* of the approximation. Between

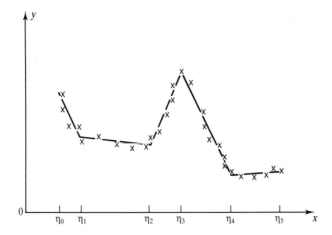

Figure 7.17 Choice of nodes.

each consecutive pair of nodes, $[\eta_0,\eta_1],[\eta_1,\eta_2], \ldots ,[\eta_{n-1},\eta_n]$, the approximation is a straight line and at each internal node $\eta_1,\eta_2,\ldots,\eta_{n-1}$ the
straight-line representation to the left of the node matches that to the right. This
means that the approximation is continuous everywhere but that it cannot be
differentiated, with respect to x, at the nodes. Note that there are fewer nodes
than data points; in general, there are usually many more data points than nodes
$(n \ll m)$.

The nodes need not be equally spaced and, because they need no longer
be points on which data is given, their positions can be chosen for convenience.
Usually, this choice depends on the distribution of data values. For example,
given the data (marked $\times$ in Figure 7.17) it seems logical to use the nodes to
split the data into approximate straight-line segments and this has been achieved
using the nodes $\eta_0,\eta_1, \ldots ,\eta_5$.

The simplest form for the piecewise linear approximation, $p(x)$, is

$$p(x) = \sum_{j=0}^{n} \alpha_j\phi_j(x) \tag{7.27}$$

where each $\phi_j(x)$ is a piecewise-linear **basis** function of the form shown in
Figure 7.18.

Note that $\phi_j(x)$ is zero at η_{j-1} and η_{j+1}, that it is zero for values of x
outside the subinterval (η_{j-1},η_{j+1}) and that the value of $\phi_j(x)$ at η_j is unity. As a
result, the coefficients α_j $\{j = 0,1, \ldots ,n\}$ represent the values of the
approximation at the nodes η_j $\{j = 0,1, \ldots ,n\}$. Thus

$$p(\eta_j) = \alpha_j \quad \text{for } j = 0,1, \ldots ,n$$

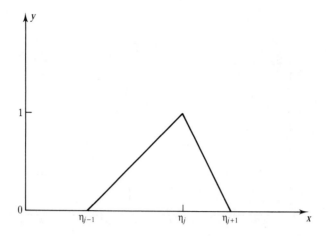

Figure 7.18 Basis function $\phi_j(x)$.

A similar property is displayed by the Lagrange polynomial of Section 7.1. The equation of each $\phi_j(x)$ is given by

$$\phi_j(x) = \begin{cases} 0, & x \leqslant \eta_{j-1} \\ \dfrac{x - \eta_{j-1}}{\eta_j - \eta_{j-1}} & \eta_{j-1} \leqslant x \leqslant \eta_j \\ \dfrac{x - \eta_{j+1}}{\eta_j - \eta_{j+1}} & \eta_j \leqslant x \leqslant \eta_{j+1} \\ 0 & \eta_{j+1} \leqslant x \end{cases}$$

Before giving an example of least squares piecewise linear approximation, we will reformulate the normal equations to take account of the new form of approximation. The residuals can be written as

$$f_i - \sum_{j=0}^{n} \alpha_j \phi_j(x_i)$$

and so we have to minimize

$$\hat{F}_2^2 = \sum_{i=0}^{m} \left[f_i - \sum_{j=0}^{n} \alpha_j \phi_j(x_i) \right]^2$$

As before, differentiating with respect to an arbitrary coefficient, α_k, gives the condition

$$2 \sum_{i=0}^{m} \left(f_i - \sum_{j=0}^{n} \alpha_j \phi_j(x_i) \right) (-\phi_k(x_i)) = 0 \qquad \text{for } k = 0, 1, \ldots, n$$

which can be rearranged to give the equations

$$\sum_{j=0}^{n} \alpha_j \sum_{i=0}^{m} \phi_j(x_i)\phi_k(x_i) = \sum_{i=0}^{m} f_i\phi_k(x_i) \qquad \text{for } k = 0,1, \ldots ,n \qquad \text{(7.28)}$$

or, in a form similar to Equation (7.26),

$$Pa = c \qquad \qquad \text{(7.29)}$$

where

$$p_{jk} = \sum_{i=0}^{m} \phi_j(x_i)\phi_k(x_i) \qquad j,k = 0,1,\ldots,n$$

and

$$c_k = \sum_{i=0}^{m} f_i\phi_k(x_i) \qquad k = 0,1,\ldots,n$$

It can be shown that the symmetric tri-diagonal system of Equation (7.28) has a unique solution.

An algorithm for determining the piecewise polynomial least squares (PPLS) fit to a set of data, given the nodes η_k, $\{k = 0,1, \ldots ,n\}$, is given in Figure 7.19. To illustrate the algorithm, we find the piecewise-linear least squares approximation to the data from Table 7.5 using nodes $\eta_0 = 0$, $\eta_1 = 1$, $\eta_2 = 3$ and $\eta_3 = 5$.

The values of the basis functions $\phi_j(x)$ $\{j = 0,1,2,3\}$ evaluated at the x_i $\{i = 0,1, \ldots ,10\}$ are presented in Table 7.6. From these values we evaluate the elements of P.

$$P_{00} = \sum_{i=0}^{10} [\phi_0(x_i)]^2 = 1.25$$
$$P_{01} = P_{10} = \sum_{i=0}^{10} \phi_0(x_i)\phi_1(x_i) = 0.25$$
$$\vdots$$

Similarly, we calculate the c_k values:

$$c_0 = \sum_{i=0}^{10} f_i\phi_0(x_i) = 4.5$$
$$c_1 = \sum_{i=0}^{10} f_i\phi_1(x_i) = 2.275$$
$$\vdots$$

Given (x_i, f_i) $\{i = 0,1, \ldots ,m\}$ and η_j $\{j = 0,1, \ldots ,n\}$
For $j = 0,1, \ldots ,n$
  For $i = 0,1, \ldots ,m$
    Set $x = x_i$

$$\phi_j(x) = \begin{cases} 0 & x \leq \eta_{j-1} \\ \dfrac{x - \eta_{j-1}}{\eta_j - \eta_{j-1}} & \eta_{j-1} \leq x \leq \eta_j \\ \dfrac{x - \eta_{j+1}}{\eta_j - \eta_{j+1}} & \eta_j \leq x \leq \eta_{j+1} \\ 0 & \eta_{j+1} \leq x \end{cases}$$

For $k = 0,1, \ldots ,n$
  For $j = 0,1, \ldots ,n$
    Set $p_{jk} = \displaystyle\sum_{i=0}^{m} \phi_j(x_i)\, \phi_k(x_i)$
For $k = 0,1, \ldots ,n$
  Set $c_k = \displaystyle\sum_{i=0}^{m} f_i \phi_k(x_i)$
Solve $Pa = c$ using tri-diagonal solver

Figure 7.19   Algorithm for PPLS approximation.

Table 7.5   Function values.

i	x_i	f_i
0	0.0	3.80
1	0.5	1.40
2	1.0	0.75
3	1.5	0.55
4	2.0	0.55
5	2.5	0.55
6	3.0	0.65
7	3.5	1.00
8	4.0	1.45
9	4.5	2.00
10	5.0	2.80

Table 7.6 Point values of basis functions.

i	x_i	ϕ_0	ϕ_1	ϕ_2	ϕ_3
0	0.0	1.00	0.00		
1	0.5	0.50	0.50		
2	1.0	0.00	1.00	0.00	
3	1.5		0.75	0.25	
4	2.0		0.50	0.50	
5	2.5		0.25	0.75	
6	3.0		0.00	1.00	0.00
7	3.5			0.75	0.25
8	4.0			0.50	0.50
9	4.5			0.25	0.75
10	5.0			0.00	1.00

and thus obtain the system of linear equations:

$$\begin{bmatrix} 1.250 & 0.250 & 0.000 & 0.000 \\ 0.250 & 2.125 & 0.625 & 0.000 \\ 0.000 & 0.625 & 2.750 & 0.625 \\ 0.000 & 0.000 & 0.625 & 1.875 \end{bmatrix} \begin{bmatrix} \alpha_0 \\ \alpha_1 \\ \alpha_2 \\ \alpha_3 \end{bmatrix} = \begin{bmatrix} 4.500 \\ 2.275 \\ 3.450 \\ 5.275 \end{bmatrix}$$

This system has the solution

$$a = \begin{bmatrix} 3.50 \\ 0.50 \\ 0.54 \\ 2.63 \end{bmatrix}$$

The graphs of the data values and the final approximation are given in Figure 7.20.

Program construction

The subroutine plan of Figure 7.21 contains the main elements of the algorithm of Figure 7.19. A separate subroutine will be written for each step of the plan and so this plan leads to the overall controlling subroutine PPLS given in Figure 7.22. The matrix P is tri-diagonal and, because the coefficients are

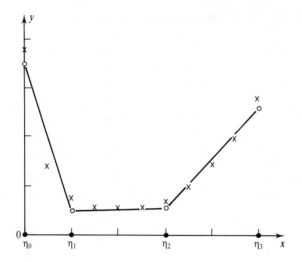

Figure 7.20 Graph of data ($\times$) and approximation (——).

Given: $n, m, (x_i, f_i) \{i = 0, 1, \ldots, m\}, \eta_j \{j = 0, 1, \ldots, n\}$
Evaluate: $\phi_j(x_i)$ *using* $x_i \{i = 0, 1, \ldots, m\}$ *and* $\eta_j \{j = 0, 1, \ldots, n\}$
  P_{jk} *using* ϕ_j *and* $\phi_k \{j, k = 0, 1, \ldots, n\}$
  c_k *using* $\phi_k \{k = 0, 1, \ldots, n\}$ *and* $f_i \{i = 0, 1, \ldots, m\}$
Solve: $Pa = c$

Figure 7.21 Plan of subroutine for PPLS.

```
SUBROUTINE PPLS (NSIZE,MSIZE,N,M,X,F,NODE,
*                A,STATUS,PSUB,PDIAG,PSUP,C,PHI)

INTEGER  M,MSIZE,N,NSIZE,STATUS
REAL     A(0:N),C(0:N),F(0:M),NODE(0:N),
*        PDIAG(0:N),PHI(0:NSIZE,0:MSIZE),PSUB(0:N),
*        PSUP(0:N),X(0:M)
EXTERNAL SETC,SETP,SETPHI,TRISL2

CALL SETPHI (NSIZE,MSIZE,N,M,X,NODE, PHI)
CALL SETP   (NSIZE,MSIZE,N,M,PHI, PSUB,PDIAG,PSUP)
CALL SETC   (NSIZE,MSIZE,N,M,F,PHI, C)

CALL TRISL2 (0,N,0,N,PSUB,PDIAG,PSUP,C, STATUS,A)

END
```

Figure 7.22 Subroutine to determine least squares approximation.

subscripted from 0, the equations are solved using subroutine TRISL2 of Figure 5.21. Accordingly, the diagonals of P are stored in three one-dimensional arrays PSUB, PDIAG and PSUP.

Subroutine PPLS makes use of a two-dimensional array PHI to store the values of the basis functions at the data points and initializes this array using the subroutine SETPHI of Figure 7.23. Making full use of symmetry, the values in PSUB, PDIAG and PSUP are set up using the subroutine SETP of Figure 7.24; those in C are set up using subroutine SETC of Figure 7.24. The arrays PSUB, PDIAG and PSUP are formed from the products of the basis functions and each component is evaluated using the function subprogram DOTPRD of Figure 7.25. This calculates the product of row I and row J of a matrix stored in Q.

There is an alternative form of least squares approximation, the **weighted** least squares approximation, in which the functional

$$W_2 = \left[\sum_{i=0}^{m} \omega_i \left(f_i - \sum_{j=0}^{n} a_j x_i^j \right)^2 \right]^{1/2} \tag{7.30}$$

is minimized rather than that of Equation (7.24). The *weights* ω_i $\{i = 0, 1, \ldots, m\}$ are positive values chosen to emphasize certain of the residuals. In this way a large weight can be attached to particular residuals that are required to be small in the final solution. The least squares technique will 'see' these residuals as being large and will calculate a solution to compensate for this.

7.2.3 Alternative approximating functions

In this chapter, we have concentrated on using polynomials to approximate the original data. In some cases this choice is inappropriate. For example, the data may be periodic (related, say, to the availability of sunlight) or may vary exponentially (many biological processes appear to behave in this way). For the first case the use of trigonometric functions seems sensible and these are the basis of the well known method utilizing **Fourier series**; in the second case the use of exponential functions is indicated. A further type of approximating function in common use is the **rational** polynomial consisting of the ratio of two polynomials. Rational polynomials are particularly useful for approximating functions; the interested reader is referred to Ralston and Rabinowitz (1978).

Figure 7.23 Subroutine to set up PHI.

```
SUBROUTINE SETPHI (NSIZE,MSIZE,N,M,X,NODE, PHI)

INTEGER I,J,M,MSIZE,N,NSIZE
REAL     NJ,NJM1,NJP1,XI
REAL     NODE(0:N),PHI(0:NSIZE,0:MSIZE),X(0:M)
```

```
C       { First and last basis functions are special cases }

        NJ  =NODE(0)
        NJP1=NODE(1)
        DO 10, I=0,M
          XI=X(I)
          IF (XI.GE.NJP1) THEN
            PHI(0,I)=0
          ELSE
            PHI(0,I)=(XI-NJP1)/(NJ-NJP1)
          END IF
10      CONTINUE

        NJM1=NODE(N-1)
        NJ  =NODE(N)
        DO 20, I=0,M
          XI=X(I)
          IF (XI.LE.NJM1) THEN
            PHI(N,I)=0
          ELSE
            PHI(N,I)=(XI-NJM1)/(NJ-NJM1)
          END IF
20      CONTINUE

C       { The rest follow the same pattern }

        DO 30, J=1,N-1
          NJM1=NODE(J-1)
          NJ  =NODE(J)
          NJP1=NODE(J+1)
          DO 40, I=0,M
            XI=X(I)
            IF (XI.LE.NJM1) THEN
              PHI(J,I)=0
            ELSE IF (XI.LE.NJ) THEN
              PHI(J,I)=(XI-NJM1)/(NJ-NJM1)
            ELSE IF (XI.LE.NJP1) THEN
              PHI(J,I)=(XI-NJP1)/(NJ-NJP1)
            ELSE
              PHI(J,I)=0
            END IF
40        CONTINUE
30      CONTINUE

        END
```

Figure 7.23 *cont.*

```
      SUBROUTINE SETP (NSIZE,MSIZE,N,M,PHI, PSUB,PDIAG,PSUP)

      INTEGER   J,M,MSIZE,N,NSIZE
      REAL      DOTPRD
      REAL      PDIAG(0:N),PHI(0:NSIZE,0:MSIZE),PSUB(0:N),PSUP(0:N)
      EXTERNAL DOTPRD

      PDIAG(0)=DOTPRD (NSIZE,MSIZE,M,PHI,0,0)
      DO 10, J=1,N-1
        PSUB(J)  =DOTPRD (NSIZE,MSIZE,M,PHI,J-1,J)
        PDIAG(J) =DOTPRD (NSIZE,MSIZE,M,PHI,J,J)
        PSUP(J-1)=PSUB(J)
10    CONTINUE
      PSUB(N)  =DOTPRD (NSIZE,MSIZE,M,PHI,N,N-1)
      PDIAG(N) =DOTPRD (NSIZE,MSIZE,M,PHI,N,N)
      PSUP(N-1)=PSUB(N)

      END


      SUBROUTINE SETC (NSIZE,MSIZE,N,M,F,PHI, C)

      INTEGER   I,K,M,MSIZE,N,NSIZE
      DOUBLE PRECISION SUM
      REAL      C(0:N),F(0:M),PHI(0:NSIZE,0:MSIZE)
      INTRINSIC DPROD

      DO 10, K=0,N
        SUM=0
        DO 20, I=0,M
          SUM=SUM+DPROD(F(I),PHI(K,I))
20      CONTINUE
        C(K)=SUM
10    CONTINUE

      END
```

Figure 7.24   Subroutines to set up values in PSUB, PDIAG, PSUP and C.

```
REAL FUNCTION DOTPRD (NSIZE,MSIZE,M,Q,I,J)

INTEGER   I,J,K,M,MSIZE,NSIZE
DOUBLE PRECISION SUM
REAL      Q(0:NSIZE,0:MSIZE)
INTRINSIC DPROD

SUM=0
DO 10, K=0,M
  SUM=SUM+DPROD(Q(I,K),Q(J,K))
10  CONTINUE
DOTPRD=SUM

END
```

Figure 7.25   Function subprogram to form product of basis.

EXERCISES

7.1 Use the appropriate Lagrange interpolation polynomial to estimate $f(0.14)$ from each of the following sets of values:

(a)

x	0.0	0.1	0.2	0.3	0.4
f	0.0000	0.1002	0.2013	0.3045	0.4108

(b)

x	-2	-1	0	1	2
f	-1.2599	-1	0	1	1.2599

(c)

x	0.11	0.12	0.15	0.16	0.19
f	1.1095	1.1194	1.1488	1.1585	1.1875

7.2 In Exercise 7.1, $f(x)$ is given by (a) $f(x) = \sinh x$, (b) $f(x) = x^{1/3}$ and (c) $f(x) = e^x \cos x$. Use the Lagrange error formula to bound the error in each case.

7.3 Use the Lagrange interpolation formula to obtain an extrapolated value of $f(2.5)$ given the data

x	0.0	0.5	1.0	1.5	2.0
f	1.0000	1.6487	2.7183	4.4817	7.3891

7.4 Given that the function of Exercise 7.3 is e^x, obtain error bounds on your answer.

7.5 In the interval $[0,1]$, the function $f(x) = e^x$ is to be approximated by a piecewise-linear polynomial whose nodes are equally spaced. Use the Lagrange error formula to determine the minimum number of nodes required to ensure that interpolated results are correct to at least four decimal places.

7.6 Given the values

x	0.5	1.0	1.5	2.0
f	−0.1733	0.0000	0.9123	2.7726

obtain the coefficients of the cubic spline interpolate that uses the end-conditions

(a) $\sigma_0 = \sigma_3 = 0$

(b) $f'_0 = -0.1931$, $f'_3 = 4.7726$

7.7 Use the coefficients obtained in (a) and (b) of Exercise 7.6 to estimate $f(1.73)$ and compare your answers with the exact value, 1.6405 (rounded to four decimal places).

7.8 Obtain the least squares fit by polynomials of degree 1 and degree 2 to the data

x	0.0	0.1	0.2	0.3	0.4	0.5
f	1.0000	1.2589	1.5849	1.9953	2.5119	3.1623

Draw the graph of the data and of the approximating polynomials.

7.9 Using the piecewise linear polynomial basis functions associated with the nodes $\eta_0 = 0.0$, $\eta_1 = 0.2$ and $\eta_3 = 0.5$, obtain a least squares fit to the data of Exercise 7.8. Draw the graph of the data and of the polynomial.

Programming exercises

7.10 Using the function LAGINT of Figure 7.5, obtain numerical values of the polynomial which interpolates the data of Table 7.1. Draw the graph of the polynomial, paying particular attention to the intervals [0,0.1] and [0.6,1.0]. Given that the data is derived from the function e^x, how accurate do you think your interpolate is outside the interval [0.1,0.6]?

7.11 Modify the function LAGINT of Figure 7.5 to take appropriate action if the interpolation point XBAR is 'close' to one of the data points.

7.12 Modify the subroutine CSPLIN of Figure 7.11 to use the boundary conditions (7.20). Use this subroutine and the function SPLNEV of Figure 7.13 to estimate $f(1.73)$ from the data of Exercise 7.6.

7.13 Modify the subroutine CSPLIN and the function SPLNEV (Figures 7.11 and 7.13) to accept unequally spaced data and end-conditions of the form given in (7.20). Using the end-conditions

$$f'_0 = 1.1143 \qquad \text{and} \qquad f'_4 = 1.2056$$

write and run a program that uses the modified routines to estimate $f(0.14)$ from the data of Exercise 7.1(c).

7.14 Write a program that uses the subroutine PPLS of Figure 7.22. Run it to determine a piecewise-linear approximation to the data of Exercise 7.1(c) using the nodes $\eta_0 = 0.0$, $\eta_1 = 0.2$ and $\eta_2 = 0.5$. By varying the position of the node η_1 and computing the least squares function value $\hat{F}_2^2$, determine the position of the node η_1 that minimizes $\hat{F}_2^2$.

Chapter 8
Differentiation and integration

8.1 Differentiation   8.2 Integration

There are essentially two situations where numerical differentiation, or integration, is necessary. The first occurs when only function values are given and so numerical differentiation or integration is the only option. The second arises when the function to be differentiated, or integrated, is complicated and an analytic differentiation, or integration, is difficult if not impossible.

To ensure that the processes we perform are meaningful we assume, throughout this chapter, that the function is sufficiently smooth, without discontinuities or singularities.

8.1   Differentiation

In Chapter 7 we described several methods for obtaining polynomial approximations to functions represented by sets of discrete data. In this section,
approximations to the derivatives of the function are obtained by differentiating
one of the polynomial approximations. However, the reader should be aware that
this process may not lead to accurate results. For example, the interpolating
polynomial $p(x)$ of Figure 8.1 is a good approximation to $f(x)$ over the interval
$[x_0, x_4]$ but the gradients of $p(x)$ and $f(x)$ differ significantly at some points.

8.1.1   Differentiating a tabulated function

We begin by considering the problem of estimating derivatives given values of
the function at discrete points. Numerical differentiation formulae can be
obtained by differentiating any interpolating function; the Lagrange interpolation
polynomial will be used here. We illustrate this by considering the situation in
which we have been given three sets of values – (x_0, f_0), (x_1, f_1) and (x_2, f_2) –
and we shall assume that the data is ordered so that $x_0 < x_1 < x_2$. The Lagrange
interpolation polynomial has degree 2 and is written as

$$p_2(x) = f_0 l_0(x) + f_1 l_1(x) + f_2 l_2(x)$$
$$= f_0 \frac{(x - x_1)(x - x_2)}{(x_0 - x_1)(x_0 - x_2)} + f_1 \frac{(x - x_0)(x - x_2)}{(x_1 - x_0)(x_1 - x_2)} + f_2 \frac{(x - x_0)(x - x_1)}{(x_2 - x_0)(x_2 - x_1)}$$

and the error, $f(x) - p_2(x)$, is given by the expression

$$E(x) = \frac{(x - x_0)(x - x_1)(x - x_2)}{3!} f^{(3)}(\xi) \qquad x_0 < \xi < x_2$$

We now approximate $f'(x)$ by $p_2'(x)$, i.e. by

$$p_2'(x) = f_0 l_0'(x) + f_1 l_1'(x) + f_2 l_2'(x) \tag{8.1}$$

where

$$l_0'(x) = \frac{(2x - x_1 - x_2)}{(x_0 - x_1)(x_0 - x_2)} \tag{8.2a}$$

$$l_1'(x) = \frac{(2x - x_0 - x_2)}{(x_1 - x_0)(x_1 - x_2)} \tag{8.2b}$$

$$l_2'(x) = \frac{(2x - x_0 - x_1)}{(x_2 - x_0)(x_2 - x_1)} \tag{8.2c}$$

Thus, the process is straightforward and so a mathematical algorithm is not
provided; an example follows directly. The derivative of $f(x) = e^x$ at $x = 0.2$ is
estimated given the data values $(0.0,1.0000)$, $(0.1,1.1052)$ and $(0.3,1.3499)$.

From Equations (8.2),

$$l_0'(0.2) = \quad 0.0000$$
$$l_1'(0.2) = -5.0000$$
$$l_2'(0.2) = \quad 5.0000$$

and so $l_0' + l_1' + l_2' = 0$. This is to be expected because, as noted in Chapter 7, $l_0 + l_1 + l_2 = 1$ and so the derivative of the sum is zero. The approximation to $f'(0.2)$ is

$$\begin{aligned} p_2' &= 1.0000(0.0000) + 1.1052(-5.0000) + 1.3499(5.0000) \\ &= 1.2235 \end{aligned}$$

The correct value of $f'(0.2) = e^{0.2}$ is 1.2214, to four decimal places, and so the numerical approximation is a reasonable estimate of the correct answer. To see how accurate an answer can be expected, the error in the differentiation process must also be studied.

Both differentiation and integration are linear operations, i.e.

$$\frac{d}{dx}[f(x) - g(x)] = \frac{d}{dx}[f(x)] - \frac{d}{dx}[g(x)]$$

and

$$\int [f(x) - g(x)] \, dx = \int f(x) \, dx - \int g(x) \, dx$$

Thus, the error in the numerical differentiation is the differential of the interpolation error. This gives

$$\begin{aligned} f'(x) - p_2'(x) &= \frac{d}{dx}[E(x)] \\ &= \frac{d}{dx}\left[\frac{(x - x_0)(x - x_1)(x - x_2)}{3!} f^{(3)}(\xi) \right] \qquad x_0 < \xi < x_2 \\ &= \frac{1}{3!}\left[\frac{d}{dx}\{(x - x_0)(x - x_1)(x - x_2)\} f^{(3)}(\xi) \right. \\ &\qquad \left. + (x - x_0)(x - x_1)(x - x_2)\frac{d}{dx}\{f^{(3)}(\xi)\} \right] \end{aligned} \qquad (8.3)$$

because the point ξ is a function of the point x at which the interpolate is evaluated. Unfortunately, the analysis is not straightforward because the dependence of ξ on x is not known and so the second differential expression in Equation (8.3) cannot be evaluated. However, by concentrating on evaluating the derivative of the interpolation polynomial at one of the data points, the second term in Equation (8.3) becomes zero and the error can be estimated.

If the data is equally spaced, the formulae for estimating derivatives at tabular points are particularly simple. Assuming that $x_i = x_0 + ih$ $\{i = 0,1,2\}$

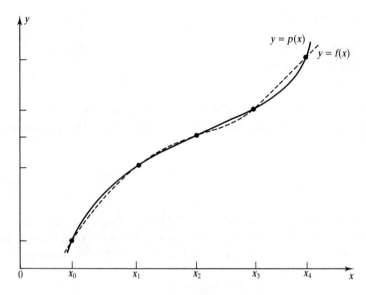

Figure 8.1 Quartic interpolation polynomial $p(x)$.

and substituting $x = x_0$, $x = x_1$ and $x = x_2$, in turn, into Equations (8.1) and (8.2) we obtain the estimates

$$f_0' \simeq \frac{-1}{2h}(3f_0 - 4f_1 + f_2) \tag{8.4a}$$

$$f_1' \simeq \frac{1}{2h}(f_2 - f_0) \tag{8.4b}$$

$$f_2' \simeq \frac{1}{2h}(f_0 - 4f_1 + 3f_2) \tag{8.4c}$$

From Equation (8.3), the corresponding errors are

$$E(x_0) = \frac{h^2}{3}f^{(3)}(\xi_0)$$

$$E(x_1) = \frac{-h^2}{6}f^{(3)}(\xi_1)$$

$$E(x_2) = \frac{h^2}{3}f^{(3)}(\xi_2)$$

where $x_0 < \xi_0, \xi_1, \xi_2 < x_2$. To illustrate the application of these formulae we estimate $f'(0.1)$ for $f(x) = e^x$ using the data $(0.0, 1.0000)$, $(0.1, 1.1052)$ and $(0.2, 1.2214)$. From Equation (8.4b),

$$f'(0.1) \simeq \frac{1}{2(0.1)}(1.2214 - 1.0000) = 1.1070$$

with error bounds

$$0.0017 = \frac{h^2}{6} f^{(3)}(x_0) \leqslant |E| \leqslant \frac{h^2}{6} f^{(3)}(x_2) = 0.0020$$

where, because $f^{(3)}$ is a monotonic increasing function, its values at x_0 and x_2 have been used to bound the error. The actual error is -0.0018 and its modulus does lie between the bounds.

8.1.2   Differentiating an analytic function

The differentiation formulae given above are designed to give estimates when the data is discrete. Obviously, they can be used when the function itself is available and can be evaluated anywhere in an interval $[a,b]$ (say). In this situation, however, the number *and* positions of the points at which the function is to be evaluated can be chosen. Consequently, a more accurate estimate of the derivative can usually be obtained but there are restrictions and these will be discussed later. First, an alternative method of deriving the differentiation formulae will be given.

Suppose that the derivative of the function $f(x)$ at the point $\bar{x}$ is required and also that the points $\bar{x} + h$ and $\bar{x} - h$ lie inside the interval $[a,b]$. Using Taylor's series (see Appendix A) we can write

$$f(\bar{x} + h) = f(\bar{x}) + hf'(\bar{x}) + \frac{h^2}{2!} f''(\bar{x}) + \frac{h^3}{3!} f^{(3)}(\bar{x}) + \cdots \tag{8.5}$$

and

$$f(\bar{x} - h) = f(\bar{x}) - hf'(\bar{x}) + \frac{h^2}{2!} f''(\bar{x}) - \frac{h^3}{3!} f^{(3)}(\bar{x}) + \cdots \tag{8.6}$$

Subtracting Equation (8.6) from Equation (8.5) and dividing by $2h$ gives the equation

$$f'(\bar{x}) = \frac{f(\bar{x} + h) - f(\bar{x} - h)}{2h} - \sum_{j=1}^{\infty} \frac{f^{(2j+1)}(\bar{x})}{(2j + 1)!} h^{2j} \tag{8.7}$$

Similarly we can obtain the expression

$$f''(\bar{x}) = \frac{f(\bar{x} + h) - 2f(\bar{x}) + f(\bar{x} - h)}{h^2} - \sum_{j=1}^{\infty} \frac{f^{(2j+2)}(\bar{x})}{(2j + 2)!} h^{2j}$$

As a result, if h is chosen to be sufficiently small, $f'(\bar{x})$ can be approximated by

$$f'(\bar{x}) \simeq \frac{f(\bar{x} + h) - f(\bar{x} - h)}{2h} \qquad (8.8)$$

and $f''(\bar{x})$ by

$$f''(\bar{x}) \simeq \frac{f(\bar{x} + h) - 2f(\bar{x}) + f(\bar{x} - h)}{h^2}$$

Note that the approximation in Equation (8.8) is equivalent to that in Equation (8.4b). Formulae for higher derivatives can be obtained in exactly the same way.

8.1.3   Rounding error versus truncation error

It might be expected that arbitrarily good approximations to the first and second derivatives of $f(x)$ at $\bar{x}$ would be obtained by taking a sequence of decreasing positive values of h. Unfortunately, rounding errors eventually dominate the calculation and it can be seen quite easily why this should be. If h in Equation (8.8) is allowed to become very small in magnitude, the two terms $f(\bar{x} + h)$ and $f(\bar{x} - h)$ in the numerator must be nearly equal and so their difference must be small. Also, the denominator $2h$ must be small because h is small and so Equation (8.8) consists of the quotient of two small numbers. In Chapter 3 we advised that this situation be avoided if possible because of the effects of rounding errors.

This error can be analysed further. Using the Mean Value Theorem (see Appendix A) to replace the infinite series for the error, Equation (8.7) can be rewritten in the form

$$f'(\bar{x}) = \frac{f(\bar{x} + h) - f(\bar{x} - h)}{2h} - \frac{h^2}{6} f^{(3)}(\xi)$$

where $\bar{x} - h < \xi < \bar{x} + h$. Now, suppose that evaluation of $f(\bar{x} + h)$ incurs a rounding error $\varepsilon_{\bar{x}+h}$ and evaluation of $f(\bar{x} - h)$ incurs a rounding error $\varepsilon_{\bar{x}-h}$. Then, the computed values $\tilde{f}(\bar{x} + h)$ and $\tilde{f}(\bar{x} - h)$ have the form

$$\tilde{f}(\bar{x} + h) = f(\bar{x} + h) + \varepsilon_{\bar{x}+h}$$

and

$$\tilde{f}(\bar{x} - h) = f(\bar{x} - h) + \varepsilon_{\bar{x}-h}$$

Consequently, the error in the approximation to $f'(\bar{x})$ is

$$f'(\bar{x}) - \frac{\tilde{f}(\bar{x} + h) - \tilde{f}(\bar{x} - h)}{2h} = \frac{\varepsilon_{\bar{x}+h} - \varepsilon_{\bar{x}-h}}{2h} - \frac{h^2}{6} f^{(3)}(\xi)$$

involving both rounding and truncation errors. If we can bound the modulus of the rounding errors $\varepsilon_{\bar{x}\pm h}$ by some value $\varepsilon > 0$ and we assume that the modulus of third derivative of f is bounded by some value F then

$$\left| f'(\bar{x}) - \frac{\tilde{f}(\bar{x}+h) - \tilde{f}(\bar{x}-h)}{2h} \right| \leq \frac{\varepsilon}{h} + \frac{h^2}{6}F \tag{8.9}$$

This error expression comprises two terms. The term $h^2 F/6$ will tend to zero as h tends to zero but the term ε/h can become large because of the division by h. Thus the effect of rounding error can dominate the approximation. This can be illustrated by an example. The values in Table 8.1, produced using a sequence of decreasing values for h in Equation (8.8), represent approximations to the first derivative of $f(x) = e^x$ at the point $x = 1$.

Initially, the approximation improves with decreasing h until it is close to the exact value, $f'(1) = 2.7183$, and then it diverges. In this case, by differentiating the right-hand side of Equation (8.9) to determine the point at which a minimum occurs, it is possible to estimate the value of h for which the smallest error should occur. This point is found to be

$$h = (3\varepsilon/F)^{1/3}$$

In our case, because we are working correct to four decimal places, $\varepsilon = 0.000\,05$. We know that F is approximately e^1 and so the optimal value of h is $h = 0.0381$ which is consistent with the results above. In general, this calculation cannot be carried out for an optimal h because there is no information about the third derivative of f.

8.1.4 Richardson extrapolation

If it is not possible to obtain an answer to the desired accuracy by decreasing h, the *Richardson* extrapolation technique can be used. This technique combines a sequence of estimates of the derivative to obtain a further estimate which is more accurate. Expanding Equation (8.7) as far as the term in h^4 gives

$$f'(\bar{x}) = \frac{f(\bar{x}+h) - f(\bar{x}-h)}{2h} - \frac{h^2}{6}f^{(3)}(\bar{x}) - \frac{h^4}{120}f^{(5)}(\bar{x}) + \cdots \tag{8.10}$$

Now we form another estimate for $f'(\bar{x})$ by replacing h by rh where r is any value other than ± 1. This results in the equation

$$f'(\bar{x}) = \frac{f(\bar{x}+rh) - f(\bar{x}-rh)}{2rh} - \frac{r^2 h^2}{6}f^{(3)}(\bar{x}) - \frac{r^4 h^4}{120}f^{(5)}(\bar{x}) + \cdots \tag{8.11}$$

By comparing Equations (8.10) and (8.11) it can be seen that the term in $h^2 f^{(3)}(\bar{x})/6$ can be eliminated by multiplying Equation (8.10) by r^2 and

Table 8.1

h	Approximation to $f'(1)$
0.10	2.7230
0.09	2.7222
0.08	2.7213
0.07	2.7207
0.06	2.7200
0.05	2.7200
0.04	2.7188
0.03	2.7200
0.02	2.7175
0.01	2.7200

subtracting Equation (8.11). After rearrangement, the equation takes the form

$$f'(\bar{x}) = \frac{1}{2hr(r^2 - 1)}\left[r^3 f(\bar{x} + h) - f(\bar{x} + rh) - r^3 f(\bar{x} - h) + f(\bar{x} - rh)\right]$$
$$+ \frac{r^2 h^4}{120} f^{(5)}(\bar{x}) + \cdots \tag{8.12}$$

This gives an expression for $f'(\bar{x})$ that is accurate to order h^4 rather than order h^2. This process can be repeated by combining yet more function values to remove further terms from the error expansion. In this way successive approximations with errors of order h^6, h^8, etc., can be obtained.

One of the most common choices for r is $r = 1/2$ in which case Equation (8.12) takes the form

$$f'(\bar{x}) = \frac{-1}{6h}\left[f(\bar{x} + h) - 8f(\bar{x} + h/2) - f(\bar{x} - h) + 8f(\bar{x} - h/2)\right]$$
$$+ \frac{h^4}{480} f^{(5)}(\bar{x}) + \cdots$$

Using this formula with $h = 0.04$ (the best value from Table 8.1) we obtain

$$f'(1.0000) \simeq \frac{-1}{6(0.04)}\left[f(1.04) - 8f(1.02) - f(0.96) + 8f(0.98)\right]$$
$$= 2.7183$$

which is correct to the accuracy quoted.

The Richardson extrapolation technique can be applied, with a few restrictions, to discrete data. In this case, substituting $r = 2$ in Equation (8.12)

Table 8.2 Values of
$f(x)$.

x	$f(x) = e^x$
-0.5	0.6065
0.0	1.0000
0.5	1.6487
1.0	2.7183
1.5	4.4817

gives the formula

$$f'(\bar{x}) = \frac{1}{12h}\left(f(\bar{x} - 2h) - 8f(\bar{x} - h) + 8f(\bar{x} + h) - f(\bar{x} + 2h)\right)$$
$$+ \frac{4h^4}{120} f^{(5)}(\bar{x}) + \cdots$$

We use this formula and the data of Table 8.2 to estimate $f'(0.5)$. From the earlier calculation the initial estimate is $f'(0.5) \simeq 1.7183$. The new estimate is

$$f'(0.5) \simeq \frac{1}{12(0.5)} [0.6065 - 8(1.0000) + 8(2.7183) - 4.4817]$$
$$= 1.6452$$

and this is considerably closer to the correct answer. The use of this formula is, of course, limited by the availability of the necessary data values.

The Richardson extrapolation technique has many applications to fields other than numerical differentiation. In fact, it is used again in the next section on numerical integration.

Before leaving this section, we note that good results can also be obtained by using either cubic splines or least squares polynomials to estimate derivatives. Cubic splines are particularly appropriate because their first and second derivatives are continuous and, furthermore, an error estimate is available.

8.2 Integration

In a direct parallel with differentiation, numerical integration formulae can be obtained by integrating functions which approximate the integrand in some way. In general, numerical integration is a very accurate process because errors introduced in separate subintervals tend to cancel each other out. This would be the case in Figure 8.1 where $f(x)$ lies above $p(x)$ in some intervals but below in others.

8.2.1 Newton–Cotes formulae

One obvious way to obtain an integration formula is to integrate an interpolation polynomial. For example, a formula can be obtained by integrating the *linear* Lagrangian interpolation polynomial. Defining $x_0 \equiv a$ and $x_1 \equiv b$ gives

$$
\begin{aligned}
\int_a^b f(x) \, dx &\equiv \int_{x_0}^{x_1} f(x) \, dx \\
&\simeq \int_{x_0}^{x_1} \left[\frac{(x - x_1)}{(x_0 - x_1)} f(x_0) + \frac{(x - x_0)}{(x_1 - x_0)} f(x_1) \right] dx \\
&= \frac{(x_1 - x_0)}{2} \left[f(x_0) + f(x_1) \right]
\end{aligned}
$$

If we let $h = b - a = x_1 - x_0$ then we can rewrite this as

$$
\int_{x_0}^{x_1} f(x) \, dx \simeq \frac{h}{2}(f_0 + f_1) \tag{8.13}
$$

where, as usual, $f_0 \equiv f(x_0)$ and $f_1 \equiv f(x_1)$. Formula (8.13) is known as the **trapezoidal rule**. The derivation of the name is obvious: the right-hand side represents the area under the line section joining the points (x_0, f_0) and (x_1, f_1) and, whenever f_0 and f_1 have the same sign, this is a trapezium.

As might be expected, a more accurate formula can be obtained by splitting the interval $[a,b]$ into two equal subintervals of size $h = (b - a)/2$ and integrating the quadratic interpolation polynomial based on the points (x_i, f_i) $\{i = 0,1,2\}$ where $x_0 = a$, $x_1 = x_0 + h$ and $x_2 = x_0 + 2h = b$. This gives

$$
\begin{aligned}
\int_a^b f(x) \, dx &= \int_{x_0}^{x_2} f(x) \, dx \\
&\simeq \int_{x_0}^{x_2} \left[\frac{(x - x_1)(x - x_2)}{(x_0 - x_1)(x_0 - x_2)} f_0 + \frac{(x - x_0)(x - x_2)}{(x_1 - x_0)(x_1 - x_2)} f_1 \right. \\
&\qquad \left. + \frac{(x - x_0)(x - x_1)}{(x_2 - x_0)(x_2 - x_1)} f_2 \right] dx \\
&= \frac{h}{3} \left[f_0 + 4f_1 + f_2 \right] \tag{8.14}
\end{aligned}
$$

This formula is known as **Simpson's rule**.

We can obtain formulae for the error incurred when using these numerical integration formulae.

Theorem 8.1

The error associated with the trapezoidal approximation to the integral

$$\int_{x_0}^{x_1} f(x)\, dx$$

is

$$E_T = -\frac{h^3}{12} f''(\eta) \tag{8.15}$$

where $x_0 < \eta < x_1$.

Proof

The error is the integral of the interpolation error, thus

$$E_T = \int_{x_0}^{x_1} \frac{(x - x_0)(x - x_1)}{2!} f''(\xi)\, dx \tag{8.16}$$

The integral cannot be evaluated directly because ξ is an unknown function of x. This problem can be circumvented by using the Mean Value Theorem for integrals (see Appendix A); the term $(x - x_0)(x - x_1)$ does *not* change sign in the interval $[x_0, x_1]$ and so Equation (8.16) can be replaced by

$$E_T = \frac{f''(\eta)}{2!} \int_{x_0}^{x_1} (x - x_0)(x - x_1)\, dx$$

where η is some value such that $x_0 < \eta < x_1$. Performing the integration we obtain

$$E_T = -\frac{h^3}{12} f''(\eta)$$

the required result.   ∎

Unfortunately we cannot obtain an error estimate for Simpson's rule in exactly the same way because the term $(x - x_0)(x - x_1)(x - x_2)$, which appears in the interpolation error formula, *does* change sign in the interval $[x_0, x_2]$. However, using a different approach, it is possible to show that the error incurred by using Simpson's rule is given by

$$E_S = -\frac{h^5}{90} f^{(4)}(\eta) \qquad \text{for } x_0 < \eta < x_2 \tag{8.17}$$

On close examination of the errors (8.15) and (8.17), an interesting result emerges. Equation (8.15) involves only the second derivative of the function $f(x)$ and so the trapezoidal error is zero if $f(x)$ is a linear polynomial; this would be expected because linear interpolation was used to obtain the trapezoidal rule. However, error (8.17) is written in terms of the *fourth* derivative of $f(x)$ and this means that Simpson's rule is exact for all polynomials of degree 3, one higher than expected.

This unexpected increase in order is associated particularly with some members of the *Newton–Cotes* family of integration formulae. The Newton–Cotes formulae are obtained by subdividing the interval $[a,b]$ into n equal subintervals of size $h = (b - a)/n$ and then integrating an interpolation polynomial defined on the points $x_i = a + ih$ ($x_0 \equiv a, x_n \equiv b$). The Newton–Cotes *closed* formulae integrate interpolation polynomials that use *all* the $(n + 1)$ points; the trapezoidal and Simpson rules are closed formulae. Newton–Cotes *open* formulae do not involve the end-points of the interval. For example, dividing $[a,b]$ into four equal subintervals using the points x_0 ($\equiv a$), x_1, x_2, x_3 and x_4 ($\equiv b$) and integrating the quadratic polynomial, defined by the function values at x_1, x_2 and x_3, over the whole interval, gives the open formula

$$\int_{x_0}^{x_4} f(x) \, dx \simeq \frac{4h}{3} (2f_1 - f_2 + 2f_3) \tag{8.18}$$

and this is known as **Milne's rule**. The error associated with Equation (8.18) is given by

$$E_M = \frac{14h^5}{45} f^{(4)}(\eta) \qquad \text{where } x_0 < \eta < x_4 \tag{8.19}$$

Theorem 8.2

(1)   For Newton–Cotes closed formulae:
  (a)   if n is odd, the error is of order h^{n+2}; and
  (b)   if n is even, the error is of order h^{n+3}.

(2)   For Newton–Cotes open formulae:
  (a)   if n is odd, the error is of order h^n; and
  (b)   if n is even, the error is of order h^{n+1}.

Proofs of these results can be found in Isaacson and Keller (1966).

The closed formulae are more accurate than the open ones and there would seem to be no reason ever to use open formulae. However, as Chapter 9 shows, these formulae have an important part to play in the solution of ordinary differential equations.

8.2.2 Composite rules

To increase the accuracy of the approximation to the integral it would appear that all that is necessary is to split the range of integration into a large number of subintervals and integrate the interpolation polynomial defined on the nodes of this partition. However, as we know, using high degrees of interpolating polynomial is not a good idea. Consequently, we split the interval into a number of subintervals and integrate the function over each subinterval separately.

Consider an interval $[a,b]$ divided into n equal subintervals. If the nodes of the partition are $x_i = x_0 + ih$ $\{i = 0,1, \ldots ,n\}$, where $h = (b - a)/n$ and $x_0 \equiv a$, $x_n \equiv b$, the integral can be written as

$$\int_a^b f(x)\, dx = \int_{x_0}^{x_n} f(x)\, dx$$

$$= \int_{x_0}^{x_1} f(x)\, dx + \int_{x_1}^{x_2} f(x)\, dx + \cdots + \int_{x_{n-1}}^{x_n} f(x)\, dx \qquad (8.20)$$

and each of the integrals in Formula (8.20) can be approximated using some numerical integration scheme. If the trapezoidal rule is used,

$$\int_{x_i}^{x_{i+1}} f(x)\, dx \simeq \frac{h}{2}(f_i + f_{i+1})$$

and so

$$\int_a^b f(x)\, dx \simeq \frac{h}{2}(f_0 + f_1) + \frac{h}{2}(f_1 + f_2) + \cdots + \frac{h}{2}(f_{n-1} + f_n)$$

$$= \frac{h}{2}(f_0 + 2f_1 + 2f_2 + \cdots + 2f_{n-1} + f_n) \qquad (8.21)$$

This is known as the **composite** form of the trapezoidal rule; its error is given by a sum of errors of the form of (8.15)

$$E_T = \frac{-h^3}{12}[f''(\eta_1) + f''(\eta_2) + \cdots + f''(\eta_n)]$$

where

$$x_0 < \eta_1 < x_1 < \eta_2 < \cdots < x_{n-1} < \eta_n < x_n$$

If each $f''(\eta_i)$ is bounded in modulus by a value F, this error expression can be bounded as follows

$$|E_T| \leq \frac{h^3}{12} nF$$

but $n = (b - a)/h$ and so

$$|E_T| \leq \frac{h^2}{12} (b - a)F$$

If, instead, the integration is split in the following way

$$\int_{x_0}^{x_n} f(x) \, dx = \int_{x_0}^{x_2} f(x) \, dx + \int_{x_2}^{x_4} f(x) \, dx + \cdots + \int_{x_{n-2}}^{x_n} f(x) \, dx$$

for some *even* n, then the composite form of Simpson's rule can be derived, replacing each of the integrals on the right-hand side using Simpson's formula, to give

$$\int_{x_0}^{x_n} f(x) \, dx \simeq \frac{h}{3} (f_0 + 4f_1 + 2f_2 + 4f_3 + 2f_4 + \cdots + 2f_{n-2} + 4f_{n-1} + f_n) \quad \textbf{(8.22)}$$

Using the same technique as for the composite trapezoidal rule and making the same assumptions, it can be shown that the error in using Formula (8.22) is of the form

$$|E_S| \leq \frac{h^4}{180} (b - a)F$$

where F is now a bound on the fourth derivative of f.

The use of the composite forms of the trapezoidal and Simpson rules is illustrated by considering an example; the two formulae are simple and so we give no mathematical algorithms. We estimate the value of

$$\int_0^{1.2} \sin x \, dx = 0.637\ 642$$

from the data given in Table 8.3.

The trapezoidal rule estimate is

$$\int_0^{1.2} \sin x \, dx \simeq \frac{(0.2)}{2} [0.000\ 000 + 2(0.198\ 669 + 0.389\ 418 + 0.564\ 642$$
$$+ 0.717\ 356 + 0.841\ 471) + 0.932\ 039]$$
$$= 0.635\ 515$$

Table 8.3

x	$sin\ (x)$
0.0	0.000 000
0.2	0.198 669
0.4	0.389 418
0.6	0.564 642
0.8	0.717 356
1.0	0.841 471
1.2	0.932 039

The error bound, using $F = \max |f''| = \sin(1.2) = 0.932\ 039$, is

$$|E_T| \leq \frac{(0.2)^2}{12}(1.2)(0.932\ 039) = 0.003\ 728$$

and the actual error, 0.002 127, is within this bound. Similarly, the Simpson rule estimate is

$$\int_0^{1.2} \sin x\ dx \simeq \frac{(0.2)}{3}[0.000\ 000 + 4(0.198\ 669) + 2(0.389\ 416)$$
$$+ 4(0.564\ 642) + 2(0.717\ 356) + 4(0.841\ 471) + 0.932\ 039]$$
$$= 0.637\ 647$$

The error bound, using $F = 0.932\ 039$, is

$$|E_S| \leq \frac{(0.2)^4}{90}(1.2)(0.932\ 039) = 0.000\ 020$$

and the actual error, 0.000 005, does lie within this bound.

Composite forms of any of the Newton–Cotes formulae can be obtained easily.

Program construction

The trapezoidal rule appears as an element of programs given in later sections of this chapter. Here, we describe a function subprogram to estimate an integral using Simpson's rule. We accumulate the value of the integral using two variables *sum2* and *sum4* to reduce the number of multiplications, *sum2* accumulates those terms to be multiplied by 2 whilst *sum4* accumulates those to be multiplied by 4. A plan is given in Figure 8.2.

Given: n {even}, a,b, f_i {$i = 0,1, \ldots ,n$}
Set: $h = (b - a)/n$
  $sum2 = 0$
  $sum4 = f_1$

for $i = 2,4,6, \ldots ,n-2$
  Set: $sum2 = sum2 + f_i$
    $sum4 = sum4 + f_{i+1}$

Set: integral $= (f_0 + 4sum4 + 2\,sum2 + f_n)h/3$

Figure 8.2 Plan of function subprogram for Simpson's rule.

The function subprogram of Figure 8.3 is a straightforward translation of the subprogram plan of Figure 8.2. It is assumed that the x_i and f_i values are stored in two one-dimension arrays X and F..

8.2.3 Romberg integration

Romberg integration is a technique that allies Richardson extrapolation, described in Section 8.1.4, to the trapezoidal rule in such a way that a high accuracy approximation to an integral can easily be found. The composite form of the trapezoidal rule approximation to the integral

$$\int_a^b f(x)\,dx$$

is

$$\int_a^b f(x)\,dx \approx \frac{h}{2}(f_0 + 2f_1 + 2f_2 + \cdots + 2f_{n-1} + f_n) \tag{8.23}$$

in which $h = (b - a)/n$, $x_0 \equiv a$ and $x_n \equiv b$. The error formula for this rule can be written as

$$E_T = \frac{-h^2}{12}(b - a)f''(\eta) \quad \text{with } x_0 < \eta < x_n$$

However, we require the alternative form given below.

```
REAL FUNCTION SIMPSN (N,A,B,F)

INTEGER I,N
REAL     A,B,H,SUM2,SUM4
REAL     F(0:N)

H    =(B-A)/N
SUM2=0
SUM4=F(1)

DO 10, I=2,N-2,2
  SUM2=SUM2+F(I)
  SUM4=SUM4+F(I+1)
10    CONTINUE
SIMPSN=(F(0)+4*SUM4+2*SUM2+F(N))*H/3

END
```

Figure 8.3 Function subprogram for Simpson's rule.

Theorem 8.3

The error formula for the composite form trapezoidal rule can be written as

$$E_T = \frac{-h^2}{12}[f'(b) - f'(a)] + \frac{(b-a)}{720} h^4 f^{(4)}(\xi) \qquad \text{with } x_0 < \xi < x_n$$

$$(8.24)$$

A proof can be found in Ralston and Rabinowitz (1978, p. 124).

In its simplest form, the Romberg method starts by evaluating approximations, of the form of Expression (8.23), to the integral for a sequence of decreasing values of h. We start with the value $h_0 = b - a$ and successively halve the subintervals   so   that $h_1 = h_0/2$, $h_2 = h_1/2$ and,   in   general, $h_k = h_{k-1}/2 = (b-a)/2^k$. If we denote the right-hand side of Expression (8.23) by $S_{k,0}$ when h is replaced by h_k (and, as a result, n is 2^k), then

$$S_{0,0} = \frac{(b-a)}{2}[f(a) + f(b)] = \frac{h_0}{2}[f(a) + f(b)]$$

$$S_{1,0} = \frac{h_1}{2}[f(a) + 2f(a + h_1) + f(b)] = \frac{1}{2}\frac{h_0}{2}[f(a) + f(b)] + h_1 f(a + h_1)$$

$$= \frac{1}{2}S_{0,0} + h_1 f(a + h_1)$$

$$S_{2,0} = \frac{h_2}{2} [f(a) + 2f(a + h_2) + 2f(a + 2h_2) + 2f(a + 3h_2) + f(b)]$$

$$= \frac{1}{2} \frac{h_1}{2} [f(a) + 2f(a + 2h_2) + f(b)] + h_2[f(a + h_2) + f(a + 3h_2)]$$

$$= \frac{1}{2} S_{1,0} + h_2[f(a + h_2) + f(a + 3h_2)]$$

$$\vdots$$

In general it can be shown that

$$S_{k,0} = \frac{1}{2} S_{k-1,0} + h_k \sum_{i=1}^{2^{k-1}} f(a + (2i - 1)h_k) \qquad \text{for } k = 1, 2, \ldots$$

We illustrate this technique by approximating the integral

$$\int_0^1 \frac{1}{1 + x} \, dx = 0.6931$$

We obtain

$$S_{0,0} = \frac{(1 - 0)}{2} \left[\frac{1}{1 + 0} + \frac{1}{1 + 1} \right] = \frac{3}{4} = 0.75$$

$$S_{1,0} = \frac{0.75}{2} + 0.5 \left[\frac{1}{1 + 0.5} \right] = 0.375 + 0.33333 = 0.708\,33$$

$$S_{2,0} = \frac{0.708\,33}{2} + 0.25 \left[\frac{1}{1 + 0.25} + \frac{1}{1 + 0.75} \right]$$

$$= 0.6970 \qquad \text{(rounded to four decimal places)}$$

The approximations $S_{k,0}$ are converging to the correct answer, but slowly. The convergence can be speeded up by applying the Richardson extrapolation technique. Combining Expressions (8.23) and (8.24) gives

$$\int_a^b f(x) \, dx = S_{n-1,0} - \frac{h_{n-1}^2}{12} [f'(b) - f'(a)] + \frac{(b - a)}{720} h_{n-1}^4 f^{(4)}(\xi_{n-1}) \quad \textbf{(8.25)}$$

where

$$a < \xi_{n-1} < b$$

Similarly, for the step size $h_n = h_{n-1}/2$,

$$\int_a^b f(x) \, dx = S_{n,0} - \frac{h_n^2}{12} [f'(b) - f'(a)] + \frac{(b - a)}{720} h_n^4 f^{(4)}(\xi_n)$$

$$= S_{n,0} - \frac{h_{n-1}^2}{48}\,[f'(b) - f'(a)] + \frac{(b-a)}{720}\,h_n^4 f^{(4)}(\xi_n) \qquad (8.26)$$

where

$$a < \xi_n < b$$

Combining Equations (8.25) and (8.26) in such a way as to eliminate the terms in h_{n-1}^2 we obtain the equation

$$\int_a^b f(x)\,dx = \frac{4S_{n,0} - S_{n-1,0}}{3} + \frac{(b-a)}{2160}\,[4h_n^4 f^{(4)}(\xi_n) - h_{n-1}^4 f^{(4)}(\xi_{n-1})]$$

Thus

$$\int_a^b f(x)\,dx \simeq \frac{4S_{n,0} - S_{n-1,0}}{3}$$

with an error of order h_n^4 provided that $f^{(4)}$ is bounded. We define

$$S_{k,1} = \frac{4S_{k,0} - S_{k-1,0}}{3} \qquad \text{for each } k = 1,2,\ldots \qquad (8.27)$$

Richardson extrapolation can be applied to the approximations given by Equation (8.27) and approximations obtained with successively higher powers of h in their error formulae. In general, it can be shown that

$$S_{k,j} = \frac{4^j S_{k,j-1} - S_{k-1,j-1}}{4^j - 1} \qquad \begin{array}{l} \text{for } k = 1,2,\ldots, \\ j = 1,2,\ldots,k \end{array} \qquad (8.28)$$

It is interesting to note that, for certain values of k and j, the approximations produced using Equation (8.28) are exactly those produced by successively higher order Newton–Cotes formulae. For example, Equation (8.27) is equivalent to Simpson's rule with $h = h_k$. (See Ralston and Rabinowitz (1978) for more details.)

It is usual to present the approximations (8.28) in the form of a table

$$
\begin{array}{llll}
S_{0,0} & & & \\
S_{1,0} & S_{1,1} & & \\
S_{2,0} & S_{2,1} & S_{2,2} & \\
\vdots & & & \\
S_{n,0} & S_{n,1} & S_{n,2} & \cdots & S_{n,n}
\end{array}
$$

Ralston and Rabinowitz (1978, p. 125) prove that the diagonal elements $S_{k,k}$

Given $a,b,f(x)$,tolerance,maximum number of steps
Set $h = b - a$
  $S_{0,0} = h(f(a) + f(b))/2$
Repeat {for $k = 1,2, \ldots$,max no of steps}
  Set $h = h/2$
$$S_{k,0} = S_{k-1,0}/2 + h \sum_{i=1}^{2^{k-1}} f(a + (2i - 1)h)$$
  For $j = 1,2, \ldots ,k$
    Set $S_{k,j} = (4^j S_{k,j-1} - S_{k-1,j-1})/(4^j - 1)$

Until converged { or limit on number of steps reached }
Set integral = last diagonal entry of S

Figure 8.4   Algorithm for Romberg integration.

converge to the integral, provided that the elements $S_{k,0}$ in the first column do so. We would expect the diagonal elements to converge faster than those in the first column.

The most efficient use of this table results from performing the calculations row by row; then, a new row of the table can be calculated using only one further application of the trapezoidal rule. Thus, the elements are calculated in the order $S_{0,0}; S_{1,0}, S_{1,1}; S_{2,0}, S_{2,1}, S_{2,2}; \ldots$ When two diagonal elements $S_{k-1,k-1}$ and $S_{k,k}$ agree to the required tolerance the process is terminated and $S_{k,k}$ is accepted as the estimate of the integral. A mathematical algorithm for this technique is given in Figure 8.4.

Again, we use the integral

$$\int_0^1 \frac{1}{1 + x} \, dx$$

to illustrate the algorithm. $S_{0,0}$ and $S_{1,0}$ have already been calculated and so

$$S_{1,1} = \frac{4S_{1,0} - S_{0,0}}{3} = \frac{4(0.7083) - 0.75}{3} = 0.6944$$

Similarly, because we have also calculated $S_{2,0} = 0.6970$ we have

$$S_{2,1} = \frac{4S_{2,0} - S_{1,0}}{3} = \frac{4(0.6970) - 0.7083}{3} = 0.6932$$

and therefore

$$S_{2,2} = \frac{4^2 S_{2,1} - S_{1,1}}{4^2 - 1} = \frac{16 S_{2,1} - S_{1,1}}{15} = \frac{16(0.6932) - 0.6944}{15}$$
$$= 0.6931 \text{ (rounded to four decimal places)}$$

Given: $a, b, f(x)$, tolerance, maximum number of steps
Set: $h = b - a$
    $sk_0 = h(f(a) + f(b))/2$
repeat {for $k = 1, 2, \ldots$,max steps}
    Set: $h = h/2$
        temps = sk_0

$$news = temps/2 + h \sum_{i=1}^{2^{k-1}} f(a + (2i - 1)h)$$

        $sk_0 = news$
   for $j = 1, 2, \ldots, k - 1$
    Set: $news = (4^j sk_{j-1} - temps)/(4^j - 1)$
        $temps = sk_j$
        $sk_j = news$
   Set: $sk_k = (4^k news - temps)/(4^k - 1)$
   if $|sk_k - temps| \leq$ tolerance **then**
     Note: 'converged'
until 'converged' {or limit on number of steps reached}
if 'converged' **then**
   Record: k, sk_k
if 'limit' **then**
   Record: max steps, $sk_{max\ steps}$

Figure 8.5 Plan of subroutine for Romberg integration.

Thus, after these calculations, the table has the form

$S_{k,j}$	$j = 0$	1	2
$k = 0$	0.75		
1	0.7083	0.6944	
2	0.6970	0.6932	0.6931

If only two decimal place accuracy is required, $S_{2,2}$ can be accepted as the estimate of the integral because $S_{2,2}$ and $S_{1,1}$ agree to this accuracy; note that $S_{2,0}$ and $S_{1,0}$ do not. If two decimal place accuracy is not sufficient, the next step is to calculate $S_{3,0}$ and then $S_{3,1}$, $S_{3,2}$ and $S_{3,3}$ which should be compared with $S_{2,2}$.

Program construction

A plan for a subroutine that implements Romberg integration is given in Figure 8.5. We have chosen a subroutine rather than a function subprogram so that the number of steps taken can be recorded as well as the estimate of the integral. The plan follows from the mathematical algorithm of Figure 8.4; however, we note that the major part of the computation involves the repeated calculation of the expression

Figure 8.6 Subroutine for Romberg integration.

```
SUBROUTINE ROMBRG (A,B,F,TOL,MAXSTP, STATUS,NSTEP,INT, SK)

INTEGER    CONVGD,FOURJ,I,J,K,LIMIT,MAXSTP,NSTEP,STATUS,TWOKM1
REAL       A,B,F,H,HCOEFF,INT,NEWS,TEMPS,TOL
DOUBLE PRECISION DBLEH,SUM
PARAMETER (CONVGD=0,LIMIT=1)
REAL       SK (0:MAXSTP)
INTRINSIC ABS,DBLE,DPROD
EXTERNAL   F

H      =B-A
TWOKM1=1
SK(0)  =H*(F(A)+F(B))/2

DO 10, K=1,MAXSTP
  H      =H/2
  DBLEH =DBLE(H)
  TEMPS =SK(0)
  HCOEFF=-1
  SUM   =DPROD(TEMPS,1.0/2)
  DO 20, I=1,TWOKM1
    HCOEFF=HCOEFF+2
    SUM    =SUM+DBLEH*F(A+HCOEFF*H)
20    CONTINUE
  NEWS=SUM
  SK(0)=NEWS

  FOURJ=1
  DO 30, J=1,K-1
    FOURJ=FOURJ*4
    NEWS =(FOURJ*SK(J-1)-TEMPS)/(FOURJ-1)
    TEMPS=SK(J)
    SK(J)=NEWS
30    CONTINUE

  FOURJ=FOURJ*4
  SK(K)=(FOURJ*NEWS-TEMPS)/(FOURJ-1)

  IF (ABS(SK(K)-TEMPS).LE.TOL) THEN
    STATUS=CONVGD
    GO TO 11
  ELSE
    TWOKM1=TWOKM1*2
  END IF
10    CONTINUE
  STATUS=LIMIT
```

```
11    IF (STATUS.EQ.CONVGD) NSTEP=K
      IF (STATUS.EQ.LIMIT)  NSTEP=MAXSTP
      INT=SK(NSTEP)

      END
```

Figure 8.6   *cont.*

$$S_{k,j} = \frac{(4^j S_{k,j-1} - S_{k-1,j-1})}{4^j - 1}$$

It is clear that each value $S_{k-1,j-1}$ is used only once, to calculate $S_{k,j}$. Thus there is no need to store more than one row of the table; each old value can be overwritten in turn. This is implemented in the plan of Figure 8.5 using the vector *sk* to represent a row of the table; the variables *temps* and *news* are used to hold values temporarily. A subroutine based on the plan of Figure 8.5 is given in Figure 8.6.

8.2.4   Gaussian quadrature

The integration, or **quadrature**, rules discussed so far have been restricted in the sense that only equally spaced quadrature points have been used. If the restriction that the points be equally spaced is removed, a more accurate formula based on a given number of points can be designed. For example, Equations (8.15) and (8.17) show that the trapezoidal rule is *exact* for polynomials of degree 1 and Simpson's rule is exact for polynomials of degree 3. The trapezoidal rule approximation to

$$\int_{x_0}^{x_1} f(x) \, dx$$

makes use of two function values, $f(x_0)$ and $f(x_1)$, and two constants, both of which are $h/2 = (x_1 - x_0)/2$. If we remove the restriction that the points x_0 and x_1 be used for the quadrature rule then we have four free parameters which can be used to design a new rule. With four parameters a polynomial of degree *three* can be integrated exactly and this is a significant increase in the precision of the integration rule. Similarly, using three points and three coefficients, the same number as for Simpson's rule, a rule that is exact for polynomials of degree *five*, rather than *three*, can be defined.

   To introduce the ideas involved in Gaussian quadrature we consider the more general integral

$$\int_a^b \omega(x) \, f(x) \, dx$$

where $\omega(x) > 0$ is a weight function.

The quadrature rules discussed so far have been derived by replacing $f(x)$ by an interpolation polynomial $p_n(x)$, leading to the following approximation to the integral:

$$I(f) = \int_a^b \omega(x)\, f(x)\, dx \simeq \int_a^b \omega(x)\, p_n(x)\, dx \qquad (8.29a)$$

$$= \sum_{j=0}^n \alpha_j f_j = I_n(f)$$

where, for example, using Lagrangian interpolation,

$$\alpha_j = \int_a^b \omega(x)\, l_j(x)\, dx \qquad (8.29b)$$

This quadrature rule is *exact* if $f(x)$ is a polynomial of degree at most n; the quadrature rule is thus said to have **precision** n. In particular the rule is exact if $f(x)$ is replaced by one of the powers x^k $\{k = 0, 1, \ldots, n\}$ and so

$$\int_a^b \omega(x)\, x^k\, dx = \sum_{j=0}^n \alpha_j \alpha_j^k \qquad \text{for } k = 0, 1, \ldots, n$$

Close examination of the right-hand side of this equation shows that there are $2n + 2$ parameters involved: $n + 1$ coefficients α_j and $n + 1$ points x_j. It is tempting to ask if it is possible to construct a rule that will integrate exactly polynomials of degree $2n + 1$. This is precisely the property possessed by Gaussian quadrature formulae.

The derivation of these formulae makes use of orthogonal polynomials.

Definition 8.1

Let the polynomial $\phi_i(x)$ have degree i; then the set of polynomials $\{\phi_0(x), \phi_1(x), \ldots, \phi_{n+1}(x)\}$ is said to be *orthogonal* on the interval $[a,b]$, with respect to the weight function $\omega(x) > 0$, if

$$\int_a^b \omega(x)\, \phi_i(x)\, \phi_j(x)\, dx$$

is zero when $i \neq j$ and positive otherwise.

One of the main properties of orthogonal polynomials is given in the following theorem.

Theorem 8.4

Let $q(x)$ be a polynomial of degree at most n, then $q(x)$ has the unique representation

$$q(x) = \sum_{j=0}^{n} \gamma_j \phi_j(x)$$

in terms of the orthogonal polynomials $\phi_j(x)$ $\{j = 0,1, \ldots ,n\}$ and the constants γ_j $\{j = 0,1, \ldots ,n\}$.

A proof of this result is given in Atkinson and Harley (1983).

The following theorem concerning the zeros of an orthogonal polynomial is proved in Johnson and Riess (1982).

Theorem 8.5

Let $\phi_j(x)$ $\{j = 0,1, \ldots ,n + 1\}$ be a set of orthogonal polynomials as given above. Then for each $j > 0$, the zeros of $\phi_j(x)$ are real and distinct and lie in the interval (a,b).

Gaussian quadrature rules make use of the zeros of orthogonal polynomials and the enhanced precision of these rules is illustrated by the following theorem.

Theorem 8.6

If $p_{2n+1}(x)$ is a polynomial of degree $2n + 1$ the formula

$$\int_a^b p_{2n+1}(x)\, \omega(x)\, dx = \sum_{j=0}^{n} \alpha_j p_{2n+1}(x_j)$$

is exact if the points x_j $\{j = 0,1, \ldots ,n\}$ are the zeros of the orthogonal polynomial $\phi_{n+1}(x)$ and the α_j are as given in Equation (8.29b).

This result also is proved in Atkinson and Harley (1983).

The following theorem, the converse of Theorem 8.6, is proved by Johnson and Riess (1982, p. 326) and shows that only by using the roots of the orthogonal polynomial ϕ_{n+1} can the optimal precision be achieved.

Theorem 8.7

The quadrature formula given above has precision $2n + 1$ only if the x_j $\{j = 0, 1, \ldots ,n\}$ are the roots of $\phi_{n+1}(x)$.

Johnson and Riess also prove the important result that the weights α_j $\{j = 0,1, \ldots ,n\}$ are positive and so the quadrature formula has good properties for the control of rounding errors.

As a consequence of the theorems above, an $(n + 1)$-point quadrature formula has the optimal precision $2n + 1$ if and only if the quadrature points are the roots of an orthogonal polynomial of degree $n + 1$ and the weights are calculated using Equation (8.29b).

The following estimate of the error involved in this type of quadrature is derived in Ralston and Rabinowitz (1978, p. 103). The appearance of $f^{(2n+2)}$ in the error expression again verifies the precision of the quadrature rule.

Theorem 8.8

If $f(x)$ has $2n + 2$ continuous derivatives in (a,b), the error associated with Gaussian quadrature is

$$I(f) - I_n(f) = \frac{f^{(2n+2)}(\eta)}{(2n + 2)!} \int_a^b q_{n+1}^2(x)\, \omega(x)\, dx$$

where $q_{n+1}(x)$ is the **monic Chebyshev** polynomial of the *first* kind.

Different choices of ω play very important roles in numerical integration and a discussion of these can be found in Ralston and Rabinowitz (1978); however, only the case $\omega(x) = 1$ will be considered here. The orthogonal polynomials corresponding to this weight function are known as the **Legendre** polynomials, denoted by $P_j(x)$ $\{j = 0,1, \ldots\}$; quadrature using these polynomials is called Gauss–Legendre quadrature or, simply, **Gaussian quadrature**. The Legendre polynomials are defined in Appendix A.

The coefficients γ_i $\{i = 0,1,2, \ldots ,n\}$ could be calculated but this is unnecessary because they, and the points x_j, have already been tabulated for a large range of values of n (see Stroud and Secrest, 1966). Some of the roots of the Legendre polynomials and their corresponding weights are given, correct to six decimal places, in Table 8.4.

Use of Gaussian quadrature formulae is not dependent on the integral being defined on the interval $[-1,1]$; any interval $[a,b]$ can be transformed into $[-1,1]$ by using the simple linear transformation

$$y = \frac{2x - a - b}{b - a}$$

from which

$$\int_a^b f(x)\, dx = \frac{1}{2} \int_{-1}^1 f\left(\frac{(b - a)y + b + a}{2}\right) (b - a)\, dy$$

Table 8.4

n	Roots x_i	Weights α_i
2	±0.577 550	1
3	0.0	0.888 889
	±0.774 597	0.555 556
4	±0.339 981	0.652 145
	±0.861 136	0.347 855

The increase in accuracy gained by using Gaussian quadrature is easily illustrated by considering an example; we evaluate

$$\int_{-1}^{1} e^x \, dx = e^1 - e^{-1} = 2.3504$$

numerically. The trapezoidal rule gives the approximation

$$\int_{-1}^{1} e^x \, dx \simeq \frac{2}{2}(e^1 + e^{-1}) = 3.0862$$

The two-point Gaussian rule uses the points $-0.577\,55$ and $0.577\,55$ and coefficients 1 and 1. This gives the result

$$\int_{-1}^{1} e^x \, dx \simeq 1(e^{-0.577\,55} + e^{0.577\,55}) = 2.3429$$

which is considerably more accurate than the trapezoidal rule estimate.

8.2.5 Adaptive quadrature

The rules discussed so far make no provision for the possibility that the function behaves non-uniformly; this is unreasonable because most functions vary more rapidly in one part of the interval than in another. An *adaptive* quadrature method takes this local variation into account. We illustrate the technique of adaptive quadrature by using the trapezoidal rule to approximate

$$I = \int_{a}^{b} f(x) \, dx$$

in such a way that S_{ap}, the approximation to the integral, is accurate to within a specified tolerance ε; that is

$$|I - S_{\text{ap}}| \leq \varepsilon$$

To achieve this accuracy, the interval $[a,b]$ is split into a sequence of subintervals $[x_{i-1}, x_i]$ of length $h_{i-1} = x_i - x_{i-1}$; from Equation (8.15) the contribution to the total error from each subinterval is

$$-\frac{h_{i-1}^3}{12} f''(\eta_i) \qquad x_{i-1} < \eta_i < x_i$$

The size of this error depends on h_{i-1} and $f''(\eta_i)$; the larger the value of $|f''(\eta_i)|$ the smaller h_{i-1} must be to control the error. Hence, the sizes of the subintervals are chosen so that all subintervals contribute approximately equally to the total error. Defining $I(h_{i-1})$ and $S_{\text{ap}}(h_{i-1})$ to be, respectively, the integral and its approximation on the interval $[x_{i-1}, x_i]$, the total error is kept below ε if

$$|I(h_{i-1}) - S_{\text{ap}}(h_{i-1})| \leq \frac{h_{i-1}\varepsilon}{(b - a)}$$

The process is started by forming the trapezoidal approximation on the whole interval $[a,b]$. Thus

$$S_0^{(1)} = \frac{(b - a)}{2}[f(a) + f(b)] = \frac{h_0}{2}[f(a) + f(b)]$$

Then a second approximation, $S_0^{(2)}$, is obtained by splitting $[a,b]$ into two equal subintervals of size $h_1 = h_0/2$. Thus

$$S_0^{(2)} = \frac{1}{2}\frac{(b - a)}{2}[f(a) + 2f(a + h_0/2) + f(b)]$$

$$= \frac{1}{2}[S_0^{(1)} + h_0 f(a + h_0/2)]$$

$$= \frac{1}{2}S_0^{(1)} + h_1 f(a + h_1)$$

From Equation (8.15) the errors in these two approximations can be written as

$$I_0 - S_0^{(1)} = \frac{-f''(\eta_1)}{12}h_0^3 \qquad a < \eta_1 < b \tag{8.30}$$

and

$$I_0 - S_0^{(2)} = \frac{-2f''(\eta_2)}{12}\left[\frac{h_0}{2}\right]^3 \qquad a < \eta_2 < b \tag{8.31}$$

In Equation (8.31), the factor 2 occurs because we are integrating over two adjacent subintervals. Assuming that $f''(x)$ is approximately constant throughout the interval $[a,b]$ (and denoted by $f''(\eta)$), Equation (8.31) can be subtracted from Equation (8.30) to obtain

$$S_0^{(2)} - S_0^{(1)} \simeq \frac{f''(\eta)}{12} \left[\frac{h_0^3}{2^3} (2 - 2^3) \right]$$

from which

$$\frac{f''(\eta)}{12} \left[\frac{h_0^3}{2^3} \right] = \frac{S_0^{(2)} - S_0^{(1)}}{-6} \tag{8.32}$$

Substituting Equation (8.32) into the right-hand side of Equation (8.31) gives the error estimate

$$I_0 - S_0^{(2)} = \frac{S_0^{(2)} - S_0^{(1)}}{3}$$

Thus, the error in the more accurate estimate, $S_0^{(2)}$, is approximately one third of the difference $S_0^{(2)} - S_0^{(1)}$ and this can easily be calculated.

If the error estimate satisfies the relation

$$E_0 = \frac{|S_0^{(2)} - S_0^{(1)}|}{3} \leqslant \varepsilon \tag{8.33}$$

then we accept $S_0^{(2)}$ as our approximation to I_0. If inequality (8.33) is not satisfied, we restrict our attention first to the subinterval $[a, a + h_1]$ and then to the subinterval $[a + h_1, b]$ and attempt to obtain approximations to the integrals in these subintervals which, in the sense of Equation (8.33), are accurate to within a tolerance of $\varepsilon/2$. This process is repeated until the approximation to the integral over each subinterval is sufficiently accurate.

A mathematical algorithm is given in Figure 8.7. This algorithm is not as detailed as earlier ones because we want to emphasize the structure of the technique as a whole. During a hand calculation, the process of saving and retrieving information would amount to writing or reading the values of the left- and right-hand end-points of the next interval to be considered along with the corresponding function values and suitable tolerance.

We illustrate this adaptive process by considering

$$\int_0^1 \frac{1}{1 + x} \, dx = [\ln(1 + x)]_0^1 = \ln 2 = 0.6931$$

which we wish to evaluate numerically to within an accuracy of $\varepsilon = 0.005$. First we evaluate $S_0^{(1)}$, an approximation to the integral over the whole range of

Given $f(x)$, a, b, *epsilon*
Set x_0 = a
    f_0 = $f(x_0)$
    x_1 = b
    f_1 = $f(x_1)$
    sum = 0
Repeat
  Set $h = x_1 - x_0$
        $xmid = x_0 + h/2$
        $fmid = f(xmid)$
        $s_1 = (f_0 + f_1)*h/2$
        $s_2 = (s_1 + h*fmid)/2$
  If $|s_2 - s_1|/3 \leqslant epsilon$ *then*
      Set $sum = sum + s_2$
      If '*interval* $[a,b]$ *not covered*' *then*
              { *retrieve information about next subinterval* }
            retrieve $(x_0, f_0, x_1, f_1, epsilon)$
  Else
      Set $epsilon = epsilon/2$
              { *save information about right-hand subinterval* }
      save $(xmid, fmid, x_1, f_1, epsilon)$
      Set $x_1 = xmid$
            $f_1 = fmid$
Until '*interval* $[a,b]$ *covered*'
Set $integral = sum$

Figure 8.7   Algorithm for adaptive quadrature.

integration.

$$S_0^{(1)} = \frac{1}{2}\left[\frac{1}{1} + \frac{1}{2}\right] = \frac{3}{4} = 0.75$$

Now, splitting the interval into two, we obtain

$$S_0^{(2)} = \left[0.75 + 1\left(\frac{1}{1 + 0.5}\right)\right]\bigg/ 2 = 0.7083$$

and

$$\frac{1}{3}|S_0^{(2)} - S_0^{(1)}| = 0.0139 \not< 0.005$$

Thus, the error test is *not* satisfied for this interval and so we concentrate on approximating the integral on the first subinterval, $[0,0.5]$, noting that it will be necessary to return to the second subinterval, [0.5,1], at a later stage. Now $h = 0.5$ and the error tolerance is $\varepsilon/2 = 0.0025$. The first approximation to the integral on [0,0.5] is

$$S_0^{(1)} = \frac{0.5}{2}\left(1 + \frac{2}{3}\right) = 0.4167$$

and the second is

$$S_0^{(2)} = \left[0.4167 + 0.5\left(\frac{4}{5}\right)\right]\bigg/ 2 = 0.4083$$

The error estimate is

$$\frac{1}{3}\left|S_0^{(2)} - S_0^{(1)}\right| = \frac{1}{3}|0.0084| = 0.0028 \not< 0.0025$$

and so the estimate $S_0^{(2)}$ is *not* sufficiently accurate. Thus, we split [0,0.5] into the two subintervals [0,0.25] and [0.25,0.5] and the integral on each is considered in turn. On [0,0.25] the error bound is $\varepsilon/4 = 0.001\ 25$ and

$$S_0^{(1)} = \frac{0.25}{2}\left[1 + \frac{4}{5}\right] = 0.2250$$

$$S_0^{(2)} = \left[0.2250 + 0.25\left(\frac{8}{9}\right)\right]\bigg/ 2 = 0.2236$$

The error estimate is

$$\frac{1}{3}\left|S_0^{(2)} - S_0^{(1)}\right| = \frac{1}{3}|0.0014| = 0.0005 < 0.001\ 25$$

and we have our first contribution to the integral over the whole interval. We will accumulate this total integral in a variable *sum* and so *sum* is set to 0.2236. Now we return to the interval [0.25,0.5] in which

$$S_1^{(1)} = \frac{0.25}{2}\left(\frac{4}{5} + \frac{2}{3}\right) = 0.1833$$

$$S_1^{(2)} = \left[0.1833 + 0.25\left(\frac{8}{11}\right)\right]\bigg/ 2 = 0.1826$$

and the error bound is $0.001\ 25$. The error estimate is

$$\frac{1}{3}\left|S_1^{(2)} - S_1^{(1)}\right| = \frac{1}{3}(0.0007) = 0.0002 < 0.001\ 25$$

and so we accumulate another contribution to the total:

$$sum = 0.2236 + 0.1826 = 0.4062$$

Now, on the interval $[0.5,1]$, as for $[0,0.5]$, the error bound is 0.0025. Here

$$S_2^{(1)} = \frac{0.5}{2}\left(\frac{2}{3} + \frac{1}{2}\right) = 0.2917$$

$$S_2^{(2)} = \left[0.2917 + 0.5\left(\frac{4}{7}\right)\right]\bigg/ 2 = 0.2887$$

and

$$\frac{1}{3}|S_2^{(2)} - S_2^{(1)}| = \frac{1}{3}(0.0030) = 0.0010 < 0.0025$$

and so the final estimate of the integral is

$$sum = 0.4062 + 0.2887 = 0.6949$$

It can be seen immediately that the actual error

$$|0.6931 - 0.6949| = 0.0018 < 0.005$$

and so the adaptive quadrature method has been successful.

Adaptive quadrature rules can be based on *any* numerical integration scheme; Simpson's rule is often used because of its accuracy (relative to the number of points involved). The major difficulty associated with adaptive quadrature methods lies in the task of keeping track of the stage that has been reached; we must, for example, know over which subinterval we are integrating and which is the next subinterval that we must consider. Obviously, if the derivatives of f change rapidly in some interval it may be necessary to create a large number of nested subintervals in order to calculate the intergral to the required accuracy.

Program construction

A subroutine plan for adaptive quadrature is a direct transcription of the mathematical algorithm of Figure 8.7. However, rather than merely reproducing the algorithm, we concentrate on the implementation of those parts of it associated with the saving and retrieving of information. The information to be saved or retrieved comprises five values: the end-points x_0 and x_1 of an interval, the function values f_0 and f_1 at these points and the local tolerance, ε. If many subdivisions are needed to obtain the integral to the required accuracy, it is

```
SUBROUTINE SAVE (SSIZE,A,FA,B,FB,EPS, STACK,STACKP)

INTEGER   BOTTOM,SSIZE,STACKP
REAL      A,B,EPS,FA,FB
PARAMETER (BOTTOM=1)
REAL      STACK(BOTTOM:SSIZE)

STACK(STACKP+1)=A
STACK(STACKP+2)=FA
STACK(STACKP+3)=B
STACK(STACKP+4)=FB
STACK(STACKP+5)=EPS
STACKP=STACKP+5

END
```

Figure 8.8   Subroutine to save information in adaptive quadrature.

possible that many such sets of information will need to be stored. It is natural to consider storing this information in a two-dimensional array, each row of which would contain five values: the information about a particular subinterval. Initially, this 'stack' of information would be empty and, if the cells were numbered from 1, a pointer to the top of the stack would be set to 0. When an unsuccessful estimate has been produced, the stack pointer would be incremented by 1 and the information about the right-hand subinterval saved. This process would be continued for each unsuccessful estimate until a successful estimate was produced. At this stage, a note would be made of the contribution to the integral and the information about the latest unsuccessfully integrated interval would be retrieved and the stack pointer decreased by 1. Thus, the information would be processed in a last-in, first-out order. This process would be repeated, with perhaps further subdivisions, until the stack was empty and the stack pointer had the value 0. Within the subroutine, the value of the stack-pointer would be checked and, if it were 0, the calculation would be terminated and the accumulation of the estimates taken from each of the subintervals to be the approximation to the integral.

In fact, to avoid the double subscript references needed when using a two-dimensional array, we use a one-dimensional array STACK, the five values are stored in successive positions STACKP+1, STACKP+2, . . . , STACKP+5 and then we increment the stack-pointer STACKP by 5. To dimension the array we use a maximum stack size SSIZE which must be given its value in the calling subprogram. Obviously, within the subroutine, we must check in case an attempt is made to save more sets of information than the stack can accommodate. The subroutines SAVE and RETREV which save and retrieve the information are as in Figures 8.8 and 8.9.

```
SUBROUTINE RETREV (SSIZE,A,FA,B,FB,EPS, STACK,STACKP)

INTEGER    BOTTOM,SSIZE,STACKP
REAL       A,B,EPS,FA,FB
PARAMETER (BOTTOM=1)
REAL       STACK(BOTTOM:SSIZE)

STACKP=STACKP-5
A  =STACK(STACKP+1)
FA =STACK(STACKP+2)
B  =STACK(STACKP+3)
FB =STACK(STACKP+4)
EPS=STACK(STACKP+5)

END
```

Figure 8.9 Subroutine to retrieve information in adaptive quadrature.

It is possible that, during the subdivision, an extremely small subinterval is required to achieve accurate integration. This is usually an indicator of some unforeseen problem concerning the original function and so we include a check for a small value of H, the size of the subinterval. If this is less than some value MINH, we will arrange for control to leave the subroutine after a suitable value has been given to a STATUS argument and the left- and right-hand end-points of the interval stored in LB and UB respectively. The repeat-loop in the algorithm is implemented using a DO loop which has as its upper limit the value MAXCYC, an integer passed as an argument to the subroutine. We would hope that this number of cycles is never necessary but a value for the STATUS argument is included in case this situation arises. The complete subroutine is given in Figure 8.10.

Figure 8.10 Subroutine for adaptive quadrature.

```
SUBROUTINE TRAPAD (SSIZE,F,A,B,TOL,MINH,MAXCYC,
*                  STATUS,INT,LB,UB, STACK)

INTEGER    BIGSTK,BOTTOM,CHOPNG,DONE,HSMALL,I,LIMIT,
*          MAXCYC,SSIZE,STACKP,STATUS
REAL       A,B,EPS,F,FMID,F0,F1,H,INT,MINH,LB,SUM,S1,S2,TOL,
*          UB,XMID,X0,X1
PARAMETER (BOTTOM=1)
PARAMETER (DONE=0,CHOPNG=1,HSMALL=2,BIGSTK=3,LIMIT=4)
REAL       STACK(BOTTOM:SSIZE)
INTRINSIC ABS
EXTERNAL   F,RETREV,SAVE
```

```
                EPS=TOL
                STACKP=BOTTOM-1
                X0=A
                F0=F(X0)
                X1=B
                F1=F(X1)
                SUM=0
                STATUS=CHOPNG
                DO 10, I=1,MAXCYC
                  H=X1-X0
                  IF (H.LT.MINH) THEN
                    STATUS=HSMALL
                  ELSE
                    XMID=X0+H/2
                    FMID=F(XMID)
                    S1  =(F0+F1)*H/2
                    S2  =(S1+H*FMID)/2
                    IF (ABS(S2-S1)/3.LE.EPS) THEN
                      SUM=SUM+S2
                      IF (STACKP.GT.BOTTOM) THEN
                        CALL RETREV (SSIZE,X0,F0,X1,F1,EPS, STACK,STACKP)
                      ELSE
                        STATUS=DONE
                      END IF
                    ELSE
                      IF (STACKP.LE.(SSIZE-5)) THEN
                        EPS = EPS/2
                        CALL SAVE (SSIZE,XMID,FMID,X1,F1,EPS, STACK,STACKP)
                        X1=XMID
                        F1=FMID
                      ELSE
                        STATUS=BIGSTK
                      END IF
                    END IF
                  END IF

                  IF (STATUS.NE.CHOPNG) GO TO 11
        10      CONTINUE
                STATUS=LIMIT

        11      IF (STATUS.EQ.DONE) THEN
                  INT=SUM
                ELSE
                  LB=X0
                  UB=X1
                END IF

                END
```

Figure 8.10   *cont.*

EXERCISES

8.1 Use Lagrangian interpolation to estimate $f'(-0.8)$ from the data

x	-1.0	-0.8	-0.6	-0.4
$f(x)$	0.3679	0.4493	0.5488	0.6703

Given that $f(x) = e^x$, obtain error bounds on your result. Compare your result with the exact answer.

8.2 Use Formulae (8.4) to estimate $f'(1.00)$, $f'(1.10)$ and $f'(1.20)$ from the data

x	1.00	1.05	1.10	1.15	1.20
$f(x)$	0.4430	0.5558	0.6754	0.8040	0.9447

Given that $f(x) = \ln(\tan x)$, compare your results with the exact answers.

8.3 In Exercise 7.6, the coefficients of cubic spline interpolates for the data

x	0.5	1.0	1.5	2.0
$f(x)$	-0.1733	0.0000	0.9123	2.7726

were obtained using two sets of end-conditions. Estimate $f'(0.7)$ and $f''(1.6)$ by differentiating the spline obtained for each set of end-conditions. Given that $f(x) = x^2 \ln(x)$, compare your results with the exact answer.

8.4 Use Richardson extrapolation with $r = 2$ to estimate $f'(1.10)$ from the data of Exercise 8.2. Compare your answer with that of Exercise 8.2.

8.5 Use the composite forms of

(a)   the trapezoidal rule and
(b)   Simpson's rule

to estimate

$$\int_{-0.6}^{0.6} f(x)\, dx$$

from the data

x	$f(x)$
-0.6	0.5488
-0.4	0.6703
-0.2	0.8187

0.0	1.0000
0.2	1.2214
0.4	1.4918
0.6	1.8221

Given that $f(x) = e^x$, compare your results with the exact answer.

8.6 Use Romberg integration to estimate

$$\int_0^1 f(x)\, dx$$

correct to four decimal places from the data

x	$f(x)$
0.000	1.0000
0.125	0.9922
0.250	0.9689
0.375	0.9305
0.500	0.8776
0.625	0.8110
0.750	0.7317
0.875	0.6410
1.000	0.5403

Given that $f(x) = \cos x$, compare your result with the exact answer.

8.7 Estimate

$$\int_0^1 \cos x\, dx$$

by splitting the interval $[0,1]$ into two, four and then eight subintervals and using Gaussian two-point quadrature in each subinterval. Compare your estimates with the exact answer.

8.8 Estimate the integral of Exercise 8.7 using Gaussian four-point quadrature in a single interval.

8.9 Use adaptive quadrature, in the form given in the algorithm of Figure 8.7, to estimate

$$\int_0^1 \sec^2 x\, dx$$

correct to two decimal places. Compare your estimate with the exact answer.

Programming exercises

8.10 Modify the function subprogram SPLNEV (Figure 7.13) to obtain an estimate of the first and second derivatives of the supplied function. Apply the modified subprogram to estimate $f'(1.125)$ and $f''(1.03)$ from the data of Exercise 8.2. Compare your results with the exact answer.

8.11 Write a function subprogram that uses the composite form of the trapezoidal rule to estimate the integral of a function $f(x)$ given the equally spaced data $(x_0, f_0), \ldots, (x_n, f_n)$. Apply this function subprogram and that for Simpson's rule (Figure 8.3) to estimate

$$\int_0^{\pi/2} \sin x \, dx$$

using the data $(ih, \sin(ih))$ $\{i = 0, 1, \ldots, 20\}$ where $h = \pi/40$.

8.12 Apply the subroutine ROMBRG (Figure 8.6), using a tolerance of 0.000 05, to estimate

$$\int_0^{\pi/2} \sin x \, dx$$

8.13 Write a function subprogram that uses two-point Gaussian quadrature to estimate the integral

$$\int_a^b f(x) \, dx$$

by splitting the interval into n equal subintervals and applying the quadrature rule in each subinterval. Use this function subprogram, with a range of values for n, to estimate

$$\int_0^{\pi/2} \sin x \, dx$$

8.14 Apply the subroutine TRAPAD (Figure 8.10), using a tolerance of 0.000 05, to estimate

$$\int_0^{\pi/2} \sin x \, dx$$

8.15 By modifying the subroutine TRAPAD (Figure 8.10) produce a subroutine that uses Simpson's rule. Apply the new subroutine to the problem of Exercise 8.14.

Chapter 9
Ordinary differential equations

In general, an ordinary differential equation has the form

$$\frac{d^n y}{dx^n} = y^{(n)} = f(x, y, y', y'', y^{(3)}, \ldots, y^{(n-1)}) \tag{9.1}$$

where y is a function of the single variable x and n is a positive integer. Equation (9.1) is said to be of *order n*, the order of its highest derivative.

Differential equations arise frequently in many fields of study including physics, chemistry, biology, engineering, medicine and economics. Unfortunately, even if a solution is known to exist, there are relatively few cases for which an analytic solution can be found. Numerical methods for the solution of differential equations are therefore extremely important. These methods enable us to estimate values of $y(x)$ for *discrete* values of x. Thus, if we wish to integrate Equation (9.1) from $x = a$ to $x = b$, we divide the interval $[a,b]$ into a number of smaller subintervals, usually of equal length h, and set x_i equal to $x_0 + ih$ $\{i = 1, 2, \ldots, n\}$ where $x_0 = a$ and $x_n = b$. Then we compute a numerical solution (x_i, y_i) $\{i = 0, 1, 2, \ldots, n\}$, where y_i is an *estimate* of the exact solution $y(x_i)$.

9.1   First-order initial-value problems

In this section we consider *first*-order equations of the form

$$\frac{dy}{dx} = f(x,y) \qquad\qquad (9.2)$$

Taken alone, this equation has an infinite family of solutions. For example, the equation

$$\frac{dy}{dx} = 2x \qquad\qquad (9.3)$$

is satisfied by any function of the form

$$y = x^2 + c \qquad\qquad (9.4)$$

where c is an arbitrary constant. To isolate a *particular* solution, we impose an *initial condition* which specifies the value of y for a given value of x. Thus, for example, if Equation (9.3) is accompanied by the initial condition $y = 2$ when $x = 1$ [usually written $y(1) = 2$], these values can be substituted into Equation (9.4), giving

$$2 = 1^2 + c$$

from which $c = 1$. Substituting for c in Equation (9.4) provides the particular solution

$$y = x^2 + 1$$

We will assume that Equation (9.2) is to be solved in the region $[a,b]$ where $b > a$ and that the initial condition is given at $x = a$, then, in general, our first-order initial-value problem takes the form

$$\frac{dy}{dx} = f(x,y) \qquad y(a) = y_0 \qquad\qquad (9.5)$$

where a and y_0 are given constants.

The following theorem states a *sufficient condition* for a solution of Equation (9.5) to exist and be unique. A proof of this theorem can be found in Henrici (1962).

Theorem 9.1

Let $f(x)$ be defined and continuous for all points (x,y) in a region D defined by $a \leqslant x \leqslant b$, $-\infty < y < \infty$ with a and b finite. If there is a constant L such that, for every $(x, y(x_1))$ and $(x, y(x_2))$ in D,

$$|f(x, y(x_1)) - f(x, y(x_2))| \leq L|y(x_1) - y(x_2)| \qquad (9.6)$$

then there exists a unique solution $y(x)$ of Equations (9.5), where $y(x)$ is continuous and differentiable for all (x, y) in D.

Inequality (9.6) is known as a *Lipschitz* condition for f, and L is known as a Lipschitz constant. It can be shown that, if $f(x, y)$ is continuously differentiable with respect to y for all (x, y) in D, then f satisfies Condition (9.6).

There is no single numerical technique that is best for all first-order initial-value problems and so we consider several methods for obtaining a numerical solution of Equations (9.5). The numerical techniques will be illustrated by applying them to the initial-value problem

$$\frac{dy}{dx} = \frac{1}{2}(x + y) - 1 \qquad y(0) = 1 \qquad (9.7)$$

It is easily shown that the analytic solution to Equation (9.7) is

$$y = e^{x/2} - x$$

and this will be used to provide a check on the numerical results.

9.1.1 Series method

This method is not strictly numerical, but is important because several numerical methods are related to it. Basically, the series method produces an infinite series of powers of x which, *near to the initial point*, is a good approximation to the analytic solution $y(x)$. Indeed, if the analytic solution can be expressed as an infinite series (this is the case with the test equation), then the method will reproduce the terms of this series exactly.

Using Taylor's theorem (see Appendix A), $y(x)$ can be expanded about $x = a = x_0$ and this gives

$$y(x) = y(x_0) + (x - x_0)y'(x_0) + \frac{1}{2!}(x - x_0)^2 y''(x_0)$$
$$+ \frac{1}{3!}(x - x_0)^3 y^{(3)}(x_0) + \frac{1}{4!}(x - x_0)^4 y^{(4)}(x_0) + \cdots \qquad (9.8)$$

The first term on the right-hand side of Equation (9.8) is given by the initial condition. The other terms, all involving derivatives, can be obtained from the differential equation as illustrated in the example below.

For the test equation, the initial condition is given at $x = 0$ and so $y(x)$ is expanded about this point. Thus

$$y(x) = y(0) + xy'(0) + \frac{1}{2!}x^2y''(0) + \frac{1}{3!}x^3y^{(3)}(0) + \frac{1}{4!}x^4y^{(4)}(0) + \cdots \quad \textbf{(9.9)}$$

From the initial condition, $y(0) = 1$ and, from the differential equation,

$$y'(0) = \frac{1}{2}(0 + 1) - 1 = -\frac{1}{2}$$

To evaluate $y''(0), y^{(3)}(0), \ldots$, we differentiate the differential equation repeatedly, setting $x = 0$ after each step. This gives

$$y''(x) = \frac{1}{2}[1 + y'(x)] \text{ from which } y''(0) = \frac{1}{2}\left(1 - \frac{1}{2}\right) = \frac{1}{4}$$

$$y^{(3)}(x) = \frac{1}{2}y''(x) \qquad \Rightarrow \qquad y^{(3)}(0) = \frac{1}{8}$$

$$y^{(4)}(x) = \frac{1}{2}y^{(3)}(x) \qquad \Rightarrow \qquad y^{(4)}(0) = \frac{1}{16}$$

$$\vdots$$

Substituting these values into Equation (9.9) gives

$$y(x) = 1 - \frac{1}{2}x + \frac{1}{8}x^2 + \frac{1}{48}x^3 + \frac{1}{384}x^4 \cdots \quad \textbf{(9.10)}$$

This series can be used to evaluate $y(x)$ for values of x close to zero. For example, suppose that we require $y(0.1)$ correct to four decimal places. We have

$$y(0.1) = 1 - \frac{1}{2}0.1 + \frac{1}{8}0.1^2 + \frac{1}{48}0.1^3 + \frac{1}{384}0.1^4 + \cdots$$

$$= 1 - 0.05 + 0.001\,25 + 0.000\,020\,8 + 0.000\,000\,3 + \cdots \quad \textbf{(9.11)}$$

and, rounded to four decimal places, this gives

$$y(0.1) = 0.9513$$

In practice, this series is truncated when a non-zero term is encountered with magnitude not exceeding some prescribed tolerance. Thus, in the above computation, the fourth and fifth terms are ignored. In Table 9.1 $y(x)$ is evaluated for various values of x using Series (9.10) truncated after 3, 4 and 5 terms respectively. For comparison, values computed from the analytic solution are included. Figure 9.1 shows a set of approximations to $y(x)$; each $S_i(x)$ represents a solution obtained from a series with i terms.

Table 9.1 Series solution to the test equation.

x	From analytic solution	Series solution		
		3 terms	4 terms	5 terms
0.1	0.9513	0.9513	0.9513	0.9513
0.2	0.9052	0.9050	0.9052	0.9052
0.4	0.8214	0.8200	0.8213	0.8214
0.6	0.7499	0.7450	0.7495	0.7498
0.8	0.6918	0.6800	0.6907	0.6917
1.0	0.6487	0.6250	0.6458	0.6484
⋮	⋮	⋮	⋮	⋮
10.0	138.4132	8.5000	29.3333	55.3750

Note that, as x moves away from x_0, more and more terms of the series are required to preserve a specified accuracy and so the method becomes very inefficient. In fact, 24 terms of the series would be required to estimate $y(10.0)$ correct to four decimal places.

An alternative approach is to use the series approximation about x_0 to evaluate only y_1, an approximation to $y(x_1)$. Then the point (x_1, y_1) provides an initial condition for the *new* initial value problem

$$\frac{dy}{dx} = f(x,y) \qquad y(x_1) = y_1$$

The series solution of this equation is used to estimate $y(x_2)$ and this provides an initial condition (x_2, y_2) for a third initial-value problem and so on. Thus, in general, the series expansion about a point (x_i, y_i) is used only to estimate the value of $y(x_i + h)$ and so relatively few terms of the series are required.

For several reasons, this technique is not applied in quite this way in practice. Clearly the series method is not easily implemented on a computer. Furthermore, it assumes that the function $f(x, y)$ can be differentiated repeatedly and also that the derivatives exist at the point at which they are to be evaluated. These constraints are more severe than those required by Theorem 9.1 for a unique solution to exist and will not be satisfied in general. Nevertheless, the technique is extremely important because the numerical methods discussed below do attempt to match terms of the series expansion of $y(x_{i+1})$ about $x = x_i$.

9.1.2 Single-step methods

As indicated above, these methods use the information at the initial point (x_0, y_0) to obtain an estimate y_1 of $y(x_1)$. Then the new point (x_1, y_1) is used to obtain an estimate y_2 of $y(x_2)$ and so on. At each stage, the value of x is increased by h and

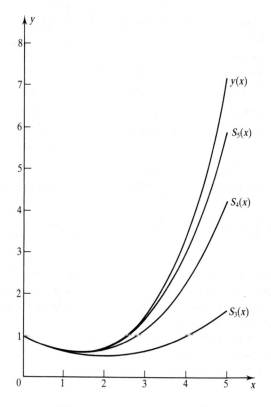

Figure 9.1   Series solutions S_i.

the corresponding increase δy in y is estimated. This leads to a formula of the form

$$y_{i+1} = y_i + \text{estimate of } \delta y \qquad i = 0,1,2, \ldots \tag{9.12}$$

The methods of this section vary only in the way they estimate δy.

Euler methods

These are the simplest of the single-step methods. They are not particularly accurate and so are rarely used in practice. However, they provide a useful introduction to the similar, but more powerful, Runge–Kutta methods described later.

Basic Euler method

A simple approximation to δy can be obtained from the gradient of the tangent to the curve at the point $(x_i, y(x_i))$. From Figure 9.2,

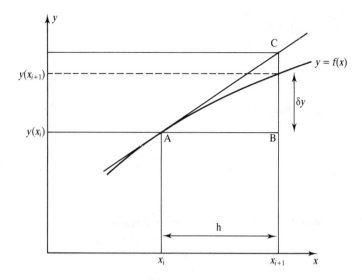

Figure 9.2   Illustration of Euler's method.

$$\left(\frac{dy}{dx}\right)_{x=x_i} = \frac{BC}{AB}$$

and, using the differential equation (9.5), this can be written

$$f(x_i, y(x_i)) = \frac{BC}{AB}$$

Now $AB = h$ and, if this is sufficiently small, $\delta y \simeq BC$ and the last equation gives the approximation

$$f(x_i, y(x_i)) \simeq \frac{\delta y}{h}$$

from which

$$\delta y \simeq hf(x_i, y(x_i))$$

Replacing $y(x_i)$ by its estimate y_i and substituting for δy in Equation (9.12) gives

$$y_{i+1} = y_i + hf(x_i, y_i) \qquad i = 0,1,2, \ldots \qquad (9.13)$$

Equation (9.13) is the basic Euler formula for the solution of first-order initial-value problems. To illustrate its use, we estimate $y(0.1)$ and $y(0.2)$ for the function defined by our test equation

$$\frac{dy}{dx} = \frac{1}{2}(x + y) - 1 \qquad y(0) = 1$$

Taking $h = 0.1$, we have

$$
\begin{aligned}
y(0.1) \simeq y_1 &= y_0 + hf(x_0, y_0) \\
&= 1 + 0.1f(0.1) \\
&= 1 + 0.1\left[\frac{1}{2}(0 + 1) - 1\right] \\
&= 1 - 0.05 \\
&= 0.95
\end{aligned}
$$

To calculate $y(0.2)$ the process is repeated starting from the point $(0.1, 0.95)$. Thus

$$
\begin{aligned}
y(0.2) \simeq y_2 &= y_1 + hf(x_1, y_1) \\
&= 0.95 + 0.1f(0.1, 0.95) \\
&= 0.9025
\end{aligned}
$$

An algorithm for Euler's method is given in Figure 9.3.

Note that the two terms that provided the estimate of $y(0.1)$ from Euler's formula are identical to the first two terms of the series approximation (9.11). There is a reason for this. The Taylor expansion of $y(x_{i+1})$ about x_i is

$$y(x_{i+1}) = y(x_i) + hy'(x_i) + \frac{h^2}{2!}y''(x_i) + \frac{h^3}{3!}y^{(3)}(x_i) + \cdots \qquad (9.14)$$

Truncating the series after the second term and eliminating the derivative using the differential equation gives

$$y(x_{i+1}) \simeq y(x_i) + hf(x_i, y(x_i))$$

which is an *approximate* relation between *exact* values. This relation forms the basic for an *exact* relation between *approximate* values

$$y_{i+1} = y_i + hf(x_i, y_i) \qquad i = 0, 1, 2, \ldots$$

and this, of course, is Euler's formula.

The above analysis shows that, if $y_i = y(x_i)$, the estimate of $y(x_{i+1})$ given by Euler's formula is exactly the same as that given by the first two terms of the Taylor series expansion of $y(x_{i+1})$ about x_i. Euler's *formula* is said to be *of order* h [written $O(h)$] because it agrees with the series expansion of $y(x_{i+1})$ up to and including the term in h. Alternatively, Euler's formula is said to be *first order*. If it is assumed that $y_i = y(x_i)$, any difference between y_{i+1} and $y(x_{i+1})$ results from neglecting terms of Series (9.14). Therefore this difference is often called

Given $f(x,y),a,b,n,y_0$
Set $h = (b - a)/n$
  $x_0 = a$
For $i = 0,1,2, \ldots ,n - 1$
  Set $x_{i+1} = x_i + h$
    $y_{i+1} = y_i + hf(x_i,y_i)$

Figure 9.3 Algorithm for Euler's method.

the **local truncation error**, although some authors use this expression in a slightly different context (see Convergence and stability, p. 322). In general, when the Taylor series expansion (9.14) is truncated after the term in h^n, the remainder R_n may be written in the following form (see Appendix A):

$$R_n = h^{n+1}y^{(n+1)}(\xi)/(n + 1)! \qquad x_i < \xi < x_{i+1}$$

Thus, the local truncation error in Euler's formula is $O(h^2)$. Clearly, Euler's method is not very accurate unless h is very small. To obtain a better estimate of $y(0.1)$ for our test equation, we could try using a smaller steplength, say $h = 0.01$, because this would reduce the truncation error. However, the Euler formula would then have to be applied ten times and the additional computation would almost certainly increase the effect of rounding errors. Thus the total error, known as the **global** error, could be quite significant. Alternatively, a better estimate of δy could be obtained by using formulae that agree more closely with the Taylor series expansion (9.14). A formula that agrees with this expansion up to and including the term in h^p is said to be pth *order*. We now consider two modifications of the basic Euler method which provide higher order methods.

Modifications to Euler's formula

In deriving Equation (9.13), we made use of the gradient of the curve at the point $(x_i, y(x_i))$ to estimate δy. Clearly, for the function sketched in Figure 9.2, this overestimated δy. If, instead, we had used the gradient of a line through $(x_i, y(x_i))$ but parallel to a tangent at $(x_{i+1}, y(x_{i+1}))$, this would have underestimated δy. Hence we might expect the average of the two gradients to provide a better approximation to δy than either taken alone. Using the average gradient, we obtain

$$\delta y \simeq \frac{h}{2}[f(x_i, y(x_i)) + f(x_{i+1}, y(x_{i+1}))]$$

$$\simeq \frac{h}{2}[f(x_i, y_i) + f(x_{i+1}, y_{i+1})]$$

and then Equation (9.12) gives

$$y_{i+1} = y_i + \frac{h}{2}[f(x_i, y_i) + f(x_{i+1}, y_{i+1})]$$

Of course, $f(x_{i+1}, y_{i+1})$ cannot be evaluated because y_{i+1} is unknown and so, inside the function evaluation, y_{i+1} is calculated using the basic Euler formula of Equation (9.13). This gives

$$y_{i+1} = y_i + \frac{h}{2}[f(x_i, y_i) + f(x_i + h, y_i + hf(x_i, y_i))] \qquad i = 0, 1, 2, \ldots \textbf{(9.15)}$$

which is known as the *improved* Euler formula. Applying it to the test equation with $h = 0.1$ gives

$$y(0.1) \simeq y_1 = 1 + \frac{0.1}{2}[f(0,1) + f(0.1, 1 + 0.1f(0,1))]$$

$$= 1 + \frac{0.1}{2}\left[-\frac{1}{2} + f(0.1, 0.95)\right]$$

$$= 1 + \frac{0.1}{2}\left[-\frac{1}{2} + \frac{1}{2}(0.1 + 0.95) - 1\right]$$

$$= 0.9513 \qquad \text{(when rounded to four decimal places)}$$

This result is more accurate than that computed from the basic Euler method. It will be shown later that the improved Euler formula can be expressed as an infinite series whose first *three* terms are identical to those of Equation (9.14). Thus, the improved Euler method is $O(h^2)$ (therefore it is said to be a *second-order* formula) and its local truncation error is $O(h^3)$.

An alternative modification of Euler's method makes use of the gradient of the curve at the estimated midpoint of $(x_i, y(x_i))$ and $(x_{i+1}, y(x_{i+1}))$ to estimate δy. Then, Equation (9.12) leads to

$$y_{i+1} = y_i + hf\left(\frac{x_i + x_{i+1}}{2}, \frac{y_i + y_{i+1}}{2}\right)$$

in which the y_{i+1} on the right-hand side is again calculated from Equation (9.13). Hence

$$y_{i+1} = y_i + hf\left(x_i + \frac{h}{2}, y_i + \frac{h}{2}f(x_i, y_i)\right) \qquad i = 0, 1, 2, \ldots \qquad \textbf{(9.16)}$$

and this is known as the *modified* Euler formula. Using this formula to estimate $y(0.1)$ for the function defined in the test equation gives

$$y(0.1) \simeq y_1 = 1 + 0.1f\left(0 + \frac{0.1}{2}, 1 + \frac{0.1}{2}f(0,1)\right)$$

Table 9.2   Euler solutions to the test equation.

x	From analytic solution	Euler	Improved/ modified Euler
0.1	0.9513	0.9500	0.9513
0.2	0.9052	0.9025	0.9051
0.3	0.8618	0.8576	0.8618
0.4	0.8214	0.8155	0.8213
0.5	0.7840	0.7763	0.7839
0.6	0.7499	0.7401	0.7497
0.7	0.7191	0.7071	0.7189
0.8	0.6918	0.6775	0.6916
0.9	0.6683	0.6514	0.6680
1.0	0.6487	0.6290	0.6484
⋮	⋮	⋮	⋮
10.0	138.4131	121.5013	138.1156

$$= 1 + 0.1f(0.05, 0.975)$$
$$= 0.9513 \quad \text{(when rounded to four decimal places)}$$

and this result is the same as that obtained from the improved Euler method.

We will show later that the modified Euler method is also $O(h^2)$ and so its local truncation error is $O(h^3)$. In Table 9.2, we have extended our solutions for each of the Euler methods, giving the results correct to four decimal places. Note that, although the two modifications give the same results for our test equation, this will not be the case in general. The table clearly illustrates the greater accuracy of the improved and modified formulae compared with that of the original.

Program construction

The three Euler methods are very similar and so we shall construct a subroutine for only one: the modified method given in Equation (9.16). We assume that the subroutine will be supplied with the function $f(x,y)$, the end-points a and b of the region of integration, the number of intervals n and the initial value y_0. A subroutine plan is given in Figure 9.4. This is based on the algorithm of Figure 9.3 but, because we are not using subscripted variables, the value of y must be updated before that of x. Also, the solution at every point x_i is of interest and, because we do not store these values, each result is output as soon as it has been computed. Of course, we could use a WRITE statement within the subroutine but, ideally, the output format should be independent of the subroutine. For this reason, in the subroutine of Figure 9.5, we have assumed the existence of a

$Given$: $f(x,y),a,b,n,y_0$
Set: $h = (b - a)/n$
  $x = a$
  $y = y_0$
$Output$: x,y
for $i = 0,1, \ldots ,n - 1$
  Set: $y = y + hf\left(x + \dfrac{h}{2}, y + \dfrac{h}{2}f(x,y)\right)$
  $x = x + h$
$Output$: x,y

Figure 9.4 Plan of subroutine for the modified Euler method.

separate subroutine to output the results and this is referred to using the *dummy argument name* XYOUT. This name must appear in the argument list and be declared as EXTERNAL.

The use of DOUBLE PRECISION would reduce the accumulation of rounding errors, particularly when the value of N is large. Inevitably, this would increase execution time and the reader is left to make the necessary modifications if required. The same remark applies to all other subroutines in this chapter.

Runge–Kutta methods

Runge–Kutta methods are also based on Equation (9.12) but use a weighted average of *several* estimates of δy to obtain a more accurate approximation. An *r-stage* Runge–Kutta method is usually written in the form

$$y_{i+1} = y_i + a_1 k_1 + a_2 k_2 \cdots + a_r k_r \tag{9.17}$$

where each k_i $\{i = 1,2, \ldots ,r\}$ is an estimate of δy and the a_i $\{i = 1,2, \ldots ,r\}$ are constants chosen so that Equation (9.17) agrees, as far as possible, with Series (9.14). The two modifications of the basic Euler method may be considered as examples of two-stage Runge–Kutta schemes. The improved Euler formula may be written

$$y_{i+1} = y_i + \frac{1}{2}(k_1 + k_2) \tag{9.18}$$

where

$k_1 = hf(x_i,y_i)$
$k_2 = hf(x_i + h, y_i + k_1)$

```
SUBROUTINE EULERM (F,XYOUT,A,B,N,Y0)

INTEGER  I,N
REAL     A,B,F,H,HBY2,X,Y,Y0
EXTERNAL F,XYOUT

H=(B-A)/N
HBY2=H/2
X=A
Y=Y0
CALL XYOUT (X,Y)

DO 10, I=0,N-1
  Y=Y+H*F(X+HBY2,Y+HBY2*F(X,Y))
  X=X+H
  CALL XYOUT (X,Y)
10   CONTINUE

END
```

Figure 9.5   Subroutine for the modified Euler method.

while the modified Euler formula may be written

$$y_{i+1} = y_i + k_2 \tag{9.19}$$

where

$$k_1 = hf(x_i, y_i)$$
$$k_2 = hf(x_i + h/2, y_i + k_1/2)$$

Note that, in both modifications, k_1 is the estimate of δy given by the basic Euler method; this is a common feature of Runge–Kutta methods.

Equations (9.18) and (9.19) suggest that, in general, a two-stage Runge–Kutta scheme can be written in the form

$$y_{i+1} = y_i + a_1 k_1 + a_2 k_2 \tag{9.20}$$

where

$$k_1 = hf(x_i, y_i)$$
$$k_2 = hf(x_i + \mu h, y_i + \lambda k_1)$$

and a_1, a_2, μ, λ are constants chosen so that Equation (9.20) agrees as closely as possible with Series (9.14). To determine the constants, we begin by substituting for k_1 in the right-hand side of the expression for k_2 and this gives

$$k_2 = hf(x_i + \mu h, \; y_i + \lambda hf(x_i, y_i))$$

Expanding the function on the right-hand side using the Taylor series expansion for a function of two variables (see Appendix A) gives

$$k_2 = h\left[f + h(\mu f_x + \lambda ff_y) + \frac{h^2}{2!}(\mu^2 f_{xx} + 2\mu\lambda ff_{xy} + \lambda^2 f^2 f_{yy}) + \cdots \right]$$

in which all functions and derivatives are evaluated at the point (x_i, y_i). Substituting for k_1 and k_2 in Equation (9.20) gives

$$
\begin{aligned}
y_{i+1} = {}& y_i + a_1 hf + a_2 h\left[f + h(\mu f_x + \lambda ff_y) \right. \\
& \left. + \frac{h^2}{2!}(\mu^2 f_{xx} + 2\mu\lambda ff_{xy} + \lambda^2 f^2 f_{yy}) + \cdots \right] \\
= {}& y_i + hf(a_1 + a_2) + a_2 h^2(\mu f_x + \lambda ff_y) \\
& + \frac{a_2 h^3}{2}(\mu^2 f_{xx} + 2\mu\lambda ff_{xy} + \lambda^2 f^2 f_{yy}) + \cdots
\end{aligned}
\tag{9.21}
$$

Now, from the differential equation,

$$y'(x) = f(x, y)$$

and so

$$y''(x) = \frac{df}{dx}$$

Using the chain rule (see Appendix A), the last equation may be written

$$
\begin{aligned}
y''(x) &= f_x + f_y \frac{dy}{dx} \\
&= f_x + f_y f
\end{aligned}
$$

Similarly,

$$
\begin{aligned}
y^{(3)}(x) &= \frac{d}{dx}(f_x + f_y f) \\
&= \frac{\partial}{\partial x}(f_x + f_y f) + \frac{\partial}{\partial y}(f_x + f_y f)\,dy/dx \\
&= f_{xx} + 2f_{xy}f + f_x f_y + f_{yy}f^2 + f_y^2 f
\end{aligned}
$$

Substituting the expressions for $y'(x)$, $y''(x)$, and $y^{(3)}(x)$ into Equation (9.14) gives

$$y(x_{i+1}) = y(x_i) + hf + \frac{h^2}{2!}(f_x + f_y f)$$
$$+ \frac{h^3}{3!}(f_{xx} + 2f_{xy}f + f_x f_y + f_{yy}f^2 + f_y^2 f) + \cdots \qquad \textbf{(9.22)}$$

where, again, all functions are evaluated at the point (x_i, y_i). Comparing Equations (9.21) and (9.22), it is clear that the two-stage Runge–Kutta scheme can be made to agree with the Taylor series, up to and including the term in h^2, by choosing the constants so that

$$a_1 + a_2 = 1$$
$$\mu a_2 = 1/2 \qquad\qquad \textbf{(9.23)}$$
$$\lambda a_2 = 1/2$$

Because the four unknowns have to satisfy only three equations, the value of one of them can be chosen arbitrarily provided that the resulting equations have a solution (this rules out, for example, $a_2 = 0$, $\mu = 0$ or $\lambda = 0$). Thus there is an infinite family of two-stage Runge–Kutta schemes each of which is $O(h^2)$. For example, if we set $a_1 = 1/2$, and solve Equations (9.23), we obtain

$$a_1 = 1/2 \qquad a_2 = 1/2 \qquad \mu = 1 \qquad \lambda = 1$$

which leads to the improved Euler method; if we set $a_1 = 0$ and solve Equations (9.23), we obtain

$$a_1 = 0 \qquad a_2 = 1 \qquad \mu = 1/2 \qquad \lambda = 1/2$$

which leads to the modified Euler method. Neither of these solutions produces agreement between the $O(h^3)$ terms in Equations (9.21) and (9.22) and so both the improved and modified Euler formulae are $O(h^2)$.

It is not, in fact, possible to obtain agreement of the $O(h^3)$ terms for any choice of the constants and so, at best, a two-stage Runge–Kutta scheme can only be $O(h^2)$. Similarly, the order of a three-stage Runge–Kutta scheme cannot exceed 3, while that of a four-stage scheme cannot exceed 4. Beyond this, the relationship is more complicated. For example, a fifth-order method requires at least six stages; further details are given in Lambert (1973).

A well known Runge–Kutta scheme is the classical four-stage fourth-order method:

$$k_1 = hf(x_i, y_i)$$
$$k_2 = hf(x_i + h/2,\ y_i + k_1/2)$$
$$k_3 = hf(x_i + h/2,\ y_i + k_2/2) \qquad\qquad (9.24)$$
$$k_4 = hf(x_i + h,\ y_i + k_3)$$
$$y_{i+1} = y_i + \frac{1}{6}(k_1 + 2k_2 + 2k_3 + k_4)$$

An algorithm for this procedure can easily be set up by replacing the Euler formula of Figure 9.3 by Equations (9.24). Applying the scheme to our test equation to estimate $y(0.1)$ we have

$$k_1 = 0.1f(0,1) = -0.05$$
$$k_2 = 0.1f(0 + 0.1/2,\ 1 - 0.05/2) = -0.048\ 75$$
$$k_3 = 0.1f(0 + 0.1/2,\ 1 - 0.048\ 75/2) = -0.048\ 718\ 8$$
$$k_4 = 0.1f(0 + 0.1,\ 1 - 0.048\ 718\ 8) = -0.047\ 435\ 9$$
$$
\begin{aligned}
y(0.1) \simeq y_1 \\
= 1 - (0.05 + 2 \times 0.048\ 75 + 2 \times 0.048\ 718\ 8 + 0.047\ 435\ 9)/6 \\
= 0.951\ 271\ 1
\end{aligned}
$$

In Table 9.3, the numerical solution is continued and compared with values obtained from the analytic solution. At $x = 0.1$ the Runge–Kutta value is correct to seven decimal places and, even at $x = 10$, it is correct to six significant figures.

Program construction

A subroutine for any simple Runge–Kutta scheme can be obtained easily by modifying that of Figure 9.5. For example, to write a subroutine for the fourth-order Runge–Kutta method of Equations (9.24), it is necessary only to replace the FORTRAN code for the modified Euler formula in Figure 9.5 by that for Equations (9.24) and to modify the declarations accordingly. This has been done in Figure 9.6. Note that, in this subroutine, X can be updated before Y because the expression for Y does not depend upon X explicitly; this was not the case for the Euler method.

Error control

We have described several single-step methods which will produce a numerical solution to a differential equation. However, to produce an *accurate* numerical solution, it is necessary to ensure that the magnitude of the local truncation error never exceeds some suitable pre-assigned tolerance. Thus, at each stage of the numerical solution, we should determine the local truncation error, T_{i+1}, in y_{i+1}. If this is unacceptably large, we must return to the previous stage of the solution and proceed with a smaller steplength. It is not possible, in fact, to

Table 9.3   Fourth-order Runge–Kutta solution to the test equation.

x	From analytic solution	From Runge–Kutta solution
0.1	0.951 271 1	0.951 271 1
0.2	0.905 170 9	0.905 170 9
0.3	0.861 834 3	0.861 834 2
0.4	0.821 402 7	0.821 402 7
0.5	0.784 025 4	0.784 025 4
0.6	0.749 858 8	0.749 858 8
0.7	0.719 067 6	0.719 067 5
0.8	0.691 824 7	0.691 824 7
0.9	0.668 312 2	0.668 312 1
1.0	0.648 721 3	0.648 721 2
⋮	⋮	⋮
10.0	138.413 116 5	138.413 033 2

derive a formula that allows exact calculation of the truncation error. Therefore it must be estimated and we can do this if we compute a second, more accurate approximation $\hat{y}_{i+1}$ to $y(x_{i+1})$. It has been noted already that truncation errors can be reduced by using a smaller steplength or a higher order method; either of these approaches can be used to obtain the second solution.

Suppose that the first solution has been obtained using a single-step method of order p with a steplength h. The local truncation error is then given by

$$T_{i+1} = y(x_{i+1}) - y_{i+1}$$
$$\simeq ch^{p+1}$$

for some constant c. Now suppose that we obtain our second solution using the *same* method but with a steplength $h/2$, so that two steps are needed to advance the solution from x_i to x_{i+1}. If we assume that $y^{(p+1)}(x)$ does not change significantly in the interval $[x_i, x_{i+1}]$, the new truncation error can be written in the form

$$\hat{T}_{i+1} = y(x_{i+1}) - \hat{y}_{i+1}$$
$$\simeq 2c(h/2)^{p+1}$$

Subtracting this relation from the previous one gives

$$\hat{y}_{i+1} - y_{i+1} \simeq ch^{p+1}(1 - 2^{-p})$$

```
SUBROUTINE RK4 (F,XYOUT,A,B,N,YO)

INTEGER  I,N
REAL     A,B,F,H,HBY2,K1,K2,K3,K4,X,Y,YO
EXTERNAL F,XYOUT

H=(B-A)/N
HBY2=H/2
X=A
Y=YO
CALL XYOUT (X,Y)

DO 10, I=0,N-1
  K1=H*F(X,Y)
  K2=H*F(X+HBY2,Y+K1/2)
  K3=H*F(X+HBY2,Y+K2/2)
  K4=H*F(X+H,Y+K3)
  X=X+H
  Y=Y+(K1+2*K2+2*K3+K4)/6
  CALL XYOUT (X,Y)
10    CONTINUE

END
```

Figure 9.6 Subroutine for the classical fourth-order Runge–Kutta method.

from which

$$ch^{p+1} \simeq \frac{\hat{y}_{i+1} - y_{i+1}}{1 - 2^{-p}}$$

Hence, the local truncation error in y_{i+1} is given approximately by

$$T_{i+1} \simeq \frac{\hat{y}_{i+1} - y_{i+1}}{1 - 2^{-p}}$$

For example, if the classical fourth-order Runge–Kutta method (9.24) is used to obtain y_{i+1} and $\hat{y}_{i+1}$, the local truncation error in y_{i+1} can be estimated from

$$T_{i+1} = \frac{\hat{y}_{i+1} - y_{i+1}}{1 - 2^{-4}}$$
$$= \frac{16}{15}(\hat{y}_{i+1} - y_{i+1})$$

Unfortunately, this approach to estimating the local truncation error involves considerable computational effort, particularly if evaluation of the function $f(x, y)$ on the right-hand side of the differential equation is expensive. If an r-stage Runge–Kutta scheme were used ($r \leqslant 4$), the function would have to be evaluated r times to calculate y_{i+1} and, assuming a common k_1, a further $(2r - 1)$ times to calculate $\hat{y}_{i+1}$. Thus, *each* stage of the numerical solution would involve $(3r - 1)$ function evaluations. Now consider the second approach.

Suppose that the second solution is obtained by using a single-step method of order $p + 1$ with a steplength h. The local truncation errors in y_{i+1} and $\hat{y}_{i+1}$ are then given by

$$T_{i+1} = y(x_{i+1}) - y_{i+1} \simeq c_1 h^{p+1}$$

and

$$\hat{T}_{i+1} = y(x_{i+1}) - \hat{y}_{i+1} \simeq c_2 h^{p+2}$$

Subtracting the second equation from the first gives

$$\hat{y}_{i+1} - y_{i+1} = c_1 h^{p+1} - c_2 h^{p+2}$$

Then, assuming that $c_2 h^{p+2}$ is small in comparison with $c_1 h^{p+1}$, the local truncation error in y_{i+1} can be estimated from

$$T_{i+1} \simeq \hat{y}_{i+1} - y_{i+1}$$

The number of function evaluations required by this approach depends on the value of p. For example, use of the classical fourth-order Runge–Kutta Scheme (9.24) to obtain the first solution would involve four function evaluations at each stage. Use of a fifth-order Runge–Kutta method to obtain the second solution would require at least a six-stage scheme which, using a common k_1, makes nine different function evaluations altogether. This compares favourably with the 11 evaluations required if Scheme (9.24) were used alone with two different steplengths.

The second approach can be made even more efficient by using fourth- and fifth-order methods based on the *same* set of k_j $\{j = 1, 2, \ldots, 6\}$ because then the number of function evaluations is reduced from nine to six. This is the basis of the *Runge–Kutta–Fehlberg* method given by

$$k_1 = hf(x_i, y_i)$$

$$k_2 = hf\left(x_i + \frac{h}{4}, y_i + \frac{k_1}{4}\right)$$

$$k_3 = hf\left(x_i + \frac{3h}{8}, y_i + \frac{3}{32}k_1 + \frac{9}{32}k_2\right)$$

$$k_4 = hf\left(x_i + \frac{12h}{13}, y_i + \frac{1932}{2197}k_1 - \frac{7200}{2197}k_2 + \frac{7296}{2197}k_3\right)$$

(9.25)

$$k_5 = hf\left(x_i + h, y_i + \frac{439}{216}k_1 - 8k_2 + \frac{3680}{513}k_3 - \frac{845}{4104}k_4\right)$$

$$k_6 = hf\left(x_i + \frac{h}{2}, y_i - \frac{8}{27}k_1 + 2k_2 - \frac{3544}{2565}k_3 + \frac{1859}{4104}k_4 - \frac{11}{40}k_5\right)$$

$$y_{i+1} = y_i + \left(\frac{25}{216}k_1 + \frac{1408}{2565}k_3 + \frac{2197}{4104}k_4 - \frac{1}{5}k_5\right)$$

$$\hat{y}_{i+1} = y_i + \left(\frac{16}{135}k_1 + \frac{6656}{12\,825}k_3 + \frac{28\,561}{56\,430}k_4 - \frac{9}{50}k_5 + \frac{2}{55}k_6\right)$$

The last two equations give fourth- and fifth-order estimates, respectively, of $y(x_{i+1})$. Thus, an estimate of the magnitude of the local truncation error in the fourth-error formula is given by

$$E = |\hat{y}_{i+1} - y_{i+1}| = \left|\frac{1}{360}k_1 - \frac{128}{4275}k_3 - \frac{2197}{75\,240}k_4 + \frac{1}{50}k_5 + \frac{2}{55}k_6\right| \qquad (9.26)$$

As for adaptive quadrature (Section 8.2.5), we divide this estimate by the steplength to produce an estimate of the *error per unit step*, which we shall call E^*. If this proves to be unacceptably large, we return to the point (x_i, y_i), reduce the steplength and compute a new y_{i+1}; note that the new y_{i+1} will correspond to a *different* value of x because of the new steplength used. Alternatively, if the error per unit step is much smaller than the specified tolerance, a larger steplength may be tried for the next stage. Burden and Faires (1985) discuss step refinement in some detail but a common practice, which we shall adopt, is to halve or double the steplength as appropriate.

To illustrate the method, we apply it to our test equation with an initial steplength of $h = 0.1$ and take 10^{-7} as the tolerance per unit step. We begin by calculating the k_i $\{i = 1,2, \ldots ,6\}$; the reader is invited to check the following values:

$$k_1 = -0.050\,000\,0 \qquad k_2 = -0.049\,375\,0 \qquad k_3 = -0.049\,053\,7$$
$$k_4 = -0.047\,637\,6 \qquad k_5 = -0.047\,434\,9 \qquad k_6 = -0.048\,734\,6$$

There is no point in calculating y_1 until we have checked that our steplength is appropriate. Consequently, from Equation (9.26), we calculate

$$E = 0.000\,000\,000\,3$$

giving

$$E^* = E/h = 0.000\,000\,003$$

as our estimate of the error per unit step. Because E^* is less than 10^{-7}, we

Table 9.4   Runge–Kutta–Fehlberg solution to the test equation.

x	From analytic solution	Runge– Kutta– Fehlberg	Step- length	$E*$
0.1	0.951 271 1	0.951 271 1	0.1	0.30×10^{-8}
0.3	0.861 834 3	0.861 834 2	0.2	0.63×10^{-7}
0.5	0.784 025 4	0.784 025 3	0.2	0.71×10^{-7}
0.7	0.719 067 6	0.719 067 3	0.2	0.76×10^{-7}
0.9	0.668 312 2	0.668 311 8	0.2	0.89×10^{-7}
1.1	0.633 253 0	0.633 253 6	0.2	0.99×10^{-7}
1.2	0.622 118 8	0.622 118 4	0.1	0.34×10^{-8}
1.3	0.615 540 8	0.615 540 3	0.1	0.56×10^{-8}
1.4	0.613 752 7	0.613 752 0	0.1	0.67×10^{-8}
1.5	0.617 000 0	0.616 999 1	0.1	0.77×10^{-8}

estimate $y(0.1)$ from the fourth-order formula and this gives

$$y(0.1) \simeq y_1 = 0.951\ 271\ 1$$

If $E*$ had turned out to be greater than 10^{-7}, we would have repeated the calculation but with $h = 0.05$.

Before proceeding with the numerical solution, we decide whether it is worth trying to double the steplength at the next stage. Note that, if we double a steplength h, the new truncation error will be of order $(2h)^5$. This might exceed our tolerance of 10^{-7} but, for $y(0.1)$, $E*$ was less than $10^{-7}/2^5$ and so we try $h = 0.2$ for the next step. In Table 9.4, the solution is continued as far as $x = 1.5$. The table shows that a steplength of $h = 0.2$ is satisfactory as far as $x = 1.1$. However, with the same steplength, $E*$ at $x = 1.3$ is 0.11×10^{-6} which exceeds the tolerance and so we return to $x = 1.1$ and halve the steplength. No further change to the steplength is required to advance the solution to $x = 1.5$.

Program construction

We construct a subroutine for the Runge–Kutta–Fehlberg method. As a precaution, a lower bound will be imposed on the steplength used and execution of the subroutine will be terminated if the steplength falls below this value. We supply an initial steplength but, because we do not know how this may be changed, the number of cycles needed to extend the solution to $x = b$ cannot be

Given: $f(x,y),a,b,y_0$, *firsth,minh,max cycles,tolerance*
Define: *small number*
Set: *fine tolerance*=*tolerance*/32
   $h = firsth$
   $x = a$
   $y = y_0$
Output: x,y,h
repeat (*not exceeding max cycles*)

   Evaluate: k_i $\{i = 1,2, \ldots ,6\}$ *from equations* (9.25)

   $$Set: error = \left| \frac{1}{360}k_1 - \frac{128}{4275}k_3 - \frac{2197}{75\,240}k_4 + \frac{1}{50}k_5 + \frac{2}{55}k_6 \right| \Big/ h$$

   if *error* > *tolerance* **then**
      Set: $h = h/2$
      if $h < minh$ **then**
         Note: '*h small*'
   else
   Set: $x = x + h$

   $$y = y + \left(\frac{25}{216}k_1 + \frac{1408}{2565}k_3 + \frac{2197}{4104}k_4 - \frac{1}{5}k_5 \right)$$

   Output: x,y,h
   if $|b - x| \le$ *small number* **then**
      Note: '*solved*'
   else
      if *error* $\le$ *fine tolerance* **then**
         Set: $h = 2h$
      if $h > b - x$ **then**
         Set: $h = b - x$
until '*solved*' **or** '*h small*' (*or max cycles reached*)

Figure 9.7 Plan of subroutine for the Runge–Kutta–Fehlberg method.

calculated in advance. So that we can use our usual repeat-loop, an arbitrary bound will be imposed on the number of cycles permitted and this bound will be supplied to the subroutine as an argument. We must also detect when the value of x exceeds b and, in this event, reset the last steplength accordingly. A plan of the subroutine is given in Figure 9.7.

A subroutine for the Runge–Kutta–Fehlberg scheme follows immediately from the plan. In Figure 9.8 we have used an extra variable YARG to represent the lengthy y-argument of the function F.

Figure 9.8 Subroutine for the Runge–Kutta–Fehlberg method.

```
SUBROUTINE RKF45 (F,XYHOUT,A,B,YO,FIRSTH,MINH,MAXCYC,TOL,
*                 STATUS)
INTEGER   HSMALL,INTGRT,LIMIT,MAXCYC,SOLVED,STATUS,STEP
REAL      A,B,BMX,ERROR,F,FINTOL,FIRSTH,H,K1,K2,K3,K4,K5,K6,
*         MINH,TINY,TOL,X,Y,YARG,YO
PARAMETER (TINY=1E-10)
PARAMETER (INTGRT=-1,SOLVED-0,LIMIT-1,HSMALL-2)
EXTERNAL  F,XYHOUT
INTRINSIC ABS

FINTOL=TOL/32
H=FIRSTH
X=A
Y=YO
CALL XYHOUT (X,Y,H)

STATUS=INTGRT
DO 10 STEP=1,MAXCYC

  K1=H*F(X,Y)
  K2=H*F(X+H/4,Y+K1/4)
  YARG=Y+3*K1/32+9*K2/32
  K3=H*F(X+3*H/8,YARG)
  YARG=Y+1932*K1/2197-7200*K2/2197+7296*K3/2197
  K4=H*F(X+12*H/13,YARG)
  YARG=Y+439*K1/216-8*K2+3680*K3/513-845*K4/4104
  K5=H*F(X+H,YARG)
  YARG=Y-8*K1/27+2*K2-3544*K3/2565+1859*K4/4104-11*K5/40
  K6=H*F(X+H/2,YARG)
  ERROR=ABS(K1/360-128*K3/4275-2197*K4/75240+K5/50+2*K6/55)/H

  IF (ERROR.GT.TOL) THEN
    H=H/2
    IF (H.LT.MINH) STATUS=HSMALL
  ELSE
    X=X+H
    Y=Y+25*K1/216+1408*K3/2565+2197*K4/4104-K5/5
    CALL XYHOUT (X,Y,H)
    BMX=B-X
    IF (ABS(BMX).LE.TINY) THEN
      STATUS=SOLVED
    ELSE
      IF (ERROR.LE.FINTOL) H=2*H
      IF (H.GT.BMX) H=BMX
    END IF
  END IF

  IF (STATUS.NE.INTGRT) GO TO 11
```

```
10    CONTINUE
      STATUS=LIMIT

11    END
```

Figure 9.8   *cont.*

Convergence and stability

In certain circumstances, it is possible that a numerical solution to a differential equation could bear little resemblance to the exact solution which it is supposed to approximate. A detailed error analysis is difficult to perform and is beyond the scope of the present text; however, it is essential that the reader is aware of possible problems and so the likely sources of error will be outlined. The reader is referred to Lambert (1973) for a detailed discussion.

First we note that, when we apply a numerical method, we do not solve the given differential equation, but an equation related to it. All the numerical methods described so far are based on an equation that relates y_{i+1} to the preceding value y_i. Such an equation is known as a **difference** equation and is not, of course, exactly equivalent to the differential equation; this gives rise to the **local truncation errors** we have already encountered.

In addition to truncation errors, the estimate of $y(x_{i+1})$ will also be affected by **rounding errors** because, in general, it is not possible to work with exact arithmetic. Furthermore, the value of y_i, from which $y(x_{i+1})$ is estimated will have been affected by *both* types of error and so errors incurred at one stage are automatically carried forward to subsequent stages. Even if a small steplength is used to reduce truncation errors and high arithmetic precision is used to reduce rounding errors, it is possible for the errors to accumulate to such an extent that, eventually, they 'swamp' the solution. When this happens, the numerical method is said to be **unstable**.

All the single-step methods of Section 9.1.2 make use of an equation of the form

$$y_{i+1} = y_i + h\phi(x_i, y_i, h) \tag{9.27}$$

For example, in the modified Euler method,

$$\phi(x_i, y_i, h) = f\left(x_i + \frac{h}{2}, y_i + \frac{h}{2}f(x_i, y_i)\right)$$

Equation (9.27) is known as a *first-order* difference equation because it relates just two *consecutive* discrete y-values, y_i and y_{i+1}. As for a first-order differential equation, a first-order difference equation has only one solution once an initial condition has been imposed. This solution approximates the solution of the initial-value problem.

In effect, when using the single-step method (9.27), the differential equation

$$\frac{dy}{dx} = f(x, y) \tag{9.28}$$

is replaced by the difference equation

$$\frac{y_{i+1} - y_i}{h} = \phi(x_i, y_i, h) \tag{9.29}$$

and so it is important that Equation (9.29) is a good approximation to Equation (9.28). If the two equations were equivalent, the exact solution $y(x)$ of the differential equation would also satisfy the difference equation. Thus, we define

$$t(x,h) = \frac{y(x + h) - y(x)}{h} - \phi(x, y(x), h) \tag{9.30}$$

as the error in the representation of the differential equation. Note that $t(x,h)$ is the local truncation error divided by h (some authors define t to be the local truncation error). Clearly, for our numerical method to be useful, we require that $t(x,h) \rightarrow 0$ as $h \rightarrow 0$.

Definition 9.1

The single-step method using Equation (9.27) is said to be **consistent** with the differential equation (9.28) if

$$t(x,h) \rightarrow 0 \quad \text{as} \quad h \rightarrow 0$$

for all x in $[a,b]$.

It follows immediately from Definition 9.1 that a consistent method must have order *at least one*. Furthermore, assuming that $\phi(x, y, h)$ is continuous, it follows from Equations (9.30) and (9.28) that, for a consistent method,

$$\phi(x, y, 0) = f(x, y)$$

The error defined in Equation (9.30) is a measure of how closely the difference equation approximates the differential equation at a given point. It is also important to consider how closely the *solution* of the difference equation approximates that of the differential equation. Clearly, it is necessary that the numerical solution *at a fixed point* approaches the exact solution as the steplength tends to zero.

Definition 9.2

The single-step method of Equation (9.27) is said to be **convergent** if, for any x_i in $[a,b]$,

$$\lim_{\substack{h \to 0 \\ ih = x_i - a}} y_i = y(x_i)$$

where $y(x)$ is the solution of the initial-value problem (9.5) satisfying the conditions of Theorem 9.1.

Note that, for x_i to remain fixed, i must tend to infinity as h tends to zero. Henrici (1962) proves the following theorem concerning the convergence of the single-step method (9.27).

Theorem 9.2

(1)   Let $\phi(x,y,h)$ be continuous in its three arguments in the region D defined by $a \leqslant x \leqslant b$, $-\infty < y < \infty$ and $0 \leqslant h \leqslant h_0$ for some $h_0 > 0$.

(2)   Let $\phi(x,y,h)$ satisfy a Lipschitz condition of the form

$$|\phi(x,y_1,h) - \phi(x,y_2,h)| \leqslant M|y_1 - y_2|$$

for all points (x,y_1,h) and (x,y_2,h) in D.

Then the single-step method of Equation (9.27) is convergent if and only if it is consistent.

All the single-step methods described in Section 9.1.2 are convergent provided that the function $f(x,y)$ satisfies the Lipschitz condition (9.6) of Theorem 9.1. The convergence property is important but it does not *guarantee* that a numerical method will produce an accurate solution to an initial-value problem. Convergence is concerned with the behaviour of the numerical solution as the steplength tends to zero. However, in practice, we work with a *fixed* steplength and so we must also consider the effect of *global errors* on the solution as more and more steps are taken. Global errors are the accumulation of both truncation errors and rounding errors and are extremely difficult to analyse in general. For this reason it is usual to consider the simple initial-value problem

$$\frac{dy}{dx} = \lambda y \qquad y(a) = y_0 \qquad (\lambda \text{ constant}) \tag{9.31}$$

whose solution is

$$y(x) = \exp [\lambda(x - a)y_0] \tag{9.32}$$

Equation (9.31) is chosen because, *locally*, any ordinary differential equation

$$\frac{dy}{dx} = f(x,y)$$

can be linearized to give an equation of the form

$$\frac{dy}{dx} = \alpha y + \beta$$

and, essentially, the solution of this equation behaves like that of Equation (9.31).

Suppose that Equation (9.31) is to be solved by the basic Euler method. In this example $f(x,y) = \lambda y$ and so Euler's formula gives

$$\begin{aligned} y_{i+1} &= y_i + h\lambda y_i \\ &= (1 + h\lambda)y_i \end{aligned} \tag{9.33}$$

In practice, the *numerical* solution of this difference equation will be the approximation to the exact solution of the initial-value problem. However, before considering the numerical solution, it is interesting to consider the *analytic* solution of the difference equation; this can be obtained very easily by back-substitution. Thus

$$\begin{aligned} y_{i+1} &= (1 + h\lambda)y_i \\ &= (1 + h\lambda)^2 y_{i-1} \\ &= (1 + h\lambda)^3 y_{i-2} \\ &\quad\vdots \\ &= (1 + h\lambda)^{i+1} y_0 \end{aligned} \tag{9.34}$$

Compare the behaviour of Equation (9.34) as $i \to \infty$ with that of Equation (9.32) as $x \to \infty$. If $\lambda > 0$, both $y(x)$ and y_{i+1} tend to infinity. However, if $\lambda < 0$, $y(x)$ tends to zero but y_{i+1} can tend to zero only if $|1 + h\lambda| < 1$. Hence the *exact* solution of the difference equation cannot approach that of the initial-value problem unless $h < 2/|\lambda|$.

Now consider the *numerical* solution of the difference equation. Because of rounding errors, the numerical solution will not satisfy Equation (9.34) exactly. Suppose that the Euler method generates a sequence of numbers $\bar{y}_1, \bar{y}_2, \ldots$, each of which is contaminated by rounding errors. From Equation (9.33),

$$\bar{y}_{i+1} = (1 + h\lambda)\bar{y}_i + r_i \tag{9.35}$$

where r_i is the rounding error incurred when calculating $\bar{y}_{i+1}$ from $\bar{y}_i$. Let ε_{i+1} denote the *global* error in $\bar{y}_{i+1}$ such that

$$\varepsilon_{i+1} = y(x_{i+1}) - \bar{y}_{i+1}$$

Using Equations (9.32) and (9.35),

$$\varepsilon_{i+1} = \exp[\lambda(x_{i+1} - a)]y_0 - (1 + h\lambda)\bar{y}_i - r_i$$

from which

$$
\begin{aligned}
\varepsilon_{i+1} &= \exp[\lambda(i + 1)h]y_0 - (1 + h\lambda)\bar{y}_i - r_i \\
&\quad - \exp(\lambda h)\exp(\lambda ih)y_0 - (1 + h\lambda)\bar{y}_i - r_i \\
&= \exp(\lambda h)y(x_i) - (1 + h\lambda)\bar{y}_i - r_i \\
&= (1 + h\lambda)y(x_i) - (1 + h\lambda)\bar{y}_i + [\exp(\lambda h) - 1 - h\lambda]y(x_i) - r_i \\
&= (1 + h\lambda)\varepsilon_i + [\exp(\lambda h) - 1 - h\lambda]y(x_i) - r_i
\end{aligned}
$$

where ε_i is the global error in $\bar{y}_i$. The last equation shows that the effect of the global error ε_i will be magnified if

$$|1 + h\lambda| > 1$$

Thus, for a given λ, h should be chosen so that

$$-2 < h\lambda < 0$$

In general, when the single-step method (9.27) is applied to Equation (9.31), the resulting difference equation has the form

$$y_{i+1} = R(\bar{h})y_i$$

where $\bar{h} = h\lambda$. For example, in the basic Euler method, $R(\bar{h}) = 1 + \bar{h}$.

Definition 9.3

A single-step method of the form of Equation (9.27) is said to be **absolutely stable** for a given $\bar{h}$ if, for that $\bar{h}$,

$$|R(\bar{h})| < 1$$

Table 9.5 Fourth-order Runge–Kutta solution to Equation (9.31) with $\lambda = -15$ and $y(0) = 1$.

x	From analytic solution	$h = 0.1$	$h = 0.2$
0.1	0.223 130	0.273 437	
0.2	0.049 787	0.074 768	1.375 000
0.3	0.011 109	0.020 444	
0.4	0.002 479	0.005 590	1.890 624
0.5	0.000 553	0.001 529	
0.6	0.000 123	0.000 418	2.599 608
0.7	0.000 028	0.000 114	
0.8	0.000 006	0.000 031	3.374 461
0.9	0.000 001	0.000 009	
1.0	0.000 000	0.000 002	4.914 884

and to be **absolutely unstable** otherwise. An interval (α, β) is said to be an interval *of absolute stability* if the method is absolutely stable for all $\bar{h}$ in (α, β). If the method is absolutely unstable for all $\bar{h}$, it is said to have *no interval of absolute stability*.

It follows from the above analysis that, for the basic Euler method, the interval of absolute stability is $(-2,0)$. It can be shown that, for a specific r (≤ 4), all r-stage rth-order Runge–Kutta methods have the same interval of absolute stability. For example, the improved Euler method, the modified Euler method and all other two-stage, second-order Runge–Kutta methods have $(-2,0)$ as their interval of absolute stability. When $r = 3$, the interval is $(-2.51,0)$ and, when $r = 4$, it is $(-2.78,0)$.

To illustrate the importance of the above discussion, we give (in Table 9.5) some solutions to Equation (9.31) with $\lambda = -15$ and $y(0) = 1$. These solutions have been obtained using the fourth-order Runge–Kutta method (9.24) with (a) $h = 0.1$ and (b) $h = 0.2$. These steplengths set $\bar{h}$ inside and outside the interval of absolute stability, respectively. The solution using $h = 0.1$ follows the general behaviour of the analytic solution although a much finer steplength is required to obtain accurate results. However, the solution using $h = 0.2$ does not even resemble the form of the analytic solution and shows clearly the effect of instability.

All single-step methods of the form of Equation (9.27) are absolutely unstable if $\bar{h} > 0$. However, if $\lambda > 0$, the numerical solution to Equation (9.31) may still be acceptable. As an example, in Table 9.6 we give the solution obtained by the classical Runge–Kutta method for the case $\lambda = 5$.

Table 9.6 Fourth-order Runge–Kutta solution to Equation (9.31) with $\lambda = 5$ and $y(0) = 1$.

x	From analytic solution	From numerical solution	Error
0.1	0.1649×10	0.1648×10	0.2839×10^{-3}
0.2	0.2718×10	0.2717×10	0.9358×10^{-3}
0.3	0.4482×10	0.4479×10	0.2315×10^{-2}
0.4	0.7389×10	0.7384×10	0.5089×10^{-2}
0.5	0.1218×10^2	0.1217×10^2	0.1048×10^{-1}
0.6	0.2009×10^2	0.2006×10^2	0.2074×10^{-1}
0.7	0.3312×10^2	0.3308×10^2	0.3988×10^{-1}
0.8	0.5460×10^2	0.5452×10^2	0.7512×10^{-1}
0.9	0.9002×10^2	0.8988×10^2	0.1393
1.0	0.1484×10^3	0.1482×10^3	0.2552

9.1.3 Multistep methods

In the numerical solution of a first-order initial-value problem, single-step methods use information from only the last computed point (x_i, y_i) to evaluate (x_{i+1}, y_{i+1}). In contrast, multistep methods use information from several points (x_i, y_i), (x_{i-1}, y_{i-1}), (x_{i-2}, y_{i-2}), ... It is immediately obvious that multistep methods cannot be used until a few points in the numerical solution have been obtained, possibly by employing the series method or a single-step method. However, there are advantages (and disadvantages) in changing over to a multistep method once a numerical solution has been started and these will be discussed later.

There are several ways of constructing multistep methods. In one of these, we integrate the differential equation (9.5) between the limits x_j and x_{i+1} $(j \leqslant i)$ and this gives

$$\int_{x_j}^{x_{i+1}} \frac{dy}{dx}\, dx = \int_{x_j}^{x_{i+1}} f(x,y)\, dx$$

from which

$$y(x_{i+1}) - y(x_j) = \int_{x_j}^{x_{i+1}} f(x,y)\, dx \qquad (9.36)$$

Now we use numerical integration to estimate the right-hand side of Equation (9.36). For example, if we set $j = i - 1$, we can use Simpson's rule, given in Equation (8.14), to perform the integration and this leads to the two-step formula

$$y_{i+1} = y_{i-1} + \frac{h}{3}(f_{i-1} + 4f_i + f_{i+1}) \tag{9.37}$$

Unfortunately, this equation is not immediately useful because we cannot evaluate the f_{i+1} term until y_{i+1} is known. However, returning to Equation (9.36) and setting $j = i - 3$, we can use Milne's rule from Equation (8.18) to perform the integration, and obtain the four-step formula

$$y_{i+1} = y_{i-3} + \frac{4h}{3}(2f_{i-2} - f_{i-1} + 2f_i) \tag{9.38}$$

Now, if the points (x_1, y_1), (x_2, y_2) and (x_3, y_3) have been evaluated either by the series method or by a single-step method, values of f_1, f_2 and f_3 can be obtained from the differential equation and then Equation (9.38) can be used to advance the solution to (x_4, y_4) and so on.

In practice, Equation (9.38) is rarely used alone because Milne's rule is based on extrapolation and, as Chapter 7 has shown, this can be an inaccurate process. Therefore Equation (9.38) is usually used in conjunction with Equation (9.37) in the manner described in the next section. Equations such as Equation (9.38) which allow us to calculate y_{i+1} directly from information available at previously computed points are said to be *explicit*, while those of the form of Equation (9.37) are said to be *implicit*. (The methods discussed in Section 9.12 are explicit.)

The Milne–Simpson predictor–corrector method

In this method, Equation (9.38) is used to *predict* the value of $y(x_{i+1})$ and the value obtained allows us to calculate f_{i+1} from the differential equation. Then Equation (9.37) is used to check, and if necessary to *correct*, the predicted value of $y(x_{i+1})$. The fact that the checking process requires only *one* extra function evaluation is an important advantage of multistep methods over single-step methods.

In practice, there are several ways in which the method may be implemented. Denoting an application of the predictor formula by **P**, an application of the corrector by **C** and a function evaluation by **E**, the most obvious implementation to advance the solution by one step is the **PEC** mode. However, having obtained a corrected estimate of $y(x_{i+1})$ in this way, it seems sensible to use it to improve the estimate of $f(x_{i+1})$ before proceeding to the next stage. Hence, another implementation is the **PECE** mode. If the predicted and corrected values of y_{i+1} do not agree to within a specified tolerance, the corrector can be used repeatedly to produce further estimates of $y(x_{i+1})$. This provides a

---

Given $f(x,y)$, (x_i, y_i) $\{i = 0,1,2,3\}$, h, n
For $i = 1,2,3$
   Set $f_i = f(x_i, y_i)$
For $i = 3,4,5, \ldots, n-1$
   Set $x_{i+1} = x_i + h$

$$y_{i+1} = y_{i-3} + \frac{4h}{3}(2f_{i-2} - f_{i-1} + 2f_i)$$

$$f_{i+1} = f(x_{i+1}, y_{i+1})$$

$$y_{i+1} = y_{i-1} + \frac{h}{3}(f_{i-1} + 4f_i + f_{i+1})$$

$$f_{i+1} = f(x_{i+1}, y_{i+1})$$

Figure 9.9 Algorithm for the Milne–Simpson method.

third implementation which we denote by $\mathbf{P(EC)}^m\mathbf{E}$ in which $(\mathbf{EC})^m$ denotes a function evaluation and an application of the corrector repeated m times. It can be shown that the successive estimates converge provided that the steplength is chosen so that $h < 3/L$ where L is the Lipschitz constant for f. However, to minimize the number of function evaluations, the usual implementation is either **PEC** or **PECE**. The reader is referred to Lambert (1973) for a detailed discussion on the choice of implementation.

The algorithm in Figure 9.9 applies the Milne–Simpson equations in the **PECE** mode. Note that the choice of steplength must be decided before the starting solution is computed.

To illustrate the algorithm, we apply it to our test equation using, as the starting solution, the initial condition and the first three entries of Table 9.3, produced using the fourth-order classical Runge–Kutta method. Working correct to four decimal places, we calculate

$$f_1 = \frac{1}{2}(0.1 + 0.9513) - 1 = -0.4744$$

$$f_2 = \frac{1}{2}(0.2 + 0.9052) - 1 = -0.4474$$

$$f_3 = \frac{1}{2}(0.3 + 0.8618) - 1 = -0.4191$$

Using Equation (9.38) with $i = 3$, we predict $y(0.4)$. Thus

$$y(0.4) \simeq y_4 = y_0 + \frac{0.4}{3}(2f_1 - f_2 + 2f_3)$$

$$= 1 - \frac{0.4}{3}(2 \times 0.4744 - 0.4474 + 2 \times 0.4191)$$

$$= 0.8214$$

Before the corrector formula can be used, we have to calculate f_4:

$$f_4 = \frac{1}{2}(0.4 + 0.8214) - 1 = -0.3893$$

and then Equation (9.37) gives

$$y(0.4) \simeq y_4 = y_2 + \frac{h}{3}(f_2 + 4f_3 + f_4)$$

$$= 0.9052 - \frac{0.1}{3}(0.4474 + 4 \times 0.4191 + 0.3893)$$

$$= 0.8214$$

The two estimates of $y(0.4)$ agree to within four decimal places and so there is no need to recalculate f_4.

Error control

In general, the two estimates of $y(x_{i+1})$ may not agree to within the specified tolerance and then it is necessary to decide whether or not the corrected value obtained from Equation (9.37) is sufficiently accurate to proceed. From the results quoted in Equations (8.17) and (8.19), the error inherent in Simpson's rule is given by

$$E^{\hat{S}} = -h^5 y^{(5)}(\eta_1)/90 \qquad x_{i-1} < \eta_1 < x_{i+1}$$

while that in Milne's rule is given by

$$E^{\hat{M}} = 28h^5 y^{(5)}(\eta_2)/90 \qquad x_{i-3} < \eta_2 < x_{i+1}$$

Thus, although the coefficient of the derivative in $E^{\hat{M}}$ is much greater than that in $E^{\hat{S}}$, both formulae are fourth order. If we assume that $y^{(5)}(\eta_1) \simeq y^{(5)}(\eta_2)$, the magnitude of $E^{\hat{M}}$ will be approximately 28 times that of $E^{\hat{S}}$. Thus, denoting our predicted and corrected estimates of $y(x_{i+1})$ by y^p_{i+1} and y^c_{i+1} respectively,

$$y(x_{i+1}) - y^p_{i+1} \simeq -28(y(x_{i+1}) - y^c_{i+1})$$

from which

$$y(x_{i+1}) - y^c_{i+1} \simeq \frac{1}{29}(y^p_{i+1} - y^c_{i+1}) \qquad\qquad \textbf{(9.39)}$$

The technique used to obtain Equation (9.39) is a special case of *Milne's device* which allows us to estimate the error in the corrected value of y_{i+1} from the difference between the predicted and corrected values. A significant difference between y^p_{i+1} and y^c_{i+1} indicates that the steplength is too large and, unless the $\mathbf{P(EC)}^m\mathbf{E}$ implementation is used, we must return to the previous stage of the solution and proceed with a smaller steplength. On the other hand, if the modulus of the difference between the two estimates of $y(x_{i+1})$ is very small in comparison with the specified tolerance, then we can try using a larger steplength at the next stage.

Unfortunately, it is not an easy matter to change the steplength when using a multistep method; this is a common disadvantage of multistep methods and does not occur with single-step methods. For example, suppose that we have computed part of a numerical solution using a steplength h, but then we find that there is a significant difference between the two estimates of $y(x_{i+1}) = y(x_i + h)$. At this stage we might decide to halve the steplength and compute $y(x_i + h/2)$. However, this calculation requires estimates of $y(x_i - h/2)$ and $y(x_i - 3h/2)$ and these values are not immediately available from the current solution. Therefore, they would have to be either interpolated from neighbouring values or computed using a single-step method; whichever method were used, formulae of order at least 4 would be necessary to maintain the accuracy of the Milne–Simpson scheme.

In hand calculations, doubling the steplength is less troublesome because estimates of $y(x_i)$, $y(x_i - 2h)$, . . . , $y(x_i - 8h)$ are immediately available from the current solution. However, a subroutine must store the appropriate values.

A more serious disadvantage of the Milne–Simpson scheme is that, in certain circumstances, the errors do not tend to zero as the steplength is reduced and the method is unstable. The concept of stability with respect to multistep methods is discussed in more detail under Convergence and stability, below. Because of this possible stability problem, we shall not construct a subroutine for the Milne–Simpson method; instead, we consider an alternative predictor–corrector method.

Adams–Bashforth–Moulton predictor–corrector methods

If we set $j = i$ in Equation (9.36) and approximate $f(x, y)$ by a third-degree polynomial passing through the points (x_i, f_i), . . . , (x_{i-3}, f_{i-3}), we obtain the four-step *explicit* formula

$$y_{i+1} = y_i + \frac{h}{24}(55f_i - 59f_{i-1} + 37f_{i-2} - 9f_{i-3}) \qquad (9.40)$$

Alternatively, if we approximate $f(x, y)$ by a third-degree polynomial passing through the points (x_{i+1}, f_{i+1}), . . . , (x_{i-2}, f_{i-2}), again with $j = i$, we obtain the three-step *implicit* formula

$$y_{i+1} = y_i + \frac{h}{24}(9f_{i+1} + 19f_i - 5f_{i-1} + f_{i-2}) \qquad (9.41)$$

Given $f(x,y)$, (x_i,y_i) $\{i = 0,1,2,3\}$, h, n
For $i = 0,1,2,3$
  Set $f_i = f(x_i,y_i)$
For $i = 3,4,5, \ldots ,n - 1$
  Set $x_{i+1} = x_i + h$
$$y_{i+1} = y_i + \frac{h}{24}(55f_i - 59f_{i-1} + 37f_{i-2} - 9f_{i-3})$$
$$f_{i+1} = f(x_{i+1},y_{i+1})$$
$$y_{i+1} = y_i + \frac{h}{24}(9f_{i+1} + 19f_i - 5f_{i-1} + f_{i-2})$$
$$f_{i+1} = f(x_{i+1},y_{i+1})$$

Figure 9.10 Algorithm for the fourth-order Adams–Bashforth–Moulton method.

Equations (9.40) and (9.41) constitute a fourth-order predictor–corrector pair and are often used in conjunction with the fourth-order Runge–Kutta method defined in Equations (9.24). Using an argument similar to that for the Milne–Simpson scheme, it can be shown that the error in the corrected estimate of $y(x_{i+1})$ is given by

$$y(x_{i+1}) - y_{i+1}^c \approx \frac{19}{270}(y_{i+1}^p - y_{i+1}^c)$$

Other predictor–corrector pairs can be derived by using polynomials of different degrees to approximate $f(x,y)$; those of explicit form are known as *Adams–Bashforth* formulae while those of implicit form are known as *Adams–Moulton* formulae. All such predictor–corrector pairs can be implemented in any of the modes described for the Milne–Simpson method and a suitable algorithm for any implementation can be obtained by modifying that in Figure 9.9. Figure 9.10 presents an algorithm for the fourth-order Adams–Bashforth–Moulton method applied in the **PECE** mode.

Program construction

At each stage of the calculation, we apply the formulae

```
yp = y3 + h(55f3 - 59f2 + 37f1 - 9f0)/24
f4 = f(x,yp)
yc = y3 + h(9f4 + 19f3 - 5f2 + f1)/24
f4 = f(x, yc)
```

in which the values on the right-hand side are obtained by updating values calculated at the previous stage. Following our usual practice of updating values

Given: $f(x,y)$, (xi,yi) $\{i = 0,1,2,3\}$, h, n, *tolerance*
Set: $x = x3$
         $yc = y3$
         $f1 = f(x0,y0)$
         $f2 = f(x1,y1)$
         $f3 = f(x2,y2)$
         $f4 = f(x3,y3)$

for $i = 3,4,5, \ldots ,n - 1$ (*unless h is too large*)
   Set: $x = x + h$
            $y3 = yc$
            $f0 = f1$
            $f1 = f2$
            $f2 = f3$
            $f3 = f4$

            $yp = y3 + h(55f3 - 59f2 + 37f1 - 9f0)/24$
            $f4 = f(x,yp)$
            $yc = y3 + h(9f4 + 19f3 - 5f2 + f1)/24$
            $f4 = f(x,yc)$
            $error = |19(yp - yc)/270|/h$
if $error > tolerance$ **then**
   Note: '*h too large*'
else
   Output: x,yc

Figure 9.11   Plan of subroutine for the fourth-order Adams–Bashforth–Moulton method.

just before they are required, we precede the above statements by

   $x = x + h$
   $y3 = yc$
   $f0 = f1$
   $f1 = f2$
   $f2 = f3$
   $f3 = f4$

Prior to entering the loop, the variables x, yc, $f1$, $f2$, $f3$ and $f4$ must be initialized.

   $x = x3$
   $yc = y3$
   $f1 = f(x0,y0)$
   $f2 = f(x1,y1)$
   $f3 = f(x2,y2)$
   $f4 = f(x3,y3)$

As for the Runge–Kutta–Fehlberg subroutine, we test the error per unit step. However, we shall not attempt to change the steplength as the solution progresses; if the error test indicates that our initial steplength should be reduced, we will terminate the iteration. A complete subroutine plan is given in Figure 9.11.

A subroutine based on this plan is given in Figure 9.12. As usual, we have included the variable STATUS in the argument list to indicate the outcome to the calling subprogram.

Convergence and stability

As for single-step methods, it is important that a multistep method uses a difference equation which is a good approximation to the differential equation and that the solution of the difference equation tends to that of the differential equation as the steplength tends to zero. Consequently, the concepts of consistency and convergence will again be discussed here. However, in contrast to the case for single-step methods, it will be seen that consistency alone is not a sufficient condition for a multistep method to be convergent.

All the multistep methods described so far use a difference equation of the form

$$\sum_{j=0}^{k} \alpha_j y_{n+j} = h \sum_{j=0}^{k} \beta_j f_{n+j} \qquad (9.42)$$

where k is the number of steps and the α_j and β_j are constants. For example, the Simpson corrector formula (9.37) may be written

$$-y_{i-1} + y_{i+1} = \frac{h}{3}(f_{i-1} + 4f_i + f_{i+1})$$

and so, in this case,

$$
\begin{array}{lll}
k = 2 & n = i - 1 & \\
\alpha_0 = -1 & \alpha_1 = 0 & \alpha_2 = 1 \\
\beta_0 = 1/3 & \beta_1 = 4/3 & \beta_2 = 1/3
\end{array}
\qquad (9.43)
$$

Because Equation (9.42) is linear in y, the methods are properly known as **linear** multistep methods.

Definition 9.4

The multistep method using Equation (9.42) is said to be **consistent** if its order is *at least one*.

To determine the order of a multistep method, we write down the truncation

Figure 9.12   Subroutine for the fourth-order Adams–Bashforth–Moulton method.

```
      SUBROUTINE ADBAMO (F,XYOUT,X0,Y0,X1,Y1,X2,Y2,X3,Y3,H,N,TOL,
     *                   STATUS)
      INTEGER   I,HLARGE,N,SOLVED,STATUS
      REAL      ERROR,F,F0,F1,F2,F3,F4,H,TOL,X,X0,X1,X2,X3,
     *          YC,YP,Y0,Y1,Y2,Y3
      PARAMETER (SOLVED=0,HLARGE=1)
      EXTERNAL  F,XYOUT
      INTRINSIC ABS

      X =X3
      YC=Y3
      F1=F(X0,Y0)
      F2=F(X1,Y1)
      F3=F(X2,Y2)
      F4=F(X3,Y3)

      DO 10 I=3,N-1
        X=X+H
        Y3=YC
        F0=F1
        F1=F2
        F2=F3
        F3=F4

        YP=Y3+H*(55*F3-59*F2+37*F1-9*F0)/24
        F4=F(X,YP)
        YC=Y3+H*(9*F4+19*F3-5*F2+F1)/24
        F4=F(X,YC)
        ERROR=ABS(19*(YP-YC)/270)/H
        IF (ERROR.GT.TOL) THEN
          STATUS=HLARGE
          GO TO 11
        ELSE
          CAL XYOUT (X,YC)
        END IF

10    CONTINUE
      STATUS=SOLVED

11    END
```

error:

$$T_k = \sum_{j=0}^{k} \alpha_j y(x + jh) - h \sum_{j=0}^{k} \beta_j f(x + jh)$$
$$= \sum_{j=0}^{k} \alpha_j y(x + jh) - h \sum_{j=0}^{k} \beta_j y'(x + jh)$$

and, using a Taylor series to expand $y(x + jh)$ and $y'(x + jh)$, express it thus:

$$T_k = C_0 y(x) + C_1 hy'(x) + C_2 h^2 y''(x) + \cdots$$

The multistep method is of order p if $C_0 = C_1 = \cdots = C_p = 0$ and $C_{p+1} \neq 0$. Thus it is consistent if $C_0 = C_1 = 0$. It is easily shown that

$$C_0 = \alpha_0 + \alpha_1 + \cdots + \alpha_k$$

and

$$C_1 = \alpha_1 + 2\alpha_2 + 3\alpha_3 + \cdots + k\alpha_k - (\beta_0 + \beta_1 + \cdots + \beta_k)$$

Hence, for a linear multistep method to be consistent, the α_i and β_i must satisfy the relations

$$\alpha_0 + \alpha_1 + \cdots + \alpha_k = 0 \tag{9.44}$$

and

$$\alpha_1 + 2\alpha_2 + 3\alpha_3 + \cdots + k\alpha_k = (\beta_0 + \beta_1 + \cdots + \beta_k) \tag{9.45}$$

Note that the equations used in the predictor–corrector methods of Section 9.1.3 satisfy Equations (9.44) and (9.45) and so are consistent.

The concept of convergence for a multistep method is similar to that for a single-step method *provided that the starting values all tend to y_0 as h tends to zero*. A formal definition of convergence for a multistep method is given in Lambert (1973). Ralston and Rabinowitz (1978) prove that consistency is *necessary* for convergence but Lambert (1973) shows that, for a multistep method, consistency is *not a sufficient* condition. The difficulty is caused by the fact that the difference Equation (9.42) is of order $k > 1$ and so it has more than one solution. For example, the second-order difference equation

$$y_{n+2} - 5y_{n+1} + 6y_n = 0$$

is clearly satisfied by

$$y_n = c_1 2^n$$

and also by

$$y_n = c_2 3^n$$

where c_1 and c_2 are arbitrary constants. Hence, the general solution of this equation is

$$y_n = c_1 2^n + c_2 3^n$$

To find the general solution of Equation (9.42), we define the *first characteristic polynomial* of Equation (9.42) to be

$$\rho(\xi) = \sum_{j=0}^{k} \alpha_j \xi^j$$

and the *second characteristic polynomial* to be

$$\sigma(\xi) = \sum_{j=0}^{k} \beta_j \xi^j$$

The general solution of Equation (9.42) comprises two parts, one defined by the left-hand side of the equation and the other by the right-hand side. Lambert (1973) shows that the part associated with the left-hand side has the form

$$y_m = \gamma_1 \xi_1^m + \gamma_2 \xi_2^m + \cdots + \gamma_k \xi_k^m$$

where $\xi_1, \xi_2, \ldots, \xi_k$ are the zeros of the first characteristic polynomial, $\rho(\xi)$. If the method defined by Equation (9.42) is consistent, it follows from Equation (9.44) that $\rho(1) = 0$. Hence, the equation

$$\rho(\xi) = 0$$

has a root at $\xi = 1$; this root is known as the **principal** root and is denoted by ξ_1. The remaining roots $\xi_2, \xi_3, \ldots, \xi_k$ are known as **spurious** roots and do not represent, in any way, the behaviour of the differential equation. Thus, it is vital that these components of the general solution are damped out as the steplength is reduced. This will happen provided that none of the roots has modulus greater than unity. Furthermore, it is essential that all roots of modulus 1 are simple (not repeated) roots.

Definition 9.5

The linear multistep method using Equation (9.42) is said to be **zero-stable** or, equivalently, to satisfy a **root condition**, if no root of the equation $\rho(\xi) = 0$ has modulus greater than 1, and if every root of modulus 1 is a simple root.

The concepts of consistency, zero-stability and convergence are drawn together in the following theorem, proved in Henrici (1962).

Theorem 9.3

The necessary and sufficient conditions for a linear multistep method to be convergent are that it be consistent and zero-stable.

Henrici also proves the following theorem concerning the order of a linear multistep method.

Theorem 9.4

No zero-stable linear k-step method can have order greater than $k + 1$ when k is odd, or greater than $k + 2$ when k is even.

With reference to this theorem, recall that the three-stage Milne predictor formula (9.38) has the same order as the two-stage Simpson corrector formula (9.37) whilst the four-stage Adams–Bashforth formula (9.40) has the same order as the three-stage Adams–Moulton formula (9.41).

We now turn our attention to the behaviour of global errors in multistep methods. Ideally, as for single-step methods, we do not want these be magnified as the solution progresses. Again discussion is confined to the initial-value problem (9.31):

$$\frac{dy}{dx} = \lambda y \qquad y(a) = y_0$$

Lambert (1973) shows that the global errors for the linear multistep method (9.42) applied to (9.31) are governed by the roots of the *stability* equation

$$\sum_{j=0}^{k} (\alpha_j - \bar{h}\beta_j)r^j = 0 \qquad\qquad\qquad \textbf{(9.46)}$$

where $\bar{h} = h\lambda$. To simplify the discussion, we shall assume that the roots r_j $\{j = 1, \ldots, k\}$ are distinct, although this is not a necessary condition for the following results to be valid.

Definition 9.6

The linear multistep method of Equation (9.42) is said to be **absolutely stable** for a given $\bar{h}$ if, for that $\bar{h}$, all the roots of Equation (9.46) satisfy

$$|r_j| < 1 \qquad j = 1, \ldots, k$$

and to be **absolutely unstable** otherwise. An interval (α, β) is said to be an *interval of absolute stability* if the method is absolutely stable for all $\bar{h}$ in (α, β). If the method is unstable for all $\bar{h}$, then it is said to have *no interval of absolute stability*.

When $\bar{h} = 0$, the roots of the stability equation are the zeros of the first characteristic polynomial. Assuming that the method is consistent and zero-stable ensures that $\rho(r)$ has a simple zero at $r = 1$. Let r_1 be the root of Equation (9.46) that tends to one as $\bar{h} \to 0$. Lambert proves the following result.

Lemma 9.1

$$r_1 = e^{\bar{h}} + O(\bar{h}^{p+1}) \qquad \text{as} \qquad \bar{h} \to 0$$

where p is the order of the linear multistep method.

It follows immediately from Lemma 9.1 that, for small positive $\bar{h}$, r_1 is greater than unity and so *every consistent zero-stable linear multistep method is absolutely unstable when $\bar{h}$ is positive*. Thus the interval of absolute stability must always be of the form $(\alpha, 0)$. There do exist methods for which α is zero.

The fact that the interval of absolute stability is always negative need not prevent the use of the method when $\bar{h} > 0$. If $\lambda > 0$, the solution of Equation (9.42) is the increasing exponential $\exp[\lambda(x - a)]$ and if the error grows at a rate similar to that of the solution of the differential equation, the numerical solution may be acceptable. For this reason, an alternative concept of stability has been introduced. The following definition is taken from Lambert.

Definition 9.7

The linear multistep method of Equation (9.42) is said to be **relatively stable** for a given $\bar{h}$ if, for that $\bar{h}$, the roots r_j of Equation (9.46) satisfy

$$|r_j| < |r_1| \qquad j = 2, 3, \dots, k$$

and to be **relatively unstable** otherwise. An interval (α, β) is said to be an *interval of relative stability* if the method is relatively stable for all $\bar{h}$ in (α, β).

We illustrate the concepts of absolute and relative stability by considering Simpson's method of Equation (9.37). Substituting the α_i and β_i of Equation (9.43) into Equation (9.46), we obtain the stability equation

$$\left(1 - \frac{1}{3}\bar{h}\right)r^2 - \frac{4}{3}\bar{h}r - \left(1 + \frac{1}{3}\bar{h}\right) = 0$$

The roots of this equation are given by

$$r = \frac{4\bar{h}/3 \pm \sqrt{[(4\bar{h}/3)^2 + 4(1 - \bar{h}/3)(1 + \bar{h}/3)]}}{2(1 - \bar{h}/3)}$$

$$= \frac{2\bar{h}/3 \pm \sqrt{(1 + \bar{h}^2/3)}}{(1 - \bar{h}/3)}$$

$$= \left[\frac{2}{3}\bar{h} \pm \left(1 + \frac{\bar{h}^2}{3}\right)^{1/2}\right]\left(1 - \frac{\bar{h}}{3}\right)^{-1}$$

Expanding the expressions in brackets using the binomial theorem gives

$$r = \left[\frac{2}{3}\bar{h} \pm \left(1 + \frac{1}{6}\bar{h}^2 \cdots\right)\right]\left(1 + \frac{1}{3}\bar{h} + \frac{1}{9}\bar{h}^2 \cdots\right)$$

$$= \frac{2}{3}\bar{h} \pm \left(1 + \frac{1}{3}\bar{h} + \cdots\right)$$

Hence, to $O(\bar{h}^2)$, the two roots are given by

$$r_1 = 1 + \bar{h}$$

and

$$r_2 = -1 + \frac{1}{3}\bar{h}$$

Clearly, r_1 is greater than 1 if $\bar{h}$ is positive and r_2 is less than -1 if $\bar{h}$ is negative. Hence, the Simpson corrector formula is absolutely unstable for all $\bar{h}$. However, by Definition 9.7, the formula is relatively stable for values of $\bar{h}$ satisfying

$$\left| -1 + \frac{1}{3}\bar{h} \right| < |1 + \bar{h}|$$

Any positive value of $\bar{h}$ satisfies this inequality and so the interval of relative stability for Simpson's formula is $(0, \infty)$. Therefore Simpson's formula is not appropriate if $\bar{h} < 0$, but, if $\bar{h} > 0$, the errors will not grow relative to the solution. This observation is supported by the numerical solutions to Equation (9.31) given in Tables 9.7 and 9.8. Both solutions were computed using the Milne–Simpson method with $h = 0.1$ and $y(0) = 1$ and were started using values obtained from the exact solution. Table 9.7 gives the solution when $\lambda = -15$ and clearly shows the instability of the method. Table 9.8 gives the solution along with the errors for the case $\lambda = 5$; in this case, the errors are increasing as the solution progresses but only at a similar rate to the solution and so this is reasonably acceptable.

Table 9.7 Milne–Simpson solution to
Equation (9.31) when $\lambda = -15$ and
$y(0) = 1$.

x	From analytic solution	From Milne–Simpson
0.4	0.002 479	0.078 593
0.5	0.000 553	0.078 434
0.6	0.000 123	0.172 770
0.7	0.000 028	0.248 030
0.8	0.000 006	0.440 297
0.9	0.000 001	0.699 483
1.0	0.000 000	1.175 997

In contrast to Simpson's formula, all Adams methods have the property that

$$\rho(\xi) = \xi^k - \xi^{k-1}$$

that is

$$\alpha_k = 1 \quad \text{and} \quad \alpha_{k-1} = -1$$

with $\alpha_j = 0 \{j = 0,1, \ldots ,k - 2\}$. Thus the principal root is $\xi_1 = +1$ and all other roots are zero. Consequently, the Adams methods generally have substantial intervals of absolute stability. For example, the interval of absolute stability for the Adams–Moulton corrector formula (9.41) is $(-3,0)$ and so this formula is appropriate when λ is negative, provided that a suitable steplength is used. Finally, we note that the stability interval of a predictor–corrector pair is the same as that of the corrector *if the latter is iterated to convergence.* (This was the case when the values of Tables 9.7 and 9.8 were produced.) Otherwise, it depends on the stability interval of the two equations and the way in which the predictor–corrector method is implemented. For example, the interval of absolute stability for the fourth-order Adams–Bashforth–Moulton method, implemented in the **PECE** mode, is $(-1.25,0)$. Further details are given in Lambert (1973).

9.1.4 Comparison of Runge–Kutta and predictor–corrector methods

It is not easy to make a fair comparison of Runge–Kutta and predictor–corrector methods; first, we have to decide on the criteria by which they are to be judged. Topics that should be considered include accuracy, stability, the cost of using the

Table 9.8 Milne–Simpson solution to Equation (9.31) when $\lambda = 5$ and $y(0) = 1$.

x	From analytic solution	From Milne– Simpson	Error
0.4	0.7389×10^1	0.7391×10^1	-0.0019
0.5	0.1218×10^2	0.1219×10^2	-0.0047
0.6	0.2009×10^2	0.2010×10^2	-0.0115
0.7	0.3312×10^2	0.3314×10^2	-0.0242
0.8	0.5460×10^2	0.5465×10^2	-0.0495
0.9	0.9002×10^2	0.9011×10^2	-0.0966
1.0	0.1484×10^3	0.1486×10^3	-0.1846

methods (measured in terms of function evaluations) and ease of programming. Lambert discusses these in some detail and we shall draw from his analysis. He points out that these properties of the methods are interrelated; for example, can we justify comparing the accuracy of two methods when one uses two function evaluations and the other six? Perhaps the property that is least complicated to compare is the ease of implementation. Here, the Runge–Kutta methods are seen to be the best; the ease with which the steplength can be changed and the lack of need for starting values count in their favour. However, it should be remembered that the need for extra function evaluations to determine error estimates makes them less efficient than predictor–corrector methods.

After some discussion, Lambert concludes that, if only methods of the same order using the same number of function evaluations per interval are compared, it would appear that predictor–corrector methods are to be preferred. Then Runge–Kutta methods are ideally suited to calculate the necessary starting values.

9.2 Systems and higher-order initial-value problems

In Section 9.1, we described several methods for the numerical solution of the *first-order* differential equation

$$\frac{dy}{dx} = f(x,y)$$

over an interval $[a,b]$, given the initial value $y(a) = y_0$. In this section we describe how these methods can be adapted to solve both a system of first-order equations and a higher order initial-value problem.

9.2.1   Systems of first-order equations

Some physical problems may be represented by a system of m equations of the form

$$\frac{dy_1}{dx} = f_1(x, y_1, y_2, \ldots, y_m)$$

$$\frac{dy_2}{dx} = f_2(x, y_1, y_2, \ldots, y_m) \qquad\qquad (9.47)$$

$$\vdots$$

$$\frac{dy_m}{dx} = f_m(x, y_1, y_2, \ldots, y_m)$$

which are to be solved for the functions $y_1(x), y_2(x), \ldots, y_m(x)$ over an interval $[a,b]$ subject to the conditions

$$y_1(a) = c_1$$
$$y_2(a) = c_2$$
$$\vdots \qquad\qquad (9.48)$$
$$y_m(a) = c_m$$

where the $c_j \; \{j = 1, 2, \ldots, m\}$ are constants. This problem is an initial-value problem because all the conditions are given for the *same* value of x. The following theorem, which is an extension of Theorem 9.1, states a sufficient condition for a solution of Equations (9.47) to exist and be unique.

Theorem 9.5

Let $f_j(x, y_1, \ldots, y_m) \; \{j = 1, 2, \ldots, m\}$ be defined and continuous in a region D defined by $a \leqslant x \leqslant b$, $-\infty < y_j < \infty$. If there is a constant L such that, for all $(x, y_1, \ldots, y_m)$ and $(x, z_1, \ldots, z_m)$ in D,

$$\left| f_j(x, y_1, \ldots, y_m) - f_j(x, z_1, \ldots, z_m) \right| \leqslant L \sum_{k=1}^{m} |y_k - z_k|$$

then Equations (9.47) have a unique solution $\{y_1(x), y_2(x), \ldots, y_m(x)\}$ where each $y_j \; \{j = 1, 2, \ldots, m\}$ is continuous and differentiable for all x in $[a,b]$.

A proof of a more general form of this theorem is given in Henrici (1962).

Any of the numerical methods described in Section 9.1 can be adapted to solve System (9.47). We will illustrate the general approach by considering a pair of equations and, to avoid confusion in the notation, write them in the form

$$\frac{dy}{dx} = f(x,y,z) \qquad y(a) = y_0$$

$$\frac{dz}{dx} = g(x,y,z) \qquad z(a) = z_0$$

(9.49)

Thus the symbol y_i will again denote an estimate of $y(x_i)$ rather than the ith member of the set $\{y_1(x), y_2(x), \ldots, y_m(x)\}$. Similarly, the symbol z_i will denote an estimate of $z(x_i)$.

Because the functions on the right-hand sides of Equations (9.49) are functions of *three* variables, the formulae used in the numerical methods must be modified. For example, to use the basic Euler method, Equation (9.13)

$$y_{i+1} = y_i + hf(x_i, y_i)$$

is replaced by the two equations

$$y_{i+1} = y_i + hf(x_i, y_i, z_i)$$
$$z_{i+1} = z_i + hg(x_i, y_i, z_i)$$

Then, after setting $x_0 = a$, these equations are used to compute the sequence y_1, z_1; y_2, z_2; ... which are the estimates of $y(x_1)$, $z(x_1)$; $y(x_2)$, $z(x_2)$; ....

Any of the Runge–Kutta methods can be adapted in a similar manner. For example, the fourth-order Runge–Kutta Equations (9.24)

$$k_1 = hf(x_i, y_i)$$
$$k_2 = hf(x_i + h/2, y_i + k_1/2)$$
$$k_3 = hf(x_i + h/2, y_i + k_2/2)$$
$$k_4 = hf(x_i + h, y_i + k_3)$$
$$y_{i+1} = y_i + (k_1 + 2k_2 + 2k_3 + k_4)/6$$

can be replaced by

$$k_1 = hf(x_i, y_i, z_i)$$
$$k_2 = hf(x_i + h/2, y_i + k_1/2, z_i + l_1/2)$$
$$k_3 = hf(x_i + h/2, y_i + k_2/2, z_i + l_2/2)$$
$$k_4 = hf(x_i + h, y_i + k_3, z_i + l_3)$$
$$y_{i+1} = y_i + (k_1 + 2k_2 + 2k_3 + k_4)/6$$
$$l_1 = hg(x_i, y_i, z_i)$$
$$l_2 = hg(x_i + h/2, y_i + k_1/2, z_i + l_1/2)$$
$$l_3 = hg(x_i + h/2, y_i + k_2/2, z_i + l_2/2)$$
$$l_4 = hg(x_i + h, y_i + k_3, z_i + l_3)$$
$$z_{i+1} = z_i + (l_1 + 2l_2 + 2l_3 + l_4)/6$$

Given $f(x,y,z)$, $g(x,y,z)$, a, b, n, y_0, z_0
Set $h = (b - a)/n$
　　$x_0 = a$
For $i = 0,1, \ldots ,n - 1$
　Set　$k_1 = hf(x_i,y_i,z_i)$
　　　$l_1 = hg(x_i,y_i,z_i)$
　　　$k_2 = hf(x_i + h/2, y_i + k_1/2, z_i + l_1/2)$
　　　$l_2 = hg(x_i + h/2, y_i + k_1/2, z_i + l_1/2)$
　　　$k_3 = hf(x_i + h/2, y_i + k_2/2, z_i + l_2/2)$
　　　$l_3 = hg(x_i + h/2, y_i + k_2/2, z_i + l_2/2)$
　　　$k_4 = hf(x_i + h, y_i + k_3, z_i + l_3)$
　　　$l_4 = hg(x_i + h, y_i + k_3, z_i + l_3)$
　　$x_{i+1} = x_i + h$
　　$y_{i+1} = y_i + (k_1 + 2k_2 + 2k_3 + k_4)/6$
　　$z_{i+1} = z_i + (l_1 + 2l_2 + 2l_3 + l_4)/6$

Figure 9.13　Algorithm for the classical fourth-order Runge–Kutta method applied to a pair of equations.

where the k_j $\{j = 1,2,3,4\}$ are estimates of δy and the l_j $\{j = 1,2,3,4\}$ are estimates of δz. Note that k_2 cannot be calculated until l_1 has been computed, nor can k_3 be calculated until l_2 has been computed and so on. The sequence of calculations is given in the algorithm of Figure 9.13.

We illustrate the algorithm by estimating $y(0.1)$ and $z(0.1)$ given

$$\frac{dy}{dx} = x + y + z \qquad y(0) = 1$$

$$\frac{dz}{dx} = 1 + y + z \qquad z(0) = -1 \tag{9.50}$$

In this example,

$$f(x,y,z) = x + y + z$$
$$g(x,y,z) = 1 + y + z$$

and so, with $h = 0.1$,

$$k_1 = 0.1f(0,1,-1) = 0$$
$$l_1 = 0.1g(0,1,-1) = 0.1$$
$$k_2 = 0.1f(0 + 0.1/2, 1 + 0/2, -1 + 0.1/2) = 0.01$$
$$l_2 = 0.1g(0 + 0.1/2, 1 + 0/2, -1 + 0.1/2) = 0.105$$
$$k_3 = 0.1f(0 + 0.1/2, 1 + 0.01/2, -1 + 0.105/2) = 0.010\ 75$$
$$l_3 = 0.1g(0 + 0.1/2, 1 + 0.01/2, -1 + 0.105/2) = 0.105\ 75$$

Given $f(x,y,z)$, $g(x,y,z)$, (x_i,y_i,z_i) $\{i = 0,1,2,3\}$, h, n
For $i = 0,1,2,3$
  Set $f_i = f(x_i,y_i,z_i)$
    $g_i = g(x_i,y_i,z_i)$
For $i = 3,4,\ldots,n-1$
  Set $x_{i+1} = x_i + h$
    $y_{i+1} = y_i + h(55f_i - 59f_{i-1} + 37f_{i-2} - 9f_{i-3})/24$
    $z_{i+1} = z_i + h(55g_i - 59g_{i-1} + 37g_{i-2} - 9g_{i-3})/24$
    $f_{i+1} = f(x_{i+1},y_{i+1},z_{i+1})$
    $g_{i+1} = g(x_{i+1},y_{i+1},z_{i+1})$
    $y_{i+1} = y_i + h(9f_{i+1} + 19f_i - 5f_{i-1} + f_{i-2})/24$
    $z_{i+1} = z_i + h(9g_{i+1} + 19g_i - 5g_{i-1} + g_{i-2})/24$
    $f_{i+1} = f(x_{i+1},y_{i+1},z_{i+1})$
    $g_{i+1} = g(x_{i+1},y_{i+1},z_{i+1})$

Figure 9.14   Algorithm for the fourth-order Adams–Bashforth–Moulton method applied to a pair of equations.

$$k_4 = 0.1f(0 + 0.1,1 + 0.010\ 75,-1 + 0.105\ 75) = 0.021\ 65$$
$$l_4 = 0.1g(0 + 0.1,1 + 0.010\ 75,-1 + 0.105\ 75) = 0.111\ 65$$

Then

$$y(0.1) \simeq y_1 = 1 + (0 + 2 \times 0.01 + 2 \times 0.010\ 75 + 0.021\ 65)/6$$
$$= 1.010\ 53$$
$$z(0.1) \simeq z_1 = -1 + (0.1 + 2 \times 0.105 + 2 \times 0.105\ 75 + 0.111\ 65)/6$$
$$= -0.894\ 48$$

These results are correct to the accuracy quoted.

If required, a solution started by a single-step method can be extended using a multistep method. Figure 9.14 gives an algorithm for solving Equations (9.49) by the fourth-order Adams–Bashforth–Moulton method implemented in the **PECE** mode.

As for a single equation, error control can be included in any of the numerical methods. The error test must be applied to *every* component of the solution; if any component fails the test, the steplength must be reduced and *all* components recalculated.

Program construction

It is a simple matter to modify the programs of Section 9.1 so that they can be applied to the System (9.47). To illustrate the general approach, we give a subroutine for solving a pair of equations using the fourth-order Runge–Kutta method. The subroutine in Figure 9.15 is a straightforward modification of that in Figure 9.6.

```
SUBROUTINE RK4TWO (F,G,XYZOUT,A,B,N,Y0,Z0)

INTEGER  I,N
REAL     A,B,F,G,H,HBY2,K1,K2,K3,K4,
*        L1,L2,L3,L4,X,Y,Y0,Z,Z0
EXTERNAL F,G,XYZOUT

H=(B-A)/N
HBY2=H/2
X=A
Y=Y0
Z=Z0
CALL XYZOUT(X,Y,Z)

DO 10, I=0,N-1
  K1=H*F(X,Y,Z)
  L1=H*G(X,Y,Z)
  K2=H*F(X+HBY2,Y+K1/2,Z+L1/2)
  L2=H*G(X+HBY2,Y+K1/2,Z+L1/2)
  K3=H*F(X+HBY2,Y+K2/2,Z+L2/2)
  L3=H*G(X+HBY2,Y+K2/2,Z+L2/2)
  K4=H*F(X+H,Y+K3,Z+L3)
  L4=H*G(X+H,Y+K3,Z+L3)
  X=X+H
  Y=Y+(K1+2*K2+2*K3+K4)/6
  Z=Z+(L1+2*L2+2*L3+L4)/6
  CALL XYZOUT(X,Y,Z)
10   CONTINUE

END
```

Figure 9.15   Subroutine for the classical fourth-order Runge–Kutta method applied to a pair of equations.

If m is large, a subprogram modified in this way will be very lengthy. Furthermore, it is difficult to adapt subroutine RK4TWO for a *general* value of m because the number of arguments in the functions depends on m. An alternative approach for the general system (9.47) is to use a one-dimensional array Y to represent the components of the solution, another one-dimensional array F to represent the values of the right-hand sides of the differential equations and a two-dimensional array K to represent the values of k. This has been done in the subroutine of Figure 9.16.

This subroutine requires the user to write and name a subroutine for calculating the elements of the array F. For example, a subroutine appropriate for

```
SUBROUTINE RK4M (M,FCALC,XYOUT,A,B,N,YO, Y,F, K,YARG)

INTEGER  I,J,L,M,N
REAL     A,B,H,X,XARG
REAL     COEFF(4),F(M),K(0:4,M),Y(M),YARG(M),YO(M)
EXTERNAL FCALC,XYOUT

COEFF(1)=0
COEFF(2)=0.5
COEFF(3)=0.5
COEFF(4)=1

DO 10, L=1,M
  K(0,L)=0
10  CONTINUE

H=(B-A)/N
X=A
DO 20, L=1,M
  Y(L)=YO(L)
20  CONTINUE
CALL XYOUT (M,X,Y)

DO 30, I=0,N=1
  DO 40, J=1,4
    XARG=X+H*COEFF(J)
    DO 50 L=1,M
      YARG(L)=Y(L)+COEFF(J)*K(J-1,L)
50      CONTINUE
    CALL FCALC(M,XARG,YARG, F)
    DO 60, L=1,M
      K(J,L)=H*F(L)
60      CONTINUE
40    CONTINUE
  X=X+H
  DO 70, L=1,M
    Y(L)=Y(L)+(K(1,L)+2*K(2,L)+2*K(3,L)+K(4,L))/6
70    CONTINUE
  CALL XYOUT(M,X,Y)
30  CONTINUE

END
```

Figure 9.16 Subroutine for the classical fourth-order Runge–Kutta method applied to a system of equations.

System (9.50) is

```
SUBROUTINE F2(M,X,Y, F)
INTEGER M
REAL    X
REAL    F(M),Y(M)

F(1)=X+Y(1)+Y(2)
F(2)=1+Y(1)+Y(2)

END
```

9.2.2 Higher-order initial-value problems

To solve the general mth order differential equation

$$\frac{d^m y}{dx^m} = f(x, y, y', y'', y^{(3)}, \ldots, y^{(m-1)}) \tag{9.51}$$

we need m conditions. If these are all given for the *same* values of x so that

$$y(a) = c_1$$
$$y'(a) = c_2$$
$$y''(a) = c_3$$
$$\vdots$$
$$y^{(m-1)}(a) = c_m$$

then the problem is an initial-value problem and can be solved by any of the methods described in Section 9.1. If the conditions are not all specified for the same value of x, the problem is a *boundary-value problem*; methods for solving problems of this type are discussed in Section 9.3.

To solve the general initial-value problem, we make the transformations

$$y_1(x) = y(x)$$
$$y_2(x) = y'(x)$$
$$y_3(x) = y''(x)$$
$$\vdots$$
$$y_m(x) = y^{(m-1)}(x)$$

and then replace Equation (9.51) by the system

$$\frac{dy_1}{dx} = y_2$$
$$\frac{dy_2}{dx} = y_3$$

$$\vdots$$

$$\frac{dy_{m-1}}{dx} = y_m$$

$$\frac{dy_m}{dx} = f(x, y_1, y_2, \ldots, y_m)$$

This system is equivalent to that in Equations (9.47) with

$$f_j = \begin{cases} y_{j+1} & j = 1, 2, \ldots, m-1 \\ f & j = m \end{cases}$$

and so can be solved using the same methods.

9.3 Boundary-value problems

As we have noted already, a differential equation of order m must be accompanied by m conditions if we are to obtain a unique solution. In the last section, it was assumed that all the conditions were given for *one* value of x. In practice, however, differential equations of order greater than one are often accompanied by conditions that specify values of y and/or its derivatives at more than one value of x. It is frequently the case that conditions are given at the end-points of an interval $[a,b]$; such problems are known as *boundary-value problems*. As an example

$$\frac{d^2y}{dx^2} = f(x, y, y') \qquad y(a) = A \qquad y(b) = B \tag{9.52}$$

is a *two-point* boundary-value problem. In general, we are interested in the solution of this problem within the interval $[a,b]$.

A boundary-value problem may have a unique solution, an infinite number of solutions or no solution at all. Theorems stating sufficient conditions for the existence of a unique solution to various types of boundary-value problem are given in Keller (1968). We shall concentrate on the problem given in Equation (9.52) for which the following theorem is appropriate.

Theorem 9.6

Let $f(x, y, y')$ be defined and continuous for all (x, y, y') in a region D defined by $a \leqslant x \leqslant b$, $-\infty < y < \infty$, $-\infty < y' < \infty$ and let $\partial f/\partial y$ and $\partial f/\partial y'$ be continuous in D. Then the two-point boundary-value problem of Equations (9.52) has a unique solution if, for all (x, y, y') in D:

(1) $\dfrac{\partial f}{\partial y} > 0$

and

(2)   there exists a constant K such that

$$\left| \frac{\partial f}{\partial y'} \right| \leq |K|$$

In general, numerical solutions to boundary-value problems are easier to obtain if the differential equation is *linear*. A second-order differential equation is said to be linear if the coefficients of y, y' and y'' are either constants or functions of x only. In this case, the two-point boundary-value problem (9.52) can be written in the form

$$\frac{d^2y}{dx^2} + p(x)\frac{dy}{dx} + q(x)y = r(x) \qquad y(a) = A \qquad y(b) = B \tag{9.53}$$

It can be shown that this equation has a unique solution provided that $p(x)$, $q(x)$ and $r(x)$ are continuous on $[a,b]$ and that $q(x) < 0$ on $[a,b]$.

Two techniques for solving two-point boundary-value problems are considered. The first makes use of the initial-value methods of Section 9.2. The second replaces the boundary-value problem by a system of algebraic equations; if the differential equation is linear, this system can be solved using the methods of Chapter 5. In practice, the boundary conditions may have the more general form

$$\begin{aligned} \alpha_1 y(a) + \alpha_2 y'(a) &= A \\ \beta_1 y(b) + \beta_2 y'(b) &= B \end{aligned} \tag{9.54}$$

where α_1, α_2, β_1 and β_2 are constants. In this case the problem is more difficult computationally; we return to this point in later sections, particularly Section 9.3.2.

9.3.1   The shooting method

If the value of $y'(a)$ (M, say) were known in addition to the given conditions, the differential equation in (9.52) could be solved over the interval $[a,b]$ using the conditions

$$y(a) = A \qquad \text{and} \qquad y'(a) = M$$

This would be an initial-value problem and so could be solved by the methods described in Section 9.2. Similarly, if the value of $y'(b)$ were known, the two-point boundary-value problem could be replaced by an initial-value problem

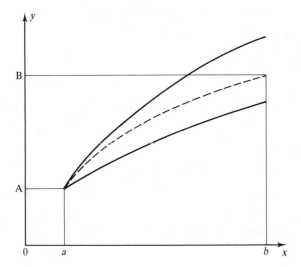

Figure 9.17 The shooting method.

involving $y(b)$ and $y'(b)$ (and integrating from b to a). Unfortunately, neither $y'(a)$ nor $y'(b)$ is known.

The idea behind the shooting method is very simple: we estimate the value of $y'(a)$ (or $y'(b)$) and thus produce an initial-value problem! Suppose we take a value M_1 as an estimate of $y'(a)$. We proceed by solving the differential equation over the interval $[a,b]$ using the conditions

$$y(a) = A \qquad y'(a) = M_1$$

As in Section 9.2, we use a steplength $(b - a)/n$ and so a set of values $\{y_1, y_2, \ldots, y_n\}$ is obtained which are estimates of $y(x_i)$ $\{i = 1,2, \ldots, n\}$ for our initial-value problem and another set $\{y'_1, y'_2, \ldots, y'_n\}$ which are estimates of $y'(x_i)$. However, at this stage, only the value of y_n is of interest. If we were extremely fortunate and had estimated the value of $y'(a)$ correctly, we would find that $y_n = B$ within the accuracy attainable from the numerical method. In this event, the numerical solution to our initial-value problem would also be the solution to the two-point boundary-value problem. Of course, in practice, it is very unlikely that our first estimate of $y'(a)$ would be correct and so, most probably, we would find that $y_n \neq B$. In this event, we could try again with a different estimate, M_2, of $y'(a)$. Figure 9.17 illustrates the solutions obtained from two incorrect estimates of $y'(a)$; the broken line represents the required solution.

Clearly we could experiment with different estimates of $y'(a)$ until we eventually 'hit the target' at (b,B). Fortunately, however, there are several ways to accelerate the procedure. Note that y_n is a function of M and so, essentially,

Given $f(x,y,y')$, a, A, b, B, n, M_1, M_2
Set $h = (b - a)/n$
Repeat (for $j = 1,2,3, \ldots$)
  For $i = 1,2, \ldots ,n$
    Set $x = a + ih$
    Evaluate y_i, z_i {by solving the system: $y' = z$ $y(a) = A$
                                              $z' = f(x,y,z)$ $z(a) = M_j$}
  Set $B_j = y_n$
  If $j \geqslant 2$ then

    Set $M_{j+1} = \dfrac{(B_j - B)M_{j-1} - (B_{j-1} - B)M_j}{B_j - B_{j-1}}$

Until converged

Figure 9.18 Algorithm for the shooting method.

the problem is that of solving the equation

$$F(M) = y_n(M) - B = 0$$

This is a non-linear equation and can be solved using, for example, the secant method. Suppose that an estimate M_i of M leads to the value $y_n(M_i) = B_i$ and another estimate M_{i+1} leads to the value $y_n(M_{i+1}) = B_{i+1}$. Then the secant formula (4.1) gives

$$M_{i+2} = \frac{F_{i+1}M_i - F_iM_{i+1}}{F_{i+1} - F_i} = \frac{(B_{i+1} - B)M_i - (B_i - B)M_{i+1}}{B_{i+1} - B_i} \tag{9.55}$$

as the next estimate of M. An algorithm for the shooting method is given in Figure 9.18.

To illustrate the shooting method, we consider the two-point boundary-value problem

$$\frac{d^2y}{dx^2} = \frac{9}{2}(x - 1) + \frac{3}{x^2} - 2yz \qquad y(1) = 1 \quad y(2) = 2 \tag{9.56}$$

In this example, we require a value M for $y'(1)$ which leads to $B = 2$. As a first approximation, we set $M_1 = 0$. Applying the transformation described in Section 9.2.2, and using z to represent dy/dx, we replace Equation (9.56) by the initial-value system

$$\frac{dy}{dx} = z \qquad\qquad\qquad y(1) = 1$$

$$\frac{dz}{dx} = \frac{9}{2}(x - 1) + \frac{3}{x^2} - 2yz \qquad z(1) = 0 \tag{9.57}$$

Table 9.9 Estimates, M_i, of $y'(1)$ and the resulting values B_i.

i	M_i	B_i
1	0	1.8535
2	1	2.1353
3	0.5199	2.0056
4	0.4992	1.9998
5	0.4999	2.0000

Any of the initial-value methods can be used to solve this system. For example, using the fourth-order Runge–Kutta algorithm of Figure 9.13 with $x_0 = 1$, $n = 10$ and

$$f(x,y,z) = z$$
$$g(x,y,z) = \frac{9}{2}(x - 1) + \frac{3}{x^2} - 2yz$$

we find that $B_1 = y_{10} = 1.8535$. Because $B_1 \neq 2$, we repeat the procedure using a different estimate of $y'(1)$. For our second approximation, we set $M_2 = 1$; this leads to $B_2 = 2.1353$ and so $y'(1)$ has still not been estimated correctly. For the third approximation to M, we use Equation (9.55). This gives

$$M_3 = \frac{(2.1353 - 2)0 - (1.8535 - 2)1}{(2.1353 - 1.8535)} = 0.5199$$

which leads to $B_3 = 2.0056$. The results of further calculations are given in Table 9.9.

After five attempts, a value M_i has been located for which $B_i = 2$ to within four decimal places and we will stop at this stage. The solutions to Equations (9.57) with $y(1) = 1$ and $z(1) = y'(1) = 0.4999$ are recorded in the third and fifth columns of Table 9.10. For comparison, values are also given of y and y' obtained from the exact solution

$$y = \frac{3}{2}(x - 1) + \frac{1}{x}$$

of the boundary-value problem (9.56). Note that, in this example, five initial-value systems had to be solved to obtain a solution to a single two-point boundary-value problem.

When the boundary conditions have the general form of (9.54), we make the following minor modification to the method. We require values M, M' of $y(a)$, $y'(a)$ that are consistent with the condition given at $x = a$ and lead to

Table 9.10 Solution to the boundary-value problem (9.56).

x	y Analytic solution	y Numerical solution	y' Analytic solution	y' Numerical solution
1.0	1.0000	1.0000	0.5000	0.4999
1.1	1.0591	1.0591	0.6736	0.6735
1.2	1.1333	1.1333	0.8056	0.8055
1.3	1.2192	1.2192	0.9083	0.9082
1.4	1.3143	1.3143	0.9898	0.9898
1.5	1.4167	1.4166	1.0556	1.0555
1.6	1.5250	1.5250	1.1094	1.1094
1.7	1.6382	1.6382	1.1540	1.1540
1.8	1.7556	1.7555	1.1914	1.1914
1.9	1.8763	1.8763	1.2230	1.2230
2.0	2.0000	2.0000	1.2500	1.2500

values C, C' of $y(b)$, $y'(b)$ satisfying the condition given at $x = b$. Beginning with an estimate M_1 of M, we compute M'_1 from

$$M'_1 = \frac{(A - \alpha_1 M_1)}{\alpha_2}$$

Then the initial-value problem

$$\frac{d^2y}{dx^2} = f(x, y, y') \qquad y(a) = M_1 \quad y'(a) = M'_1$$

is solved to provide C_1 ($= y_n$) and C'_1 ($= y'_n$). Repeating the procedure with a different estimate M_2 of $y(a)$ gives values M'_2, C_2 and C'_2. At this stage the secant method can be used to solve the non-linear equation

$$F(M) = \beta_1 y_n(M) + \beta_2 y'_n(M) - B = 0$$

and so give successive estimates of M.

Now consider the application of the shooting method to the *linear* two-point boundary-value problem (9.53)

$$\frac{d^2y}{dx^2} + p(x)\frac{dy}{dx} + q(x)y = r(x) \qquad y(a) = A \quad y(b) = B$$

In this case, only *two* initial-value problems need be solved:

$$\frac{d^2u}{dx^2} + p(x)\frac{du}{dx} + q(x)u = r(x) \qquad u(a) = A \quad u'(a) = 0$$

$$\frac{d^2v}{dx^2} + p(x)\frac{dv}{dx} + q(x)v = 0 \qquad v(a) = 0 \quad v'(a) = 1$$

(9.58)

because the solution of the boundary-value problem can be expressed directly as a linear combination of the solutions of these equations. Let $u(x)$, $v(x)$ denote the exact solutions of Equations (9.58) and u_i, v_i $\{i = 0,1, \ldots ,n\}$ denote their numerical solutions. Consider the function defined by

$$Y(x) = u(x) + \lambda v(x)$$

where λ is a constant. Now

$$Y'(x) = u'(x) + \lambda v'(x)$$
$$Y''(x) = u''(x) + \lambda v''(x)$$

and so

$$Y'' + p(x)Y' + q(x)Y = u'' + p(x)u' + q(x)u + \lambda(v'' + p(x)v' + q(x)v)$$
$$= r(x) + 0$$
$$= r(x)$$

Hence $Y(x)$ is a solution of the differential equation (9.53) for any value of λ. Furthermore, when $x = a$,

$$Y(a) = u(a) + \lambda v(a)$$
$$= A + 0$$
$$= A$$

and so $Y(x)$ satisfies the condition given in Equations (9.53) for $x = a$. Furthermore, λ can be chosen so that, in addition, $Y(x)$ satisfies the condition for $x = b$ given in Equations (9.53). We require

$$Y(b) = u(b) + \lambda v(b) = B$$

and so λ is given by

$$\lambda = \frac{B - u(b)}{v(b)}$$
$$\simeq \frac{B - u_n}{v_n}$$

Thus, to solve the linear two-point boundary-value problem (9.53) by the shooting method, we compute numerical solutions u_i, v_i $\{i = 1, 2, \ldots, n\}$ to Equations (9.58) and then set

$$y_i = u_i + \frac{B - u_n}{v_n} v_i$$

In fact, other values for $u'(a)$ and $v'(a)$ can be chosen (with the restriction that $v'(a) \neq 0$) without affecting the numerical solution y_i.

We shall not construct subroutines for the shooting method because we can make use of subroutine RK4TWO (Figure 9.15) and also, in the non-linear case, the subroutine SECANT (Figure 4.12).

9.3.2   Finite-difference methods

Finite-difference methods enable us to replace a differential equation by a system of algebraic equations. If the differential equation is non-linear, the algebraic equations will be non-linear also. The solution of such a system is beyond the scope of the present text and so, for this method, only linear two-point boundary-value problems will be considered. Initially, we assume that the boundary conditions are $y(a) = A$ and $y(b) = B$.

We begin by dividing the interval $[a,b]$ into n subintervals, each of width h, and define $x_0 = a$, $x_i = x_0 + ih$ $\{i = 1, 2, \ldots, n\}$ so that $x_n = b$.

The problem is to estimate $y(x_i)$ $\{i = 1, 2, \ldots, n - 1\}$. At the general point x_i, the differential equation gives

$$\left(\frac{d^2 y}{dx^2}\right)_{x=x_i} + p(x_i)\left(\frac{dy}{dx}\right)_{x=x_i} + q(x_i)y(x_i) = r(x_i) \tag{9.59}$$

In Chapter 8 we derived the approximations

$$f'(x) = \frac{f(x + h) - f(x - h)}{2h} + O(h^2)$$

and

$$f''(x) = \frac{f(x + h) - 2f(x) + f(x - h)}{h^2} + O(h^2)$$

For the function $y(x)$, these approximations may be written

$$\left(\frac{dy}{dx}\right)_{x=x_i} = \frac{y(x_{i+1}) - y(x_{i-1})}{2h} + O(h^2) \tag{9.60}$$

and

$$\left(\frac{d^2y}{dx^2}\right)_{x=x_i} = \frac{y(x_{i+1}) - 2y(x_i) + y(x_{i-1})}{h^2} + O(h^2) \tag{9.61}$$

Equations (9.60) and (9.61) are known as the *central three-point finite-difference approximations* to $y'(x_i)$ and $y''(x_i)$ respectively and enable us to replace the derivatives in Equation (9.59). Substituting Equations (9.60) and (9.61) into Equation (9.59) and multiplying through by h^2 gives

$$\left[1 - \frac{1}{2}hp(x_i)\right]y(x_{i-1}) - [2 - h^2q(x_i)]y(x_i)$$
$$+ \left[1 + \frac{1}{2}hp(x_i)\right]y(x_{i+1}) = h^2r(x_i) + O(h^4) \tag{9.62}$$

Ignoring the error term and replacing $y(x_j)$ by its estimate y_j $\{j = i - 1, i, i + 1\}$, we obtain the second-order finite-difference equation

$$\left[1 - \frac{1}{2}hp(x_i)\right]y_{i-1} - [2 - h^2q(x_i)]y_i + \left[1 + \frac{1}{2}hp(x_i)\right]y_{i+1} = h^2r(x_i) \tag{9.63}$$

Setting $i = 1, 2, \ldots, n - 1$ in Equation (9.63) produces a system of $(n - 1)$ linear algebraic equations relating the $(n + 1)$ values $y_0, y_1, \ldots, y_n$. However, the values of y_0 and y_n are known from the boundary conditions and so the system can be solved for $y_1, y_2, \ldots, y_{n-1}$. For example, if we set $n = 5$, Equation (9.63) leads to the system

$$-[2 - h^2q(x_1)]y_1 + \left[1 + \frac{h}{2}p(x_1)\right]y_2 = h^2r(x_1) - \left[1 - \frac{h}{2}p(x_1)\right]y_0$$
$$\left[1 - \frac{h}{2}p(x_2)\right]y_1 - [2 - h^2q(x_2)]y_2 + \left[1 + \frac{h}{2}p(x_2)\right]y_3 = h^2r(x_2)$$
$$\left[1 - \frac{h}{2}p(x_3)\right]y_2 - [2 - h^2q(x_3)]y_3 + \left[1 + \frac{h}{2}p(x_3)\right]y_4 = h^2r(x_3) \tag{9.64}$$
$$\left[1 - \frac{h}{2}p(x_4)\right]y_3 - [2 - h^2q(x_4)]y_4 = h^2r(x_4) - \left[1 + \frac{h}{2}p(x_4)\right]y_5$$

Note that Equations (9.64) have tri-diagonal form. Clearly, Equation (9.63) will

Given $p(x)$, $q(x)$, $r(x)$, a, A, b, B, n
Set $h = (b - a)/n$
For $i = 1, 2, \ldots, n - 1$
  Set $x_i = a + ih$
    $a_i = 1 - hp(x_i)/2$
    $d_i = -[2 - h^2 q(x_i)]$
    $c_i = 1 + hp(x_i)/2$
    $b_i = h^2 r(x_i)$
Set $b_1 = b_1 - a_1 A$
    $b_{n-1} = b_{n-1} - c_{n-1} B$

{ Solve the tri-diagonal system }

Figure 9.19   Algorithm for the finite-difference method.

always produce a tri-diagonal system, regardless of the value of n. It follows from Theorem 5.2 that this system will have a unique solution if the coefficient matrix is strictly diagonally dominant. When $q < 0$, this condition can be achieved by choosing h so that $(h/2)|p(x_i)| \leq 1$ {$i = 1, 2, \ldots, n - 1$}. An algorithm for the finite-difference method is given in Figure 9.19. The tri-diagonal algorithm of Figure 5.19 provides a convenient method for solving the finite-difference equations.

To illustrate the finite-difference method, we consider the two-point boundary-value problem

$$\frac{d^2 y}{dx^2} + \frac{1}{x}\frac{dy}{dx} - \frac{y}{x^2} = 3 \qquad y(1) = 2 \qquad y(2) = 3 \tag{9.65}$$

For this problem,

$$a = 1 \qquad b = 2 \qquad A = 2 \qquad B = 3$$
$$p(x) = \frac{1}{x} \qquad q(x) = -\frac{1}{x^2} \qquad r(x) = 3$$

Dividing the region of integration [1,2] into five intervals,

$$h = 0.2 \quad x_0 = 1 \quad x_1 = 1.2 \quad x_2 = 1.4 \quad x_3 = 1.6 \quad x_4 = 1.8 \quad x_5 = 2$$

Hence, from Equations (9.64), we obtain the system

$$
\begin{aligned}
-2.0278y_1 + 1.0833y_2 &= 0.12 - 1.8333 \\
0.9286y_1 - 2.0204y_2 + 1.0714y_3 &= 0.12 \\
0.9375y_2 - 2.0156y_3 + 1.0625y_4 &= 0.12 \\
0.9444y_3 - 2.0123y_4 &= 0.12 - 3.1667
\end{aligned}
$$

Table 9.11   Solutions to boundary-value problem (9.65).

x	From analytic solution	Numerical solution h = 0.2	Numerical solution h = 0.1	Extra-polated solution
1	2	2	2	2
1.1	1.9282		1.9285	
1.2	1.9067	1.9083	1.9071	1.9067
1.3	1.9285		1.9289	
1.4	1.9886	1.9904	1.9890	1.9885
1.5	2.0833		2.0837	
1.6	2.2100	2.2115	2.2103	2.2099
1.7	2.3665		2.3667	
1.8	2.5511	2.5520	2.5513	2.5511
1.9	2.7627		2.7627	
2	3	3	3	3

The solution of these equations is given in the third column of Table 9.11. For comparison, the table also gives values calculated from the analytic solution

$$y = x(x - 1) + \frac{2}{x}$$

The numerical solution is correct to two decimal places.

The truncation errors in the finite-difference approximations (9.60) and (9.61) are $O(h^2)$ and so we would expect to obtain a significant improvement in the numerical solution by using a smaller steplength. The fourth column of Table 9.11 gives the solution to Equation (9.65) computed by the finite-difference method with $h = 0.1$; this solution is correct to three decimal places.

Unfortunately, as the steplength is halved, the number of finite-difference equations increases from $(n - 1)$ to $(2n - 1)$. To reduce the computational effort, a useful technique is to compute a solution y^* using a steplength h, and a second solution y^{**} with a steplength $h/2$, and then use Richardson extrapolation (Section 8.1.1) to obtain the $O(h^4)$ solution

$$y_i = \frac{4y_i^{**} - y_i^*}{3} \qquad i = 1, 2, \ldots, n - 1$$

It is permissible to use Richardson extrapolation because the errors in the central finite-difference approximations (9.60) and (9.61) may be written in terms of even powers of h. If the extrapolated solution differs significantly from y^{**}, a

Table 9.12 Solutions to boundary-value problem (9.67).

x	From analytic solution	From scheme (9.63)	From scheme (9.66)
0.2	0.3611	0.3600	0.3611
0.4	0.6465	0.6449	0.6465
0.6	0.8547	0.8531	0.8547
0.8	0.9776	0.9765	0.9776

third solution is computed by the finite-difference method using a steplength $h/4$ and further extrapolations are carried out. The last column of Table 9.11 shows the benefit of just one application of the extrapolation process.

It is possible to derive finite-difference approximations that are more accurate than those given in Equations (9.60) and (9.61). However, these higher order approximations lead to systems of equations which, in general, are not of tri-diagonal form and so are more difficult to solve. One notable exception is **Numerov's method**. This is an $O(h^4)$ method which does lead to a tri-diagonal system but it can be applied only to second-order differential equations in which the coefficient of y' is zero. For the equation

$$\frac{d^2y}{dx^2} + q(x)y = r(x)$$

Numerov's method uses the finite-difference scheme

$$\left[1 + \frac{h^2}{12}q(x_{i-1})\right]y_{i-1} - \left[2 - \frac{5}{6}h^2q(x_i)\right]y_i + \left[1 + \frac{h^2}{12}q(x_{i+1})\right]y_{i+1}$$
$$= \frac{h^2}{12}[r(x_{i-1}) + 10r(x_i) + r(x_{i+1})] \tag{9.66}$$

Table 9.12 gives numerical solutions obtained by the standard finite-difference scheme (9.63) and by Numerov's method for the two-point boundary-value problem

$$\frac{d^2y}{dx^2} - y + x + 2\cosh x = 0 \qquad y(0) = 0 \quad y(1) = 1 \tag{9.67}$$

Both solutions were obtained with $h = 0.2$. Comparison of these solutions with values obtained from the exact solution

$$y = (1 - x)\sinh x + x$$

illustrates the greater accuracy of the Numerov method.

$$
\begin{array}{l}
\textit{Given}: p(x),q(x),r(x),a,A,b,B,n \\
\textit{Set}: h = (b - a)/n \\
\textbf{for } i = 1,2, \ldots ,n - 1 \\
\quad \textit{Set}: x = a + ih \\
\qquad a_i = 1 - hp(x)/2 \\
\qquad d_i = -[2 - h^2 q(x)] \\
\qquad c_i = 1 + hp(x)/2 \\
\qquad b_i = h^2 r(x) \\
\textit{Set}: b_1 = b_1 - a_1 A \\
\qquad b_{n-1} = b_{n-1} - c_{n-1} B
\end{array}
$$

Figure 9.20   Plan of subroutine to construct the tri-diagonal system.

Program construction

We construct a subroutine to calculate the coefficient matrix and the right-hand-side constants of the tri-diagonal system produced by Equation (9.63). The subroutine plan of Figure 9.20 follows directly from the algorithm of Figure 9.19. A subroutine based on this plan is given in Figure 9.21. Note that the variables X0 and XN are used to represent a and b, and the variables Y0 and YN to represent A and B.

The output from this subroutine is in a form suitable for direct input to either subroutine TRISOL of Figure 5.20 or subroutine TRISL2 of Figure 5.21. It is a simple matter to modify the subroutine FINDIF so that it uses Numerov's method and this is left as an exercise for the reader.

Derivative boundary conditions

When the boundary conditions are given in the form of Equation (9.54), y_0 and y_n are not known explicitly and so the finite-difference method leads to a system of $(n - 1)$ equations in $(n + 1)$ unknowns, $\{y_0, y_1, \ldots, y_n\}$. To obtain two more equations to complete the system, Equation (9.63) is applied for $i = 0$ and $i = n$. This gives

$$
\begin{aligned}
\left[1 - \frac{h}{2}p(x_0)\right]y_{-1} - [2 - h^2 q(x_0)]y_0 + \left[1 + \frac{h}{2}p(x_0)\right]y_1 &= h^2 r(x_0) \\[2mm]
\left[1 - \frac{h}{2}p(x_n)\right]y_{n-1} - [2 - h^2 q(x_n)]y_n + \left[1 + \frac{h}{2}p(x_n)\right]y_{n+1} &= h^2 r(x_n)
\end{aligned}
\tag{9.68}
$$

The values y_{-1} and y_{n+1} are estimates of $y(a - h)$ and $y(b + h)$ respectively and are known as 'fictitious' values because the solution may not exist at the points $x_{-1} = a - h$ and $x_{n+1} = b + h$.

```
SUBROUTINE FINDIF (P,Q,R,XO,YO,XN,YN,N, A,B,C,D)

INTEGER  I,N
REAL     H,HPXBY2,P,Q,R,X,XN,XO,YN,YO
REAL     A(N-1),B(N-1),C(N-1),D(N-1)
EXTERNAL P,Q,R

H=(XN-XO)/N

DO 10, I=1,N-1
  X=XO+I*H
  HPXBY2 =H*P(X)/2
  A(I)=1-HPXBY2
  D(I)=-(2-H*H*Q(X))
  C(I)=1+HPXBY2
  B(I)=H*H*R(X)
10  CONTINUE
B(1)=B(1)-A(1)*YO
B(N-1)=B(N-1)-C(N-1)*YN

END
```

Figure 9.21   Subroutine to construct the tri-diagonal system.

The next step is to eliminate the fictitious values from Equations (9.68) and, to do this, the boundary conditions are used. Replacing the derivatives in Equations (9.54) by the approximation (9.60) leads to

$$\alpha_1 y(x_0) + \alpha_2 \frac{[y_1 - y_{-1}]}{2h} = A$$

$$\beta_1 y(x_n) + \beta_2 \frac{[y_{n+1} - y_{n-1}]}{2h} = B$$

(9.69)

Using Equations (9.69) to eliminate the fictitious values from Equations (9.68) produces the two equations required to complete the tri-diagonal system.

To illustrate the finite-difference method when derivative boundary conditions are present, consider the two-point boundary-value problem

$$\frac{d^2y}{dx^2} + 2x\frac{dy}{dx} - 3y + 6e^{-x}(1 + x^2) = 0 \qquad y'(0) - y(0) = 3$$

$$y'(1) = 0$$

(9.70)

365 BOUNDARY-VALUE PROBLEMS 365

In this case

$$a = 0 \quad b = 1 \quad \alpha_1 = -1 \quad \alpha_2 = 1 \quad \beta_1 = 0 \quad \beta_2 = 1$$
$$p(x) = 2x \quad q(x) = -3 \quad r(x) = -6e^{-x}(1 + x^2)$$

and, with $n = 5$,

$$h = 0.2 \quad x_0 = 0 \quad x_1 = 0.2 \quad x_2 = 0.4 \quad x_3 = 0.6 \quad x_4 = 0.8 \quad x_5 = 1$$

Hence, setting $i = 0,1,2,3,4,5$ in Equation (9.63) gives the system

$$
\begin{aligned}
y_{-1} - 2.1200y_0 + \quad\quad\quad y_1 &= -0.2400 \\
0.9600y_0 - 2.1200y_1 + 1.0400y_2 &= -0.2044 \\
0.9200y_1 - 2.1200y_2 + 1.0800y_3 &= -0.1866 \\
0.8800y_2 - 2.1200y_3 + 1.1200y_4 &= -0.1791 \\
0.8400y_3 - 2.1200y_4 + 1.1600y_5 &= -0.1769 \\
0.8000y_4 - 2.1200y_5 + 1.2000y_6 &= -0.1766
\end{aligned}
\quad\quad \textbf{(9.71)}
$$

From the boundary condition at $x = 0$,

$$\frac{y_1 - y_{-1}}{2(0.2)} - y_0 = 3$$

and so

$$y_{-1} = y_1 - 0.4(3 + y_0)$$

From the boundary condition at $x = 1$,

$$\frac{y_6 - y_4}{2(0.2)} = 0$$

and so

$$y_6 = y_4$$

Hence, eliminating the fictitious values y_{-1} and y_6 from the first and last of Equations (9.71), the tri-diagonal system becomes

$$
\begin{aligned}
-2.52y_0 + \quad 2y_1 \quad\quad\quad\quad\quad\quad\quad\quad\quad &= \quad 0.9600 \\
0.9600y_0 - 2.1200y_1 + 1.0400y_2 \quad\quad\quad\quad\quad &= -0.2044 \\
0.9200y_1 - 2.1200y_2 + 1.0800y_3 \quad\quad\quad &= -0.1866 \\
0.8800y_2 - 2.1200y_3 + 1.1200y_4 \quad &= -0.1791 \\
0.8400y_3 - 2.1200y_4 + 1.1600y_5 &= -0.1769 \\
2y_4 - 2.1200y_5 &= -0.1766
\end{aligned}
$$

Table 9.13   Solutions to the boundary-value problem (9.70).

x	Analytic solution	Numerical solution		Extra-polated solution
		h = 0.2	h = 0.1	
0	0.0000	0.0169	0.0043	0.0001
0.1	0.2715		0.2748	
0.2	0.4912	0.5013	0.4938	0.4913
0.3	0.6667		0.6687	
0.4	0.8044	0.8098	0.8058	0.8045
0.5	0.9098		0.9108	
0.6	0.9879	0.9898	0.9885	0.9881
0.7	1.0428		1.0430	
0.8	1.0784	1.0773	1.0782	1.0785
0.9	1.0977		1.0773	
1	1.1036	1.0996	1.1027	1.1037

The solution of these equations is given in Table 9.13. For comparison, we have included values computed from the analytic solution

$$y = 3xe^{-x}$$

of the boundary-problem. A more accurate numerical solution obtained with $h = 0.1$ is also given in this table, together with an extrapolated solution.

Modification of the subroutine in Figure 9.21 to take account of derivative boundary conditions is straightforward and this is left as an exercise for the reader.

EXERCISES

9.1   Using the Taylor series method, obtain the first four non-zero terms in the series solution of each of the initial-value problems

(a) $y' = x + y$ $y(0) = 0$

(b) $y' = y \cos x - 1$ $y(0) = 1$

(c) $y' = 1 - x^2 + y^2$ $y(1) = 0$

9.2   Use the classical fourth-order Runge–Kutta method, with $h = 0.1$, to compute $y(0.1)$ and $y(0.2)$ for the problem given in Exercise 9.1a. Check your results using the series solution.

9.3 Working to four decimal places, evaluate $y(-0.1)$, $y(0.1)$ and $y(0.2)$ from the series solution obtained in Exercises 9.1b. Extend this solution as far as $x = 0.4$ using

(a)   the Milne–Simpson predictor–corrector method,

(b)   the fourth-order Adams–Bashforth–Moulton predictor–corrector method.

9.4 Obtain sufficient terms in the series solution of the second-order initial-value problem

$$y'' - y' - y + x^2 = 0 \qquad y(0) = 0 \quad y'(0) = 1$$

to evaluate $y(-0.1)$, $y(0.1)$ and $y(0.2)$ correct to four decimal places. Check your result for $y(0.1)$ using the Runge–Kutta algorithm of Figure 9.13.

9.5 Using the Adams–Bashforth–Moulton algorithm of Figure 9.14, extend the solution obtained in Exercise 9.4 as far as $x = 0.4$.

9.6 Using the finite-difference method (9.63), with $n = 4$, formulate the tri-diagonal system for the differential equation

$$y'' + xy' - 2y + x = 0$$

given that

(a) $y(0) = 1 \qquad y(1) = 3$

(b) $2y(0) + y'(0) = 3 \qquad y(1) - y'(1) = 0$

In each case, solve the finite-difference equations using the tri-diagonal algorithm and compare your results with values obtained from the analytic solution

$$y = 1 + x + x^2$$

Explain the accuracy of the results obtained from the finite-difference method when, as in this case, the solution of the differential equation is a quadratic function.

9.7 Use Numerov's method, with $n = 4$, to formulate the tri-diagonal system for the two-point boundary-value problem

$$y'' - y + x + 2e^x = 0 \qquad y(0) = 1 \quad y(1) = 1$$

Use the tri-diagonal algorithm to solve the system and compare your results with values obtained from the analytic solution

$$y = x + (1 - x)e^x$$

Programming exercises

9.8 Using the subroutine EULERM of Figure 9.5 as a guide, write a program based on the *improved* Euler method to solve a first-order initial-value problem. Run your program with $h = 0.1$, 0.05 and 0.025 to estimate $y(x)$ over the region $[0,1]$ given that

$$y' = 4xy^{1/2} \qquad y(0) = 1$$

Compare your results with values obtained from the analytic solution

$$y = (1 + x^2)^2$$

9.9 Write a program that uses the Runge–Kutta–Fehlberg subroutine of Figure 9.8 to estimate $y(0.1)$, $y(0.2)$ and $y(0.3)$ for the problem in Exercise 9.8. Use a tolerance of 10^{-6} and an initial steplength of 0.05.

9.10 Write a program which uses the Milne–Simpson predictor–corrector method to solve a first-order initial-value problem, given suitable starting values. Use your program to solve the problem in Exercise 9.8 for $x = 0.4, 0.5, \ldots ,1$ taking the results of Exercise 9.9 as the starting values.

9.11 Write a program to solve a second-order initial-value problem by the Runge–Kutta–Fehlberg method. Hence, using a tolerance of 10^{-4}, estimate $y(0.1)$, $y(0.2)$ and $y(0.3)$ given that

$$y'' + xy' - y + xe^{-x} = 0 \qquad y(0) = 1 \quad y'(0) = 0$$

Compare your results with values obtained from the analytic solution

$$y = x + e^{-x}$$

9.12 Write a program to solve a second-order initial-value problem by the fourth-order Adams–Bashforth–Moulton method. Hence extend the solution obtained in Exercise 9.11 as far as $x = 1$ and compare your results with values obtained from the analytic solution.

9.13 Write a program that uses the subroutine RK4M of Figure 9.16 to solve the third-order initial-value problem

$$y^{(3)} + xy'' + 3y' + xy = x(1 - 4 \sin x) \qquad \begin{aligned} y(0) &= 1 \\ y'(0) &= 1 \\ y''(0) &= 0 \end{aligned}$$

for $x = 0.1, 0.2, \ldots ,1$. Compare your results with values obtained from the analytic solution

$$y = x \cos x + 1$$

9.14 Write a program to solve a *linear* two-point boundary-value problem using the shooting method. Hence solve the problem

$$y'' - (2x - 1)y' - 2y = 1 - 4x \qquad y(0) = 1 \quad y(1) = 2$$

Compare your results with values obtained from the analytic solution

$$y = e^{x(x-1)}$$

9.15 Write a program to solve a *non-linear* two-point boundary-value problem using the shooting method. Hence solve the problem

$$y'' - yy' = \frac{2}{x^2}\left(1 + \frac{4}{x}\right) \qquad y(1) = 3 \quad y(2) = 2$$

Compare your results with values obtained from the analytic solution

$$y = 1 + \frac{2}{x}$$

9.16 Modify your program of Exercise 9.15 so that it can accept boundary conditions in the form of Equations (9.54). Hence obtain a numerical solution to the differential equation

$$y'' - yy' = \frac{2}{x^2}\left(1 + \frac{4}{x}\right)$$

given that

$$2y(1) + y'(1) = 4$$
$$y(2) + 2y'(2) = 1$$

Compare your solution with that obtained in Exercise 9.15.

9.17 Write a program that uses the subroutine FINDIF of Figure 9.21 and the subroutine TRISOL of Figure 5.20 to solve a two-point boundary-value problem with boundary conditions of the form $y(a) = A$, $y(b) = B$. Run your program with (a) $h = \pi/20$ and (b) $h = \pi/40$ for the problem

$$y'' + 2xy' - y = 2(1 + x^2)\cos x \qquad y(0) = 0 \quad y(\pi/2) = \pi/2$$

Modify your program so that it also produces an extrapolated solution and compare all your results with values obtained from the analytic solution

$$y = x \sin x$$

9.18 Modify your program of Exercise 9.17 so that it can accept boundary conditions of the form of Equations (9.54). Hence, solve the problem

$$y'' + 2xy' - y = 2(1 + x^2)\cos x \qquad y'(0) = 0 \quad y'(\pi/2) = 1$$

using (a) $h = \pi/20$ and (b) $h = \pi/40$. Compare your solutions with those of Exercise 9.17.

9.19 Write a program that uses Numerov's method to solve the two-point boundary-value problem

$$y'' + q(x)y = r(x) \qquad y(a) = A \quad y(b) = B$$

Hence, using a steplength $h = \pi/30$, obtain a numerical solution of the problem

$$y'' - y \cos^2 x + \sin x \, e^{\sin x} = 0 \qquad y(0) = 1 \qquad y(\pi) = 1$$

Obtain a second solution using your program of Exercise 9.17 with the same steplength and compare both numerical solutions with values obtained from the exact solution

$$y = e^{\sin x}$$

Appendix A
Useful mathematical results

In the results that follow it is assumed that the functions are sufficiently differentiable for the conclusions to be valid.

Mean Value Theorem

For a given x_0 and h, there exists a value ξ such that

$$f(x_0 + h) = f(x_0) + hf'(\xi) \qquad \text{with } x_0 < \xi < x_0 + h$$

Taylor's Theorem

For a given x_0, h and n, there exists a value ξ such that

$$f(x_0 + h) = f(x_0) + hf'(x_0) + \frac{h^2 f''(x_0)}{2!} + \cdots + \frac{h^n f^{(n)}(x_0)}{n!} + \frac{h^{n+1} f^{(n+1)}(\xi)}{(n+1)!}$$

with $x_0 < \xi < x_0 + h$.

Taylor's theorem is often written in terms of the infinite series

$$f(x_0 + h) = f(x_0) + hf'(x_0) + \frac{h^2 f''(x_0)}{2!} + \cdots + \frac{h^n f^{(n)}(x_0)}{n!} + \cdots$$

Taylor's Theorem in two dimensions

For a given x_0, y_0, h and k

$$f(x_0 + h, y_0 + k) = f(x_0, y_0) + \left[\left(h\frac{\partial}{\partial x} + k\frac{\partial}{\partial y} \right) f(x,y) \right]_0$$
$$+ \frac{1}{2!} \left[\left(h^2 \frac{\partial^2}{\partial x^2} + 2hk \frac{\partial^2}{\partial x \partial y} + k^2 \frac{\partial^2}{\partial y^2} \right) f(x,y) \right]_0 + \cdots$$

Alternatively, using f_x, f_y, f_{xx}, f_{xy} and f_{yy} to denote $(\partial f/\partial x)$, $(\partial f/\partial y)$, $(\partial^2 f/\partial x^2)$, $(\partial^2 f/\partial x \partial y)$ and $(\partial^2 f/\partial y^2)$ respectively, this series may be written

$$f(x_0 + h, y_0 + k) = f(x_0, y_0) + (hf_x + kf_y)_0$$
$$+ \frac{1}{2!}(h^2 f_{xx} + 2hk f_{xy} + k^2 f_{yy})_0 + \cdots$$

Mean Value Theorem for integrals

If the function $f(x)$ is continuous on the interval $[a,b]$ and the function $g(x)$ is integrable and does not change sign on $[a,b]$, then there exists a value ξ such that

$$\int_a^b f(x)\, g(x)\, dx = f(\xi) \int_a^b g(x)\, dx$$

where $a < \xi < b$.

Chain rule

If y is a function of x then the derivative of the function $f(x, y(x))$ can be obtained using the formula

$$\frac{d}{dx} f(x, y(x)) = \frac{\partial}{\partial x} f(x, y(x)) + \frac{\partial}{\partial y} f(x, y(x)) \frac{d}{dx} y(x)$$

Descartes' rule of signs

Given the polynomial equation

$$p(x) = a_n x^n + a_{n-1} x^{n-1} + \cdots + a_1 x + a_0 = 0$$

the number of *positive* real roots is either equal to the number of sign changes in the sequence of coefficients

$$a_n, a_{n-1}, \ldots, a_1, a_0$$

or is smaller by an *even* integer. The number of *negative* real roots is related to the coefficients of $p(-x)$ is a similar manner.

Legendre polynomials

The Legendre polynomials $P_n(x)$, $n = 0,1,2, \ldots$, are given by

$$P_0(x) = 1$$
$$P_1(x) = x$$
$$P_{n+1}(x) = \frac{2n + 1}{n + 1} xP_n(x) - \frac{n}{n + 1} P_{n-1}(x) \qquad n \geqslant 1$$

and are orthogonal with respect to the weight function $w(x) = 1$ on the interval $[-1, 1]$.

Appendix B
FORTRAN operators and intrinsic functions

The following symbols are used for the different types of operand: I, integer; R, real; Z, complex; D, double precision; C, character; and S, string constant. If an operator can be applied to operands of different types a composite type formed from the letters representing those types will be used. For example, if an operator can be applied to real or double precision operands, its operands will be described in the following list as RD.

FORTRAN 77 operators

Operator	Type of left operand	Type of right operand	Type of result	Definition
**	RD > 0	R	RD	exponentiation
	I > 0	R	R	
	IRD	I	IRD	
*	R	IR	R	multiplication
	IR	R	R	
	I	I	I	
	D	IRD	D	
	IRD	D	D	
	Z	IRZ	Z	
	IRZ	Z	Z	
/	R	IR	R	division
	IR	R	R	
	I	I	I	
	D	IRD	D	
	IRD	D	D	
	Z	IRZ	Z	
	IRZ	Z	Z	

375

FORTRAN 77 operators (continued)

Operator	Type of left operand	Type of right operand	Type of result	Definition
+	R	IR	R	addition
	IR	R	R	
	I	I	I	
	D	IRD	D	
	IRD	D	D	
	Z	IRZ	Z	
	IRZ	Z	Z	
−	R	IR	R	subtraction
	IR	R	R	
	I	I	I	
	D	IRD	D	
	IRD	D	D	
	Z	IRZ	Z	
	IRZ	Z	Z	
−		IRDZ	IRDZ	negation
.EQ.	scalar	scalar	logical	equal to
.NE.	scalar	scalar	logical	not equal to
.LT.	scalar	scalar	logical	less than
.GE.	scalar	scalar	logical	greater than or equal to
.GT.	scalar	scalar	logical	greater than
.NOT.		logical	logical	changes .TRUE. to .FALSE. and .FALSE. to .TRUE.
.AND.	logical	logical	logical	logical 'and'
.OR.	logical	logical	logical	logical 'or'
.EQV.	logical	logical	logical	logical 'equivalence'
.NEQV.	logical	logical	logical	logical 'non-equivalence'

Intrinsic functions

Function	Type of result	Description
ABS(IRD)	same as argument	$\lvert IRD \rvert$
ABS(Z)	real	$((REAL(Z))^2+(AIMAG(Z))^2)^{1/2}$
ACOS(RD)	same as argument	arccos (RD)
AIMAG(Z)	real	imaginary part of Z
AINT(RD)	same as argument	truncation, REAL(INT(RD))
AMAX0(I1,I2, . . .)	real	REAL(MAX(I1,I2, . . .))
AMIN0(I1,I2, . . .)	real	REAL(MIN(I1,I2, . . .))
ANINT(RD)	same as argument	nearest whole number, REAL(INT(RD+0.5)) if RD≥0 otherwise REAL(INT(RD−0.5))
ASIN(RD)	same as argument	arcsin (RD)
ATAN(RD)	same as argument	arctan (RD)
ATAN2(RD1,RD2)	same as argument	arctan (RD1/RD2)
CHAR(I)	character	character in position I of lexicographic order
CMPLX(IRD)	complex	complex number (REAL(IRD),0)
CMPLX(IRD1,IRD2)	complex	complex number (REAL(IRD1),REAL(IRD2))
CMPLX(Z)	complex	Z
CONJG(Z)	complex	complex conjugate, (REAL(Z),−AIMAG(Z))
COS(RDZ)	same as argument	cos(RDZ)
COSH(RD)	same as argument	cosh(RD)
DBLE(IRZ)	double precision	double precision version of REAL(IRZ)
DBLE(D)	double precision	D
DIM(IRD1,IRD2)	same as argument	positive difference, MAX((IRD1−IRD2),0)
DPROD(R1,R2)	double precision	double precision product R1*R2
EXP(RDZ)	same as argument	exp(RDZ)
ICHAR(C)	integer	integer equivalent of single character C, dependent on lexicographic order
INDEX(S1,S2)	integer	position of first appearance of S2 in S1, if S2 does not appear in S1 then 0
INT(RDZ)	integer	integer part of REAL(RDZ)
INT(I)	integer	I
LEN(S)	integer	length of S
LGE(S1,S2)	logical	true if S1=S2 or S1 follows S2 in lexicographic order, otherwise false

Intrinsic functions (continued)

Function	Type of result	Description
LGT(S1,S2)	logical	true if S1 follows S2 in lexicographic order, otherwise false
LLE(S1,S2)	logical	true if S1=S2 or S1 precedes S2 in lexicographic order, otherwise false
LLT(S1,S2)	logical	true if S1 precedes S2 in lexicographic order, otherwise false
LOG(RDZ)	same as argument	natural logarithm $\log_e$(RDZ)
LOG10(RDZ)	same as argument	$\log_{10}$(RDZ)
MAX(IRD1,IRD2, . . .)	same as argument	largest of IRD1, IRD2, . . .
MAX1(R1,R2, . . .)	integer	INT(MAX(R1,R2, . . .))
MIN(IRD1,IRD2, . . .)	same as argument	smallest of IRD1,IRD2, . . .
MIN1(R1,R2, . . .)	integer	INT(MIN(R1,R2, . . .))
MOD(IRD1,IRD2)	same as argument	remainder, IRD1-INT(IRD1/IRD2)*IRD2
NINT(RD)	integer	nearest integer, INT(ANINT(RD))
REAL(ID)	real	real equivalent of ID
REAL(Z)	real	real part of Z
REAL(R)	real	R
SIGN(IRD1,IRD2)	same as argument	$\|IRD1\|$ if IRD2 > 0, $-\|IRD1\|$ if IRD2 < 0
SIN(RDZ)	same as argument	sin(RDZ)
SINH(RD)	same as argument	sinh(RD)
SQRT(RDZ)	same as argument	$(RDZ)^{1/2}$
TAN(RD)	same as argument	tan(RD)
TANH(RD)	same as argument	tanh(RD)

Standard functions from FORTRAN IV that are not mentioned above will be recognized by a FORTRAN 77 compiler. A list of these functions is given in Ellis (1982).

Appendix C
Programs, subroutines and functions

Answers to exercises

Chapter 4

4.1 1.327

4.2 −1.325

4.3 0.589

4.6 1.0000, −0.9900, −1.0100

4.8 1.2500

4.9 (a) 1.4063 (b) 0.4746, −1.3953

4.10 $x^2 + 1.9413x + 1.9502$

Chapter 5

5.2 (a) $(-1,1,1,-1)^T$ (b) $(5,-10,10,-5,1)^T$

5.3 (a) $(126,-20,12)^T$

5.5 (a) $(11,25,3)^T$ (b) $(1,3,5,7)^T$

5.8 $(1,2,3,4)^T$

5.9 $(9,7,5,3,1)^T$

5.10 $\begin{bmatrix} 9 & 68 & -24 \\ -2 & -14 & 5 \\ 0 & -3 & 1 \end{bmatrix}$

5.11 $(3,2,1)^T$

Chapter 6

6.1 5.236 07, $(0.447\ 21, 0.894\ 43, 1)^{\mathrm{T}}$,
3, $(1, -0.5, 0)^{\mathrm{T}}$,
0.763 93, $(-0.447\ 21, -0.894\ 43, 1)^{\mathrm{T}}$

Chapter 7

7.1 (a) 0.1405 (b) 0.1569 (c) 1.1391

7.2 (a) $1.1648 \times 10^{-7} \leqslant |E| \leqslant 1.2592 \times 10^{-7}$
(b) $0.0007 \leqslant |E| \leqslant \infty$
(c) $1.9182 \times 10^{-10} \leqslant |E| \leqslant 1.9740 \times 10^{-10}$

7.3 12.0680

7.4 $0.031\ 25 \leqslant |E| \leqslant 0.3807$

7.5 84

7.6 (a)

i	a_i	b_i	c_i	d_i
0	1.0709	0	0.0789	-0.1733
1	0.5573	1.6064	0.8821	0
2	-1.6283	2.4424	2.9065	0.9123

(b)

i	a_i	b_i	c_i	d_i
0	0.4451	0.8568	-0.1931	-0.1733
1	0.2590	1.5245	0.9976	0
2	0.1910	1.9130	2.7164	0.9123

7.7 (a) 1.6902 (b) 1.6406

7.8 (a) $0.8488 + 4.2802x$ (b) $1.0107 + 1.8517x + 4.8570x^2$

7.9 $(0.9985, 1.5252, 3.1012)^{\mathrm{T}}$

Chapter 8

8.1 0.4490, $2.4525 \times 10^{-4} \leqslant |E| \leqslant 4.4688 \times 10^{-4}$

8.2 numerical: 2.188, 2.482, 2.935; exact: 2.200, 2.474, 2.961

8.3 natural spline: 0.2074, 3.9078; clamped spline: 0.2030, 3.9406; exact: 0.2007, 3.9400

8.4 2.4732

8.5 (a) 1.2775 (b) 1.2733; exact: 1.2733

8.6 0.8415

8.7 numerical: 0.841 452 6, 0.841 468 7, 0.841 470 6; exact: 0.841 471 0

8.8 0.841 471 0

8.9 numerical: 1.56; exact: 1.56

Chapter 9

9.1 (a) $\dfrac{x^2}{2} + \dfrac{x^3}{6} + \dfrac{x^4}{24} + \dfrac{x^5}{120}$ (b) $1 - \dfrac{x^3}{6} - \dfrac{x^4}{24} + \dfrac{x^6}{72}$

(c) $-(x-1)^2 - \dfrac{1}{3}(x-1)^3 + \dfrac{1}{5}(x-1)^5 + \dfrac{1}{9}(x-1)^6$

9.2 0.005 17, 0.021 40

9.3 $y(0.3) = 0.9951$, $y(0.4) = 0.9883$

9.4 $x + \dfrac{x^2}{2} + \dfrac{x^3}{3} + \dfrac{x^4}{24}$

9.5 $y(0.3) = 0.3543$, $y(0.4) = 0.5026$

9.6 (a) 1.3125, 1.7500, 2.3125
(b) 1.0000, 1.3125, 1.7500, 2.3125, 3.0000

9.7 1.213 04, 1.324 39, 1.279 27

Bibliography

Atkinson L.V. and Harley P.J. (1983). *An Introduction to Numerical Methods with Pascal*. Wokingham: Addison-Wesley

Birkhoff G. and de Boor C. (1964). Error bounds for spline approximation. *J. Math. Mech.*, **13**, 827–35

Burden R.L. and Faires J.D. (1985). *Numerical Analysis*. Boston, Mass.: Prindle, Weber and Schmidt

Ellis T.M.R. (1982). *A Structured Approach to FORTRAN 77 Programming*. Wokingham: Addison-Wesley

Fehlberg E. (1970). Klassische Runge–Kutta Formeln vierter und niedrigerer Ordnung mit Schrittweiten–Kontrolle und ihre Anwendung auf Wärmeleitungs-probleme. *Computing*, **6**, 61–71

Golub G.H. and Van Loan C.F. (1983). *Matrix Computations*. Oxford: North Oxford Academic

Gourlay A.R. and Watson G.A. (1973). *Computational Methods for Matrix Eigenproblems*. Chichester: Wiley

Henrici P. (1962). *Discrete Variable Methods in Ordinary Differential Equations*. New York: Wiley

Isaacson E. and Keller H.B. (1966). *Analysis of Numerical Methods*. New York: Wiley

Johnson L.W. and Riess R.D. (1982). *Numerical Analysis*. Reading, Mass.: Addison-Wesley

Keller H. B. (1968). *Numerical Methods for Two-point Boundary-value Problems*. Waltham, Mass.: Blaisdell

Lambert J.D. (1973). *Computational Methods in Ordinary Differential Equations*. Chichester: Wiley

McKeown G.P. and Rayward-Smith V.J. (1982). *Mathematics for Computing*. London: Macmillan

Ralston A. and Rabinowitz P. (1978). *A First Course in Numerical Analysis*. New York: McGraw-Hill

Stroud A.H. and Secrest D. (1966). *Gaussian Quadrature Formulas*. Englewood Cliffs, NJ: Prentice-Hall

Wilkinson J.H. (1959). The evaluation of zeros of ill-conditioned polynomials. *Numerische Mathematik*, **1**, 150–66, 167–80

Wilkinson J.H. (1963). *Rounding Errors in Algebraic Processes*. Englewood Cliffs, NJ: Prentice-Hall

Wilkinson J.H. (1965). *The Algebraic Eigenvalue Problem*. Oxford: Oxford University Press

Wilkinson J.H. and Reinsch C. (1971). *Handbook for Automatic Computation*, Vol II, *Linear Algebra*. New York: Springer-Verlag

Young D.M. (1971). *Iterative Solution of Large Linear Systems*. New York: Academic Press

Index